GLIMPSES
OF
TRUTH

by
Thomas W. Shepherd

9/0.5

Portions of this book first appeared in *Glimpses of Truth, Volume I*,
© 1999 and *Glimpses of Truth,* 2nd Edition, © October 1999 by Thomas W. Shepherd

Printed in the United States of America
First Printing: July 2000

Universal Foundation for Better Living, Inc.
21310 N.W. 37th Avenue
Carol City, FL 33056

In Memory of Marcus Bach

who studied so many religious traditions
with such lovingkindness
and skillful scholarship
that every group he blessed with his words
thought he belonged to them,
and they were right.

Open my eyes, that I may see

Glimpses of truth thou hast for me;

Place in my hands the wonderful key

That shall unclasp, and set me free.

Silently now I wait for thee,

Ready my God, thy will to see;

Open my eyes, illumine me,

Spirit divine!

—Clara H. Scott

(1841-1897)

CONTENTS

FOREWORD

When Albert Einstein said, "Never lose a holy curiosity," he was speaking the language of the theologian. As a scientist, Einstein understood that curiosity could not only be holy, but was necessary to discovery. For just as the scientist seeks to uncover reality in the physical world and make it clear to humankind, theological inquiry seeks to uncover the reality of God as it is experienced by a community of faith and make it clear to that community.

Maybe you've noticed that in your own community of faith, there are those who prefer to experience God rather than to think about God. On the other hand, there are also those who use thought about God to replace the experience of God. Neither position works very well. True theological inquiry brings both the experience of God and our thinking about God together. Jesus not only experiences God, but reasons with us, asking us to think deeply about God, to engage in logos—divine reasoning, about Theos—God.

For example, out of His own experience with God, we find Jesus addressing His disciples, and through them His own community of faith, about the form of prayer. The theological issue He raises goes to the heart of the very nature of God. He notices that there is a tendency to "heap up empty phrases" when praying—"for they think that they will be heard because of their many words" (Mt. 6:7 NRSV). He tells them it is a waste of time. And why? He tells them with the now familiar and astounding theological statement, "Your Father knows what you need before you ask him" (Mt. 6:8 NRSV).

It should be obvious that this insight is not "the experience of God," but the insight it communicates makes possible the authentic experience we all seek. This is the way theology functions. This is the work of theological inquiry and in one way or another every serious Truth student is called to this vocation.

Tom Shepherd is just such an inquirer. He brims over with a "holy curiosity" that seeks to make clear to us in the metaphysical Christian community in a systematic way, the essence of our tradition. If you feel called to think with him as he ponders the deep questions of metaphysical Christian faith, you will enjoy this book immensely. Perhaps Einstein, who allowed the universe to reveal some of its secrets said it as well as anyone:

"The important thing is not to stop questioning. Curiosity has its own reason for existing. One cannot help but be in awe when he contemplates the mysteries of eternity, of life, of the marvelous structure of reality. It is enough if one tries merely to comprehend a little of this mystery every day."

Enjoy your journey through Tom Shepherd's *"Glimpses of Truth."*

Philip White, M. Div.
Editor, *Unity Magazine*

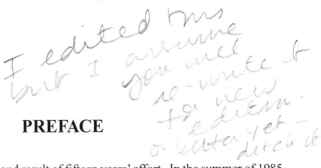

PREFACE

The volume you hold in hand result of fifteen years' effort. In the summer of 1985 Pamela Yearsley, then-editor of Unity Books, wrote a letter which caught up to me in Graffenwoehr, Germany, where I was assigned as a U.S. Army chaplain. In the letter she congratulated me on the success of the *Unity Magazine* series "Friends in High Places" and its upcoming publication as a Unity book. She then suggested I begin a new work, not a magazine series but a book-length project of my choice. I replied that I wanted to write a systematic theology for Metaphysical Christians, which to my knowledge had never been done. Ms. Yearsley found the project to be of sufficient interest that she encouraged me to begin the research.

Preparing to write such a comprehensive book required extensive study of theological, historical, and biblical materials. However, I was living in Germany, where very little scholarly material was available in English, and my tourist-quality German wasn't ready to tackle Karl Barth's *Church Dogmatics* in the original tongue. So, my wife, Carol-Jean, and I stuffed our infant daughter into her backpack carrier and crossed the stormy English Channel during the coldest winter in fifty years. We spent a week at Oxford University as guests of the faculty of Manchester College, the British Unitarian institution at the Oxford collegium.

Returning to Germany with armloads of research books and stacks of photocopied notes, I set to work at home in the evening, pecking away on my word processor in a tiny, six-by-six maid's quarters we had converted to an office space. Two years later, the first draft of *Glimpses of Truth* was completed. Sending the manuscript to Unity Books, I waited for the verdict. And waited. And waited. And waited. Months became years. By 1990, the book had been passed around Unity School and read by several key people, including Philip White and James Gaither. At one point, Connie Fillmore looked over part of the manuscript. The problem was that *Glimpses* represented a wholly different direction in religious writing, an attempt to do metaphysical theology the way it is done in Protestant and Catholic traditions, i.e., critically, thoughtfully, and systematically, while working through the major issues of the Christian faith. It wasn't a new approach; it was simply too new for the approval people at Unity School. There was also a marketing consideration; I was told repeatedly that the book would not sell because Unity readers were not interested in academic theology.

More years passed. All the while, everyone who read the work seemed to like it, or so they told me. One senior editor said, "Nobody wanted to say 'No', because it was so good." By the mid-1990s, I realized Unity was never going to issue this work which they had commissioned. Finally, in the late 1990s, Michael Maday told me the book had no chance of being published by Unity.

So, in the summer of 1999, my wife and I created our own publishing company, Mimosa Books, and issued the first half of *Glimpses*. This version came to the attention of the Rev. Dr. Mary Tumpkin, president of the Universal Foundation for Better Living, when Rev. Michael Smith gave her a copy for Christmas. Mary contacted me and asked if I might consider letting the UFBL publish the whole work. Eagerly, I agreed, and began to re-write and edit the manuscript. The revised and updated book you hold is the result of that process.

I cannot begin to express my gratitude to the many people who have shaped this volume, but there are a few who deserve special mention. First, Pamela Yearsley, who started the process almost fifteen years ago and encouraged me as the pieces of the book took shape. The faculties of Manchester College at Oxford, the University of Idaho, Lancaster Theological Seminary in Pennsylvania, and Unity School of Christianity, for the things I learned at those institutions which found their way into this work, and for the use of their research facilities. My former teacher and friend Phil White, whose tireless efforts at Unity publications have raised the discussion of metaphysics to the level of authentic theology for the benefit of everyone in the New Thought movement. My good friend Rev. Robert Hungerford, who hammered out the Historical-Metaphysical Method of interpretation with me in a series of discussions way back in the summer of 1981. My good friend and theological discussion-partner since seminary days at LTS, the Very Reverend Nathan D. Baxter, who today serves as Dean of the National Cathedral of the Episcopal Church in Washington, D.C. And my oldest friend on the planet, Gerald W. Jarsocrak, a career policeman and original thinker whose theological reflections with me way back in grade school helped to shape my direction in life.

I also want to thank the people at Universal Truth Center and the UFBL headquarters at Carol City, Florida, especially Janell Walden Agyeman, whose editorial midnight oil burned long to get this book to press; Ghislaine "Mimi" Douze, who prepared the actual copy; Dr. Mary Tumpkin, who supervised and motivated everyone involved in the project and without whom *Glimpses of Truth* never would have been published; and Michael Smith, who brought the book to Mary's attention.

Finally, I'd like to thank my wife, Carol-Jean, for her comforting confidence in my writing and her support when I retreated behind the study door to wrestle with the pesky angels of systematic theology.

The aim of *Glimpses of Truth* was to produce a readable, competent statement of the basic themes in Systematic Theology from a Metaphysical Christian perspective. If the quality of this volume is reflective of the caliber of people who helped me do the creative and technical work, then I have accomplished my goal.

[handwritten: change the word metaphysical lower or upper case throughout.]

[handwritten: I don't think the changing style + boldness + the overuse of quotation marks is unprofessional + continuing]

CAVEAT

Do not read this book expecting to find an authoritative Statement of Faith or the ultimate definition of Truth. The intent of this work is something quite different. *Glimpses Of Truth* is a new kind of book, an attempt to do theology from a Metaphysical Christian point of view, and make it interesting and applicable to the lives of non-scholarly readers. As such, we require some preparatory remarks about 1) the wide variety of writing grouped under the general heading of **Metaphysical literature**, and 2) the **nature of theology** itself.

1) Metaphysical Literature: *One Presence / One Power*

As most participants in the genre know, the term "metaphysical" comes from Aristotle, who discussed the physics of the Cosmos and then proceeded to discuss things which went beyond physics (Greek, *meta-physics*). In philosophy "meta-physics" refers to a comprehensive effort to explain the nature of Ultimate Reality. In popular religious literature, the adjective "metaphysical" refers to a conglomerate of beliefs and practices loosely grouped around a central idea, ordinarily summarized:

> *"There is only One Presence and One Power in my life and in the Universe, God the Good, Omnipotent."*

No mere aphorism, this statement judiciously presents all the essentials for a profoundly "metaphysical" theology. We shall discuss its implications in great detail during the course of this study. Of course, not every author claiming to be "meta-physical" would also claim to be a Christian. Some, in fact, are pointedly anti-Christian; others strive for an innocuous syncretism which treats all religions as equals and stake no claim in any camp. Other "metaphysical" books attempt to graft Eastern philosophy and theology onto the tree of Western thought, with mixed successes and failures, not unlike the Christian effort to evangelize the East. Other varieties dot the shelves of "metaphysical" bookstores—some thoughtful, some capricious.

A few non-Christian metaphysical writers teach by *personal authority* and quite frankly proceed by begging the question. Other works are *highly speculative*, tiptoe-ing dangerously close to the occult. Some generic metaphysical teachers write *devotionally*; their books are exquisite hymns to the Divine Presence and Power, love letters to God which overflow with insights drawn from daily living. Still others write inspirationally, encouraging and uplifting men and women by reminding them of their divine potential. Finally, the best of them follow Charles Fillmore's penchant for experiential religion and *teach only what they have discovered* by trial and error; these are the "how-to-do-it" books, filled with metaphysical principles to increase prosperity, reclaim radiant health, improve self-esteem, and build better relationships.

Most of these approaches are important, meaningful, and valid. However, if this book hits the target, we'll accomplish none of the above.

2) Theology: Critical Analysis Of Religious Beliefs

Glimpses of Truth is a work of *theology,* which is a way of looking critically at religious beliefs. (For a better definition of the term, see Chapter 2). We aim to develop a self-consciously Christian system of thought which will speak the language of twenty-first century men and women. Our route will take us close to non-Western traditions, but we shall keep within the boundaries marked by metaphysical authors who describe themselves as New Thought, Practical, Mystical, or Metaphysical Christians.

MORE "SCIENTIFIC"

In the nineteenth century, theology was called the *"Queen of the Sciences,"* although it was neither queenly nor scientific. Our goal is to re-introduce a more "scientific" method to the discussion of Metaphysical Christian thought, and to combat-test each idea by ruthlessly submitting it to crossfire from other points of view. Good theology more correctly deserves to share the nickname of the United States Army's Infantry Corps, the *"Queen of Battle."*

There is nothing particularly new about theological analysis; Catholic and Protestant scholars have applied the method to their doctrines for centuries. However, Metaphysical Christian writers have been so concerned with maintaining a positive outlook and giving "no power to negative thinking" that their works have shown a palpable reluctance to sift through the issues, analyze options, and discuss the pros and cons of religious beliefs. Sometimes in the Christ-like spirit of loving all God's children—other times for fear of giving offense—Metaphysical Christian authors have been by-and-large wholly positive in their work, refraining from criticism of other ways of thinking.

While this reluctance to apply Occam's razor to the religious thought of others is commendable in a devotional work, it has no place in Christian theology, which must be critical, analytical, aggressive, vigorous, demanding, and uncompromising in its pursuit of Truth.

Addressing the whole range of Christian subjects usually classified under Systematic Theology, we shall try to demonstrate how to do theology by providing a competent example. Theology is dialogue and discussion, often proceeding in good Hegelian fashion from thesis to antithesis to synthesis, sometimes just raising thorny problems while acknowledging that grasping for answers can prick our fingers.

Although it is critical, good theology is not hostile to any beliefs, but requires all religious thought to present itself to the most rigorous scrutiny we can employ. When second century theologian Tertullian said of the Christian gospel, "I believe, because it is absurd!" he had departed from sound methodology. If absurdity lingers, theology has not done its homework.

THEOLOGY—NOT STATEMENT OF FAITH

This book is not the official statement of any denomination or movement. It is one theologian's attempt to bring the tools of theological inquiry to Metaphysical Christian studies. As such, it is an attempt at bridge building. Historic Christianity and its dynamic young stepchild, Metaphysical Christianity, have much to offer each other. If thinkers from older Protestant and Roman Catholic traditions would dialogue with their counterparts in the newer metaphysical churches, the traditional church could gain insights about prayer, meditation, and spirituality—at which the Metaphysical Christian churches excel—while we non-traditionalists reclaim our heritage as full members in the Christian community through modern biblical studies, better appreciation of church history, and increased theological sophistication. We have much to share in the family of Christ.

This book does not initiate the dialogue; others did that years ago. What it does is to raise the level of dialogue to the plane of Systematic Theology. It is written for intelligent laypeople, clergy and teachers, not professional theologians.

Glimpses of Truth aims to spark discussions, raise provocative issues, and exemplify the kind of theologizing which could energize the Christian church at large. Every chapter ends with six questions, which allow you, the reader/student, to test your knowledge of the material presented, and six questions to discuss among your community of faith. Eric Butterworth noted: "A religion, to be a contemporary influence, must be redefined for every generation in the light of that day's thought."[1] This process of redefining plants the very cornerstone of Systematic Theology.

LOOK BOTH WAYS WHEN CROSSING MILLENNIA

As we enter the twenty-first century, we hear a call to look both ways—backward and forward—when crossing into the new millennium. Legitimate Christian theology always restates the ancient Truth of the gospel of Jesus Christ for today and invites thoughtful consideration of the central issues which have excited and outraged Christians for the past two thousand years.

None of this theologizing is meant to take the place of prayer, meditation, and other spiritual disciplines. Our goal will be to develop what H. Emilie Cady called an "understanding faith," a religious viewpoint which integrates the heart and the head, the thinking and the feeling natures of humanity. Just as a bird needs two wings to fly, we need to love God with heart and mind. Such are the lofty goals of this first volume of Systematic Theology from a Metaphysical Christian perspective.

CAVEAT

1. Eric Butterworth, *Unity: A Quest for Truth* (Unity Village, MO: Unity Books, 1985), p. 3.

THEOLOGY AND LIFE

Chapter One

The Christmas Faith in an Easter World

Dietrich Bonhoeffer was a German pastor who tried to kill Adolf Hitler. Although he never handled a gun or planted a bomb, Bonhoeffer was unquestionably involved in the conspiracy which led to an abortive attempt on Hitler's life by military officers on July 20, 1944. As early as 1940, Bonhoeffer had told friends:

> "If we claim to be Christians, there is no room for expediency. Hitler is the anti-Christ. Therefore we must go on with our work and eliminate him..." [1]

In his willingness to act without regard for "expediency," Dietrich Bonhoeffer was a lonely figure. I am deeply saddened—as an ethnic German-American and a clergyman—by the historic fact that most German clergy of the Nazi era either enthusiastically supported the Führer, whom they hailed as the opponent of godless Communism, or implicitly condoned Hitler's policies by a conspiracy of silence.

Paul Johnson says in his book *A History of Christianity* that the German church early in this century was poorly prepared to resist a powerful leader who went astray. European Christianity has long a history of allegiance to the government. To this day, German priests and ministers are paid their salaries from tax money and consider themselves civil servants. In a political system gone awry, that proved to be fatal for the faith of Jesus. For the faith of those who greeted Hitler with wild enthusiasm, listen to the incredible resolution passed April 3, 1933, by the first National Conference of the Faith Movement:

> For a German, the church is the community of believers who are under obligation to fight for a Christian Germany...Adolf Hitler's state appeals to the church: the church must obey the appeal. [2]

One pastor told a gathering of church leaders:

> Christ has come to us through Adolf Hitler..., the Saviour has come...We have only one task, be German, not be Christian... [3]

Personally, Hitler despised Christianity, even though he required his high officials to pretend otherwise. Hitler said on one occasion that the conspiracy of silence would prevail:

> Do you really believe the masses will ever be Christian again? Nonsense. The tale is finished...but we can hasten matters. The parsons will be made to dig their own graves. They will betray their God to us. They will betray anything for the sake of their miserable little jobs and incomes. [4]

NAZI STATE CHURCH: HYMNS TO HITLER

The Nazi's spurned the Faith, even while German Christianity was wooing the fascists like an unrequited lover. In fact, Hitler planned to replace the church of Christ with a Nazi State Church. There were Nazi creeds, baptism ceremonies, burial and wedding services. Sometimes propaganda became religious absurdity. Bizarre lyrics were written to make old hymns fit Nazi theology:

> Silent night, holy night,
> All is calm, all is bright,
> Only the Chancellor steadfast in fight,
> Watches o'er Germany by day and night,
> Always caring for us. [5]

The motto of the nationalistic "German Christian" organization was, "The Swastika on our breasts, the Cross in our hearts." Johnson reports that at church council meetings, "the pastors dressed in Nazi uniforms, and Nazi hymns were sung." [6]

GERMAN CALIGULA

By 1942, Dietrich Bonhoeffer's patience had expired. He flew secretly to Sweden and conferred with his friend, British churchman George Bell. Bonhoeffer revealed to Bell the details of the plot against Hitler, asking him to relay to his government the hopes of many Germans for a speedy end to the war and Nazi terror. Pushing for unconditional surrender, the Allies refused any support, but the fledgling resistance movement still tried to assassinate their German Caligula.

The conspirators arranged to have a bomb slipped under the table in a bunker briefing room, but it detonated without seriously harming Hitler. In the aftermath of the botched assassination, Hitler went on a rampage of revenge. Hundreds of people died, including General Erwin Rommel, the famed "Desert Fox." Rommel, too, wanted to be rid of Hitler.

MODERN MARTYRDOM

Dietrich Bonhoeffer was not immediately implicated because he was already in prison when the bomb exploded, but his part in the conspiracy was impossible to conceal. T. A. Kantonen describes what finally happened to him:

> ...in February, 1945, he disappeared from the Berlin prison and his family did not learn his fate until the war was over...from Berlin he

was taken to Buchenwald and then to Flossenberg. On Sunday April 8 he conducted a worship service for his fellow prisoners. He had hardly finished his closing prayer when two men came in and said, "Come with us." After a court martial that night he was hanged at dawn on Monday, April 9, 1945. [7]

Five days later, Flossenberg was liberated by the Allies. Bonhoeffer had been executed by special order of Heinrich Himmler as World War II was ending. He was 39.

A THEOLOGIAN, TOO...

If that were his only contribution—a heroic involvement in the fight for freedom and a martyr's death—he would have made a worthy contribution to humankind. However, Dietrich Bonhoeffer was not just a pastor, but a theologian. He acted from deeply held Christian beliefs which he sketched in a scant few books, poems, and letters smuggled from his prison cell during the madness of war. The day after Hitler escaped assassination, Bonhoeffer penned a poem containing these lines:

> Faint not nor fear, but go out to the storm and the action,
> trusting in God whose commandment you faithfully follow;
> freedom, exultant, will welcome your spirit with joy. [8]

We may not agree with all the points of his doctrine, but something in the tragic heroism of Dietrich Bonhoeffer evokes appreciation from Christians of diverse theological persuasions. Bonhoeffer suffered the dilemma of the philosopher-king; called to live by high principles, he nevertheless had to practice in a world, which he perceived to be ruled by brute force. He had to decide whether to dwell in a land of academic exercises—a safe, happy place where truth and goodness always rule—or descend to the muddy battlefield where the children of God were hacking each other to pieces. It was a nasty choice.

THE LAST SHIP

Few of Bonhoeffer's contemporaries in the German clergy had the courage to abandon their ivory towers for a perilous journey down the valley of the shadow of death. Most found it easier to preach theoretical sermons about the eventual triumph of God's goodness than to speak out against a tyrannical regime that was plunging the world into a holocaust.

Dietrich Bonhoeffer—safe in New York City, teaching at a major Protestant Seminary, knowing full well the peril he would face—caught the last ship home to Germany on the eve of World War II. It was the cost of his discipleship, and he paid in full.

RELIGIONLESS CHRISTIANITY

Bonhoeffer took a look at the churches of his day and called for a "religionless Christianity," a Christian faith cut free from ritualism and dogmatism so that it can

Tom - Can you take me all that but related to mercy?

speak its eternal Truth in the language of modern humanity. "I should like to speak of God," he wrote, "not on the borders of life but at its center." [9]

For Bonhoeffer, religionless Christianity meant a belief system liberated from both the the irrelevant other-worldliness of traditional Christianity and the brooding cynicism of modern secular thinking. We shall not use the word "religion" in this narrow sense. In this book, "religion" will be our term for "a community of faith distinguished by a generally held system of beliefs and practices which are advocated by a recognizable body of believers."

Bonhoeffer's distinction was really between ritualism and healthy faith. He called for a commitment to Jesus Christ, which for him included a willingness to change, grow, and "die" to oneself so that we might live for God and neighbor.

This is not achieved by dint of efforts to 'become like Jesus,' which is the way we usually interpret it. It is achieved only when the form of Jesus Christ itself works upon us in such a manner that it molds our form in its own likeness. [10]

CHRISTLIKE, NOT JESUS-LIKE

At first glimpse, this seems diametrically opposed to one of the central ideas of Metaphysical Christianity, i.e., that we are all as capable of out picturing the Christ-within, as was Jesus of Nazareth. However, closer scrutiny of Bonhoeffer's words suggests his analysis is not necessarily antithetical to this concept. We can never "become like Jesus" because Jesus Christ was absolutely unique, just as everyone is absolutely unique. For Bonhoeffer, Jesus Christ is not a hero whose exploits we mimic but a life-transforming Lord.

Certainly, when "the form of Jesus Christ itself works upon us in such a manner that it molds our form in its own likeness," we shall become Christlike. But Christlike does not require us to become Jesus-like. We must allow the process to happen. Bonhoeffer never lived to follow this idea through to its logical conclusion: when we let God mold us, we become the Christ in still another form, an idea which brings a whole new meaning to the words of Paul, "Christ in you, the hope of glory." [11]

"CHEAP GRACE" AND THE COST OF DISCIPLESHIP

Bonhoeffer believed that change comes by commitment to God. He called all attempts to become "religious" without changing the inner person "cheap grace." It is one of his most powerful and important terms. Against this superficial religiosity he set "costly grace," which is total commitment to Christ.

> Cheap grace is grace without discipleship, grace without the Cross, grace without Jesus Christ, living and incarnate... costly grace is the gospel which must be sought again and again, the gift which must be asked for, the door at which a man must knock. Such grace is costly because it calls a man to follow Jesus Christ. It is costly because it costs a man his life, and it is grace because it gives a man the only true life. [12]

Dietrich Bonhoeffer knew following Christ takes moral courage. Yet, only when we accept *The Cost of Discipleship* can we become what God intends us to be. In his lifetime Bonhoeffer watched men and women trade their Christian principles for temporary security. We can understand how this happened. We all want stability and safety in our lives. "Why should I be the one to act?" the fear-motivated ego asks. "I don't want to get involved." Who has not heard reports from news media about victims who bleed to death while people hurry by?

However, to focus on the failure of humanity is to miss the point of Dietrich Bonhoeffer's life. He was one of us, too. He remained faithful unto death. If he can do it, so can we.

Some may not admire his decision to conspire in an act of violence, but when put to the supreme test Bonhoeffer returned to the forgiving, loving faith of Jesus even while imprisoned by a world gone mad. Hitler was wrong. Bonhoeffer didn't betray everything for the sake of worldly security, nor did many others, most of whose names are lost to history but known to God.

THEOLOGY'S FAILURE

Even those Germanic theologians who stood up for the faith had little impact upon their world. I find it a frustrating feature of twentieth century Christianity that, while the flames of war were spreading across Europe, continental theology was experiencing a renaissance. Karl Barth, Rudolf Bultmann, Emil Brunner, and Paul Tillich were developing their theological systems from safe enclaves in Switzerland or behind the ocean barrier in North America. For all their academic brilliance, these German-speaking theologians were powerless to slow the stampede to World War II. And although all those mentioned above actively opposed Fascism—some had to flee for their lives when Hitler came to power—Christianity had already ceased to influence European socio-political life before the Nazi era began. By the middle of the twentieth century, Christian thought had become an intellectual game, played by professional theologians, generally ignored by everyone else. Where abided the faith to move mountains? Not in the church.

OURS A SECULAR AGE

What happened? How did so powerful an institution as the Church, which had once de-throned kings, become so impotent that no one listened to her any more?

Modern secular culture arose during the Enlightenment of the eighteenth century but has triumphed during our time. Today the socio-intellectual trend is to consider the Church peripheral to daily life. Questions of social and political ethics and are seldom referred to contemporary churches, unless an official "religious position" is sought by the news media. Quaint relics of a bygone era, churches give us someplace to go on Christmas and Easter, sanctified spaces in which to be married and buried.

Even so the institutional church of today, totally oblivious to her inability to sway the multitudes, keeps churning out dictums and position papers which the faithful keep ignoring. People seem to have decided, in large numbers, that they can make decisions of great importance without benefit of clergy.

Strangely, surveys indicate that people are not leaving their birthright churches when they encounter teachings which are unacceptable to them. They are just doing whatever they want and overlooking the teachings of their own faith on the matter. For example, let's look at the deepening chasm between North American Roman Catholicism and the Vatican party line preached by Pope John Paul II. The following quote is from a major American news magazine:

> Today, the polling data show, the average Catholic believes
> that it is possible to disagree with the church's teaching on
> moral issues and still remain a good Catholic. Despite Rome's
> prohibition on birth control, for instance, a majority of
> (American) Catholic women say they practice it. [13]

One might argue that the unique conditions of American church life contribute to this perfidy by the laity. We have noted that most European churches, Catholic and Protestant, still receive the bulk of their income from tax revenues and not offerings, making European Christianity less dependent upon the good will of its parishioners than highly competitive, North American Christianity. Since American church-goers can literally overturn religious institutions by voting with their dollars, American churches *must* pay attention to the needs and beliefs of their congregations. Both systems have their defenders and critics.

European church leaders might reasonably argue that a clergy independent of the pressure to conform to the whims of parishioners can provide a more effective witness against the excesses of secular culture. However, the very fact that churches must meet the needs of secular men and women suggests the major strength of American churches. If Christianity does not exist to meet actual human needs, why does it exist at all? It is no coincidence that cathedrals in Europe remain virtually empty on Sundays, while big churches in the U.S.A. either pack in the crowds or close their doors.

FREE-MARKET RELIGION

A sample of the articles and books published by American Catholic scholars shows that the Catholic laity, although powerless to affect the doctrinal anachronisms proclaimed by Rome, have nevertheless influenced the tone of theology preached by the American Catholic clergy. But more importantly, Christianity in North America operates in a free market consciousness. Many Catholics and Protestants, not to mention non-observant Jews, have decided to affirm their basic religious identities while ignoring those teachings which require practices that run contrary to their actual belief systems.

Not only do North American laity shrug off troublesome official beliefs but, contrary to their European counterparts, they ignore church teachings—while continuing to attend church regularly! How can a person stay a member of a religious faith that espouses ideas contrary to what he/she actually believes? Very easily, given the individualistic mindset of North Americans.

It's rather like having an eccentric old aunt who rails against this or that newfangled idea. Dissenters just smile and say, "You can't take her seriously. She lives in the past, you know."

FLIGHT FROM FEAR

If we accept the thesis that thriving churches are meeting some kind of need, we must then ask, "What needs are being met?" One researcher's answer was disquieting. As long ago as 1972, Dean M. Kelley contrasted the religious groups that were popping up like dandelions with religious groups withering on the vine. Presenting an impressive battery of charts and statistics, Kelley divided the American churches into two groups:

1) Liberals: reasonable, rational, ecumenical, tolerant, easy-going, non-dogmatic, nonsectarian churches

2) Conservatives: unreasonable, irrational, exclusivist, intolerant, demanding, dogmatic, sectarian churches

We might assume that, given the enlightened age in which we live, the former group of tolerant, liberal churches would be attracting members and the intolerant, sectarian churches would be turning people off. Kelley's data indicated the opposite:

> ...precisely the sectarian and theologically conservative religious groups have made amazing gains in recent years. Amid the current neglect and hostility toward organized religion in general, the conservative churches, holding to seemingly outmoded theology and making strict demands on their members, have equaled or surpassed in growth the yearly percentage of the nation's population. [14]

Instead of attending church to find better ways to live in the world, Kelley's data suggested that many people came to church to escape the complexities of a world hurling change at them at an accelerating pace, a world both too large and too shrunken, too hidebound and too innovative, too banal and too ghastly for the human mind to entertain, encompass, endure. Rather than seek new answers to age-old questions, these rapidly growing churches offered sanctuary and a full-scale retreat from modern life. It was a conclusion which Kelley, a member of the "liberal" United Methodist Church, did not find at all satisfying. [15]

BLACK PLAGUE AND PIN-HOPPING ANGELS

If the most "successful" churches in North America have been encouraging people to retreat from scary contemporary reality, then Kelley's research tracks with the data indicating that the most passionate religionists are not looking to the church for ways to interface with modern life. Large numbers of people, explicitly wanting to avoid the crisis of modernity, find sanctuary in religion. No wonder the most successful denominations preach other-worldly escapism.

Once the very center of the community, the church now finds herself standing on tippy-toes peeking in the window at the shops where movers and shakers transact the truly important business of our society. Once the custodian of knowledge and the educator of Western civilization, the church—which abused her position through suppression of new discoveries that contradicted ancient views on the world, human origins, and the Cosmos—is today regarded in academia as the repository of quaint opinions, not true knowledge.

And justifiably so. Instead of preaching a courageous faith that gave people insights into Divine Truth, Christian clergy have too often become embroiled in petty controversies such as the earth-shattering medieval debate about how many angels could dance on the head of a pin. Meanwhile, outside on the cathedral steps, people starved and died of the Black Plague.

Shame on us for being so petty.

A faith which does not help people live more effectively in the real world is not faith but fantasy. Christianity began as a healing movement, and when theology fails to remember the immediacy of those origins it risks mutating into a mere religious computer game, sizzling with brilliant answers to questions no one is asking. Kelley insisted that churches exist to provide religious answers to the great questions of life and to weave what Peter Berger called a *Sacred Canopy*. Here is Kelley's rather poetic analysis:

> If a man can see his sufferings—the bad things that befall
> him and those he loves—as part of a cosmic purpose or a long
> range good, he can often overcome them, or at least regain
> some of his zest and resilience and possibly go on to
> significant achievements. Meaning...has historically and
> repeatedly proven to be the remedy for severe disorganization
> of persons and groups. It has been the antidote for anomy,
> the rehabilitation of criminals, the rescuer of alcoholics,
> the deliverer of drug addicts, the preventer of suicide, the
> cure for psychosomatic disabilities, and the sure solution
> for many cases of poverty, failure, and despair. [16]

"ALL DINOSAURS, PLEASE REPORT TO THE NEAREST TAR PIT"

Metaphysical Christianity might quibble over Kelley's word choice—we prefer not to dwell on "sufferings" and "bad things that befall" us, but his essential sentiment about the power of meaning to heal mind, body, and affairs rings true to our deepest religious sentiments. Could the answer to Kelley's questions be a strongly spiritual view of the world, providing a framework of meaning, by which men and women can understand life religiously in the twenty-first century, while still affirming the unity of scientific and religious truth? If a greater vision of life captures the mind, empowering us to live more effectively, does this not provide the strongest of all religious systems, i.e., a comprehensive worldview integrating heart and head?

Authentic Christian theology always responds to human needs with healthy interpretations of the ancient faith grounded in the real world, not by nourishing the fears of its clientele. Promising heaven does nothing to correct ineffective living in this world.

While fear-based fantasies like Christian fundamentalism may be popular—indeed, it fills the pews of countless churches, floods the airwaves and erects cathedrals in the cornfields of the American hinterlands—fundamentalism is a dinosaur in search of a tar pit, large and vital but totally incapable of adapting to survive the social and intellectual climatic changes that will surely come in the twenty-first century.

FIRST PARADOX: ASCETICISM VS. ACTIVISM

This is the first paradox which confronts religionists who want to live their faith: Shall we withdraw from the noisome pestilence to dwell exclusively in the secret place of the Most High, or sally forth to launch the Kingdom of God by our good deeds? Shall we look for a spiritual high or a righteous cause? Seek personal salvation or convert the world? Withdraw to work on our spiritual growth or teach others? Contemplate the Divine or confront injustice? The question can be framed in many ways, but when corrected for differing emphases among conservative, moderate and liberal theologies, the picture is essentially the same: Asceticism or Activism?

Bonhoeffer saw the danger for Christianity from these two extremes: either flight from this world to the ivory palaces of heaven on one hand, or a cynical "God helps those who help themselves" attitude on the other. Both represent real religious needs, the need to find Divine Order in an apparently mad world, balanced by the equally important need to make this world a better place because of our commitment to Jesus Christ. The New Testament clearly shows that Jesus took time to pray and center Himself, then marched back to the marketplace to engage contemporary people with His words and healing touch. His spirituality flowed directly to action.

Sometimes, however, the followers of Jesus become, in the old preacher's cliché, "So heavenly minded they ain't no earthly good." Spiritual pursuits are delightful, but acute other-worldliness can lure us so far from the marketplace that we cannot, or will not, hear the cries of the poor in spirit.

During my days at theological seminary I heard a about a professor who staged a dramatic lesson for his students. On the day that he was lecturing on the parable of the Good Samaritan, the professor stationed an actor—broken, bloody and moaning, smelling and looking like a homeless drunkard who had fallen among bad company—beside a bush outside the classroom. All the students rushed by, eager to get to their lecture on the Good Samaritan! Apparently the idea of actually touching a ragged, bloody man (an AIDS victim, perhaps?) never jilted their eagerness to contemplate academically the parable of Jesus.

One wonders: Why study religion, if it helps us evade our responsibilities to live a godly life? Yet, doesn't religion comfort us precisely because it offers sanctuary from a world which can be so unpleasant at times?

Today, the pendulum has swung far from medieval pin-splitting. Theologians struggle to keep their work relevant to the real world. However, many theologians have become so hot for social and political justice that they've grown cold to their calling as spiritual leaders. Late in the twentieth century, two forms of this activism arose, one conservative and the other liberal.

In the 1980s and 1990s, fundamentalist Christians—spurred by electronic evangelists like Jerry Falwell and his Moral Majority and Religious Right groups like Pat Robertson's Christian Coalition—rallied around conservative political leaders to battle for a multitude of socio-political causes. Anti-abortion, anti-gay activism became the litmus test for Christian faithfulness; cutting the size of government became a mission field.

On the far left, *Liberation Theology* attempted to crossbreed Marxism with Christianity, sometimes promoting armed revolution for the oppressed people of the Third World. Liberal Christians created shibboleths of their own: feminists insisted on gender-neutral translations of scripture and pro-choice politics; African-American theologians defended affirmative action and condemned cuts in social programs.

Although avowed enemies, the goals of the Religious Right and Liberation Theology are essentially the same: to bring their vision of the ideal Christian community and the just society into existence by taking direct action in the outer world. Making the world a better place is an admirable goal (which we shall consider at length in Chapter 15), but too often socio-political activism submerges spiritual teachings and drowns true believers of the Left and the Right in a sea of bitterness. Too frequently, campaigns are waged *against* institutions, *against* groups, *against* opposing viewpoints.

Theologies which advocate socio-political activism run the risk of becoming intolerant, self-righteous, and prone to anger. They seem to say, "If we don't act now, God's kingdom won't come." Yet, as Dietrich Bonhoeffer discovered, the church must address the problems of the world or risk dissolving into trivia. He prayed, but saw no alternative to Hitler's overthrow. As we grapple with the *Asceticism-Activism paradox* we immediately discover a sea of gray where black and white issues float free.

IS THERE AN ANCHOR?

Anchoring the paradox requires answers to questions about appropriate involvement. When does theology need to concentrate on spiritual matters (hunger for God so rampant in our world), and when does theology need to turn its attention to socio-political issues (human rights, racism, gender discrimination, homophobia, poverty, drugs/crime, teen pregnancy, economic justice)? This book will steer a middle course between the twin poles of otherworldly asceticism and socio-political activism. We shall attempt to hold these two poles in tension as we explore Christian theology.

One solution to the paradox was suggested by Charles Fillmore, i.e. to acknowledge the troubles of the world and help the cause of justice when possible, never forgetting our primary function as students/teachers of Practical Christianity. "The church of Christ covers every department of man's existence and enters into every fiber of his being," Mr. Fillmore said. "He carries it with him day and night, seven days of the week. He lives in it as a fish lives in water and is transformed into a new creature." [17]

SECOND PARADOX: PESSIMISM VS. IDEALISM

Historically, Christian orthodoxy has resolved the Asceticism-Activism problem either by withdrawing from society to form cloisters of the Elect (as did the Jewish Essenes of the Qumran community and Christian monastics of the high Middle Ages), or by attempting to control all aspects of life (as did Rabbinical Judaism and the Medieval Church). The problem is exactly the same for Ascetics and Activists: How shall we live in an imperfect world full of imperfect people?

Belief systems in recent years have reflected this age-old question about the worth of humanity. Glancing at history, we can understand how sensitive souls might ask whether human society is incontrovertibly evil. This is going to be a point of contention between Metaphysical Christianity and virtually every other Christian perspective.

Most modern theologies are grounded in extreme pessimism about the perfectibility of human beings. However, most of the metaphysical churches were founded during the latter part of the 1800s when a different intellectual climate dominated the philosophical and theological worldview of Christendom.

The closing years of the nineteenth century were exciting times. Science had come of age; empirical research was beginning to enrich human life. First telegraph then telephone shrank distances for the first time, making instant communications possible from the other side of the world. Edison lit the night, then gave us recorded music and moving pictures. Henry Ford perfected an automobile almost everyone could afford that was mass produced on an assembly line. New advances in health brought vaccines against smallpox, the pasteurization process, and the long-overdue comprehension of the part microorganisms play in disease. Charles Darwin capped the progress of that brilliant century by quietly observing birds and animals for years and publishing his world-shattering *Origin of Species*, laying the foundation for modern biology by showing how life evolved from simpler to more complex organisms. It seemed like humanity would progress smoothly to a world of peace and harmony, governed by reason and law.

In the intellectual realm of the late nineteenth century, *Absolute Idealism* dominated the philosophical and theological landscape. Absolute Idealism was metaphysical; spiritual categories were identified with Ultimate Reality. It was monistic, believing in One Power/One Presence without a distinct line between Creator and creatures. It spoke about things as universal rather than particular; it looked at the incarnation of Jesus Christ as typical (universal) rather than unique. Absolute Idealism also espoused an unhesitant optimism. British theologian John Macquarrie reports:

> At the present day there will be no ready response to the optimism
> of idealists like Sir Henry Jones, who concluded his Gifford
> Lectures by assuring his audience of "the friendliness and helpful-
> ness of man's environment"; or like Josiah Royce, who asserted
> that "the world, as a whole, is and must be absolutely good." [18]

The "friendliness and helpfulness" of the world; One Presence/ One Power; reality itself is "absolutely good;" science and education are the magic keys to social progress and spiritual evolution: These were the dominant themes of the late nineteenth century. It seemed things would continue to get better until God's Kingdom or at least a human utopia, was established.

And then the system began to unravel.

Nation-states squared off in two world wars. Humanity compelled its scientists to design more efficient ways to kill people. First, poison gas and machine guns; then dive bombers, gas chambers, and atomic bombs. But two world wars didn't slake the human appetite for carnage. Korea, Vietnam, the Kennedy and King assassinations, drive-by homicides, drug related crime—small wonder a cynical pessimism settled over the world, replacing the sunny optimism of the nineteenth century.

Newer, gloomier philosophies appeared, like *Existentialism*, which promised nothing but full awareness of squalid human life. Existentialism became the world-view of Western intelligentsia. And since professional clergy are educated by the intellectual community, religious thinking quickly followed suit. Mid-twentieth century theologians, like Reinhold Niebuhr, were soon proclaiming that humanity is unqualified to follow the model of Jesus because we are fatally flawed. Salvation must break into human existence by God's action; we are part of the problem and cannot be part of the solution. [19]

Science and education as the answer? The Nazi's flourished in Germany, among some of the most highly educated, scientifically advanced people on earth. By mid-twentieth century we learned that when you educate a bigot you often get a better educated bigot. Still worse, we learned that education could be a weapon of tyranny as totalitarian states indoctrinated millions in their school systems.

Given the events of the twentieth century, it's not hard to see how disbelief in the perfectibility of humankind has become the only acceptable viewpoint, not just in theology but across society. Anyone who expects the best is seen as hopelessly naive. Next time you watch the evening news, listen carefully. The only people predicting good results today are politicians claiming success and their spin doctors trolling for votes. "Sure things are getting better, because our policies are working!" Anyone else "reached for comment" looks at the future as guarded at best.

Negativism is so pervasive that if news people announce an encouraging statistic they feel compelled to drain the optimism from their news item in the name of balanced reporting. When covering a government report of a nationwide lower-than-expected unemployment rate, watch the news media scour the nation until they find someone standing in an unemployment line in Boise, Idaho, to show that not everyone has benefited from the trend.

Ours has become an age of shameless pessimism.

Founded in an era of bright hopes, metaphysical Christianity now finds itself in sole possession of the optimistic highlands once crowded by theologians from virtually every major denomination. Yet, we would be living in cloud castles if we did not admit that the pessimists have a point. Humans have done terrible things to each other, often in the Name of God. But is their conduct normal or aberrant? Was the Nazi movement an isolated phenomenon, or a typical episode in human history?

As we ask ourselves whether Pessimism or Optimism is the appropriate attitude for Christian thought, we are really asking questions about our views on metaphysical anthropology. What is the nature of humanity—devil or angel, evil or good?

THIRD PARADOX: HUMAN VS. DIVINE

How can we believe that humanity, with its many flaws, is somehow related to the Divine? Are we lowly beings, dust of the earth, given permission to raise our eyes to heaven only by Divine mercy? In the words of the Episcopal prayer book:

> We have erred, and strayed from thy ways like lost sheep. We have followed too much the devices and desires of our own hearts. We have offended against thy holy laws. We have left undone those things which we ought to have done; And we have done those things which we ought not to have done; and there is no health in us. [20]

Or, are we powerful sons and daughters of God, unaware of our birthright because we have not yet learned how to claim it? Can we blithely affirm, with Sir Henry Jones, "the friendliness and helpfulness of man's environment", or with Josiah Royce, that "the world, as a whole, is and must be absolutely good"?

Are we miserable wretches, or Divine offspring?

EMERGING FROM THE SHADOWS

Metaphysical Christianity, as the surviving archipelago of nineteenth century Idealism, offers a compromise to the tension of the Human-Divine Paradox. Those who stand in the idealist tradition believe in the perfectibility of men and women, not because we blind ourselves to the atrocities humans have visited upon their brothers and sisters, but because, to paraphrase a popular epigram, God isn't finished with us yet.

Walk into a second grade classroom. Ask a bright seven-year-old this question: "Jessica, how do you find the area of a rectangle?" You'll draw a blank stare, frown, or nervous giggle. Seven-year-olds aren't ready for math problems that complicated. But that doesn't mean they're flawed, evil, or corrupt with "no health" in them. It means they are at another level of development, the proper stage for them, now.

Ask the same question of a Ph.D. candidate in computer science and you'll draw the same stare or nervous frown, but this time it's because she'll be wondering if you're serious or if you're merely insulting her intelligence. A graduate student isn't better than a second grader; she's just further along the path of knowledge.

So with humanity. Certainly, we have a long way to go. We are still capable of extreme cruelty. Nevertheless, homo sapiens has leaped forward in modern times, as all but the most bitter cynics must admit. Slavery has been abolished except in small pockets far from civilization. Colonialism is almost gone, racism is socially unacceptable, and the East-West Cold War has melted away. World peace no longer seems a wild dream, and democracy is winning the worldwide battle against totalitarianism. The good side of humanity emerges from the shadows.

Instead of adopting the wide-eyed optimism of the nineteenth century or the cold cynicism of the mid-twentieth, a balanced theology might solve the Human-Divine Paradox by acknowledging the problems of humanity while boldly affirming our indwelling Divine spirit. Isn't that the model of Jesus Christ? Instead of forcing a choice between humanity and divinity for the starting point of our theology, the Jesus Christ model gives us both: God-with-us and God-in-us. We have a long way to go, but we are eager to get on with the journey. Jesus Christ is guide, destination, and map.

THE ECLIPSE IS OVER?

As stated in the Caveat, our perspective begins with the central premise of Metaphysical Christianity—there is *One Presence and One Power* in our lives and in the Cosmos, God the Good, Omnipotent. The three paradoxes (*Asceticism vs Activism, Pessimism vs. Idealism, Human vs. Divine*) will emerge again and again as we survey the vast domain of Christian theology.

Since the emphasis in current Christian thought remains pessimistic, I am convinced the insights of metaphysical Christianity will fall like raindrops on a parched land. Christendom thirsts for Truth, hungers for hope. Writing in the turbulent 1960s, John Macquarrie first brushed aside nineteenth century idealism, then asked a prophetic question:

> Idealist theologians (like idealist philosophers) are likewise in eclipse, and the doctrine of divine immanence has been replaced by a stress on transcendence. Of course, it is a question whether, if the Western world should come through its present turmoil—political, social, and intellectual—to a settled and stable period once more, something like absolute idealism may not reappear. For the present,

however, it is out of favor, and is not even seriously discussed, much less defended. [21]

Since Macquarrie wrote this passage, the winds of change blowing across the "political, social and intellectual" seas have indeed carried us to "a settled and stable period once more." Economics and the Internet seem to be succeeding in uniting the world where armies of conquest have failed. Perhaps the global village is ready once more to discuss seriously the possibility that human beings are the children of God.

Which brings us to the next question: Which biblical event serves as the best model to understand God's relationship to humanity?

EASTER OR CHRISTMAS?

In recent years there has been an increasing pressure from clergy in traditional churches to de-emphasize Christmas in favor of Easter. Though ordinary believers (non-believers as well) seem to identify with the Nativity, the most important event in Church history for clergy has long been the Crucifixion-Resurrection. This has been especially true for theologians. Browse the index of any book on Systematic Theology; you will find plenty of Easter images and virtually nothing about Christmas.

A lot of cross, very little manger.

Contrast this theological emphasis with the popular/secular celebrations of each holiday. The Christmas euphoria begins in November and lingers until January. For a month and a half, the Western world dreams about peace on earth while sending gifts and greetings to folks we ignore the rest of the year. Christmas gathers a huge cloud of humanity into a quasi-religious community, which lingers until well after the New Year's Day clean up.

Easter gets a half-day. Even then, the Christian church has to share its most sacred observance with a big white bunny pushing chocolate figurines and pastel painted, hard-boiled eggs; an ersatz Halloween with Roger Rabbit as master of ceremonies. Certainly, Santa Claus has eclipsed the baby Jesus in some celebrations of Christmas, but at least he's a saint, theoretically based on a real person, who represents the virtues of love, kindness, and generosity. As much as I love fuzzy rabbits and colored eggs, the Easter Bunny represents new clothing and carbohydrates, a secularized holiday silenced of every whisper of religiosity. I would not eliminate the rabbits and the jelly beans in green straw baskets—I would place them at the foot of the cross, love-offerings from a gentler world to the child of humanity-divinity born in a manger, crucified on that cross.

Does the widespread embrace of Christmas—even in lands like Japan, where Christianity is a distinct minority—reflect deeper religious yearnings than the Crucifixion-Resurrection emphasis of Easter? What makes Christmas so special?

Ask children why they love Christmas, you'll get a straightforward answer: *"The presents!"* And so it is. Christmas gift-giving is love-giving, pure and simple. It's too easy to chalk holiday presents up to crass commercialism. Nothing sells unless people buy it, and advertising alone can't generate a market. Ask Hollywood producers.

Although we harry ourselves by all the holiday activities we squeeze into our busy lives, Christmas rings the love bell, even if while we grouse about it. Not by accident, people have discovered Christmas is the holiday of hope, the day when people dare to believe that it's really possible to hear the angels sing and know that God comes to us in every newborn child. Although this will sound like rank heresy to most orthodox clergy and theologians, it is possible to contend that the main event of the Christian Faith occurred not at Calvary but Bethlehem.

The Birth of the Christ—God-within-us—is at the very least equal to the Crucifixion-Resurrection event. Easter shows us God's triumph in the face of suffering and despair; Christmas reveals God's brightest hopes for every human child. Who says which message is more important?

MATTHEW FOX: FALL/REDEMPTION CENTERED THEOLOGY

Theologically, the cross has been central in Christian thought because our religious frame of reference has been built upon what Catholic theologian Matthew Fox calls a Fall-Redemption centered theology. Fox sees this as a mutant offshoot, not representing the main branch of Jewish and Christian biblical tradition.[22]

In my book, *Friends in High Places*, I described the fifth century A.D. controversy which arose between St. Augustine and the Celtic monk Pelagius. Augustine pushed for a nonbiblical Fall-and-Redemption Christianity based on his dualistic, pessimistic, Manachean background. In a Fall-Redemption centered religion, humans "fell" from some kind of pristine goodness to a state of brokenness. Humanity wallows in its fallen state, sinful and lost, until a divine agent cleanses and restores us to wholeness and harmony with God.[23]

In its Christian expression, Fall-Redemption theology interprets the Garden of Eden story as both an historic and a metaphysical event which led to original sin that stains every human soul. We inherit sinfulness from our parents, a spiritual disease transmitted *in utero*.

The biblical worldview is quite different from this alien, non-Christian, pagan viewpoint which sneaked into the church through the writings of frustrated, woman-hating celibates like St. Jerome and St. Augustine. A fresh look at the Bible shows very few passages which mutter about the dark side of humanity but a lot of verses, chapters, and whole books proclaiming creation's wholeness before God.

Matthew Fox points out that in the Middle Ages Meister Eckhart had said that God created the world good, and it stayed good. Viewed this way, the central category of Christianity is not *Fall/Redemption* but *Creation*. It's a short hop from Eckhart's mysticism to a faith based not just on the Cross but also the Incarnation. Furthermore, as we shall better see after we study Christology, Christmas is the world's birthday, because every cradle is the manger and every child is the Christ. The hunger for something to believe in bursts forth each December, when even stolid cynics must allow themselves a moment of "maybe."

> *Maybe it could be true.*
> *Maybe there could be peace on earth.*
> *Maybe God comes to us this way.*
> *Clothed in flesh.*
> *Cradled in ordinary straw.*

A world of challenges still awaits us as we walk back from candlelight services each Christmas Eve, but for one shining moment, heaven has touched earth. If we could bottle that feeling and carry it with us all year around, we might be able to handle any circumstance with courage and faith. In a Creation centered theology, Christmas gives us the light to walk by, for God dwells within us, empowering our every step on the upward path. The world is still a dangerous place; "bad" things can still happen to us. But the Nativity reveals God's presence and power reaching the weakest link in the human chain; even a newborn baby has the Divine Spirit within. Despite appearances to the contrary, God has everything under control. Life is trustworthy and good, even life which leads to apparent tragedy, such as Jesus faced at Calvary.

This, then, is the goal of Metaphysical Christianity: To be the Christmas faith in an Easter world.

CHECK YOUR KNOWLEDGE

1. "Bonhoeffer suffered the dilemma of the philosopher-king." What does this mean, and what choice did he make?

2. What does recent data indicate about people who find the teachings of their religious faith difficult to follow? Are they leaving to join other groups?

3. Three paradoxes are discussed. Name and explain each.

4. Explain "Creation-Centered" Theology. How is it helpful to Metaphysical Christians?

5. Is most Christian theology today pessimistic or optimistic? How did theology achieve its current position?

6. Why does the author call Metaphysical Christianity the "Christmas faith in an Easter world"?

QUESTIONS FOR DISCUSSION

1. Should Christians concern themselves with making this world a better place or concentrate on spiritual pursuits?

2. Was Dietrich Bonhoeffer correct when he said that discipleship is always costly?

3. If you had been a German Christian pastor during WW II, would you have joined Bonhoeffer in fighting the Nazi's or fled the country as soon as you knew how terrible life would become?

4. Is violence justified in war? What about trying to kill Hitler? Would Jesus Christ approve?

5. How can Metaphysical Christianity maintain its sunny optimism about human perfectibility after the Holocaust?

6. In what ways is Jesus Christ calling us today? What's "The Cost of Discipleship" for us?

NOTES

1. Dietrich Bonhoeffer in Paul Johnson *A History of Christianity* (NY: Atheneum, 1980), p. 494.

2. *IBID.*, p. 484.

3. *IBID.*, p. 485.

4. *IBID.*, pp. 485-486.

5. *IBID.*, p. 487.

6. *IBID.*, p. 484.

7. T.A. Kantonen, *Christian Faith Today: Studies in Contemporary Theology* (Lima, OH: C>S>S> Publishing Co., 1974), pp. 65-66.

8. Dietrich Bonhoeffer, *Letters and Papers from Prison* (NY: MacMillan, 1972), p. 371.

9. Bonhoeffer in Kantonen, p. 72.

10. Bonhoeffer in John Macquarrie, *Twentieth Century Religious Thought* (London: SCM Press, 1971), p. 331.

11 *RSV*, Colossian 1:27.

12. Dietrich Bonhoeffer, *The Cost of Discipleship* (NY: MacMillan, 1963), p. 47.

13. Merril McLoughlin, et al, "The Pope Gets Tough," *U.S. News and World Report,* November 1986, pp. 64-71.

14. Dean M. Kelley, *Why Conservative Churches Are Growing* (NY: Harper & Row, 1972), p. viii.

15. *IBID.*, p. 86.

16. *IBID.*, p. 43.

17. Charles Fillmore, *Dynamics for Living* (Unity Village: 1967), p. 288.

18. Macquarrie, p. 20.

19. Kantonen, pp. 49-50.

20. John Wallace Suter, Custodian, *The Book of Common Prayer* (NY: Harper & Brothers, 1952), p. 6.

21. Macquarrie, p. 44.

22. Matthew Fox, *Breakthrough: Meister Eckhart's Creation Spirituality in New Translation* (NY: Doubleday, 1980), pp. 24-25.

23. Thomas Shepherd, *Friends in High Places* (Unity Village: Unity Books, 1985), pp. 40-48.

THE TOOLS OF THEOLOGY

Chapter Two

In the introduction to his *History of Christian Thought*, Paul Tillich admitted the task was impossibly large:

> Actually, nobody would dare to present a complete history of what every theologian in the Christian Church has thought. That would be an ocean of contradictory ideas. The purpose of this (work) is quite different, namely, to show those thoughts which have become accepted expressions of the life of the church.[1]

As every theologian must, Tillich went beyond simply describing the ideas which "have become accepted expressions" of religious thinkers. His writings teem with analysis, critique, and synthesis. How could it be otherwise, since he frankly admitted that theology is a process of sifting through "an ocean of contradictory ideas"?

THE WORD FOR TODAY IS "THEOLOGY"

Theology is, as the root words suggest, the "study of God". We'll attempt a comprehensive, inclusive definition.

> *Theology:* Organized, rational reflection on ideas and practices pertaining to the Divine, God and Ultimate Concerns, evaluated from within the boundaries of a chosen circle of faith.

This definition is power-packed, so let's begin unpacking it. We say theological inquiry is "organized, rational reflection." This separates theology from devotional, inspirational or strictly personal studies about divine actions or ideas. It is *organized* because it proceeds from point to point in a logical sequence, and it is *rational* because the whole picture should fit together without blatant contradictions in our *reflections*.

Theology concerns itself with *ideas* and *practices*. Not just concepts but the deeds we do in the name of God are fair game for theological analysis. One theologian might examine a concept like Divine Order while another studies the Lord's Supper as it is celebrated by several different communions. Both are doing theology.

Subject matter for theological reflection must be *pertaining to the Divine, God and Ultimate Concerns*. Anything which concerns humanity in an ultimate way

Such questions as

(What happens after death? How shall we treat neighbors? What is the purpose of life?) can be studied as a theological subject. Religious ethics, human relationships, healing, prosperity anchored in a Jesus Christ consciousness—any subject which opens itself to the influx of Divine power is a theological topic. Since these questions of Ultimate Concerns move beyond data available to the physical sciences, they are inherently metaphysical.

Lastly, our definition acknowledges that all theology occurs *within the boundaries of a chosen circle of faith.* This is how a study in the "philosophy of religion" differs from doing theology. Theoretically, philosophy begins without commitment to any particular world-view. Philosophers of religion examine the writings of the prophets of all faiths without following any of them as their personal Wayshower. Theologians, however, begin with certain ineluctable assumptions.

If a Jewish theologian decides the Koran is true and Mohammed is the prophet of God, she can no longer call herself a "Jewish" theologian. If a Muslim theologian studies Buddhism and decides to embrace the Noble Eightfold Path, he is no longer a Muslim theologian. Jews do theological analysis of the Koran, of course, and Muslims study Buddhism, but they study these books from *"within the boundaries of a chosen circle of faith."* The yardstick for the Jew is Torah and Talmud. For Muslims it's the Koran. The yardstick for the Christian is...?

Answer that question, and you're doing Christian theology.

At first blush, the way of the philosopher of religion seems closer to the self-image of most Metaphysical Christians. After all, don't we pride ourselves in affirming that Truth (with a capital T) can be found in all the religions? Why not follow Truth wherever it leads, even far beyond the boundaries of the Christian faith? Aren't "boundaries" just arbitrary barriers fencing people in or out? Why not call ourselves the "Church of Truth" and recognize no single religious tradition as our home?

Because, my friends, it simply isn't true.

If we are faithful to the historical evidence, we must acknowledge that the Metaphysical Christian heritage flows from the river of Protestant thought, especially nineteenth-century Unitarian and Universalist thought as sketched by Ralph Waldo Emerson. (Marcus Bach rightly named Emerson, not Phineas P. Quimby, as the true founder of New Thought Christianity.) Metaphysical Christianity is not a free floating island, but part of the Christian mainland. We may honor the teachings of Buddha, but when we look at those teachings we do so through a stained glass window that is irrevocably shaped like Jesus Christ. Our very God-concept is not so much a God concept as it is a Jesus concept.

What are the attributes of God? Selfless love, healing mercy, infinite kindness, overwhelming forgiveness, endless warmth, non-judgmental intelligence, life-empowering confidence, vast oceans of grace. Where do we get these ideas? From the life and teachings of Jesus. My favorite definition of a Christian comes from Catholic theologian Hans Küng:

> A Christian is not just any human being with genuine conviction, sincere faith and good will. No one can fail to see that genuine conviction, sincere faith and good will also exist outside Christianity. But all those can be called Christian for whom in life and death Jesus Christ is ultimately decisive. [2]

I especially like Küng's prescription because it's a maximum definition, including virtually everyone who claims to follow Jesus. Theologians often erect elaborate screening devices to filter out the heretics, yet here we have a Catholic thinker—albeit a delightfully heretical one himself—proposing an almost fenceless Christian pasture for all the sheep of Jesus to range far and graze freely.

I said "almost fenceless" because even Küng's definition sets boundaries. Limitations are not inherently bad. Every choice necessarily eliminates other options. When we choose to marry one person we shut ourselves off from certain kinds of social interactions with members of the opposite sex, for life. When we decide to buy *this* car instead of *that* car, we have limited ourselves. Structure is not always equal to bondage, if the structure is freely chosen and provides space within it to operate in some measure of freedom. The rules in a football game provide necessary structure without which no game could be played. Rules become a problem only when they are imposed, arbitrary and oppressive.

Metaphysical Christianity straddles a paradox. We acknowledge the nature of cultural influence on religious thought, yet we freely choose to affiliate ourselves with the dominant religion of Western culture, the Judeo-Christian faith.

Why? Because it works for us. For Metaphysical Christians—as with everyone who fits under Hans Küng's rainbow definition of Christianity—birth, life, teachings, death/resurrection, and the ongoing presence of Jesus Christ provide a yardstick by which we measure Truth. There are other systems of measurement afoot in the world; doubtless many are effective for those who use them. But Jesus Christ works for us. His example shows us the way to be human and divine. That's why we call our studies Metaphysical Christianity.

SIX FUNCTIONS OF THEOLOGY

Now that we understand the place of Metaphysical Christianity in the mainstream of Christian thought, we turn next to an analysis of what theology should be doing if it does its job. To better understand what we are about in this book, we shall examine *Six Functions of Theology.* These are not the only functions of religious inquiry, but they will serve as a handy framework to introduce theological thinking for now.

1. ONGOING RE-INTERPRETATIONS OF THE FAITH.

When theology is doing its job, theology challenges the clichés and outmoded ideas of previous generations, translating the Christian faith into the language of today. The first function of theology, then, is to provide an *ongoing re-interpretation* of Truth for each new generation. Scientific research methods have taught us a valuable lesson: Truth must be faced and accepted even if it kicks the pillars out from under our most cherished hypotheses.

When Charles Darwin expounded his theory of evolution he was in no way endangering God's Truth; he just shot holes through our limited concepts of Truth. Since Darwin's day scientists have learned to be more open to new ideas. Although "orthodoxy" exists in the scientific community, science is much more willing to accept radically new concepts than almost any other field of knowledge.

A case in point is what happened when the deep space Voyager I probe passed near Saturn on its way out of the solar system in late fall-winter 1980-81. When the first computer-enhanced photographs flowed back across millions of miles of space the researchers were enthralled at the beauty of Saturn's ring system. Then their rapture turned to astonishment as Voyager focused on the inner rings of the sixth planet.

To their utter amazement they found the clear images of the F-rings showed a intertwined pattern. How could orbiting particles of frozen gas twist themselves into an elongated braid around the girth of Saturn's atmosphere?

One scientist moaned that this new discovery meant they might have to throw out everything they knew about orbital physics. "Braiding defies the laws of orbital mechanics for several reasons," he said. "But obviously these rings are doing the right thing."[3]

In an earlier age, people consulted ancient authorities if they wanted to know what was true. If Aristotle or St. Augustine said it was true, then it was true forever. No one considered examining nature to learn what is true, because learned men had already passed judgment. "Who are we to contradict the great ones?" the medieval scholar demanded.

The problem, of course is that ancient authorities, wise though they may be, are often dead wrong when they stray into the scientific realm. If scientists were still functioning from the authority model they would have looked at those crisp, color photographs of the braided rings of Saturn and said, *"Well, that can't be right. The camera must be broken. Our books on astronomy say those F-rings can't be braided, so the pictures must be wrong."*

Saturn, having never read those books, didn't know it wasn't allowed to braid its rings. The objective of science is not to prove theories but to find out what is true. Scientists studying the Voyager data had to get right with Saturn, because the ringed planet wasn't about to change its physical properties to suit their theories.

A more rational approach to religious studies might also be to accept the probability of change and to welcome it. What is important, after all, is not one particular religious theory, comfortable though it may be, but Truth itself. A faith to live by in the ages to come must be absolutely fearless when facing the accelerating pace of new knowledge streaming into human consciousness. Rather than deciding what God has done and requiring all new data to comply with our self-made religious systems, religious thinkers will need to modify their cherished beliefs as we learn what actually exists, what is actually true, what God has actually wrought. Anything less is an insult to the Creator and Source of all life, love, and intelligence.

New knowledge is no threat to God; it only threatens those who have closed their windows to the light of God's Truth. An *ongoing re-interpretation of Truth* will allow us to correct the blind spots and move closer to knowledge of God and His/Her cosmos. This brings us to the second function of theology.

2. PROVIDE CRITICAL ANALYSIS OF RELIGIOUS IDEAS.

When theologians are doing their jobs, theology becomes the science of religious analysis, a gadfly pestering us to re-think assumptions and re-design paradigms. In short, effective theology is *critical.* This is a new concept for Metaphysical Christians, deserving special attention.

The word "criticism" has fallen on hard times. Originally it meant "to evaluate and analyze," but these days criticism is almost always equated with negative comments. In today's language, "Don't criticize me!" actually means, "Don't find fault with me!"

Some exceptions reflect the original sense of the word: art critics, movie critics, and drama critics tell us about new offerings from their respective fields. These specialists do an evaluation in their specialty and pass the information along to us. Since everyone is a layperson in someone else's field, we often rely on experts to give us their critical opinion before plunking down our cash for a Broadway show, a movie, or a new car. This is the sense in which the term is used in theology.

For example, *biblical criticism* is objective study of the Bible, sometimes facing hard evidence which suggests that the author of a well known passage probably didn't mean what we've always thought he meant when he wrote the words for his target audience. Critical analysis of theological ideas means to investigate those concepts from the most objective viewpoint we can achieve. Since theology always begins within a circle of faith, we must continually check our assumptions to see if we are being faithful to gospel of Jesus Christ as understood in our faith community. We need not fantasize that we have captured Absolute Truth, but at minimum we ought to be logically consistent.

POSITIVE HERITAGE

Students of Christian metaphysics have usually emphasized points of agreement and tried to play down conflicting ideas. In a world frequently torn by religious strife, we have rightly seen that to follow Jesus Christ means, in the words of a well-known ditty, it's important to

> Accentuate the positive,
> Eliminate the negative,
> Hold fast to the affirmative
> an' don't mess with Mr. In-between.[4]

Although we want to be positive, we can't help but be analytical as well. Everyday life forces us to choose among alternatives based on analysis of the situation. For example, some people are comfortable with Roman Catholicism, others with Judaism; still others find some variety of mainstream Protestantism meets their religious needs. Those who like the spirit, excitement and freedom of Metaphysical Christianity have elected it as their religious homebase. But every selection implies non-selections. To choose one church is to reject the others. It doesn't mean to dislike, disapprove of, or even disagree with the other churches. It means to pick what works for us, the best one for our needs.

CRITICAL ANALYSIS AND ITS LIMITATIONS

Theological analysis is that sort of work. Many are the ways to look at the great issues, as Paul Tillich indicated. When we examine the concepts, practices and lifestyles offered in the religious marketplace, then select one for our personal faith, we have done critical analysis.

Practical Christianity has always encouraged people to think for themselves, i.e., be independently minded and prove Truth ideas in their lives. One of the goals of this book is to open dialogue on the subject of theological analysis and to offer help for people as they now self-consciously do what they have intuitively been doing all along. Hopefully, any critical analysis of theological topics will retain the positive tone of our Metaphysical Christian tradition while still remaining faithful to the principles of religious scholarship.

However, a note about the limitations of theology is in order before we proceed. Not only those ideas which we can fathom are true. Some religious questions will remain open, forever. A healthy religious faith rejoices when it doesn't have all the answers.

As Eric Gill said in a moment of outrage, *"Good Lord! The thing was a mystery and we measured it!"*[5]

Thankfully, some things are immeasurably deep.

ANALYTICAL HERITAGE

The Metaphysical Christian heritage affirms analytical thinking from central principles. In a remarkable passage from *Dynamics for Living,* a "best of Fillmore" compilation, Charles Fillmore laid the foundation for systematic theologies of future. Because of its significance, we quote in its entirety:

> To think in an independent, untrammeled way about anything is foreign to the habit of the races of the Occident. Our lines of thought and act are based upon precedent and arbitrary authority. We boast much of our freedom and independence, but the facts are that we defer from custom and tradition. Our whole civilization is based on manmade opinions. We have never thought for ourselves in religion, consequently we do not know how to think accurately and consecutively upon any proposition.

We have not been trained to draw conclusions each for himself from a Universal Pivotal Truth. Consequently, we are not competent to pass judgment upon any statement so predicated. Our manner of deciding whether or not certain statements are true or false is to apply the mental bias with which heredity, religion, or social custom has environed us, or else fly to some manmade record as authority.

In the study of practical Christianity all such temporary proofs of Truth are swept aside as chaff. We entertain nothing in our statements of Truth that does not stand the most searching analysis, nothing that cannot be practically demonstrated. [6]

When theology does its job, it offers us *Glimpses of Truth* from a new vantage. Our method will be analytical rather than devotional/inspirational, since we are seeking "to think in an independent, untrammeled way" about central concepts of theology from "a universal pivotal truth" turning upon solid, Metaphysical Christian foundations. Mr. Fillmore also insisted that religious Truth must "be practically demonstrated." We heartily agree. This brings us to the third function of theology.

3. INTEGRATION OF RELIGIOUS IDEAS WITH EVERYDAY LIFE.

When I was a boy, I attended a Sunday school at a mainline Protestant church. We kids enjoyed the Bible stories, but we soon noticed that we were always reading about events which happened when men wore sandals and rode camels. Jesus met the woman at the well because she had to go down to the village square to draw water. We had indoor plumbing, paved streets and sewage systems. Why was everything religious also so ancient?

Our teacher applied the stories, of course. Johnny and Susie decide to tell the truth rather than lie about finding some money in a hollow tree. Truthful children are important to any society. But what was the specifically "religious" content of such an application?

When problems crashed through our Ozzie-and-Harriet world, bringing health challenges and relationship problems never shown on 1950s television, how could ancient Christianity help? Visiting patients in the hospital, many Christian pastors report feeling utterly helpless. What can they do for a sick person but sit by his side and attempt to do Rogerian therapy: *"Could you say more about that?"*

Ministerial training at theological seminaries helps only slightly. Prospective ministers are taught to let the people express their feelings and to be a caring person, which is certainly important for a pastor to be. However, pastoral education rarely progresses beyond the psychological treatment phase of ministry. During my years of graduate theological education, I can't recall hearing a seminary professor express the belief that God could heal people of disease, let alone that we should encourage people to have faith in their God-given power to overcome any obstacle. Thumbing through the index of books on Christian theology, "healing" is almost never listed as a discussed topic.

The same is true for relationships. We were trained as therapists, treating people for marriage problems by applying the principles of non-directive counseling. And, of course, there was no mention of prosperity consciousness, even though we learned in the first year at seminary that the number one problem couples fight about is money. Essentially, we were taught the clergy's job is to help people suffer with dignity while remaining faithful to the Church.

Where is God today?

Or did He only act in the days of camels and sandals? When theology is doing its job, it helps people apply religious insights to everyday life. Shouldn't clergy talk about prosperity when people are hungry, healing when people are sick, and wholeness in relationships when marriages are faltering? If there is a central heresy in modern religious thought it is this: Pastors and theologians of mainline Protestant churches believe that God is incapable of doing anything in the real world.

Because the Metaphysical Churches grew up as lay movements within Protestantism, they were free of ecclesiastical strings and they could, like Pinocchio, dance freely wherever they wanted to go. This gave the new Luthers tremendous opportunity to develop a Practical Christianity. For example, Charles Fillmore assured readers of his magazine as early as 1897 that he taught nothing which he had not proved for himself.[7]

However, also like Pinocchio, the Metaphysical Christian churches have wandered homeless for a long while. The very freedom we enjoyed has given us a sense of independence which cuts us off from our own heritage as part of Western mystical Christianity. I wrote *Friends in High Places* to re-introduce Truth students to their long-lost relatives in Church History. The continuing popularity of that book suggests that people in the Metaphysical Churches are as eager to see themselves as "real Christians" as Pinocchio wanted to be a "real boy." Mystical Christianity has much to contribute to the greater Christian community and, of course, much to gain. This takes us to the fourth function of theology.

4. ESTABLISH DIALOGUE WITHIN THE THEOLOGICAL CIRCLE.

Scientific research begins with known facts and proceeds to learn about the unknown. Religious inquiry is different. We have certain "pivotal truths" from which we begin and to which we must return. For example, belief in God is fundamental to Christian theology, however differently we may understand what "belief" and "God" mean. A theologian who refuses to acknowledge God in his work can scarcely call himself a Christian theologian. Tillich named this space, in which religious thinkers must operate, the "Theological Circle."[8]

There are certain givens within which every theoretician must function if he/she is doing theology. Real theological dialogue is not a hostile harangue but a marketplace/meeting place for exchange of ideas. Lively, lovely disagreements have regularly brightened dry, theological discussion, as with the famous exchanges between Karl Barth and Emil Brunner. The Barth-Brunner "paper debates" lasted for years and were characterized by mutual respect and a sincere desire of both for new insights. Sadly, the history of Christian thought has seen a lot of scathing denunciations and too few instances of real dialogue.

Theological dialogue within the circle of faith should include discussions with other Christian traditions. We have much to learn from each other. Yet, how seldom it is that people from divergent Christian traditions have sat together to discuss our common bonds, let alone tackling those points at which we part company. Responsible dialogue across and within faith circles can only enrich everyone. Good theology is tolerant and promotes that sort of openness. Good theology is a bridge of light.

5. INTERPRETATION OF SYMBOLISM.

Nearly everything we say about God is symbolic, because human language cannot hope to encompass the Divine. Even spiritual experiences must be translated into word symbols when people share those encounters.

Hence all religious writings are symbolic, some more than others. Theology interprets those symbols and explains their meanings to each new generation.

Our grandchildren will rediscover the excitement we felt when we grasped the basic principle of Metaphysical Christianity: God's one presence and power. How will language and symbols change in the next hundred years? In the next thousand? We have no way to know.

New, young theologians will arise whose task it will be to restate the ancient Truths for the children of the twenty-first and twenty-second centuries and beyond. This brings us to the final category.

6. RAISE NEW ISSUES AND SUGGEST ANSWERS.

Could any religious thinker envision the moral/political crisis which shook the United States during the second half of the twentieth century? Suddenly, we became aware that our institutions were promoting racism, war, and sexism. Could anyone dream big enough to see the Berlin Wall toppling and the winds of democracy blowing through the gap to melt the Cold War? Free elections in Eastern Europe; the dissolution of the last great empire state, the Soviet Union? Attitudes have changed, and theology must address those changes. In fact, some of the changes were first brought to our attention by "radical" theological opinions, notably in the areas of world peace and civil rights.

Dr. Martin Luther King, Jr., was more than a political leader: King was a brilliant thinker with a Ph.D. in Systematic Theology from Boston University. His activism grew from a deep spirituality; his theological interpretation of Jesus and Gandhi in terms of nonviolent struggle gave him strength and courage. Like Bonhoeffer, he remained faithful to his vision until death.

What will be the new issues that motivate the "radicals" of the future to re-interpret the ancient message and find new answers? We cannot guess. But theology must never let itself become the private chaplain to the status quo, smiling approvingly as powerful people try to keep their power at the expense of needed change. Theology carries a divine mandate to seek, understand, and speak the Word of God to each new generation. *The Methodist Quadrilateral*

TOOLS: THE FANTASTIC FOUR

Our purpose in this book is to offer a broad overview of theology from a Metaphysical Christian perspective. A second aim is to interface those two thought-worlds so we can dialogue across that "bridge of light" linking islands of modern Truth churches with the liberal Protestant mainland from which they floated free a hundred years ago. It is a task fraught with peril. John Naisbitt, author of the *Megatrends*, summed up the plight of the systematic thinker when he noted that his work was

> ...synthesis in an age of analysis. Its purpose is to provide an overview. To do that, it is necessary to generalize...Yet, I think it is worth the risk. In a world where events and ideas are analyzed to the point of lifelessness, where complexity grows by quantum leaps, where the information din is so high we must shriek to be heard above it, we are hungry for structure. With a simple framework we can begin to make sense of the world. And we can change that framework as the world itself changes. [9]

To erect a "simple framework" from which to discuss modern Christian theology, we shall borrow a set of tools from a major Protestant denomination, four "guidelines" for doing theology as outlined by the United Methodist *Book of Discipline*. I call these the *"Fantastic Four."* To prepare the workbench for the task ahead, we'll take a brief look at each.

SCRIPTURE - TRADITION - EXPERIENCE - REASON

Where do we get our religious ideas? As we shall see in the next chapter, this is not the same question as "How do we know what's true?" To think theologically means to examine what we already believe as well as striking out in new directions. While many people question beliefs and practices, few have paused to consider the *sources* of religious ideas. For example, most people believe God is good, but what causes them to decide that? Where do we get the concept which says, *"God is good?"*

#1 - SCRIPTURE

One possible answer is *Scripture*. The Bible is often called the textbook of Christianity; its students and teachers are legion. We study the Bible to gain new insights and hear what God is saying to us through the voice of prophets, teachers and apostles. We shall dig deeper into biblical interpretation in Chapter 5, but for now let's just say the Bible alone can never serve as the basis for faith.

All branches of Christianity have access to the Bible, yet look how differently a Catholic charismatic or a Russian Orthodox priest, a Mormon or a Presbyterian reads this same Bible. Each person brings to the Bible his/her own peculiar brand of Christian *Tradition*.

#2 - TRADITION

Narrowly defined, tradition is that which our branch of the Christian family has believed. A wider definition might include the whole of the Christian history, even at the risk of sailing onto that ocean of contradictions. The whole body of Christian history belongs to all of us, although we certainly won't want to affirm every absurdity which has ever been declared in the name of Jesus. Tradition tells us who we are and what we accept as true.

For example, virtually all Metaphysical Christians affirm, "There is only one Presence and one Power in my life and in the universe, God the Good, Omnipotent." This is the cornerstone belief, the *"Universal Pivotal Truth"* on which modern Metaphysical Christianity is built. We are absolutely certain that One Power/One Presence, OP^2, is a true Christian teaching.

All right, *who says?*

It isn't biblical.

It isn't found in a creed or a decision of church councils.

It isn't advocated by the majority of Christian churches.

It isn't widely accepted by theologians or laity beyond our circle of faith.

Where, then, do Truth churches get the idea that God is the only Presence/Power in the Cosmos? It is a part of mystical tradition going back to Meister Eckhart, the medieval preacher, and other thinkers who both predated and followed him. Certainly, we can see OP^2 in the pages of the Bible when we look for it, but nowhere is this doctrine (teaching) elucidated as a plain statement of fact in the pages of Holy Scripture.

Alluded to? Yes. Required by the life and teachings of Jesus? Certainly. But given as an outright teaching? No where in the Bible.

Don't worry, though. Quite a few highly orthodox doctrines are non-biblical, also. To list a few: the *Trinity*, meeting on *Sundays*, and the existence of a discorporate *soul* are all traditional ideas which were developed externally and then read back into Scripture.

In fact, how did Scripture become Scripture? Who decided that the strange *Letter of Jude* would be a New Testament book, and the excellent early Christian treatise known as the *Didache* or *"Teaching of the Apostles"* wouldn't get in?

You guessed it.

Take the familiar Christmas story for an example. Ask anyone to describe the events and they will eventually come up with something like this: Joseph and Mary (his wife) come to Bethlehem in late December because of a census ordered by the Roman Emperor Augustus. They are given a stable to stay in by a kindly innkeeper and Jesus is cradled in straw. Earlier that night, angels sang while in hovering flight over shepherds who are dazzled by the star hanging over Bethlehem. Going to the stable, the shepherds meet the three Kings—Balthazar, Melchior, and Caspar (one of whom is black) —who have just arrived. The shepherds and the magi kneel, along with the animals, and worship the Christ child in the stable. Thus we have our familiar scene in the Christmas creche. *"Gloria in excelsis deo."*

Except for one small glitch: *None of the above is in the Bible.*

First we must separate the two birth narratives, one from Luke and the other from Matthew. Luke has the shepherds, the angels (who nowhere sing, fly, or hover) and the census (by Augustus, who never ordered it). Luke shows us the manger, but he never mentions straw or even a stable. And the kindly innkeeper and adoring animals are also absent from Luke's nativity. So are the star, the wise men, and the kneeling worshippers. And—with apologies to those who thought this was a G-rated narrative—Luke's Mary isn't Joseph's wife; she's his pregnant girlfriend (technically, "betrothed wife," which meant a fiancée that had vowed fidelity). Prudish Matthew has them married but chaste.

But that isn't Matthew's only problem with Luke. Matthew stages the whole affair in a house, mentioning nothing about a manger or a crowded city. He assumes Joseph lives in Bethlehem so he needs no census to bring him there. There are wise men, but the text never names them or describes their ethnic origins or even says how many there were. (We surmise three because three gifts are mentioned.) The word kings is nowhere to be found, nor are the shepherds or the angel bands which Luke hired for the gala occasion.

Most profoundly, Luke's Jesus is announced as "good news of great joy which will come to all the people; for unto you is born this day in the city of David a Savior, who is Christ the Lord." That fits Luke's universalism very well. Matthew, however, was a Jewish Christian and not at all interested in a savior for the whole world. He wanted the Messiah. Listen to how the "wise men from the East" inquired after the baby at the palace of Herod the king: "Where is he who is born the king of the Jews? For we have seen his star in the East, and have come to worship him."

Finally, why do we celebrate Christmas in December? Because the Roman holiday of *Sol Invictus*, the Unconquerable Sun, fell on December 25th, so early Christians borrowed that date as the birth of the Son of God, cleverly converting the pagan festival of winter solstice to *Christ's Mass.*

Our model for the first Nöel is really a collage of interwoven traditions. And why not? Tradition is just history that sticks. If an idea or practice works for a community of faith, it binds with the thought patterns and lifestyle as part of that church's traditions.

No one is immune from this tendency. Even avowed non-traditional groups like the Metaphysical churches have quite a few traditional ways of doing things, i.e., using guided meditation as a regular part of the worship service.

Tradition terrorizes when it withers into traditional-ism. The *Book of Discipline* recognizes this danger:

An uncritical acceptance of tradition amounts to traditionalism, deliverance from which requires an adequate understanding of history as well as a resource for acquiring new wisdom. Traditions are the residue of corporate experience of earlier Christian communities. A critical appreciation of them can enlarge our vision and enrich faith in God's provident love.[10]

Many Christians are uncomfortable with traditional-ism. However, when we set up our Christmas creches and sing about angel choirs and stars leading three kings of orient to the stable, do we need to prune the creche, segregating Luke's shepherds from Matthew's wise men? The stories have merged, not because they happened as historical events, but because together they tell a more complete truth than they ever could as separate narratives. They are the genesis myths of Christian faith, a testimony in tales, proclaiming that something special happened when Yeshua ben Joseph was born in Palestine nearly two thousand years ago.

The Bible is whatever God wanted it to be, and apparently God wanted the birth of Jesus to be a good story. Tradition enriches life.

#3 - EXPERIENCE

But we are more than just products of events long ago; we have been shaped by life *Experience* to believe certain things and doubt others. Beyond the obvious accidents of geography (most Algerians are Muslim, most Italians are Catholic) other factors which shape our religious thinking can be traumatic life experiences (such as the death of a parent) ecstatic life experiences (a powerful love relationship) or dramatic life experiences (near death encounters, serving in war, surviving a divorce, discovering a new spiritual dimension to life). Also important to our belief system are encounters with parents, peers, and professors. These people shape the way we think; we come to the study of Christianity with a basketful of beliefs already in full bloom.

And what of the cultural influences on our thought world, subtly shaping our values and expectations? A bright kid growing up in the ghetto has different role models than a bright kid growing up in suburbia. The center city child sees the effects of street crime, drug use, and violence. The suburban child sees neatly manicured lawns, white-collar workers driving their BMW's, and old people out for a stroll in the evening wearing designer jogging suits.

How will these vastly different environments slant the development of the two? The suburban child might become a great embezzler, while the ghetto youth might be a great civil rights lawyer. (Did I catch you?) Do you see how culture shapes what we expect to find?

#4 - REASON

The final formative factor we'll consider is *Reason*. We've been using this factor more than any of the others during the course of our study. I have presented a series of ideas and developed them more-or-less logically; you have read and analyzed what I have written. We both are using our capacity to reason.

Mystical Christianity has rightly observed that there really are two different types of reasoning. One is *intellectual,* the other *intuitive.* Sometimes these are associated with the two hemispheres of the brain, but most research seems to suggest that both hemispheres contain intellectual and intuitive processes. There is a recorded case of a 47-year-old man whose entire left hemisphere had to be removed due to cancer. Remarkably, his other hemisphere was able to adjust and take up the bodily and logical/intuitive functions normally found in the missing hemisphere.

Left brain/right brain chitchat is popular and trendy but perhaps not as conclusive as some would like to believe. As we shall use the term, *Reason* includes both intellectual and intuitive thought.[11]

No doubt we use *Reason* to chart our theologies. Even those groups which claim to depend on nothing but the Bible will have used their powers of reason to interpret *Scripture.* Actually, we exercise all four formative factors. No one exists without some personal history, i.e., *Experience.* Everyone brings a spiritual background to the religious quest, i.e., *Tradition.* Because the *"Fantastic Four"* are ineluctable sources for Christian thinking, we shall continually refer the topics under discussion to them as we work toward our understanding of systematic theology.

Scripture, Tradition, Experience, and *Reason* can provide us with tools to produce new insights, but how do we judge whether an idea is true or false? That is the next subject.

CHECK YOUR KNOWLEDGE

1. How does the author define *theology?* Explain the elements of the definition.
2. What is the difference between *philosophy of religion* and *theology?*
3. List and explain the *Six Functions of Theology.*
4. When theologians speak of "biblical criticism" what do they mean?
5. What are the *"Fantastic Four"* the author discusses?
6. Why does the author think *Tradition* is a good thing?

QUESTIONS FOR DISCUSSION

1. The author says theology must be done within a circle of faith. Agree?
2. Do you see yourself more like a philosopher of religion or theologian?
3. Discuss the *Six Functions of Theology.* Which ones did you recognize in your church?
4. Is the Bible "true"? What kind of biblical criticism is practiced at your church?
5. Draw a graphic representation of the way your church uses the *"Fantastic Four."*
6. Do you think churches should be more or less traditional? Discuss the *Four Sources* in an ideal church.

NOTES

1. Paul Tillich, *A History of Christian Thought* (NY: Touchstone, 1968), p. xxxviii.
2. Rick Gore, "The Riddle of the Rings," *National Geographic,* July 1981, pp. 3-31.
3. Hans Kueng, *On Being A Christian* (NY: Simon & Schuster, 1978), p. 125.
4. Johnny Mercer and Harold Arlen, "Accentuate the Positive," *The American Bicentennial Songbook* (NY: Charles Hansen Music & Books, Inc., 1978), p. 160-163.
5. Eric Gill quoted by Walter J. Burghardt, "Contemplation: A Loving Look at What's Real," in Vol. 35, March-April '90 of *Praying* magazine (Kansas City, MO: National Catholic Reporter Publishing Company, Inc., 1990), p. 11.
6. Fillmore, *Dynamics of Living,* pp. 13-14.
7. James Dillet Freeman, *The Story of Unity* (Unity Village: Unity Books, 1978), p. 165.
8. Tillich, *Systematic Theology Vol. I* (Chicago: University of Chicago Press, 1973), pp. 8-11.
9. John Naisbitt, *Megatrends* (NY: Warner Books, 1984), pp. xxxi-xxxii.
10. United Methdodist Church, *Book of Discipline* (Nashville, TN: Abingdon, undated), p. 79.
11. Jerome Kagan and Ernest Havemann, *Psychology: An Introduction* (NY: Harcourt, Brace & World, 1963), p. 259.

EPISTEMOLOGY

Chapter Three

How Do We Know What's True?

And they went into Capernaum; and immediately on the Sabbath he entered the synagogue and taught. And they were astonished at his teaching, for he taught them as one who had authority, and not as the scribes. Mark 1:21-22 (RSV)

Here's an old joke about St. Peter answering the bell at the Pearly Gates.

PETER: *Who's there?*

NEWCOMER: *It is I.*

PETER: *(Groan) Oh, no. Not another English teacher!*

Changing the scenario slightly, we might imagine the following...

PETER: *Who's there?*

NEWCOMER: *Should a position of such importance be held by someone who lacks a comprehensive grasp of the flow of individual consciousness past this point in their existential quest? In City of God, his greatest treatise, Saint Augustine wrote—and I quote verbatim—*

PETER: *(Groan) Not another theologian!*

Seminary students often come to graduate study for the professional ministry with wide-eyed innocence. It's all so simple that first Fall semester: The Bible is God's Word, Jesus' clear teachings can be found in the Gospels, and all we have to do is love the people and they'll grow under our wise pastoral guidance.

Although each of these illusions shelters a germ of truth, the new seminary student at most mainline Protestant schools of theology often approaches studies for the professional ministry with a benign ignorance as to the problems he/she is about to encounter. Students learn that modern biblical scholarship has established that humans wrote the Bible and that it reflects the struggling, striving for higher understandings which all products of the human-divine paradox will exhibit. The position held by most modern biblical scholars is that the Bible *contains the Word of God* rather than the Bible *is* the Word of God.

Furthermore, biblical scholarship today is more apt to see the words of Jesus in the Gospels as interpretive statements of the first century Church than as news bulletins quoting Jesus verbatim. When the student gets to classes on pastoral care and management of a church the professors frankly admit that we Christians are not always teachable. Books like Jim Glasse's *Putting It Together in the Parish*[1] and *Profession: Minister*[2] dispel myths about a carefree life among God's Elect. Being a pastor is tough work. Even the most faithful Christians will resist your leadership from time to time. A popular book among religious professionals discusses ways to handle *Church Fights*. There would be no market for the book if in-fighting in small and large churches were not rampant. If only the fantasies of first year seminarians held true...[3]

In some respects, religious leadership is a strange job. What gives someone the right to stand in front of a group of people and teach them about God Almighty? Everyone who has ever spoken at a gathering of believers has asked himself the question Martin Luther struggled with for so many years as he was formulating his theology of the Reformation: *"Are you alone right?"* What is the authority you call upon to stand here and tell other people how to live their lives? Every religious seeker— minister or layperson—who has ever explained the faith to another has faced the question, *"How do I know this is so?"* Many people shuffle the question into a "hold" box in their brains, but prophets, mystics, and theologians won't let us get away with that for very long.

Theologians throughout history have challenged us to think through our assumptions and re-think our prejudices. Like new seminarians, this may cause us some pain at first, but the growth which results from pruning dead ideas from our trees of knowledge makes the pangs of progress worthwhile. Prophets among us seldom explained themselves. They taught *"as one who had authority, and not as the scribes."*

Prophets seldom disagree with one another.

Theologians always do.

But without the creative re-interpretations of theologians, prodded by skeptics and free-thinkers, the dynamic quality of the prophet's message chills to cold stone as we carve idols of the prophet who walked in our midst. In a provocative passage from his book *Discover the Power Within You*, Eric Butterworth makes this observation:

> What did Jesus really teach? The answer is not easy to formulate, simply because we have been so conditioned by the about Jesus. For the religion of Jesus, we can only turn to the four Gospels of the New Testament and read the words as they have been recorded.[4]

James Dillet Freeman adds:

We like to say that we are not so much the religion about Jesus as thereligion of Jesus. We believe that He is the Son of God; we believe that everyone is a Son of God, yes, even the least of us. We believe that this is true, whatever your faith, Christian or other, and we respect your faith...a new different approach to Christianity ...interprets Jesus Christ's teachings in a slightly way than some of the religions that have been around for a longer time. [5]

What gives anyone the right to interpret things differently? Freeman is right when he says that the metaphysical churches have a distinctive flavor not found elsewhere in Christianity; he could have strengthened his argument by recalling that, although the wrapper may be only a century old, the goods inside are as ancient as anything taught by the Christian faith.

That's why metaphysical thinkers claim to be teaching the religion of Jesus instead of the religion *about* Jesus. However, Metaphysical Christianity is more than a rediscovery of ancient principles which we believe Jesus taught; it is built upon work done throughout the history of the Christian Faith by those pesky mystics and theologians.

Wherever Christianity has blossomed, good teachers have asked the hard questions and found solutions very similar to those espoused by modern Truth churches. All these thinkers have operated from the assumption that they possessed, within themselves, the ability to know Truth when they encountered it. The idea is so widely accepted today that we may wonder why it needs to be discussed. Yet, there are schools of thought which remain dubious to the ability of sinful humanity to achieve Truth. We cannot summarily dismiss these doubts as error-belief without hearing what they have to say, any more than a new Truth student can continue in old consciousness just because a new idea scratches him where he doesn't itch.

Metaphysical Christianity has much to say to these matters. Many questions resolve in answers from that school of Christian thought. These are questions people are asking today. Therefore, before we can plunge into a study of topics like *Biblical Theology* (Chapter 5), *Christology* (Chapter 8), or *Ecclesiology* (Chapter 13) we must first examine the standards by which we judge truth from un-truth.

We turn first to a brief review of epistemology's classic answers to the problem of how to know Truth, followed in each case by a critique of the various solutions. Then we shall create an epistemology which incorporates the insights of the mystical path and yet is faithful to the faith of Jesus Christ as presented in the gospels. If we do our work well, the emerging whole should affect a balance between head and heart, speaking to the great paradoxes of the faith as well.

REVIEW OF CLASSICAL EPISTEMOLOGIES

1 - AUTHORITY

Aristotle insisted that two objects of different weights, like a coin and a ship's anchor, would fall to the earth at different speeds, the heavier faster. Since Aristotle was the authority for western civilization, nearly two thousand years passed before anyone challenged this idea. Then Galileo climbed to the top of the leaning tower of Pisa and dropped two objects of varying weight. They plopped to the ground simultaneously, overturning centuries of erroneous thinking.

This, of course, is the problem with *Authority* as a source of Truth. Even though we like to think of ourselves as self-sufficient, in reality we moderns trust authorities every day. Very few of us can fly a jumbo jet, inspect the cables of an elevator, or cut away an infected appendix. When we wander beyond our specialties, we must rely upon other specialists to make the highways go where the maps point and then to keep food inside those wrapped packages fit to eat. Modern life makes us unavoidably dependent on the expertise of others, but dependence need not be blind faith. We must be educated consumers, requiring our authorities to toe the line and provide the services we need.

When thinking theologically, we can listen to what other thinkers have said and gain insights from their wisdom. We unconsciously do this whenever we quote the Bible, which is seen as somehow authoritative by most Christians. Why reinvent the wheel every generation? Isn't it better to defer to greater minds who have struggled with these problems and let them guide us?

Although we can learn from authorities in any field, there have been too many instances when religious authority turned authoritarian. Today's practical solution becomes tomorrow's dogma which must be followed even though life situations change.

Because Jesus spoke with his own authority instead of arguing from external authorities, people said he taught "not as the scribes." He did not hesitate to cite those religious thinkers of previous generations; Jesus quoted scripture freely throughout his ministry. He also reserved the right to reinterpret Truth by looking at the circumstances even if some venerated person in Hebrew history had said otherwise. Jesus felt comfortable both invoking and breaking with *Tradition*.

2 - TRADITION

Simpler societies are often steeped in tradition. One social science textbook remarks:

> Of all sources of truth, tradition is one of the most reassuring. Here is the accumulated wisdom of the ages, and he who disregards it may expect denunciation as a scoundrel or a fool. If a pattern has "worked" in the past, why not keep on using it? [6]

This is a highfalutin variation of the old truism: *"If it ain't broke, don't fix it!"*

Let's take an example. For as long as anyone can recall, *slash-and-burn* agriculture has fed the rural peoples of the Philippines. Find a level place in the jungle; cut down everything and burn the vegetable matter to ash; plant a crop in the charred plot after it cools; and in a short while you will harvest yams or whatever you have planted.

It works. Rural Filipinos have farmed this way for generations. Bring in new methods fertilizers, crop rotation, new machinery, exotic crops—and the people face a serious problem: Shall they try the new ways and risk starvation when the old ways have fed their families for so long? Tradition, for simpler societies, is more than just a system of beliefs; it's a father-to-son, mother-to- daughter technical manual about what to do in the most common situations.

This is the healthy function of tradition. However, we noted in Chapter Two that tradition can be so overbearing that it deteriorates into traditional-*ism*, preventing new ideas from improving the system just because they are new. Sometimes, new ideas are eagerly accepted but twisted by an incomplete understanding so that, instead of an improvement, the new idea becomes part of a reconstructed network of superstition. There have been some recent examples of this latter phenomenon which have been studied by social scientists.

CARGO CULTS

One of the most fascinating instances of new ideas upsetting an established culture is the bizarre phenomenon of *cargo cults*. These religious revitalization movements have flourished spasmodically for almost a century among the Melanesian islands of the South Pacific.

Western missionaries came to teach the native populations the Christian faith, but what the native peoples learned was more than the spoken word. They saw affluent people with bright new gadgets like rifles and steamships. They saw great bags of foodstuffs. They listened to Christian promises about the return of Christ and a day of judgment when good would be rewarded and the dead shall rise. Then they promptly translated this into Melanesian thought, deciding:

1) the End is Near
2) our dead ancestors will rise and
3) they will load up steamships with rifles, rice and flour
4) bringing the cargo here to us.

The earliest account of cargo cult activity comes in 1893 at Milne Bay in New Guinea where a "prophet" arose to foretell volcanic eruptions and tidal waves which would herald the arrival of the ancestors' ship and the cargo. All available food had to be consumed before the ship would dock, so they slaughtered all their pigs and went on an eating frenzy. After the tidal wave failed to appear, the prophet was jailed by colonial officials to prevent further disturbances. [7]

Other experiences were not so benign. Prophets began to point accusing fingers at European settlers and colonial officials when the cargo did not arrive as predicted. On the island of Espiritu Santo in the New Hebrides in 1923, a plantation owner was murdered by cultists when the prophet Ronovuro predicted the Europeans would prevent the cargo ships from landing. Government officials suppressed the movement for a while but it reappeared in 1939. [8]

The following analysis of cargo cult phenomena by anthropologist Marvin Harris borders on theological inquiry and points to the power tradition holds over people, especially when that tradition is the worldview itself:

> The confusion of the Melanesian revitalization prophets is a confusion about the workings of sociocultural systems. They do not understand how the productive and distributive functions of modern industrial society are organized, nor do they comprehend how law and order are maintained among statelevel peoples. To them, the matertial abundance of the industrial peoples and the penury of others constitutes an irrational flaw, a massive contradiction in the structure of the world. Their attempt to resolve this contradiction strikes us as a pathetic or even ludicrous aberration. It should be pointed out, however, that almost all of the cargo cults have occurred among people who have been exposed to intensive conversion efforts by Christian overseas missions...they have been provided with a view of the world that is fundamentally supportive of the logic and standards of that revitalization process...After all, strong justification for the logic of the cargo prophets is to be found in the New Testament. Here, too, there are prophecies, visions, ghosts, and reunion with ancestors. While Christ did not offer cargo he did offer an even greater gift, "the gift of eternal life." [9]

Tradition, as a source of Truth, is limited by its inability to adjust to new circumstances. Sometimes, as in the case of the cargo cults, when it does adjust to new circumstances that adjustment is irrational, superstitious. Tradition can be a valuable source of ideas and customs which give us a link with our heritage. But traditionalism can hold us back from growth necessary to thrive, while radical, irrational changes in tradition can put us even further out of touch with effective living in the real world. Tradition alone is insufficient for a modern Christian epistemology.

3 - INTUITION

Transcendentalists of the nineteenth century supposed that *Intuition* was the key to knowledge. Real insights come not by step-by-step procedures of logic but by flashes of creative inspiration. Where did those flashes of truth come from, if not from within?

The problem with intuition is twofold. First, it is not a dependable source because it relies upon chance insights. What do we do if inspired flashes don't come and we must decide anyway? As a supplement to other ways of understanding, intuition is fine, but we cannot rely on intuition alone. That is why Truth students read the Bible, pray, and discuss ideas with other Christians. Second, these supplementary methods are needed because intuition is really a source of Truth, not a way to determine what is true.

Intuition is one half of the formative factor of Reason, discussed in the previous chapter. We can get an idea by intellectual, step-by-step procedures or by a burst of insight, but is the idea true or false? Intuition works subjectively, like a baker sampling fresh bread to see if it tastes good. Whether we cook our ideas by intuitive insights or rational processes, we must find an objective way to taste them to see if they are wholesome fare for a spiritual life.[10]

4. REVELATION

The same applies to *Revelation*, which is intuition received from a divine Source outside the individual consciousness, presumably God. Some Christian epistemologies have been developed that identify revelation as the only source and criterion of Truth. Those who take the message of Jesus Christ as recorded in the Bible as the sole source of Truth can further use that message as a standard of what is true and judge everything else that claims to be true by the yardstick of scripture.

Obvious problems arise as soon as we identify any fixed source of Truth like a set of sacred writings which are considered *special revelations* from God. Even granting that God speaks to us through the pages of scripture, how shall we understand what those pages mean? How shall we interpret the revelation? Whatever criteria we use, they are the real basis for our epistemology. Since so many people read the same message in scripture and arrive at such diverse conclusions, how can anyone assert that the Bible is a clear, apparent yardstick by which we can measure all Truth?

We shall delve into biblical theology more thoroughly in Chapter 5. For right now let's just say that Scripture also constitutes a source of ideas, but by itself cannot test those concepts. Hence Revelation fails to provide a working basis for an epistemology because it is susceptible to all the problems we encountered when considering Intuition.

Our brief look at cargo cults shows us what can happen when *special revelations* crowd other factors from the worldview. We shall address this crucial issue more completely in Chapter 19.

Are we foiled in our search? Is there no way to verify ideas and insights that is available to anyone and repeatable under similar conditions?

5 - SCIENTIFIC METHOD

When Galileo dropped those weights off the tower at Pisa, he was employing the *scientific method*. Science tests ideas by experimentation under controlled conditions in a way that is repeatable by anyone and will produce similar results. If you want to test Aristotle's hypothesis, take two weights and drop them from a tower. You should get the same results as Galileo did, provided some other factor doesn't intervene (like high winds, or one weight striking the side of the tower) Controlled experiments allow researchers to vary one factor and see how this change will affect the outcome.

Let's take an example, drawn from the author's household. A few years ago my son, Bill, needed to come up with a science fair project. He took three plants and exposed the greenery to different types of music for one hour each evening. Two little pepper plants listened to either classical or hard rock music while the third got an hour of silence. His hypothesis was, not surprisingly for a young man, that rock music is better for living things than that stale, old junk to which Dad listens.

All three plants were about the same size when the experiment began; all three received the same, measured amount of moisture and sat in the same window the rest of the time.

Which grew tallest?

With blissfully reinforced prejudices, I can report the triumph of classical tunes over the tone-deaf mayhem of rock music. Nature herself validates the great masters.

But there were problems with Bill's research technique.

1) The *sample was too small.* How do we know that the classical plant was not going to grow taller than it did and that Mozart, Bach, and Handel did not stifle its growth?

2) There were *too many other variables.* Plants were carried to different rooms to hear their music. Humidity, temperature, and outside noises varied from room to room.

3) *Bill cheated.* He talked to the rock music plant, telling it he was hoped it would win.

That may have had no effect, but who knows? Because rock music failed to win hardly means an outside factor had no influence on the outcome. That's why conventional scientific research is useless for spiritual endeavors. The sampling we are dealing with is always too small. Emily wants to know what's true, so she tests idea *A* and concept *B*. Concept *B* works for her; idea *A* leaves her cold.

Lindsey runs the same "test" and finds *neither A nor B* will work for her. She opts for *C*, producing immediate results. Why? Because humans are absolutely unique and react in different ways to exactly the same stimulus. There were also too many variables.

Good research occurs in highly controlled environments with masses of subjects to study. Sociologists Paul B. Horton and Chester L. Hunt frankly admit that religious topics are not within the charter of scientific study:

> Since science is based on verifiable evidence, science can only deal with questions about which verifiable evidence can be found. Questions like, "Is there a God?" "What is the purpose and destiny of man?" or "What makes a thing beautiful?" are not scientific questions because they cannot be treated factually. Such questions are terribly important, but the scientific method has no tools for handling them.[11]

Scientific methods work quite well when dealing with quantifiable, measurable results, even given the fact that there will be erratic events within the framework of the best research techniques. However, science stops where religious inquiry begins. Horton and Hunt rightly note that science does not—can not—answer questions about Ultimate Concerns.

SO FAR, SO BAD

We have seen so far that the classical solutions to epistemological questions all have good and bad points. *Authority* can be helpful, since all of us are laypeople when we stray beyond our fields of expertise. But authority too easily becomes *authoritarianism,* demanding concurrence without bothering to show evidence.

Tradition is a kind of community authority, a collection of do's and don'ts which tell members of a society what the ancestors did and how they did it. Tradition can be helpful, in that it allows us to relate to our heritage and provides tried and true methods for doing things which have worked before. It can also be harmful in that it often deteriorates to *traditional-ism,* where new ideas never receive a fair hearing and the group suffers because it cannot learn and grow, or *superstition* based on a corrupt understanding of new ideas without a fundamental change in the religious worldview.

Intuition seems, at first, a likely candidate for an epistemological model, since mystics have usually held that each person has the Divine Spirit within which can guide and direct him/her. However, a belief system built strictly on intuition leaves us without a readily available, really dependable method for dealing with everyday situations. But intuition is actually a method for obtaining insights, not for checking their validity. Since epistemology asks the question, "How do we know it's true?", intuition alone falls short for the model we are seeking to construct. You may answer, intuitively, "It's true because I feel it is true." Your spouse may answer, "It's false because I feel it is false." If intuition alone is our standard then reasonable discussions about rightness/wrongness, better/worse, health/unhealth are meaningless and impossible. Intuition can't answer questions with repeatable, consistent results.

Neither can *Revelation*, which purports to originate in a divine source outside of the individual. At best, revelation is the source of ideas which then must be tested by another method.

The *Scientific Method* of experimentation can be helpful in dealing with questions about the physical universe, but has nothing to say about values, ethics, or Truth. Science is value neutral, unable to even ask the question, "Does God exist?" Anything which goes beyond study of observable phenomena, goes beyond science, too.

IS THAT ALL THERE IS?

This has been a hurried look at classical ideas about how we know Truth; it has not been a comprehensive survey of epistemology. We could have mentioned Truth-judging methods like *Common Sense, Majority Rule,* or *Instinct.* None of these meet our need for a yardstick by which we can measure Truth ideas, either. Perhaps, one might wonder, there is no standard against which we can measure religious concepts other than personal preference.

After all, isn't all religious opinion just that—*opinion* about *religion*?

LET'S TRY THIS ONE...

Without suggesting that we can solve all the problems of epistemology for time immemorial, let's take a look at a system of Truth-testing suggested by Charles Fillmore and other great mystical Christian thinkers. For lack of another term, let's call the process *Pragmatic Enlightenment. Pragmatism* is a philosophical school which says that which is true is that which works. Dr. William James (1842-1910), the philosopher/ psychologist and perhaps the best known Pragmatist, wrote: *"True ideas are those that we can assimilate, validate, corroborate and verify. False ideas are those that we can not..."*[13]

In other words, Truth works. If it doesn't, it isn't truth. But aren't we back to scientific method again? How can we verify religious questions? James would never push his system this far, but could we say that true religious ideas are those which demonstrate good results in the real world? In February 1897, Charles Fillmore placed an announcement in describing a new class which he would begin teaching March 15 of that year. The little note reads, in part:

> These lessons are in a large measure the outgrowth of my experi-
> ence in the regeneration through which I have been passing for
> several years, and are therefore very practical. I do not follow any
> teaching, but give the Truth as I have gotten it from spiritual expe-
> riences, which I find corroborated in a wonderful way in the
> Hebrew Scriptures.[14]

Charles Fillmore found ideas which he could "assimilate, validate, corroborate and verify" in his own life. He spoke of "going to headquarters," by which he meant spending time in contemplative prayer. The insights he received were then tested in the laboratory of daily living and referred to other Christians for discussions, testing, and application. His enlightenment had become pragmatic; he knew it was true because it worked. It was faith enlightened, practical Christianity. More than just working, it was repeatable. Other people tried the insights gleaned by Charles and Myrtle Fillmore and the same principles brought healing, prosperity, and wholeness to their lives as well. It was also Bible-based, because the gospels are fully staffed with people who received healings, enlightenment, and prosperity by applying the Jesus Christ principles to their daily lives. Nearly every issue of the most widely circulated magazine in the New Thought movement carries this declaration:

> Our objective is to discern the Truth and prove it. The Truth we
> teach is not new, neither do we claim special discovery of new reli-
> gious principles. Our purpose is to help and teach mankind to use
> and prove the eternal Truth taught by the Master.[15]

This is the basic definition of Pragmatic Enlightenment, as we are coining the term: *True religious ideas are those which demonstrate good results in the real world.* Religious ideas which are demonstrated true by existential reality have inner-person-al validity. You prove them true when they work for you.

INTERPRETING EXISTENTIAL REALITY

How else does one "prove" religious ideas if not by living them and enjoying their fruits? We noted Paul Tillich describes the "theological circle," as the place a theologian begins to work. Philosophers, in theory, proceed empirically toward who-knows-where as they develop their systems. Theologians begin within a community of faith and interpret existential reality (i.e., life's experiences) for that community. As a religious movement, Metaphysical Christianity begins within the circle of the faith of Jesus. Our epistemology starts with this pragmatic question: *What Christian interpretation of everyday life works for me?*

PERSONAL VALIDITY

The result of such an inquiry will not be scientifically valid because God cannot be measured or quantified. A person-centered epistemology provides personally valid theology, which is the only kind worth having, anyway. Beliefs which make textbook sense but fail to out picture in the lives of people are more examples of those theo-logical computer games.

Jesus said to the people of His day, "You have heard it said...but I say unto you..." People were attracted to His teaching. It changed lives; it brought peace that passes understanding. The validity of any theology is closely bound up to its value as a faith to live by. Spiritual principles may or may not repeat always in the lives of others because there are too many variables, but because they work for many people they constitute an aggregate system of "proof" that they are basically true.

FOUR TESTS OF PRAGMATIC ENLIGHTENMENT

Our epistemology builds on the sources for Truth—*Scripture, Tradition, Experience*, and both intellectual and intuitive *Reason*. Because this method stresses action, we test religious ideas four ways:

1) EXISTENTIALLY (everyday life) - "Does this idea work?"

2) COMPARATIVELY (dialogue with other believers) -"Does it make sense, intellectually and intuitively?" (Does it think/feel right?)

3) HOLISTICALLY (cultivating spirituality) - "Does it promote wholeness/growth?"

4) CHRISTOLOGICALLY (measuring it by Jesus) - "Does it meet the toughest standard of all—is it worthy of the faith of Jesus Christ?"

BUT IS IT SCIENCE?

Some will claim the above system, the elements of which certainly did not orig-inate with this author, is an example of scientific Christianity. The word "scientific" has been popular in Metaphysical Christian circles since the turn of the twentieth century, when a lot of New Thought groups were trumpeting the "scientific basis" of their beliefs.

Indeed, they were not alone. Even secular philosophers of the era were defining their enterprises as "the scientific treatment of the general questions relating to the universe and human life."[16]

That might be an appropriate description of the goals of astronomy, evolutionary biology, or physical anthropology, but it hardly describes the scope of theology, whose very subject matter—Ultimate Concerns—by definition lies beyond the scientist's domain.

To be intellectually honest, we must admit that this is not truly a "scientific" method, because different persons will receive differing results from the same treatment. There is no such thing as scientific Christianity, but admitting this does not doom religious thought to congenital absurdity. Our methodology must be as rigorously objective as theology can be, given the metaphysical (beyond-the-physical) nature of epistemological questions.

APPLICATION IS CRUCIAL

Truth is a dynamic, growing process. All theological ideas must be brought into contact with reality by application and dialogue or suffer the fate of a cargo cult. Jesus "taught with authority" but demonstrated what He said was true by His willingness to be faithful to Divine Principles even unto death.

We cannot teach with authority until we are willing to leave the blackboard for the marketplace, testing our beliefs in the only arena that counts, everyday life. Jesus Christ calls us to go and do likewise, to put feet on our prayers and test the ideas we cherish, and then to speak with the authority such experience will bring.

INWARD/OUTWARD

These first three chapters have discussed Christian faith as it meets the needs for spiritual understanding, both inside the believer and outside as we look at ways to interact with the world at large. This *Inward/Outward* movement will continue during the whole course of our study because it is imperative that theology deal with both inner needs and social needs. It is not enough for one person to reach enlightenment in isolation. Jesus came back from the desert to practice love among His people.

Today the world shrinks with every new technology. Communications make us one world, even though political and social harmony are far from being achieved. No Christian theology can ignore the stark reality that followers of Jesus are a minority faith of humanity at large, and that most human beings are not and never shall be Christian. Therefore we turn next in our study to a discussion of the relationship of the Christian faith and the other religions of our world.

CHECK YOUR KNOWLEDGE

1. What is *Epistemology?*

2. Give the advantages/disadvantages to the following as standards for Religious Truth: *Authority, Tradition, Intuition, and the Scientific Method.*

3. Why can't everyone read the Bible to get the same Truth? What's wrong with *REVELATION?*

4. How did Melanesian tradition, modified by contact with Christian missionaries, emerge as the superstitions of the cargo cult phenomena? What danger does this disclose for theologies leaning too heavily on tradition?

5. Define *Pragmatic Enlightenment,* and tell how it works. *repeatable + tru*

6. Explain the author's four tests of *Pragmatic Enlightenment.* p5 1

QUESTIONS FOR DISCUSSION

1. What kind of traditions are helpful? Harmful? Where is the line?

2. Do Metaphysical Christians really have the religion "of Jesus"? Isn't that arrogant? What gives us the right to interpret the faith our special way and then insist this is what Jesus taught?

3. The writings of Metaphysical teachers—like Charles Fillmore, Ernest Holmes or Mary Baker Eddy—are studied and treated as important documents in some churches. What kind of implicit "authority" do great teachers have, and how do you think they would view their status as authority figures?

4. If Truth cannot be "proved" but can be "demonstrated", what happens when a given technique works for you but not for me?

5. Is Metaphysical Christianity "scientific"? In what way?

6. What gave Jesus His authority? Will we ever have that kind of certainty? How and when?

NOTES

1. James D. Glasse, *Putting It Together In the Parish* (Nashville, TN: Abingdon, 1972).

2. James D. Glasse, *Profession Minister* (Nashville, TN: Abingdon. 1958).

3. Speed Leas. *Church Fights* (Philadelphia: Westminster, 1973).

4. Eric Butterworth, *Discover the Power Within You* (NY: Harper & Row, 1969), p. 14.

5. James Dillet Freeman, "Is Unity a Cult?" pamphlet published as reprint from *Unity* magazine. p. 3.

6. Paul B. Horton and Chester L. Hunt, *Sociology* (NY: McGraw-Hill. 1964). p. 5.

7. Marvin Harris, *Culture, Man, and Nature: An Introduction to General Anthropology* (NY: Thomas Y. Crowell Company, 1972), p. 565.

8. IBID., p. 566.

9. IBID., p. 567-568.

10. William S. Sahakian and Mabel Lewis Sahakian, *Ideas of the Great Philosophers* (NY: Barnes & Noble, 1966), p. 6.

11. Horton & Hunt. p. 33.

12. IBID., p. 7.

13. William James in *Treasury of World Philosophy,* Dagobert D. Runes, ed. (Patterson, NJ: Littlefield, Adams & Co., 1959), p. 605.

14. Charles Fillmore in Freeman, *Story of Unity,* p. 165.

15. Charles Fillmore, Untitled Excerpt from *Unity* magazine, February 1985, p. 55.

16. Macquarrie, p. 21.

CHRISTIANITY AND OTHER RELIGIONS

Chapter Four

Before we can consider specific problems of Christian theology we must complete our study of the basics. So far, we have analyzed *Theology* and discovered why thinking about the Divine in an organized way is important. We have also seen that a dynamic Epistemology is possible only if we are willing to test our ideas by action and dialogue. Now we must apply these tools to the difficult question of how Christian faith interfaces with other world religions.

THEOLOGICAL "TRUTH" ALWAYS TENTATIVE

Our methodology is theological, i.e., we organize our reflections on the meaning of life according to religious presuppositions. No one needs to prove God exists for a Christian because God's existence is part of the structure of reality for us.

Another way of saying this is to use the yardstick analogy. When measuring three feet of cloth we take the fabric to the yardstick; we don't figure the length of the yardstick from the cloth. God's existence and other basic beliefs (i.e., God's Absolute Goodness) are the standard against which we measure other ideas. They are neither provable nor disprovable; they are accepted on faith. Note carefully: not blind faith. These presuppositions have demonstrated their validity in the crucible of life. Accepting ideas on faith is no excuse for embracing any absurdity that comes along. All theological ideas must stand before the judgment seat of Scripture-Tradition-Experience-Reason, and then submit themselves to the ultimate standard of all, the life and teachings of Jesus Christ.

Having passed those tests, the idea must work in the real world, demonstrating its Truth by application. Since very few religious beliefs can meet such tough standards, healthy skepticism is the best insurance policy for a healthy theology. Therefore, virtually everything beyond the basic premises of our religious system must continually come under review and correction.

Like scientific truth, theological truth must always be tentative. This may be a little disconcerting to those who seek an absolute standard, but the alternative to such open-mindedness is to embrace dogmatism and etch the religious understandings of our generation onto millstones to hang around the necks of generations to come. We could do that, but they will throw our stone-carved idols overboard and find their own ways to worship the unknown God.

SOCIAL SCIENCE OR THEOLOGY?

Before proceeding to explore the relationship of Christianity to other world faiths, we needed to review and understand the very tentative nature of religious ideas. Yet there are some definite things we can say about theology that makes it similar to other forms of knowledge.

It has *content,* meaning specific beliefs and systems of belief. It is *organized* into a system that can be analyzed to detect any contradictions or blatant factual errors. Finally, theology must interact with other ways of knowing and not separate itself into a special category wherein the rules of knowledge do not apply; it must be *compatible* with other established truths. The job of the systematic theologian is to make sure all of the above happens.

Looking at religious systems and how they interact, some might suggest that a better way to go would be via sociology or anthropology or a history of religions approach. There is much theologians can learn from the humanities and social sciences, especially since those studies represent an objective methodology and theoretically have no points to prove, no axes to grind.

Of course, social scientists and historians have religious viewpoints and their work will be shaped, even slightly, according to those assumptions. We would do well to remember that science is no longer the god-replacement it seemed to be earlier in this century. Scientific methods, although admirable, are certainly not foolproof. (As one cynic said, "Foolproof? Give a fool enough time and he'll prove anything!") Theology needs no apologies for its methods or results. But it does need to continue dialogue with its sister studies in the social sciences and humanities. Religion without science degenerates into superstition and dogmatism; science without religion becomes amoral and inhumane.

SCIENTIFIC INPUT: EXCITING AND CHALLENGING

Let's take a quick look at some social science ideas which can point our theological inquiry in the right direction. We'll begin with a model for understanding how religious beliefs develop drawn from anthropologist Marvin Harris, whose book *Culture, Man and Nature* provided us with fascinating data about cargo cults in Chapter 3. Then we'll move on to a discussion of *Ethnocentrism* and *Cultural Relativism*, which are pretty much standard fare in introductory courses in sociology. All this sounds a lot more complicated than it really is, so hang in there. If we do it right, there will be some exciting new ideas presented during this digression into the social sciences, which may forever change the way you look at your religious system.

UNIVERSAL SOCIAL-SYSTEM MODEL OF MARVIN HARRIS

Human beings everywhere have arranged themselves into social systems that display remarkable differences. Yet, among all that diversity there seem to be universal patterns which social scientists can identify. Marvin Harris has drawn some startling conclusions. His work is based on social theory going back to Frederick Engels, but Harris organizes the ideas into a highly original and controversial model.

Harris's system, as it was presented in a series of lectures by Professor Richard Lane of the University of Idaho when I attended that school as an undergraduate, consists of enviro-cultural elements which interact in sequence. *(See figure 4-1, below)*

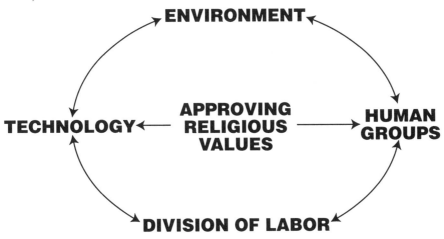

Fig. 4-1.

First environment interacts with technology. No culture exists in empty space. Geography, weather, terrain, and food availability will influence group behaviors. Yet, *Environment* alone does not determine culture. There is also technology, which social scientists define as *tools plus knowledge of how to use them.*

Give a Stone Age hunter a tractor, and his cultural level still has not leaped forward to the modern age. Why? Because he lacks knowledge of how to operate complicated machinery. By the same principle, a farm family stranded on the proverbial desert island does not have a tractor technology either, because they lack to tools necessary to implement their knowledge—no tractor.

ILLUSTRATION: SEACOAST TRIBE TO DEEP WOODS DWELLERS

Tools/knowledge must realistically apply to the environment or the group will not survive. Let's suppose a society of seacoast dwellers are chased away from their fishing nets and driven inland to the forest by another, stronger group. They face an immediate problem: Life in the deep woods requires a different technology than life along the seacoast. If a deep-woods clan insisted on fish as their main source of protein they would likely starve until someone was able to convince the pacesetters of the group that modifying their technology—*"Let's hunt deer and gather nuts"*—could feed their families. Then the tribe would need to learn how to track and kills wild animals, identify edible plants and cook what they bagged.

Next, according to the Harris system, *Technology* interacts with the *Division of Labor*. Once a group establishes its technology in a given environment, they will then divide up the work to be done.

Continuing with our illustration of a seacoast clan driven into the deep woods, if hunger forces them to change their technology from fishing to hunting and gathering, they must next decide who will do the hunting and who will do the gathering. Perhaps everyone will do both, or the women will hunt and the men gather, or young people of both sexes will hunt and old people gather. Many combinations are possible.

Techno-environmental factors will play a key role, too. If the supply of animals to be hunted is great, both sexes may hunt locally. If animals are scarce, requiring long trips to bring back large game, most probably young men will go off and leave women of child-bearing age to perform that most vital of all functions. Please note: we are not passing judgment on the ethical values of this kind of arrangement. What works well in a culture of hunters-gatherers will hardly work in a post-industrial, computer-driven society like ours.

Techno-environmental factors and the *Division of Labor* interact to influence the next category, *Human Groups*. In our tribe of uprooted sea coasters, their technology and the forest environment will give them an opportunity to divide the work among themselves in various ways. When they choose who will do what, this will influence the way their family structure and other social groupings take shape. For example, if the men do go off for long periods of time there will most likely be some kind of extended family arrangement where several generations share one large dwelling or a complex of dwellings, children will be raised communally by the extended family, and domestic work will usually be organized by the senior women of the sub-group.

Arrangements like this often lend themselves to *polygyny*, one husband married to more than one wife. But not necessarily so. Single-family dwellings are more likely had the clan lingered by the sea, where the men would not be gone for long periods of time, thus promoting—but not requiring—monogamous marriage. An interesting variation on family systems is *polygandry*, one wife married to more than one husband. Some cultural conditions have occurred under which a pair of living brothers will share a wife or a group of wives. This has happened, but quite rarely in human societies, notably among the Lohari villagers in Northern Uttar Pradesh.

The point here is that no single system of marriage and family has been baptized from On High as the "correct" one. Any combination will work if people believe in the practice and if it meets the needs of society to regulate child-raising, sexual access, and other economic/ educational functions which must take place in the family.

The single most important factor in every culture is human ingenuity. We might call it craftiness or adaptability or, to use a metaphysical term, *wisdom*. Many possible combinations can work under the same conditions, but humans are so creative that they work out solutions to their techno- environmental and social problems that are astoundingly varied and diverse.

THE RELIGIOUS FACTOR

When all these problems have been resolved, social scientists contend, the belief system will change to reinforce the new status quo. More than accepting change, the religious/ethical thinking of the clan will now display a marked preference for the new way of life. That's what happens to our uprooted seacoasters, now comfortable as woodspeople. Before, the society worshipped sea gods and prayed to the moon goddess for favorable tides. Now they worship spirits of the deep woods, praying to the goddess of the hunt to insure that deer and elk are plentiful. Along the coast they could not imagine anyone living away from the magnificent, roaring waves and they celebrated their rites of passage under a tent of stars that stretched to the rim of the world. Now they feel safe under the shelter of the Eternal Wooded Canopy, celebrating their rites of passage in meadows where only a glimpse of the sky is allowed because they are unprotected from its glare. Soon, they will not be able to imagine why anyone would want to live along the seacoast, away from their home in the deep woods.

Religion steps in and tells them that what they are doing is right, proper, and good. It is manly to hunt deer and gather nuts. Who would want to catch squiggling fishes with a net? Why get wet and risk exposure to the dangerous sky when a man can be safe under the eternal canopy of Father Forest?

BEHAVIOR CAUSES IDEOLOGIES

At this stage the model has become quite controversial. Most people believe that ideologies cause behavior. Harris's model suggests that *behavior causes ideologies.* We act in a certain way and then develop religio-political systems of thought that ratify our existing practices, giving what we do the sanction of church and society. Dr. Harris writes:

> Ideology also embraces all thoughts and patterned expressions of thought that describe, explain, and justify the parts of social structure; that give meaning and purpose to domestic and political economy and to the maintenance of law and order in domestic and political relations; that describe, justify, and plan the delegation of authority, the division of labor, the exchange of products, the sharing or non-sharing of resources.[1]

Historians of religion lend their support for Harris's contentions. When any of the four primary factors *(Environment, Technology, Division of Labor,* or *Human Groups)* has changed, human religious faith has adapted to the new circumstances by insisting this is the way things were always meant to be.

HISTORICAL ILLUSTRATION: DESTRUCTION OF THE TEMPLE

A case in point is the destruction of the Temple by the Babylonians in the sixth century B.C. Judean ideology had said that Jerusalem was the very throne of God and that the House of David would be established forever. When the Assyrians carried off the Northern Kingdom in eighth century B.C. (the so-called "lost tribes" of Israel), Jerusalem rejoiced that she was spared. Was this not vindication of her special status as the Chosen People?

Jubilation was not to last. Nebuchadnezzar, King of Babylon, marched against Judah early in the sixth century B.C. and took the city of Jerusalem. The Temple was denuded of sacred relics and treasure and burned to the ground. (Apparently, the Ark of the Covenant disappeared from history until Harrison Ford recovered it in the movie *Raiders of the Lost Ark.)*

How did Hebrew religion deal with this crushing blow to its self-esteem? At first, quite bitterly. Read Psalm 137 for the reaction of some temple musicians enroute to captivity in Babylon. It will shock you. But other voices began to rise. This was not a failure—it was the Hand of God, punishing our people for their faithless-ness. Instead of a defeat, the exile in Babylon and subsequent "return" of a small number of next-generation Jews to rebuild the Temple with the approval of the new conqueror, Cyrus the Persian Emperor, the Prophets reinterpreted these events and insisted that the God of Israel was behind it all.

Religion often comes along after the fact to give its blessings upon what has happened. That is the controversial but historically undeniable conclusion which anthropologists like Harris have drawn. Theology has begun to acknowledge this link between religious thought and socio-cultural practice which was previously noticed only by secular scholarship. On my desk as I write this is an issue of *Christianity and Crisis*, a journal of ethical-political issues from a liberal religious viewpoint. The following is from an article by the Right Reverend Dr. John S. Spong, Episcopal Bishop of Newark, New Jersey:

> The relativity of truth is as established today in theology as it is in the world of physics. A study of its history reveals that Christian theology emerges out of debate and compromise within the church as Christian thinkers interact with their understanding of truth as well as with the culture and the times in which they live. Only later, long after the smoke of battle has cleared, do these debates get codified into doctrines and dogmas that are called infallible. Then those who have no sense of history proclaim that they were received by revelation.[2]

The idea that religious thinking often comes after behavior poses no threat to the principles of Christian Truth churches. Recall, we said that Truth must be proved in everyday experience and that all good theology is dialogue among *Scripture-Tradition-Experience-Reason.* If life compels us to draw other conclusions than what is taught by our religion, we are better off with the changes which emerge from those new circumstances. Just like good science, good theology is willing to overturn its most cherished beliefs in the relentless pursuit of Truth.

Only those religions which seek to carve the ideas of today on the milestones of tomorrow will be threatened by a frank acknowledgment of religion's debt to cultural influences. We must admit that even those cornerstone concepts, by which we define ourselves as people of faith, are subject to review and reconsideration. Only a few beliefs, which serve as yardsticks, shall we cling to with tenacity, because without yardsticks there can be no measurement of truth.

Of course, the possibility exists that someone will invent a better "yardstick" (meter stick?) and that our whole religious orientation will change sometime in the future. Certainly, that is what happened to the Jews who left their religious practices to embrace the teachings of Jesus Christ. Yet, even that was not a complete break with their yardsticks of the past but a fulfillment of all the promises God had made to His people, Israel.

Metaphysical Christians will cheer new circumstances and new discoveries as gifts wrapped by the hands of God. The Prophets were right after all. God did not cause the terrors of the Babylonian exile, but He stood with the Children of Israel as they sought to understand how to sing the Lord's song in a faraway land.

SOME TERMS WE NEED TO KNOW

What we have been discussing is the cultural element in religious thought. To better comprehend how pervasive culture can be in theology, we need a few more terms from sociology. This will not be a crash course in that discipline but a quick brush-up for those who have studied the social sciences and a running summary of a few basic ideas for those who have not previously looked at human groups and their practices.

The source for this material is the popular college textbook *Sociology* by Paul B. Horton and Chester D. Hunt, whose work we quoted in the previous chapter. We shall look at *norms* (which will take in *taboo, folkways,* and *mores*), then *institutions, cultural integration,* and *ethnocentrism*. From this light-speed survey we'll move on to consider the key concept addressed by this chapter, *cultural relativism*, and see how it applies to the study of world religions.

IF IT'S NORMAL, IT'S PROBABLY A NORM

All cultures develop ways of doing things that become normative. In Western societies we shake hands with the right hand, but we may use either hand to scratch our heads. If certain parts of our bodies itch, we may not use either hand in public to scratch. Our culture has a right-hand norm for hand shaking, no norm for head scratching, and a prohibition or *taboo* on scratching genitals and other areas publicly. Norms divide into two basic types.

Folkways "... are simply the customary, normal, habitual ways a group does things...eating with knives and forks, wearing neckties on some occasions and sports shirts on others...and eating toast for breakfast are a few of our many American folk-ways."[3]

Mores. Some norms are more important that others. Choosing the wrong fork for a salad is embarrassing; choosing public nudity will land you in jail. Horton and Hunt explain the two types of norms:

> "Those which SHOULD be followed as a matter of good manners and polite behavior" and "those which MUST be followed because they are believed essential to group welfare."[4]

These "must" behaviors are called mores (pronounced MOR-ays). To understand religious behavior it is vital we realize how powerfully our sense of right and wrong are shaped by the unspoken assumptions we are taught to make. Cultures like the Aztec made it a religious act to tear the heart from a living person and burn it to their bloodthirsty gods. Today, such religious ceremonies would be considered murder.

> Our mores define the killer as either a villain or a hero according to the circumstances. Medieval mores made it right for the church to tolerate prostitution and even share in its income. Most of the Reformation churchmen, both Protestant and Catholic, who ordered the torture and burning of heretics were not cruel or evil, but were decent and often kindly men who did what the mores of the time and place required them to do Mores of our recent past have approved child labor, slavery, and persecution of minorities, and have condemned pacifism, women's suffrage, and sex education. And at all times and places, good people feel pure and righteous when following the mores, whatever they may be.[5]

Nothing could speak more eloquently for the constant review of religious beliefs and the need for dialogue. Unchecked and unexamined standards of conduct, heavily sanctioned by church and society, can retard social progress and hamper personal freedom. When a culture stones its prophets for raising unpopular issues, later generations come along, shaking their heads and sighing, "How could they have been so blind?"

DO YOU BELONG IN AN INSTITUTION?

Groups of folkways and mores organized into a complex pattern which centers on a major human activity are called institutions Industrial societies have five basic institutions which are the family (in its many forms), religion, the government, education, and economic activities.[6]

These separate institutions are not islands unto themselves.

CULTURAL INTEGRATION: BUFFALO AND TEMPLE

"Just as a pile of bricks is not a home," write Horton and Hunt, "a list of traits is not a culture."[7] Cultures are integrated into a system that works smoothly. Cultures which do not provide *cultural integration* can suffer the spasms of disunity, normlessness, and lack of self-identity. Modern Western society, many would contend, fits the description of a culture lacking integration. A culture can even be intentionally denuded of its identity, as were the Native Americans.

> The culture of the Plains Indians centered upon buffalo. From its carcass they drew most of their material culture, as they used its flesh, hides, tendons, bones, sacs, membranes, and many other parts for one purpose or another. Their religion was mainly direct-ed at ensuring the success of the buffalo hunt. Their status system measured success largely according to a man's hunting skill. Their nomadic way of life was attuned to the buffalo migrations. In other words, the different parts of the culture all fitted together in an interrelated system of practices and values. When the white man killed off the buffalo, he did so in a deliberate and successful effort to demoralize the Indian by destroying the focal point of his culture.[8]

Exactly this kind of crisis faced the ancient Israelites when the center of their religion, the Temple, was destroyed first by the Babylonians and again by the Romans. When an integrated culture suffers such a traumatic injury to its self-image, seldom does it survive without radical change. Judaism developed the synagogue worship system to replace its Temple ritual, making the written Word the new focal point of Jewish faith. Native American culture is still recovering from the shock of its amputation from its heritage. Some members of that culture have been absorbed total-ly by the white-European social order that replaced its ancient ways. Others have tried to recover the tribal practices of pre-European America with some success. It is too soon to tell whether Native American culture will survive as coherently as Judaism has.

Cultural Integration means the building blocks of a functioning society must fit together. "It is no accident," sociologists Horton and Hunt say, "that hunting peoples worship hunting gods, fishing people worship sea gods, and agricultural peoples worship sun and rain gods."[9]

The sobering realization which must follow is that we are greatly shaped by our culture. As the old axiom says: *There are no tiger gods where there are no tigers.* Our religious faith shapes the way we look at the world, but our world shapes the way we look at religious faith.

ETHNOCENTRISM

Every group assumes their way the proper, correct, natural way for humans to live. This called is *ethnocentrism*, i.e., the tendency for each group to assume the superiority of its beliefs and practices.[10]

Every culture is ethnocentric to some degree. It may come as a shock to Americans, but not everyone wants to be like us. Members of simpler societies, while often admiring the material goods of industrial nations, frequently feel quite superior to us in other ways. Look at Western society through the eyes of the native people of New Guinea:

> The Europeans were not regarded as all-powerful, but rather pathetic, ignorant people who could be easily cheated or stolen from. Their ignorance of sorcery was lamentable.[11]

Some degree of ethnocentrism is necessary for group cohesion and self-respect. It is healthy and helpful for a black American to feel proud of his African heritage, to enjoy soul music and soul food. Hispanics, Asians, Indians, and other identifiable groups justifiably revel in their uniqueness. How could anyone grow up anywhere in the world, speak the native language, belong to a religious tradition, participate in an ethnic community—and *not* see his cultural neighborhood as normative?

WASHINGTON AND FRANKLIN: *THOSE TRAITOROUS DOGS!*

Ethnocentrism only becomes a problem for a group when it draws the negative conclusion: If our way is good, your way is un-good. The damage becomes obvious when groups segregate themselves from "inferior" or "unsaved" members of alien cultures or other religions. Love of country becomes *nationalism* that spills over into *fanaticism* and provokes wars of conquest. We must not forget that those whom Western society brand as terrorists are called "heroes" and "freedom-fighters" in other religio-political settings.

What fate awaited George Washington and the other "heroes" of the American Revolution if that rebellion had failed? Would our textbooks speak of them today as our "Founding Fathers," or as the traitors who almost caused us to break away from our beloved and rightful King? In the Broadway musical *1776*, Benjamin Franklin remarks that a rebellion is always legal in the first person—*"Our rebellion."* It is only in the third person—*"Their rebellion"*—that it is illegal.

Ethnocentrism is everyone's enemy when it justifies acts of brutality against any of the children of God. Any government which sponsors "freedom fighters" in one hemisphere and opposes "terrorists" in another is either lying to its people or has sunk so deeply into ethnocentrism that it does not recognize the contradiction in its foreign policy. Virtually every government has fallen prey to the excesses of ethnocentrism at one time or another in its history. Nazi Germany is the most blatant example, but compassionate men and women of every society must be on guard against the dangers of racism, sexism, and nationalism.

TWO BLIND TRAILS: INTOLERANCE AND WISHY-WASHINESS

If modern cross-cultural studies chip away at intolerance and outright rejection of other religious views, over-eagerness to embrace alien belief systems presents a danger in the other extreme. Speaking with Christian Truth church members, one encounters a significant number of persons who have rejected the "One Way" mentality of their backgrounds and have moved in healthier directions.

To overcome narrowness is no small task, and those who have embarked on the long pilgrimage from "Turn or Burn" religions to Christian universalism have come a long way. Many of their fellow Christians have yet to realize how outrageous, how sub-Christian, the concept of hellfire-and-damnation truly is.

However, there is always the possibility that the pendulum might swing too far in the opposite direction. In their eagerness to leave ethnocentrism behind, some modern-thinking people have moved so far from narrowness that they have become wishy-washy about their own Christian heritage. Dangerous as ethnocentrism may be, lack of commitment is no answer to the problem, either. And while open-mindedness is absolutely essential to real spiritual growth, ambivalence about one's religious faith is not.

Those of us in the "liberal" churches—by which I mean the associations of Christians who strive for religious tolerance and tend to see value in any sincerely held belief or practice — must ask ourselves some hard questions when contemplating the relationship between modern Christianity and other world faiths:

1) At what point does tolerance become lack of commitment?

2) If your faith is as true as mine, why follow any?

3) How do I dialogue with followers of another faith while remaining faithful to mine?

HELP FROM THE HINDUS

To answer the first question, we need only look at the most successful tolerant religious system the world has ever known, that complex of mini-faiths practiced in the Indian Subcontinent in some form for at least five thousand years, *Hinduism* (which is a useful misnomer). Hindu religion assumes there is truth everywhere but still retains its distinctive flavor. Seeing God incarnate in many ways, the sophisticated Hindu is not threatened when others find God elsewhere. He/she does not feel the need to worship every way possible, but recognizes many possible ways.

This model is not universal; there are Hindu fanatics who insist their way is the One True Faith. But the age-old spirit of Hinduism breathes open-mindedness and tolerance without the signature lack of commitment so prevalent in some people today.

The difference? A tolerant faith is not a tolerant skepticism. Hindu emphasis is on belief, not unbelief.

A REFUGEE CHURCH

The author often tells some congregations, tongue-in-cheek, that they are not really Metaphysical Christians, they're ex-Baptists, ex-Catholics, and ex-Methodists. We truly are a refugee church. Tolerance and commitment go hand in hand, when that tolerance is based on religious principles and not on the absence of belief.

Fortunately, just that kind of spirit dominates Christian Truth churches today. There are exceptions. Credit the founders of modern Metaphysical Christianity, for they attracted open-minded men and women with positive faith who perpetuated that spirit in the generations which followed. Every generation faces the challenge to continue in the spirit of tolerance without withering our commitment to Jesus Christ. Healthy self-examination and dialogue with other Christians safeguards against the dangers of religious ethnocentrism.

IT WORKS: SIX FUNCTIONS OF THEOLOGY

The second question ("Why mine instead of yours?) is easier to answer: We embrace Christianity because it works for us. If it did not work for us, we would abandon this form of the faith and find another expression of God's Truth that better suited our needs. A religious faith "works" when it fulfills the six functions of Theology: 1) provides ongoing re-interpretation of the faith that makes sense to us, 2) critically analyzes ideas and practices, 3) helps us integrate religious concepts into everyday life, 4) gives us a place to dialogue with others within our theological circle, 5) interprets the symbolism of the faith in a way that makes it intelligible to us, and 6) raises new questions and provides new answers to problems we may face. There are many other reasons why Metaphysical Christianity suits our needs, but most can be grouped under these.

Healing/Prosperity/Relationship issues are "integration of religious ideas with everyday life." Coherent interpretation of the Bible is "symbolism," and the chance to exchange ideas without fear of criticism or threats of excommunication is "establishing dialogue within the theological circle."

THE KEY CONCEPT: CULTURAL RELATIVISM

Finally, we asked, "How do I dialogue with followers of another religious faith while remaining faithful to my own?" This is potentially a difficult question. If we approach the "gentile" as a nonbeliever who must be converted, tolerance is in jeopardy. If we come to the other person acknowledging the truth in his faith, our own commitment is suspect and he might see us as a poor representative.

To avoid both intolerance and unbelief, we have said, a positive, tolerant religious faith must be nurtured. *Cultural relativism* is a social science concept which may be extremely helpful when seeking a link between tolerance and commitment. Anthropologist Melville J. Herskovits (1895-1963) forcefully advocated this position. According to Herskovits, we must view each culture as having intrinsic value. He saw the norms and institutions of any culture to be of self-validating, since they held their respective societies together. All social systems are worthy of respect because they evolved to meet some kind of need.[12] Horton and Hunt add:

> A trait is neither good nor bad in itself. It is only good or bad with reference to the culture in which it is to function. Fur clothing is good in the arctic, but not in the tropics. Premarital pregnancy is bad in our society, where the mores condemn it and where there are no comfortable arrangements for the care of illegitimate children; premarital pregnancy is good in a society such as that of the

Bontocs of the Philippines, who consider a woman more marriage-able when her fertility has been established, and who have a set of customs and values which make a secure place for the children. Adolescent girls in the United States are advised that they will improve their marital bargaining power if they remain chaste until marriage. Adolescent girls in New Guinea are given the opposite advice, and in each setting the advice is probably correct...any cultural trait is socially "good" if it operates harmoniously within its cultural setting to attain the goals which the people are seeking.[13]

Does this mean that anything goes? As long as society says it is acceptable, can we cut loose and do it? Not quite. Read on:

The concept of cultural relativism does not mean that all customs are valuable nor does it imply that no customs are harmful. Some patterns of behavior may be injurious in any milieu...The central point in cultural relativism is that in a particular setting, certain traits are right because they work well in that setting, while other traits are wrong because they would clash painfully with parts of that culture. This is another way of saying that a culture is inte-grated, and that its various elements must harmonize passably if the culture is to function efficiently in serving human purposes.[14]

This sounds a lot like St. Paul's advice to the Corinthians: "Someone will say, 'I am allowed to do anything.' Yes, but not everything is good for you."[15]

ADAPTIVE OR MALADAPTIVE?

There are two subterms which clarify the apparent *carte blanche* that social scien-tists issue to behaviors within a culture. All behavior is either *adaptive* or *mal-adap-tive*. Adaptive behavior contributes to the health, well-being, and competitive success of a group. Maladaptive practices are harmful to group health and prosperity.

Some social scientists believe that maladaptive traits cannot long endure because either the group will cease doing business the maladaptive way or the social system will cease to exist in its present form. Unfortunately, maladaptive traits often take a long time to extinguish and the price in human suffering can be quite high.

QUICK REVIEW: GETTING IT TOGETHER

We now have a vantage point from which to look at religion, provided by social scientists. Religious behavior consists of *norms*, which are made up of common ways of doing things (*folkways*) and strict rules (*mores*) which require some kinds of behavior while prohibiting other actions (*taboos*). Theologies are built on *organized reflection upon the beliefs and practices within the theologian's institution (circle of faith)*. A society which functions harmoniously (with a minimum of *maladaptive* behavior) displays *cultural integration*, which is another way of saying that its prac-tices are *adaptive* to the circumstances and provide for the health, well being and competitive success of the larger group. Attitudes which say that our folkways/mores are the "natural" way and other behaviors are "unnatural" or wrong are called *ethno-*

centrism. Finally, *cultural relativism* suggests that we accept all cultures/beliefs as having value as long as they are not harmful to the group which is practicing the behavior.

Of course, we do not have to approve customs which seem foreign and unnatural to us in order to use cultural relativism as a working hypothesis. We merely have to accept that others see the world quite differently than we do.

AFFIRMING OURS, UNDERSTANDING THEIRS

Aren't there some standards which apply everywhere? Probably, but how do we know for certain? How does one measure the measuring stick? What perch can we find to look down upon our own worldview without being prejudiced by our values and assumptions? Modern Christian theology has tried to find such a lofty pinnacle and failed miserably. Neo-orthodoxy claimed it was the revealed Word of God, but biblical criticism shows that the Bible is a different book in each person's hands.

Traditionalists in various churches claim this or that authority, but the day of unquestioned religious authority is over. Theology came of age during the twentieth century when some thinkers began to admit that no transcendent vantage point exists: we all do our ethical/religious thinking within a *circle of faith.*

A worldview comes with the baby shower. All people are to some degree ethnocentric. This really isn't so bad as long as we keep an open mind and are aware of our ethnocentrism. If we assume that God does speak through all the religions of humankind, then He must speak through our religion, too.

For a member of Western society, this means exploring the Judaeo-Christian heritage to find the voice of God as He spoke through our prophets, apostles, and teachers. It does not mean blindly following whatever nonsense has ever been taught by a prophet, apostle, or teacher in the name of God. It means finding our own peculiar brand of "nonsense" and allowing our neighbor to go and do likewise. To be grasped by a religious faith requires faith. To accept that God may speak differently to someone of another worldview calls for the rest of St. Paul's equation, hope and love.

CHECK YOUR KNOWLEDGE

1. How is theology similar/dissimilar to other forms of knowledge?

2. Draw and explain Marvin Harris's controversial social system model.

3. Episcopal Bishop John S. Sprong said that after the *"smoke of battle has cleared,"* doctrines which were open to debate are declared infallible, then proclaimed infallible, and finally *"those who have no sense of history proclaim that they were received by revelation."* What does this mean for Christian thought?

4. Explain the following: *Norms, Taboos, Folkways, Mores, Institutions, Cultural integration, Adaptive/maladaptive.*

5. How does *Cultural Relativism* overcome some of our *Ethnocentrism?*

6. What does the old adage "There are no tiger gods where there are no tigers" mean?

QUESTIONS FOR DISCUSSION

1. If God speaks through all the religions of humanity, why worship the Christian way instead of the Muslim way?

2. Make a list of religio-cultural Do's and Don'ts. What kind of adaptive significance can you find for each?

3. Is *cultural relativism* possible when looking at atrocities like those committed by the Aztec? Where does tolerance draw the line?

4. What is the difference between *appreciating* and *approving* a belief system other than your own?

5. The author suggests we should "affirm ours, understand theirs." Do you agree? Why?

6. What ideas do you take for granted as "normal" that are not necessarily accepted by every culture on the planet?

NOTES

1. Harris, p. 146.

2. John S. Spong, "Women: Crux of Ecumenism," *Christianity and Crisis Magazine*, December 9, 1986, p. 431.

3. Horton & Hunt, pp. 49-50.

4. IBID., p. 50.

5. IBID., p. 51.

6. IBID., p. 52.

7. IBID., p. 56.

8. IBID.

9. IBID., pp. 56-57.

10. IBID., p. 74.

11. IBID., p. 75.

12. Alan Bullock and Oliver Stallybrass, ed., *The Harper Dictionary of Modern Thought* (NY: Harper & Row, 1977), p. 535.

13. Horton & Hunt, pp. 80-81.

14. IBID., p. 81.

15. I Corinthians: 6-12 *(TEV)*

BIBLICAL THEOLOGY AND METAPHYSICAL INTERPRETATION

Chapter Five

Biblical theology - historical/theological analysis of the canonical writings to determine, as closely as possible, what the author meant to say to his target audience.

Metaphysical interpretation - symbolic, allegorical interpretation of the Bible based on One Power/One Presence and the Divine-Human paradox found in the life of Jesus Christ.

Biblical theology mingles historical research with theological analysis. Biblical theologians ask: *"What did the author mean to convey to his readers?"* This is a vastly different question from, *"What does it mean for us today?"*

Biblical theology tries to arrive at just that—the theology expressed in the Bible. A person studying the actual message contained in a section of the biblical library might ask these questions: What God-concept shapes the book of Genesis, as opposed to the gospel of John? Did Paul believe in hell? How is Matthew's Jesus different from the Jesus found in Luke-Acts?

Mining the text for the author's message is called *exegesis* (reclaiming the original meaning of the text by in-depth study.) To do exegesis properly we must acquaint ourselves with the *hermeneutical principles* (techniques of interpretation) used by virtually all modern biblical scholars.

HISTORICAL-CRITICAL ANALYSIS

 # Definition of the Bible

Today's biblical theologians begin by assuming that the Bible is the recorded memories of our spiritual ancestors, written to express to their generation what they believed God was doing in their lives and in the life of the greater community of faith. The Bible speaks of issues, concepts, and expectations which make sense only when we understand the time in which each piece was written, which is the task of the biblical theologian.

This is known as the *Historical-Critical* (or *Historical-Analytical*) method of biblical study. Historical-Critical studies treat the Bible as literature produced by a partisan community of faith, not as a divinely dictated source of infallible guidance.

In the words of a seminary professor under whom the author studied, "The Bible wasn't lowered from heaven in a basket." It functions by a few basic rules.

RULE #1 / KNOWING THE DATE WHEN THE PIECE WAS WRITTEN IS MORE IMPORTANT THAN KNOWING THE ERA IT DISCUSSES.

A work of art or literature better represents the time in which it was produced than the period it portrays. Walk through the Louvre and study the magnificent Renaissance paintings of biblical scenes. You will be mildly amused to see the Virgin Mary wearing fifteenth century velvet dresses, sitting inside a gothic arch, with steep-roofed houses in the background. There may even be a gondola floating by or a medieval castle towering on the horizon.

Ancient Palestine? Hardly.

Those paintings give us a marvelous glimpse into fifteenth century Europe, since that was the only world the artist knew. He used the fashions, architecture, and topography of his era when painting biblical scenes. Historians study the paintings, not to learn about ancient Israel, but to peek into the daily life of fifteenth century Europe.

GOOD GUY WEARS A WHITE HAT, RIGHT?

Another clue to understanding the Bible is found in the history of American cinema. If you are old enough to recall the 1950s movies, or have seen vintage re-runs, you know the scenario. Good Guy wears white hat, Bad Guy wears black hat. Good Guy goes to the saloon and orders—remember?—*milk!* Or, at the most, sarsaparilla. They fight, and Good Guy never loses his hat. He needs it to keep his head warm, since he wore his hair short. Good Guy is always good; Bad Guy is always bad. Villains had no disturbed childhoods or psycho-social problems—they were just bad guys.

If you have read or studied the American West during the late 1800s you know that this model is plainly ridiculous. Photographs of that era show ragged, bearded, long-haired men in dark hats. It is impossible to tell the good guys from the bad guys without footnotes on each picture page. Milk would have spoiled in the heat rather promptly, if a saloon even bothered to carry such a drink. Saloons were usually gambling dens and houses of ill repute as well as watering troughs for whiskey-and-beer drinkers. Gunfights weren't the "High Noon," quick-draw affairs of Hollywood fantasy, either. The combatants drew slowly and blasted away, trying to hit each other first. Handguns weren't accurate enough for long-range, one-shot combat.

However fanciful those old westerns may have been, they do give us a look at the morality, dress codes, lifestyles, and attitudes of another era—the 1950s. Good was good, bad was bad, hair was short, and heroes always played fair. Or so we believed, back in the "Happy Days."

If an historian two thousand years from now comes across some of these old westerns she will face the same problem we encountered when approaching the biblical text. To unscramble the context, she would have to realize that a work of art or literature better represents the period in which it was produced than the period it portrays.

This is especially important for biblical studies, since almost every passage was written well after the events it describes by generations of believers whose issues, insights, and interests were not the same as those of the earlier time. When we approach the Bible, carrying our agenda of interests and looking for supportive texts, the problem multiplies.

RULE #2 - AUTHOR, NOT HIS CHARACTERS, IS SPEAKING TO US.

To do biblical theology, meaning to understand what the authors meant to say to their audiences, we must find out when the passage of scripture was written and for what purpose. When a biblical theologian reads the Sermon on the Mount he asks, "What did Matthew mean to say to his readers?" Not, "What did Jesus teach us?"

This is only a disturbing thought if we are operating out of a model of biblical literalism. Biblical theology seeks the intent of the author, not the intent of the characters portrayed within the narrative. Disturbing though it may be to some people, the overwhelming historical evidence suggests that the gospels are not impartial biographies of Jesus. They are shared memories of the Christian community, less like evening news reports, more like pamphlets displayed in a church lobby.

The best guess of modern scholarship is that no apostle wrote a gospel, a fact apparently confirmed by Luke in the first four verses of his gospel. The closest reference to a possible author of Luke was made by Paul in Colossians 4:14 and by the unknown author of II Timothy (4:11). Mark may have been the John Mark mentioned frequently in Acts and in various New Testament epistles, but we have no direct evidence for this assumption. John Mark was not an apostle anyway but a traveling companion and assistant to Paul.

ARAMAIC OR GREEK ORIGINALS?

Matthew was long thought to be the tax collector called by Jesus (Matthew 9:9), but scholarship has established fairly well that whoever wrote that gospel used Mark's gospel as a source document and that both were written in Greek. Our apologies to Dr. George Lamsa, but his theories about an Aramaic New Testament are not shared by the vast majority of scholars. We may gain insights into Semitic idiom by studying Dr. Lamsa's works, but the bulk of reputable New Testament scholarship stands firmly behind an all-Greek original edition.

Certain concepts, such as the logos of John 1:1, are nearly meaningless in Aramaic, a Semitic tongue related to biblical Hebrew. Aramaic shares the richness of Hebraic pictorial imagery but lacks the capacity to abstract such ideas as the *logos*. Koine Greek, on the other hand, is highly abstract. The difference comes across vividly, even in English translation.

Read Genesis 1:1-5 then skip to John 1:1-5 for two Creation accounts, the first translated from Hebrew and the latter from Greek. Notice the action-oriented imagery in the Semitic idiom and the intellectual abstractions offered by the Greek.

Because Dr. Lamsa's ideas frequently lean in the direction of mysticism, metaphysical Christians find it tempting to embrace his scholarship with open arms, proclaiming the Lamsa Bible as the "real" Bible. However, the bulk evidence of modern scholarship calls us to face the probability that there was no Aramaic New Testament, regardless how helpful Dr. Lamsa's re-wording might be to our theologies.

We can certainly learn about the thought-world of the Aramaic-speaking community from Lamsa's studies. Aramaic teachings of Jesus must stand behind the New Testament's koine Greek as part of an oral tradition, now and forever lost. Were these some of the sources cited by Luke? Or were the words of Jesus translated into Greek almost immediately? We don't know.

Since Aramaic was the language of Palestine, it is doubtful that the Apostle Matthew, a Jewish tax collector, would compose in Greek that was intended for an Aramaic-speaking audience. Of course, the book could have been written for Jews in Diaspora. Then Greek, as the universal language of educated people throughout the Roman Empire, would make more sense. However, we still have Matthew's reliance upon the gentile-Greek format of Mark's gospel. Since Mark was probably written after 70 A.D., Matthew's book could be dated in the early 80s. By that time an original apostle of Jesus would have been a very old man by ancient standards.

John's gospel is written in such good Greek that scholars doubt it could have been penned by an Aramaic-speaking fisherman. It is usually dated last, around 90 A.D.

RULE #3 - WHAT WAS THE AUTHOR SAYING, AND TO WHOM?

Because these books came late in the first century, we need to know what Matthew's theology was, to note what special interest keeps cropping up in Luke, to wonder about the rough simplicity of Mark's writing and to realize what John means when he calls upon the logos of Greek philosophy to explain the Christ-event.

Does this mean Jesus Christ is unavailable to us in scripture? Of course not. It means we must sift the biblical record for traces of the historical Jesus. Struggling, growing human beings, like us, wrote down their insights for their communities of faith. When we read the Bible, we are looking over their shoulders. In the words of the Prophet Isaiah:

> And now, go, write it before them on a tablet,
> and inscribe it in a book,
> that it may be for the time to come
> as a witness for ever.

WILL THE HISTORICAL JESUS PLEASE STAND UP?

We must constantly remind ourselves, when reading the words of Jesus, that these thoughts come to us through a series of filters, beginning with the mind of the author/editor and ending with our own particular screening process as mystical/metaphysical Christians. To look behind the filters and find the historical Jesus is always an "iffy" task, as Albert Schweitzer discovered in his book, *The Quest of the Historical Jesus.*

Schweitzer, the great medical missionary, was also a first-rate theologian. He decided it is impossible to peel off the layers of tradition and arrive at the authentic, undoubted Jesus of history. Perhaps he was right; there are limits to historical scholarship. Yet, even Schweitzer believed he found in the teachings and life stories about Jesus a spiritual force which he called the "religion of love." [3]

Jesus of history is the energy-force that stirred the New Testament authors to tell their tales. There can be no doubt that Jesus existed and that He stands behind the gospel traditions as their driving, motivating Force. As such, He is present in personalized accounts of the Christ-event, an event played out in the generation immediately before theirs.

There are times we come upon His footprints in the gospels, only the faintest hint that a flesh-and-blood Human-Divine paradox walked the earth. Some stories test our credulity, tales which smack of mythology—virgin birth, walking on water, magically transforming water into wine. But other times the historical person juts like a mountain over the plain editorializing by gospel authors: His parables, His treatment of women and children, His ringing words of faith in the Sermon on the Mount, His triumph over doubt and fear at Gethsemane.

We must frankly admit that even these mountain-top experiences are subject to the filtration process and have been colored by the stained-glass windows of human imagination—our own included. However, the task of biblical theology is not completely impeded by these problems because its goal is to determine *what the author meant to say to his target audience*, regardless of how historically valid we think his sources were. This is both the advantage of biblical theology and its greatest limitation.

INTERPRETATION IS CRUCIAL AND UNAVOIDABLE

If God speaks to us through Scripture, as Christians believe He/She does, the question becomes how can we hear His voice through the clatter of countervailing opinions, ancient concepts, and mythological language of the biblical authors? Biblical theology gives us a starting point, but we must push beyond antiquarianism, which is mere fascination with the past, and find a way to release the spiritual power the Bible authors experienced.

As a starting point, the gospel narratives give us the only reputable information about the life and teachings of Jesus. Even an arms-length encounter is welcome. The

Bible is the raw material of the Christian faith. *If the historical Jesus isn't here, He's unavailable to us.*

Perhaps we will be able to discover a way to refine the ore of scripture into the fine gold of spiritual insights. Meanwhile, I've posted a 3x5 card beside my computer screen with these words:

> *WANTED: A METHOD OF BIBLICAL INTERPRETATION*
> *THAT IS FLEXIBLE, APPLICABLE TO MODERN LIFE,*
> *AND FAITHFUL TO CHRISTIAN TRADITION.*
> *(DOGMATISM NEED NOT APPLY.)*

Jesus must be more than just a literary character employed by ancient authors to act out dramas about issues that excited Christians two thousand years ago. Yet, that is all we can hope to gain from biblical theology if we stop there.

Biblical theology is an attempt to clarify the message of scripture in its ancient context. To go beyond this we need another element in our hermeneutic. We need a way to interpret the Bible that is theologically sound (fulfilling the *six functions of theology*), that is compatible with the four formative factors of theological thinking (*Scripture/Tradition/Experience/Reason*) and that gives us insights into the three paradoxes which religious thinkers encounter when trying to live a Christian life (*Divine-Human, Asceticism-Activism, Realism-Optimism*).

Preferably, our method of interpretation would be one which has been used throughout the history of Christianity and not some gadgety new system. It would allow us to do exegesis and to apply these insights to everyday life, striking the spark of inspiration which fired the scripture-writers themselves. It would also be a method of scriptural interpretation approved by scripture itself. Since there are quite a few instances of New Testament authors interpreting Old Testament passages, we should develop a simple method which falls in line with examples of interpretations within the canon of scripture itself.

For the best of all possible worlds—why not settle for the best?—our method would allow continual re-evaluation and re-interpretation and would neither tie us down to the pre-scientific worldview of the biblical authors nor commit us to a slavishly literal pattern of belief.

ALLEGORY TO THE RESCUE

Fortunately, such a method of biblical interpretation exists. As early as the second century A.D., Alexandrian Christianity was busily painting a universalist picture of the faith under the bold brush strokes of Clement, Origen, and host of lesser figures. They believed that Christian Truth was the same as philosophical Truth. Armed with Plato's understanding of the world, these early interpreters found images, illustrations, and hidden insights tucked between the lines of Scripture.

Their method? *Allegorical Interpretation.* Today we call it *Metaphysical Interpretation.* It is both a simple and dangerous way to interpret Scripture. We would be less than candid if we did not acknowledge both its benefits and its potential pitfalls.

METAPHYSICAL INTERPRETATION: SYMBOLIC THEOLOGY IN ACTION

Any approach to scripture which is non-literal falls under the broad category of Symbolic Theology. Symbolic Theology deals with any illustration which represents God's presence or activity. Symbolism is an arrow pointing to Divine Truth. It may be an action (like the *Lord's Supper*), a physical artifact (like a *Celtic cross*), or a concept (like the *Trinity*). When we study the words of scripture to learn their deeper meaning we are doing symbolic theology. If we discover insights which relate to spiritual growth, we have done Metaphysical Interpretation of the Bible.

"Metaphysical" is not really an accurate label for this kind of interpretation and causes some confusion when Christian Truth students interface with people from other traditions. A better name might be *Mystical Interpretation*, or just calling the process by its historic name, *Allegorical Interpretation*. However, the term "metaphysical" is so entrenched that it will doubtless continue for some time, and there really is no good reason for changing it when talking within the circle of faith to other metaphysical Christians. When engaging in dialogue with people from other denominational families, the Truth student needs to be aware of these differences.

According to the landmark work in this subject, the *Metaphysical Bible Dictionary*, Metaphysical Interpreters seek "...the inner or esoteric meaning of the name defined, as it applies to every unfolding individual and to his relationship to God."[3]

DANGER! ALLEGORY MUST BE CONTROLLED BY A GUIDING PRINCIPLE

By its very flexibility, allegory can be bent to serve any master. Allegorical interpretation has been used to justify racism, sexism, and homophobia. In fact, allegory is so plastic that it was the weapon of choice when theologians battled over difficult texts in earlier times. If one side in a dispute quoted scripture that seemed to support its position, the other side would offer an allegorical interpretation that "proved" otherwise.

Today, however, theologians proceed differently. They seldom quote scripture as the authority for their ideas; that is called proof-texting and is considered an exercise in futility because of the above. Since there are so many scripture passages that could be called upon to contradict other texts, any discussion which resorts to proof-texting has deteriorated from legitimate theology to legalistic nit-picking.

Theology today tends to refer to biblical concepts and ideas rather than citing Isaiah to prove some abstract idea first enunciated by Luther or Calvin. However, fundamentalists continue to proof-text, blithely ignoring the reality of modern biblical research. One very popular example of this approach is Billy Graham whose

"Crusades" always involve biblical preaching that is usually an exciting jaunt through theologies of yesteryear. Writes Lutheran theologian T. A. Kantonen:

> It (fundamentalism) is the theology under girding mass evangelism such as that of Billy Graham. With complete disregard for the original connotations and situations as elucidated by biblical scholarship, the evangelist proves his point with a simple indiscriminate *"the Bible says..."*[4]

A QUESTION OF AUTHORITY

Biblical authority is the issue. If we see the Bible as the only source of Truth—*sola scriptura,* the cry of the Reformation—then we must make sure it agrees with what we are doing. One way to achieve harmony with Scripture is to change our practices to bring them in line with biblical mandates. This is important if one believes, in the words of *Luther's Small Catechism*: "Every word of the Bible is God's word, and therefore the Bible is without error."[5]

A more common way to reach accord between Bible and practice is to apply creative methods of interpretation to places where contradictions or difficulties appear. Even Luther claimed the right to do this, calling the Letter of James an "Epistle of straw" because he felt it contradicted his basic premise that salvation comes only through faith and not through works (James 2:14-17).

Even a cursory reading of the biblical library shows it contains an amazing array of ideas. One would have to be a titan of interpretation to harmonize the unapologetic brutality of the Book of Nahum with the words of forgiving love spoken by Jesus. And even if we accepted the idea of an inerrant Bible, with the denominational smorgasbord of Sunday worship available in the average North American town, we would have to conclude that an error-free text still manages to confuse most of Christendom.

More importantly, the religious thinker must frankly admit that he/she is not an unbiased observer. No one comes to the Bible without opinions about God, Jesus Christ, heaven, and hell. We all see scripture through that stained-glass window of our beliefs. This is not to say that an objective Bible study is impossible; it merely means we need to guard against uncritical assumptions when doing exegesis.

For example, do all those passages in Isaiah which are read every Christmas really prophesy the birth of Jesus? Our Jewish friends would politely disagree. Does the book of Revelation really talk about the future, about the time of the end? Or is it best understood as underground literature of the first century Christian community with symbolism that refers exclusively to people, places, and events which occurred during their lifetimes? Most modern biblical scholars argue the latter.

TOUGH JOB

Interpreting the Bible is a tough job. If we choose to go after the original intent of the author, we find ourselves wandering an ancient, alien culture. If we just read the Bible and let it speak to us in whatever images come to mind, we may as well be reading *Don Quixote* or *Paradise Lost* or any other piece of classical literature. Great ideas come to mind whenever we immerse ourselves in great thinking.

But isn't the Bible more than great thinking? Isn't it great inspiration? Isn't there some way to plumb the depths of biblical Truth without drowning in:

1. theology's "ocean of contradictory ideas" or sinking into sub-Christian beliefs,

2. like historic justifications of racism,

3. which were rationalized either by proof-texting or by resorting to an irresponsible allegory?

Perhaps if we begin with a healthy premise the chance for unhealthy conclusions is greatly mitigated, and there can be no healthier premise than *One Presence/One Power.*

THE BOTTOM LINE: OP/OP

Like all the departments of Metaphysical Christianity, biblical interpretation takes as its central starting point the *sine qua non* of mystical Christianity: *"There is only one Presence and one Power in my life and in the Cosmos—God the good, Omnipotent."*

If metaphysical Christianity had a creed—which, I pray, it never will—this would be it. We shall examine this concept in detail in the chapters to come, but for now let it suffice to say that any belief which falls short of this affirmation cannot truly call itself monotheism. God must be the Source and Power behind everything, or He is neither the God of Jesus Christ nor the Omnipotent Ruler of the Universe.

One Presence/One Power becomes our Occam's razor. We bring all religious ideas to this one concept to cut away everything which is contrary to God the Good, Omnipotent. This is the outer boundary of our theological circle as well as the starting point for our whole study. It serves as the "central pivotal truth" to which Charles Fillmore alluded. It is the basis for our allegories drawn from the names, places, and images of scripture. On this concept we stand or fall in systematic theology, practical Christianity, and everyday life.

Let's see how a modern allegorical method of interpretation might proceed from the belief in One Presence/One Power and still bring with it the treasures of biblical theology.

We'll call this *HISTORICAL-METAPHYSICAL INTERPRETATION.* It is a product of long, lively discussions with the Reverend Mr. Robert Hungerford, a fellow minister and good friend. He came from a strictly metaphysical background; the author was schooled in the historical-critical approach. We began wondering if there weren't some way to link the great insights of biblical criticism with the mystical truths found through metaphysical interpretation. After months of exploring both types of interpretation, we devised a five-step system to bridge both worlds.

HAVING IT ALL: HISTORICAL-METAPHYSICAL INTERPRETATION

To interpret the Bible intelligently we need the right tools. A good commentary, like the *Interpreter's One-Volume Commentary* is absolutely essential. To do metaphysical research we'll need a Bible dictionary which delves into the root meanings of the Greek and Hebrew words. *The Metaphysical Bible Dictionary (MBD)* is still the best, but other fine biblical reference works will give you root meanings. Best of all would be to study Greek and Hebrew, but few of us have the time to study that deeply.

A good translation of the Bible is also essential: Some prefer the *Revised Standard Version* or the *NRSV*. Personally, the author likes *the Good News Bible* for clarity and the *New English Bible* for scholarly accuracy. Check with your local minister for advice about other translations. Once we have the proper tools—a good historical/critical commentary and an *MBD* or another root-word source book—we can get to work.

The process is actually quite simple. We are trying to set the biblical passage in its historical context and discover what the author was trying to say to his readership, then find a concept-bridge in the root meanings which can enable us to see deeper meanings in the text through metaphysical analysis. It's actually kind of fun, too. We'll take it step-by-step.

CAUTION: THIS IS AN AVOWEDLY SUBJECTIVE METHOD

Before we begin, let's remind ourselves that we are not unlocking some deep secret meaning that the author really meant for us to find. We are taking the pieces handed to us by Matthew, Mark, or Luke and rearranging them in other patterns, quite possibly in ways that would scandalize the editor-writers of the Bible. Our license to create new images draws its authority from two sources:

    1) The Historical Context. We must begin with the best insight into what the author really did mean to say to his target audience. When the unknown author of Ephesians went off on a jag about slaves obeying their masters, we need to know he meant it. But we don't have to stop there, because we know God speaks to us through all sorts of media. Now we're ready for the second reference point.

    2) One Presence/One Power. God the good is the only power that exists. There are not two forces, light and dark; there is only light and shadow (non-light).

These provide a starting point. Of course, as with all religious ideas, we submit the insights of allegorical interpretation to the *Scripture-Tradition-Experience-Reason* test, ask that they meet our epistemological criteria for *Pragmatic Enlightenment* (Chapter 3), and hold them up against the yardstick of Jesus Christ. Disciplined by a guiding principle and aware of the method's limitations, we can venture into the exciting world of biblical allegory.

It is a method that few understand, even though doing allegory is simple. When attending a conference in Colorado, the author asked eminent biblical scholar Krister Stendahl if allegorical interpretation was justifiable today. His response startled the learned assembly but delighted the questioner: "Yes, it is a wonderful way of playing in God's garden." Dr. Stendahl went on to warn that it could become a way to rationalize ideas that were unhealthy unless we check our interpretations out with the broader community of faith.

Historical/metaphysical analysis will breathe life into some otherwise dead, airless places in Scripture and throw light upon highly obscure verses. Fair enough. Open your Bibles—any number can play! With apologies for the lame acronym, we call this: *THE B-I-B-L-E METHOD:*

B   BACKGROUND OF THE BOOK. Read the introduction to the book from your commentary, studying when it was written and for what purposes. Who were the bad guys? Did the author try to make us believe he was somebody else? (Often this is the case.) What was happening in the world and in the target community when this passage was written? Remember, some books (Psalms, Isaiah, Genesis, and others) were written by more than one author over a period of time longer than one lifetime. Focus down to your specific scripture passage by using the commentary. This brings us to the next step.

I   INTERPRETER'S INSIGHTS. Go to the textual commentary and see what the interpreter has to say about your passage of scripture. Try to set the verses in their context. What does the interpreter suggest that the biblical author wanted to say or accomplish with this passage? When you feel you understand what the ancient author probably meant to convey to his readers, you are now ready to move into symbolic interpretation.

B   BREAKDOWN TO BASICS. Find the names, objects, and places mentioned in the text. Personal names such as *Aaron, Moses, Jesus, Zedekiah, or Jezebel.* Objects like animals, plants, or mountains. Structures like temples, inns, shrines, tents, and houses. Places like *Jericho, Egypt, Syria,* or the *Red Sea.* Make a list of all the persons, places and things mentioned in your text—animal, vegetable, or mineral. And don't forget abstract nouns: *love, hate, war, peace, faith, hope.* Next, take your *Metaphysical Bible Dictionary* in hand and move to step four.

L   LOOK UP LIST. Find the key concept-words from your passage in the *MBD,* looking for root meanings and variant readings. See if patterns emerge.

E   EXCHANGE AND EDITORIALIZE. Using the new insights based on the root meanings of the text and recalling the historical context, try to find an allegorical or symbolic teaching in the passage. Listen to the new meanings you've uncovered and see if the mists rise over your verses. This is the fun part, because you get to play with the meanings until some new ideas snap into focus.

H/M SAMPLER

Let's try a quick example. Remember, biblical authors often use self-conscious symbolism when they choosing place names, character names, or physical objects. However, not every verse in the Bible can be interpreted "metaphysically", because a lot of passages are lyrical hymns of praise or already contain abstract significance and need no substitution of name/place/object values. (An example which springs to mind is Paul's *"Hymn to Love"* in I Corinthians 13.) Pick a passage with strong images and action. For example, here's how we might do a H/M workup on Mark 10:32.

> And they were on the road, going up to Jerusalem, and Jesus was walking ahead of them; and they were amazed, and those who followed were afraid.

First, we learn the <u>Background of the Book</u>. Open the *Interpreter's One-Volume Commentary* to the section on Mark. Come with me on a stream-of-consciousness study of this passage and we'll walk through the B-I-B-L-E method.

Let's see, Mark's commentary begins on page...644. Okay, now we want to find out when the book as a whole was written and for what purpose. A-ha! According to Lindsey P. Pherigo, the commentator on Mark, the book was probably written after the death of the Apostle Peter (ca. 64 A.D.) by a missionary companion of Peter and Paul. It was written far from the local traditions about Jesus, perhaps at Rome, by someone who did not participate in the events himself.

Pherigo says this is a "Gentile Christian" gospel, as opposed to the "Jewish Christian" message of Matthew. Hmmm. That means Mark was an advocate of Paul's concepts about the message of Jesus being for everyone and not just for the lost sheep of Israel, as Matthew's gospel suggests. Let's flip to the textual commentary and find our passage.

Here the commentator notes that the disciples did not understand what was happening; that's typically Marcan. He often minimizes the importance of the Apostles because he's trying to establish a world-wide Christian message that need not be linked strictly with the leadership in Jerusalem. Also, Pherigo says to notice the way they were walking, strictly in order of seniority with Jesus leading. He says that was a formal procedure in first century Palestine. This suggests we have a piece of authentic history here. If Mark was not one of the original circle but his storyline reflects a local custom he could not have known otherwise, it probably happened. Jesus leads the way, followed by his disciples...and the disciples are scared and amazed that He is going to Jerusalem, the commentator notes.

So far so good. Time for step three. OK, we've got the following characters and places:

> *1 - Jesus*
>
> *2 - disciples* (not specifically mentioned in this passage, but present)
>
> *3 - Jerusalem*

4 - road to Jerusalem

Other significant relationships to note:

they were going up to Jerusalem

the first group behind Jesus was amazed

the second group was afraid ("those who followed")

Now we move on to the *MBD*, with help from Fillmore's *Revealing Word (RW)*.

Jesus - the *MBD* lists these meanings for the name:

"...whose help Jehovah is; deliverance; safety; salvation; Savior; Deliverer; helper; prosperer; deliverance through Jehovah.

It also says that Jesus is God's idea of man in expression.

Jerusalem - habitation of peace; dwelling place of peace; possession of peace; foundation of peace; constitution of harmony; vision of peace; abode of prosperity

Disciples -   *MBD: the faculties*

RW: (cross-reference to *apostles*) *those sent forth; messengers; ambassadors; active spiritual thoughts*

Road to Jerusalem - no references in either.

Armed with these informative bits, let's move on to the interpretation stage. Jesus represents our deliverance. He leads the way and the active spiritual thoughts we have follow him. But on the upward path toward the abode of prosperity/peace/harmony, our thoughts become confused, falling into two camps. First we have those spiritual thoughts which are simply amazed. "Can all this be true?" Amazement is not necessarily bad, but if we are paralyzed by the wonder of our unfolding spiritual growth—if we feel this can't be happening—our confidence will erode into doubt.

The second group represents fearful thoughts and attitudes. They are behind and therefore lower than the amazement-thoughts, since we are moving upward after Jesus. These thoughts could stop altogether, but if we continue on the upward path we shall break through fear into amazement, which is directly beyond fear. The important thing is to keep pressing on, traveling upward after Jesus, who is safety and deliverance from all lesser states of consciousness. Just as the First Century church broke through their fears about the unknown (gentile world), so must we move beyond our fears that lack or apparent disharmony will prevail. Jesus leads us onward toward a habitation of peace; our deliverance is secure because God is within us.

LET'S BE HONEST...

This was a rough-cut example of how we can link historical insights with metaphysical methods. Wherever names, places or objects are present, a symbolic interpretation is possible. However, we must face a tough question before moving on to our next topic: Is Metaphysical Biblical Interpretation an authentic method of study, or is this merely a Bible word-game invoked by Christian Truth churches to "prove" points of doctrine that are not otherwise biblical?

Just how "biblical" is this method? What right do we have to turn the meaning of scriptural words inside-out and make them say what we want them to say? Can anyone honestly believe that Mark (whomever he was) meant for us to interpret the text the way we did in the above example from his gospel? Or shall we fall back on that old Gnostic drivel about hidden, secret meanings in the text which only specially initiated persons—members of our elite group—can comprehend?

To be honest, we must admit the most serious challenge to our method of interpretation is that allegorical reading does not faithfully represent the ideas which motivated the pen of the author so long ago. Facing the issues squarely, we must acknowledge that a metaphysical interpretation is not a truer, deeper meaning which God intended for only a select few. If we think that the writer meant anything but the plain, literal meaning when he said Jesus was *"on the road, going up to Jerusalem,"* we are fooling ourselves and doing no justice to the profound insights of metaphysical interpretation.

Given the tendency of metaphysical Christianity to slide into gnosticism, I cannot say this strongly enough: *There is no secret key which unlocks the true, hidden meaning of the Bible.* Except for a few instances of self-conscious symbolism, such as the books of Genesis and Revelation, no significant "secret" meanings exist. What, therefore, gives us the right to do metaphysical interpretation? We have grounds to interpret the Bible symbolically for three basic reasons.

FOR OPENERS, JESUS DID IT

1. It's in the Bible. First, interpreting symbolically is one of the methods used by biblical authors themselves. New Testament authors often see references to Jesus Christ throughout the pages of the Hebrew Scriptures. Remember, there was no *New Testament* when Paul and the apostles went barn-storming around the Mediterranean with their evangelical message.

Paul didn't hand out pocket New Testaments, but he did quote the Hebrew Bible—the only Testament at the time. Fortunately, the Jewish Scriptures were translated into Greek long before the time of Jesus, so the Greek-speaking world knew about the sacred writings of the Jews.

Paul and his fellow evangelists quoted the Old Testament freely, using this Greek translation (called the Septuagint or LXX). They also freely reinterpreted the symbolism of Psalm, Prophet and Torah to find references to Jesus Christ everywhere.

Jesus Himself re-interpreted and spiritualized the Scriptures. What gave Him the authority to change the meanings? If John 10:34 is authentic, He even misquoted out of context Psalm 82:6 to show that there is ample authority for His claim to be divine, since we are all divine. If it is not authentic, then the first century church felt free to reinterpret for Him.

But what about metaphysical interpretation? There are several examples, the most obvious is where Paul explains the meaning of Abraham's two wives. Significantly, he begins: *"Now this is an allegory: these two women are covenants..."* (Gal. 4:24) How can allegorical interpretation be "unbiblical", when New Testament authors use it themselves?

Dangerous, yes. We have already addressed the fact that allegorical interpretation opens us up to all sorts of weird tangents and unchristian extremes. That does not invalidate the method; it just makes us aware of our responsibility to ground our mystical interpretation in principles which meet the criteria of a sound Christian theology. If we are faithful to our principles of interpretation and those principles are in harmony with the metaphysical Christian perspective, no one can say our methods are beyond the pale of Christian theology.

ALLEGORICAL INTERPRETATION IS NOT NEW

2. It is at least as old as literalism. Two schools of biblical interpretation developed in the first Christian centuries. One, which was centered in Antioch, stressed literal interpretations of both the Jewish Bible and those Christian documents which were vying for a place in a new Testament. The other school of thought sprang from the rich intellectual/spiritual soil of Alexandria on the Egyptian coast. This second center of Christian interpretation followed the lead of Greek stoicism and the great Jewish philosopher Philo, who lived during the missionary period of the Apostle Paul.

Philo learned allegorical interpretation from the Stoics, who were uncomfortable with a literal interpretation of Greek mythology. As a Jew who was schooled in both Torah and philosophy, Philo sought to synthesize those two thought worlds by interpreting the Jewish scriptures allegorically. When Christianity came to town, its learned adherents—notably Clement and Origen—adopted the same method of interpretation. Allegorical interpretation was widely popular among educated Christians for the first few centuries after Christ.

Only later did Antiochan-style literalism become the dominant method of biblical interpretation, and then only after the light of Greek scholarship had been snuffed out by anti-intellectual zealots who ushered in the Dark Ages.

A TRUE WORK OF ART ALLOWS FOR CREATIVE INTERACTION

3. Appreciation is a creative act. As compelling as these arguments from scripture and history may be, there is a still stronger reason for doing metaphysical interpretation. Any work of art or literature will evoke a response in us which goes deeper than words. Poets write of the Mona Lisa with little thought of what DaVinci had in mind when painting his masterpiece. In fact, one researcher has concluded that DaVinci's greatest work is a secret self-portrait: the eyes, mouth and other facial features provided a perfect computer-enhanced match. Will that affect the way our grandchildren see her? Probably not.

Millions hear the *William Tell Overture* and associate it with the "Lone Ranger," a connection which scarcely occurred to the composer, Gioachino Antonio Rossini (1792-1868). Christians read prophecies in the Hebrew Bible and point to these as proofs of Jesus' messiahship, yet Jews read that same Bible and have decided these proofs do not apply to the man of Nazareth.

Who is right? Is it possible that both are? Is it possible that a true work of art or literature will speak with a voice that people can hear whether or not the artist/author intended to say exactly that?

One of Robert Frost's best beloved poems is *"Stopping by Woods on a Snowy Evening."* Listen to the haunting simplicity of the closing verse:

> These woods are lovely, dark and deep.
> But I have promises to keep,
> And miles to go before I sleep,
> And miles to go before I sleep.[6]

Countless English teachers have swooned over Frost's picture of life's journey which will end in rest one day. This noble soul has paused along the path of life, anticipating the sleep of death, but knowing there are hard times ahead and feeling the need to press onward faithful to that calling.

Then someone asked Mr. Frost what he meant by the poem, and the poet shrugged and said it was a straightforward narrative about a person who stops to see the snowfall on his way home. English teachers have never forgiven him.

When so many people see the symbolism of life and death in a poem, do we say to them? *"No, you are wrong. That is not what Robert Frost meant to say. You may not hear that in this poem!"* If the words of Scripture touch something in us and if that something expresses itself as insights which the author never intended to convey, can we not legitimately interpret the passage by its symbolism as it speaks to us? As long as we have a theological system which cogently and consistently touches base with the central Truths of the Christian faith, as Metaphysical Christianity certainly does, then a method of biblical interpretation based on allegory is valid if its insights are in harmony with the central, pivotal Truths of that belief system.

SELF-CONSCIOUS CREATIVITY

We must add a further caveat: This method is only valid if we practice self-conscious re-interpretation of the author's message into the images of Christian metaphysics. As noted above, mental integrity means we can't fool ourselves into thinking that this is what the author really meant to say and that we are merely unlocking his coded message.

What we are doing is breaking down the message and re-coding it into symbolism once more. Allegorical interpretation gets people into trouble only when they refuse to acknowledge what they are actually doing: creating something new from the energy source of the original. It is more art than science.

NO EASY JOB

Even for scholars, exploring the Bible is a difficult, complex task. But there are certainly many good ways of reading our Holy Scriptures, for surely God speaks to us with many voices depending on our level of comprehension. The Bible is a different book in everyone's hands, as it must be. It is a treasure chest from which we can receive deep insights and high standards, good stories and fine poetry, inspiration to reach for goals beyond our grasp, and power to make our dreams come true.

No single method of biblical interpretation will meet the needs of every Christian. We have merely suggested one method which seems to blend the best elements of historical-critical study with metaphysical-allegorical interpretation.

Let us reiterate: all these ideas must be continually brought to the ultimate standard of all Christian theology, the life and teaching of Jesus Christ, and any insights we glean from adventuresome reading in the allegorical hinterlands must be compared with the ideas current in the Christian community through dialogue and discussion in an atmosphere of mutual respect.

A rabbi once told the author, "You cannot be a Jew alone. It takes a community—it is a lifestyle as much as a religious faith." Hillary Clinton recently popularized an ancient African maxim when she said that it takes a village to raise a child. We know from our study of cultural influences that every one of us has been powerfully influenced by the norms of our communities, and that this influence is not inherently bad but provides a necessary context for living an effective, rich, and meaningful life. We can say the same about Christian theology and biblical interpretation. These need to be part of a community of faith, which is constantly cross-referencing itself with other forms of knowledge and ideas of the "elders", i.e., those who have walked this path before us.

Good biblical interpretation is therefore both intensely personal and irrevocably public, because it links our private communion with God's Word to the beliefs, practices, and thoughts of people in our religious tradition, and through that window we should be able to see the world.

BASICS MASTERED? LET'S GET TO WORK!

With a better understanding of the tools, terms, and limitations of theology, we turn next to examine our God-concept as interpreted in the ancient doctrine of the *Trinity* which, we shall see, was created by that Christian community as it reflected on the faith delivered to us from prophets, apostles, and teachers.

CHECK YOUR KNOWLEDGE

1. What is *biblical theology*; how does it differ from a *metaphysical interpretation* of the Bible*?*

2. List and explain the three rules for Historical-Critical Interpretation.

3. Why does the author think George Lamsa's translation of the New Testament from the Aramaic is not as accurate as Dr. Lamsa claims?

4. How is allegory at once an exciting yet dangerous tool?

5. What is Historical-Metaphysical Interpretation?

6. Explain the *B-I-B-L-E* system of Historical-Metaphysical Interpretation.

QUESTIONS FOR DISCUSSION

1. If modern biblical scholars are right when they say the people in the Bible are literary characters, what does it mean for our faith when we learn the "words of Jesus" are really the "words of Matthew"? Is Jesus Christ really present in the New Testament? How?

2. You are asked by your minister to do an Historical-Metaphysical Interpretation of either the Good Samaritan story (Luke 10:25-37) or the New Jerusalem vision of Revelation 21:1-8. Which do you choose? Why?

3. Why is metaphysical interpretation both exciting and dangerous?

4. Do you find the Bible easy or difficult to understand?

5. What are some advantages/disadvantages to Historical-Metaphysical Interpretation in your opinion?

6. How important should the Bible be in our churches today?

NOTES

1. Charles M. Layman, ed., *The Interpreter's One-Volume Commentary on the Bible* (Nashville, TN: Abingdon, 1971), pp. 609, 655-645, 672-673, 707-709. *IOVC* remains the finest single-volume biblical commentary available in English at this writing. The vast array of monographs and articles at the rear of this comprehensive commentary alone make it worth the relatively modest price.

2. Isaiah 30:3 (RSV).

3. Charles Fillmore, ed., *Metaphysical Bible Dictionary* (Unity Village: Unity Books, 1942), p. 7.

4. Kantonen, pp. 24-25.

5. Martin Luther, *Luther's Small Catechism* (St. Louis, MO: Concordia, 1971), p. 41.

6. Robert Frost, "Stopping by Woods on a Snowy Evening," in *Robert Frost's Poems* (NY: Washington Square Press, 1968), p. 194.

HOLY SPIRIT: DYNAMIC EXPRESSION

Chapter Six

The Holy Spirit is continually inspiring me. My thoughts are fresh,
and new, and clear, and powerful with the might of Omnipotence.
My prayers are the handiwork of the Holy Ghost—powerful as the
eagle and gentle as the dove.

Emmett Fox, *"The Word of Power"*[1]

Traditionally, studies of the *Trinity* begin with *God the Father* and sooner or later get around to the *Holy Spirit*, as though this aspect of God's activity were an after-thought. We Metaphysical Christians have elected to reverse this tendency and begin with Spirit because the mystical Christian point of reference is upon spirituality as opposed to the creative/ruling facility of Divinity. Neglect of the Spirit's importance is not limited to modern theologians. The author of Luke-Acts reports that Paul found the same sort of benign ignorance in his missionary encounters with new Christians:

Paul passed through the upper country and came to Ephesus.
There he found some disciples. And he said to them, "Did you
receive the Holy Spirit when you believed?" And they said, "No,
we have never even heard that there is a Holy Spirit." [2]

Apparently, whoever taught the first Christians at Ephesus didn't consider the Holy Spirit important enough to include in the basic course on being a Christian! This tendency lingers in theology, partly because the idea of Spirit is so vague when juxtaposed against such readily comprehensible symbols as Father and Son. We have all known fathers and sons; few have held conversations with a Spirit.

Another reason mainstream Christian thinking has shied away from Spirit is that Its very vagueness has allowed for some exotic interpretations in the past. Several radical sects have financed their assault on orthodoxy by claiming special revelations from the Holy Spirit. [We'll discuss the dangers in such special "messages from God" in Chapter 19.]

The final reason for Western theology's reluctance to acknowledge the impor-tance of Spirit is the whole problem of charismatic experiences, especially the phenomenon of glossolalia or "speaking in tongues." In several mainline Protestant denominations this phenomenon has driven away long-standing members, split some churches, and yet revived sagging spirituality in others.

We'll examine all these problem/objections as we look at God through the first window, Spirit, in our three-sided cathedral of faith known as the Trinity. First, however, we need to step back and take a broad look at the whole category of *Spirit* and things spiritual. Then we'll look at the concept of *Holiness*, which gives us the combination term *Holy Spirit*.

From a discussion of the Holy Spirit in biblical and theological perspectives, we'll move on to *Gifts of the Spirit/Fruit of the Spirit* and see how these special gifts and ubiquitous fruit can help us understand what God is like.

It is our contention that knowledge of God comes through knowing the divine-human nature of people. The summit of God's ultimate Nature remains forever shrouded in mystery; any God we can look down upon would scarcely be God. But although we can never fully comprehend God, we can follow a trail of clues to a clearer vantage point. Those clues come from observing God at work in the lives of other people—made in the image and likeness of the Eternal—and from organized reflection on the basic categories of belief, the task we call systematic theology. To improve our model of what God is like, we must first look at the word most common to religious talk, Spirit.

ESSENTIAL: UNDERSTAND "SPIRIT" FIRST
IF STUDYING THE TRINITY

Spirit is an ephemeral concept. As we said earlier, its very vagueness leads to confusion and can allow excesses done in the Name of Spirit. But before we talk about God the Father or the Son, we need to understand Spirit because it is the under-lying reality that stands behind all matter and energy, all thought and all creativity. "God is Spirit," says Jesus to the Samaritan woman at the well, "and those who worship him must worship him in spirit and in truth."[3]

We need not delve too deeply into philosophical studies before we encounter a serious problem with theologies based on the existence of Spirit. First, as Immanuel Kant (1724-1804) showed, all knowledge comes to us through the senses, and things of the Spirit are not sensory phenomena. Theologian John Macquarrie explains:

> Kant, as everyone knows, showed in his Critique of Pure Reason
> that human understanding is limited to the phenomena of sensory
> experience. When we try to go beyond these and ask questions
> about transcendent objects—God, freedom, immortality—we land
> ourselves in contradictions. The ultimate reality is unknowable, and
> rational metaphysics is impossible.[4]

What this means is that we learn through our senses. We hear ideas, see things happen, and make religious/ethical decisions based on this sensory input. We do not really experience the essence of "things-in-themselves" (Kant's term) but receive images from our senses. Looking at a chair, we are not in contact with the chair's true nature but merely perceive the image of the chair as reproduced in our brain. If this is true for an object as simple as a chair, how much more is it true that sensory input gives us all our knowledge about God?

But where do we get that sensory input? From other believers, who have already decided to believe. Kant held that we cannot prove anything about religion because all evidence comes through our senses and the transcendent realm of God lies beyond sensory experience.

LEAP OF FAITH

To believe in God we must make what Danish philosopher Soren Kierkegaard called a "leap of faith," taking us from the limitations of sensory input to a place of certainty which philosophy cannot provide. Things of God are beyond the physical world (*meta*-physical); they cannot be comprehended by the senses, and therefore are not legitimate knowledge. Kant insisted that a rationalistic metaphysic is impossible; Divine Ideas must be understood through a combination of faith and intuition.

If we understand what the Kantians were saying, we can appreciate why many of the founders of modern metaphysical Christianity nearly snarled when they wrote about sensory knowledge and those who claimed it was the only source of information. Charles Fillmore, among others, believed "pure reason" was capable of achieving perfect knowledge of God, although he never replied directly to Kant's critique.

INNER DIMENSION

Again, space for a full reply to the Kantian position is not available in a work this broad, but a few remarks seem appropriate since we have already cast our lot with Spirit as the underlying Reality upon which all matter and energy and consciousness is built.

First, we must frankly admit that Kant was right when he asserted that all knowledge comes to us through the senses, if we define "knowledge" as learning about things external and detached from ourselves. But if there is an inner dimension to human consciousness, then we can look within ourselves to find direct information which does not come through the senses. If God is within us, as metaphysical Christianity believes, then we should be able to make contact with God internally. We should be able to "go to headquarters" directly, as Fillmore claimed.

Secondly, we have more than sensory input; we have our own response to that input. Why do humans feel love if there is not some kind of power moving through us? Why do we respond with anger sometimes and with astonishment other times? What is consciousness itself, if not evidence of Spirit?

Most importantly, we have Jesus Christ to hold before us. If all things about God are necessarily symbolic, as we said in the previous chapter, then sensory input is just another form of symbolism. Jesus Christ, the ultimate symbol for things divine, comes to us through senses, through emotions, through meditation and prayer, through intuition, and through insight. Our knowledge about the Jesus of history may come strictly from our senses, but our knowledge of the Christ-within comes from that data as it is processed by the faith faculty. Kant would agree that belief is more than a hopeful guess. It is input plus faith plus a willingness to let some questions hang unanswered in space.

SPIRIT: THE FINAL FRONTIER

Paul Tillich believed that God is not a Being but being-itself, that God does not "exist" the way we exist but is existence itself or the very power to be. Imagine a lamp hooked into a power source, spreading warm light across a room. Electricity flows through the cord and the lamp squeezes light from the raw energy, thanks to Thomas Edison.

Now let's step off into the realm of science fiction for a moment. Suppose there were a power source that not only produced light but generated the lamp as well. Flip a switch and the power-package causes a lighted lamp to appear. (If you're a *Star Trek* fan, think holodeck and you'll have little trouble envisioning this. If not, bear with us a little longer.)

Turn off the switch and the physical lamp, as well as the light, disappears. Energy and matter are the same thing in different form, according to current scientific theory, so the idea of an energy generated lamp is not entirely beyond possibility. We are not talking about the image of a lamp, like a holographic model, but an actual, touchable, solid object which comes into existence because energy is transmuted into matter.

Got it?

Now think about the Universe. God is the very power-to-be. Everything exists because God is the Energy Source which causes everything to exist. "In him we live and move and have our being," said the Apostle Paul, paraphrasing Epimenides the Cretan poet (Acts 17:28). Spirit is the true underlying Reality that causes everything to be.

Of course, as Kant showed, this cannot be proved. It also cannot be disproved, Kant admits. But the reality of Spirit can be demonstrated by the inward life of each person and the out-picturing of Spirit through application of spiritual principles in the world. As we said in our discussion of Epistemology (Chapter 3), things spiritual must be practically demonstrated, not proved after the manner of empirical science or deductive reason. Kant is on our side in this case because he readily agrees that things of the Spirit are the province of faith and cannot be apprehended by human intellect. In fact, he goes as far as to say that the way we look at the world shapes the world itself:

> In metaphysical speculations it has always been assumed that all our knowledge must conform to objects; but every attempt from this point of view to extend our knowledge of objects...has ended in failure. The time has now come to ask, whether better progress

may not be made by supposing that objects must conform to our knowledge.[5]

Our perception of reality, far from originating in the outer world, begins within us. We all have that stained-glass window of personal beliefs and imagination through which we filter all the helter-skelter sensory and intellectual data flying at us. Take snow for an example. When most people see snow they see a white mass; but a Native Alaskan looks at snow and sees many types, textures, and weather indications. The languages of the circumpolar peoples are rich in snow words, most of which are not translatable without complex descriptive phrases.

GREEN JUMBLE OR PRECISION PARTS?

Another example comes from the author's personal experience. One day a friend and I went for a walk in the woods in rural Missouri. My friend is a wildlife ecologist, not an ignorant city-boy like me. It soon became apparent that we were not seeing the same forest or even sharing the same world. Instead of a jumble of green and brown, he saw order and organization, a magnificent ecosystem of interdependent animals and plants. He strolled down the forest paths through a world he knew well.

I got poison ivy.

We shape the world perceptually, but our ability to influence the reality in which we live extends beyond perception alone. We shall look at this highly controversial concept in Chapter 17 (A Theology of Prayer). For now let us just say that Spirit, as the Reality under girding all that exists, operates through and with us because It *is* us, and we are *It*. We begin our discussion of the Trinity with Spirit because Spirit is all that truly exists. This assertion cannot be proved or disproved, but it can be demonstrated in practical experience.

SPIRIT IN PRE-CHRISTIAN THOUGHT

In earliest form, the idea of Spirit probably found expression through *anamatism* a term coined by anthropologist Robert R. Marett. Anamatism is the belief that rocks, cooking utensils, storms, mountains, or any other person, place, or thing may have special divine power. It is the life force in both animate and inanimate objects. Anamatism differs from the more common anthropological term *animism* because the former does not require a soul-force behind it. Some anthropologists believe primitive people looked at the majestic peaks and felt the mountains had spiritual power without personifying the mountain as a spirit or a god. To the anamatist, nature does not have a spirit; nature is Spirit.[6]

Later, humans began to worship the power of spirit wherever it broke through: sunrise, flood, rainstorm, thunder, seasons. These and other powerful occurrences took their place beside mountaintops and forests, stars and meteors, to become separate spirits which eventually acquired names and personalities as gods and goddesses.

If we take Hinduism as a typical model of religious evolution, the gods and goddesses continue to grow in stature until they all become omnipotent and omnipresent. How could there be hundreds of deities, each omnipotent? Perhaps, the only logical answer is that they are all expressions of the One Presence and One Power. Thus we come full circle, back to undifferentiated spirit power which is everywhere present. The circle is really a spiral which brings us back to an entirely different level.

Modern Hinduism is not really anamatistic (i.e., believing in ambiguous spirit-force behind nature) but *pantheistic* or *monistic*, seeing a conscious Intelligence at work and present in all things. Dr. John B. Noss wrote in his widely read textbook, *Man's Religions*:

> Ultimately, (in Hindu thought) all things are bound together, not only by likeness of activity but in actuality, that is to say, in Being. Man comes to see not his separateness from the gods and his fellows but his and their identity with an eternal, all-inclusive Being or Reality, and begins to seek his deliverance (moksha) from separateness by mystical union with it.[7]

Since Hindu monistic belief arose from polytheistic religion, one cannot help but play with a fascinating question: What might have happened to Greco-Roman paganism if the Christian takeover had not radically altered the religio-cultural direction of Hellenistic society? Would the gods and goddesses of Rome have merged into a form of cosmic monism? Already in the first century there were large numbers of "God-fearing gentiles" (i.e., monotheists) who attended public meetings at Jewish synagogues and openly professed disbelief in the existence of so many mini-gods. A few centuries before Jesus, Plato was executed for teaching, among other things, that there was only one God. These proto-monotheistic tendencies are interesting, but will ever remain speculative. Greco-Roman religion was ill-equipped to deal with a vital, new faith that proclaimed one God and maintained connections with antiquity through the history of a well known ethnic group, the Jews. Spirit, as understood by this new faith, would take Hellenistic religion to a very different place than the Spirit-concepts found among the mini-religions of the Indian subcontinent which we call by the collective misnomer of Hinduism.

SPIRIT IN BIBLICAL CONTEXT

Interestingly, the Old and New Testaments chose similar words for the concept of Spirit. The Hebrew *ruach* is roughly equivalent to the koine Greek *pneuma*; both mean "wind, breath, and, by extension, a life-giving element."[8]

It is likely some ancients quite literally believed that the wind stirring in the tree-tops was the very breath of God, the Divine Spirit passing overhead. However, most biblical descriptions of God's spirit as breath or breeze must have been poetic license not unlike these words from a well-known hymn:

> This is my Father's world: He shines in all that's fair;
> In the rustling grass I hear him pass,
> He speaks to me everywhere.[9]

THREE MODES: CREATIVE, INSPIRATIONAL, AND COMMUNAL

Hebrew scripture describes three modes as movements of the Spirit.

First, there is the *creative* aspect. God's presence and power can be awesome, as in Genesis 1:2 and Ezekiel 37:1-10.

Second, Spirit manifests as *inspiration* in Old Testament passages. This mode breaks through as prophetic utterances, wisdom literature, and courageous acts by heroes—Joshua, Gideon, David—empowered by divine prompting.

Finally, there is a special presence of Spirit in the whole *community* of Israel. In the minds of some biblical authors, Israel had a unique destiny among nations and a singular status as the platform from which the Messiah would address the world. God's Spirit (read: inspiration) may depart from individuals like King Saul or Eli the Priest because of their disobedience, but He can never renounce His pledge to love Israel.[10]

Of course, "Israel" is not just a religio-cultural group but the whole body of humanity..Thus later prophets would cry that Israel must become "a light to the gentiles," a prophecy which, Christians believe, came true in the life and teaching of Jesus Christ. It must be noted before we go further that Old Testament (OT) writers, although virtually unanimous in describing God as Spirit, were not at all convinced that humans shared this spiritual nature.

The idea of a disembodied spirit is totally foreign to Hebrew thinking; most of the OT passages which are translated with the English word *soul*, for example, could just as easily read *life force*. This difference surfaces abruptly in the Hebrew view of life after death.

For most of the OT period, few Israelites believed in life after death. When Hellenistic Jewish thinkers, under pressure from Greek-dominated culture, began to tinker with the idea of personal survival, the model they built bore no resemblance to the Platonic idea of life after death as a disembodied spirit. Hebrew thought has usually held that life and bodily existence go hand-in-hand. Liberal-thinking Pharisees in the days of Jesus believed in life after death, but they taught a doctrine of *bodily resurrection* to eternal life, not immortality as a soul or spirit.

It was the only option ancient Judaism allowed.

NEW TESTAMENT, NEW NAME FOR GOD

New Testament (NT) authors carry over most of the Hebrew ideas about God's Spirit. Christian innovation on Jewish thought begins when NT writers start describing "Holy Spirit" as the activity of both the Father and the Son. We find this in Paul's letter to Galatia:

> And because you are sons, God has sent the Spirit of his Son into our hearts, crying, 'Abba! Father!' So through God you are no longer a slave but a son, and if a son then an heir.[11]

Paul uses the word *pneuma* (spirit) several ways, but he usually speaks of Spirit as a power which is available to everyone (Romans 8:6, 8:13; I Corinthians 2:10,

3:16; etc.). If Luke's account of the Sermon at Mars Hill is accurate (Acts 17:22-31), Paul quotes two Hellenistic philosophers to show that we "live and move and have our being" in God's Spirit, "For we are his offspring." Quite an advanced concept for first century Christianity. These two quotes taken in context seem to move toward understanding Spirit as the Reality under girding all existence. Is this a hint of Platonism?

Probably not. Or if it is, then it probably isn't Paul but Luke speaking to us. Paul leaned more toward the Stoic metaphysic than the Platonist, although he was not above flavoring his messages to suit the tastes of his target audience. True Christian Platonism will come two centuries later, funneled through people like Clement and Origen. However, Paul is unhesitant about the benefits we can receive from Spirit. We shall say more about that later.

Looking at the gospels—which were written after Paul, probably by his supporters and opponents—we note that Jesus sometimes regards Spirit as equal to God the Father. This is especially apparent in the episode of His baptism (Mark 1:10). Other times the gospels refer to Spirit as the life force within each person (Mark 14:38, Luke 23:26), and still other verses show Spirit as the empowering divine presence within the believers (John 3:6, 6:63, 7:39, 14:17). This clip-and-paste selection suggests that the New Testament authors were neither certain what Spirit meant nor in agreement on what part this concept should play in the emerging Christian faith. Very early they began calling an aspect of God's activity "the work of Holy Spirit," which quickly became the Holy Spirit and acquired distinct characteristics.

Hebrew Scripture refers to God's holy spirit twice (Ps. 51:11, Isa. 63:10), but both are descriptive phrases much like "God's justice and great mercy" or "God's steadfast love." In the Hebrew Bible "holy spirit" is adjectival, never a noun. For the OT authors, God *has* a holy spirit; in the NT, He *sends* the Holy Spirit.

The difference is crucial for theology. OT texts lend almost no support to the doctrine of the Trinity, but NT authors use Holy Spirit as a proper noun. This new name for God gives Christianity a whole new way of looking at the Divine and prepares us for refinements which will come later, when the Church begins to see that God is the Holy Spirit.

HOLINESS IS WHOLENESS

To understand what "Holy Spirit" means we must digress briefly and review the concept of holiness as presented in Jewish and Christian scripture. Fortunately, like Spirit, the idea of holiness is virtually identical in both Testaments. Let's look at the word from *Harper's Bible Dictionary*:

> *Holiness,* a term in Hebrew probably meaning separate from the ordinary or profane. Also in Hebrew and Greek "holy" implies connection with God or the divine. Thus God is holy and people, things, and actions may be holy by association with God. Holiness

may also include the ideas of consecration to God and purity from what is evil and improper.[12]

The Revealing Word, emphasizes that connection with God:

Holiness is wholeness in Spirit, mind, and body. In this state of consciousness man is aware of the all-pervading glory of God.[13]

Since mysticism is the identification of self with and movement toward the Divine, Charles Fillmore identified holiness with awareness of "the all-pervading glory of God." Awareness is all that is required by this definition to achieve holiness. Getting that kind of awareness is the obvious difficulty. Note that the difference between the two definitions comes down to the question of dualism again. For orthodoxy, holiness means association with something divine, a *wholly Other* that is a *Holy Other.* This also means avoiding evil or things improper.

For the mystical Fillmore, holiness is consciousness that God is not "out there" as a separate entity but dwells within as an all-pervasive Presence and Power. If God is the very structure of reality, as Paul Tillich said, then goodness and holiness lie at the heart of all things. However we may pervert that inherent goodness by using our divine power of free will, we nevertheless "live and move and have our being" in God's Spirit, "For we are his offspring."

Most Christian Truth students would be skeptical about holiness as a result of avoiding evil. Such a negative concept says nothing about what holiness is, unless our definition of holiness means simply to refrain from sin. Mystical Christianity has usually emphasized holiness as wholeness, completeness. Human beings are more than flesh-and-blood creatures with a body and mind: we are also spiritual. There is something within every person that tells of our kinship to God. As we flow with the divine will, we experience wholeness. When we move against our higher nature, brokenness and estrangement results.

This is the classical definition of sin. Paul Tillich, himself no mystic, correctly identified sin as separation—from our fellows, from ourselves, from our God. But separation occurs in mind, not in reality. How can we really be separated from an Omnipotent/Omnipresent God? For the Christian Truth student, holiness means identification of the person with God's intentions for us. This comes close to the *HDB* definition of "connection with God" or "consecration to God," but lacks the negative implications of "avoiding evil."

PURITY: MORE THAN AVOIDING EVIL

The *HBD* definition of "holiness" also mentioned *Purity,* which is a concept closely related to holiness. Again, this term is frequently defined in the negative; we more often learn what to avoid than what to accomplish when seeking purity. This odd tendency to see goodness as a double negative (lack of evil-doing) is not limited to the Judeo-Christian mythos. Listen to an abridged version of the seemingly endless

"Negative Confession" found on the walls of the tomb of Nu, a high official in Eighteenth Dynasty (1570-1305 B.C.) Egypt:

> Homage to thee, O Great God (Osiris) Lord of Double Maati, I have come to thee, O my Lord, I have brought myself hither that I may behold thy beauties...I have expelled wickedness for thee.
>
> I have not done evil to mankind.
> I have not oppressed the members of my family.
> I have not wrought evil in the place of right and truth.
> I have no knowledge of worthless men.
> I have not brought forward my name for exultation...
> I have not ill-treated servants.
> I have not belittled a god.
> I have not defrauded the oppressed one of his property.
> I have not given the order for murder to be done for me.
> I have not inflicted pain upon mankind.
> I have not committed fornication.
> I have not encroached upon the fields of others.
> I have not carried away the milk from the mouths of children.
> I am pure! I am pure! I am pure![14]

One wonders whom he was trying to convince, the god or his wife? His attitude is not confined to the ancient world. How many people do we know who define holiness and purity as non-action, not breaking certain behavioral taboos?

"I DON'T DO NOTHIN'..."

Pastor James Dyson, who was minister of the Community Church of Moscow, Idaho, when the author was attending the University of Idaho in the early 1970s, liked to tell the story about the man who came up to him and said:

> "Preacher, I'm trying to live a pure, holy life. I don't smoke; I don't drink; I don't cuss; I don't play cards and I don't dance."
>
> Rev. Dyson replied: "Congratulations. You've got a lot in common with a rock. Now, tell me—what do you do?"

Purity is more than avoiding wrong, or we would all be better off comatose. Language gets in the way here, because we speak of "impurities" in a formula, and we see fresh snow as spotless, "pure."

BLOOD SACRIFICE TO ACHIEVE HOLINESS/PURITY

Perhaps the ancients are still with us in many ways. Biblical Hebrews believed in a ritual purity which included washings, cleansing, and proper handling of food. These customs survive today in observant Jewish homes. In biblical times, women were required to perform special acts of purification after menstruating and after childbirth.

There was an intricate system of Hebrew taboos which rendered a person "unclean" (impure) which then required other actions to reinstate the alienated one to purity. To enter the house of a gentile, to touch the dead, to contact swine or a leper—

any number of events in the daily life of a first century Jew could render him impure and require ritual acts of cleansing.

Actually, the whole system of animal sacrifice was about recovering lost purity. In a sense it was a system which depended on taboo. Without sacrifice there was no forgiveness of sin; without sin (violation of taboo) there would have been no need for sacrifice.

If a person broke a taboo or committed some kind of offense, the ancients believed there was a blood-curse upon him. Something literally had to die, shedding blood to lift the curse. It was an objective transaction, and the ancients believed it functioned as immutable law. If the offender did not provide a sacrificial animal to die, he would pay the price himself.

During sacrificial worship the priest, as representative of the god, often placed one hand on the head of the sinner and the other hand on the sacrificial animal thus transferring the guilt from the offender to his blood offering. The priest or his assistant then ritually killed the animal and, depending on what type of an offering it was, burned its blood along with other inedible parts of the carcass. Since in most cases the priests kept the meat offered on the altar, taboo was good business for the clergy.

Small wonder there were so many offenses possible!

This type of ceremony can be found in the history of peoples around the world and is still practiced among people who believe angry spirits must be placated. We can see how early Christians, searching for euphemisms to describe the great sacrificial offering of Jesus upon the cross, succumbed to the metaphor of animal sacrifice, so that by the end of the first century the author of John's gospel could proclaim: "Behold, the Lamb of God, who takes away the sin of the world!"[15] How literally the early church took this prescription is a matter for scholarly debate. But the majority of Christian communions finally accepted this as a doctrinal position, even though they differ on what that sacrifice means and how Jesus took that sin away. We shall explore this in depth later as we first look at Christology (Chapter 8), then sin and atonement in our study of Soteriology (Chapter 9).

HOLINESS COMES FROM WITHIN

To the metaphysical Christian, holiness is not something poured into the believer from outside but an ever-increasing awareness of the Christ within. Several NT authors provide us with theological support for this viewpoint. Paul wrote to the church at Corinth:

> Do you not know that your body is a temple of the Holy Spirit within you, which you have from God? But it is God who establishes us with you in Christ, and has commissioned us; he has put his seal upon us and given us his spirit in our hearts as a guarantee.[16]

However, a great number of NT passages can be interpreted to mean that the Holy Spirit does in fact come from outside a person and takes up residence in our bodily temples only after we accept Jesus Christ. Paul is inconclusive on this point, as the above quote shows.

The difference is not sophistry but a fundamental variance in the way theologians look at the work of the Holy Spirit. Do all human beings—perhaps all sentient beings—*have* God's spirit within them? Or must God *send* His Spirit in a special way to those who achieve some sort of select status by virtue of their correct beliefs and practices? Is the goal of spiritual growth to open ourselves to the inflow of the Holy Spirit, or to open ourselves to the Spirit's presence within us and let it shine forth?

I call this the *Let Him In/Let Him Out* controversy. It is absolutely crucial for mystical theology, and we must pause to discuss its implications before we press on to a fuller exploration of the Holy Spirit.

"LET HIM IN/LET HIM OUT" CONTROVERSY

Traditional thinking has pictured the Holy Spirit as an sacred, alien power which benignly takes possession of human nature and either causes us to do good things or opens us to divine blessings. How else could the dichotomy between human sinfulness and an in-dwelling Spirit of God be overcome?

ANTHROPOLOGICAL DEADLOCK

The problem is *anthropological*. If our theology of humanity (theological anthropology) says that we are bad guys who need outside help to climb even an inch toward God, then there is no alternative but to provide outside intervention in a downward movement from a Righteous God to sinful humanity. Some theologies insist that God must prepare us to accept His blessings by giving the gift of faith. The term for this is *Prevenient Grace*, which suggests God runs ahead of us and makes us able to accept His good gifts. It is defined in Van A. Harvey's *Handbook of Theological Terms*:

> GRACE, PREVENIENT, is, according to Roman Catholic teaching, the supernatural power that quickens and assists the will to have faith. In Protestantism, it is often used more generally to refer to the grace preceding man's decision but is not always identified with a specific quickening power.[17]

Such a view makes it impossible to decide that humanity has any in-dwelling divinity to let out; only the *"let Him in"* theory will work here. If we are so utterly helpless that God must make us willing to accept Him before we have faith, then all talk about the Divine within must be sheer nonsense. Since much of traditional Protestantism was constructed on this idea of Prevenient Grace, built squarely on a foundation of Calvinist notions about the "total depravity" of humanity, the mystical vision of union with God has seemed far-fetched indeed. When clergy do talk about the in-dwelling divinity of all people, the idea sometimes sounds blasphemous to listeners brought up in Western Christianity. Even liberal churches today seem to enjoy stressing the sinfulness of human nature and our total inability to do anything to improve ourselves without massive infusions of divine power from beyond.

However, taking a cue from Jesus Christ, some mystical Christians find the whole idea of human depravity to be slightly depraved. What kind of person can look into the eyes of a toddler and say with conviction: "You are born a miserable sinner and have no power to grow closer to God without His pulling you toward Him against your own perverted will!"?

If everyday experience is any indication, we know there are people who seem "evil" and others who seem "saintly," with most of us falling into that vast spectrum between these extremes. If experience tells us that our theology is wrong, we'll need better arguments than the theological abstractions of John Calvin to convince us.

Jesus-the-Christ shows us a flesh and blood man who knew His Oneness with God yet called us His brothers and sisters. If Jesus had a divine Spirit and we are His kinfolk, one could reasonably assume that same Spirit dwells in each of us. Why else did Jesus continue to exhort His followers to do what He had done? If we are incapable of self-directed goodness, His words spoken in the Sermon on the Mount ("Be perfect, even as your Father in heaven is perfect...") amount to nothing but divine teasing.

Besides scriptural and existential evidence, Christian history abounds with individuals who looked within and discovered the radiance of God's Holy Spirit. People like George Fox, founder of the Society of Friends (Quakers), believed that each of us has an "inner light" which guides us. Mystics like Meister Eckhart taught what they knew from spiritual searching and prayer, that God and humanity are essentially one and that progress depends on our willingness to receive what we already have. Eckhart wrote:

> The authorities in the schools ask often how it is possible for the soul to know God. It is not from God's strictness that he requires so much of man, but rather from his kindness that he expects the soul to progress to that point where it may receive much, as he gives so much to it. No one ought to think that it is hard to attain this, however hard it sounds and however hard it may be at first...God is always ready but we are not ready. God is near to us but we are far from him. God is within; we are without.[18]

One way around the *"Let Him In/Let Him Out"* controversy is to find a middle path. Certainly, God in His majesty is out there in the Universe—working, whispering, motivating, comforting, nudging all Creation toward His divine plan. But God must also dwell within every sentient being, or the gap between our finite consciousness and Infinite Goodness becomes impossibly vast.

Some theologians do hold this latter position, insisting that only an infinite sacrifice by God Himself in the form of Jesus Christ could bridge the infinite gap. But even if that were the case, we would be back to the same problem: How does finite humanity avail itself of an infinite sacrifice unless we are somehow part of the program, somehow related to Divinity itself?

Programming Jesus into the Godhead doesn't solve the equation; it merely puts more distance between people and Jesus, Who claimed kinship both to humanity and to God. He is the link, but not by virtue of His special status as the only God-man. Jesus is our link to divinity because He is not special; He is ultimately normal for a human being. Jesus is what we shall be.

The middle path would accept both God-out-there and God-within. Sometimes we feel the presence and power of God in the world; other times we can go within and hear that still, small voice. Why must theology opt for an either/or? Can we not *"let God in"* when we experience Him beyond ourselves and *"let God out"* when we contact the Inner Light?

We have insufficient space in a survey of Christian theology to discuss such problems at the length they deserve. However, raising questions is often as important a task for theology as providing answers, especially if the question is both vital and neglected. As metaphysical Christianity continues to grow and expand its agenda to include greater emphasis on legitimate theology, other thinkers doubtless will find themselves pressed to untangle complex controversies like *"Let Him In/Let Him Out."*

One of the more satisfying aspects of being an author of a work that breaks new ground is that one can introduce problems to those who will provide solutions in the generations to come. It is also a sneaky way of confessing that I don't have all the answers and of inviting you to share the joyful headaches of constructive theology.

HOLY SPIRIT: PUTTING IT ALL TOGETHER

So far we have looked at the concepts of Spirit, Holiness, and Purity. We have discussed the difference of opinion as to whether God dwells within us in kinship relationship or stands aloof and send His Spirit to infuse us with divine power, calling this problem the *"Let Him In/Let Him Out"* controversy. Along the way we touched on themes such as sacrificial worship, theological anthropology, and the attitude of biblical and traditional mystics toward in-dwelling Spirit. Now we turn to the main event. What do we mean when we speak of the Holy Spirit? What does the Holy Spirit do, and why is it essential to understand Spirit before we discuss the Father and the Son in our study of the Trinity? We'll conclude with a brief look at the *Gifts of the Spirit* and the *Fruit of the Spirit* as taught by the Apostle Paul, hopefully showing how all this fits together in metaphysical theology.

1. WHAT DOES "HOLY SPIRIT" MEAN?

Harper's Bible Dictionary defines Holy Spirit as "the mysterious power or presence of God in nature or with individuals and communities, inspiring them with qualities they would not otherwise possess."[19]

Again, the traditionalist position. If the Holy Spirit did not inspire individuals, *"they would not otherwise possess"* those *"qualities"* of the Spirit. But note the careful wording. The author of this definition walks a fence between both sides of the *"Let Him In/Let Him Out"* controversy. Nowhere does the *Harper's* entry say whether the Holy Spirit comes from outside or from within. It is a foreign element in our natures, to be sure. But does it well up from inside us or crash over us like a divine avalanche?

Charles Fillmore is more helpful, but he, too, very carefully avoids pontifications about Spirit always coming from within or without. If you know Charles Fillmore's work, you must recognize that he was no fence-straddler and frequently leaped at the chance to take sides in a debate. Listen to Fillmore's delicate handling of the controversy:

> SPIRIT, HOLY. The source of all manifestation is in mind...The Holy Ghost, or Holy Spirit, is the law of God in action; and in that action it appears as having individuality. From this the Hebrews got their concept of the personal, tribal God... The Holy Spirit may also be defined as the whole Spirit of God, and can be known by man only through his spiritual nature. The prayer of the soul alone in its upper room (state of high spiritual aspiration) brings down the Holy Ghost. (Parenthesis original)[20]

Comparing the above to Fillmore's mini-treatise in The *Revealing Word*, we find the fence-walking continues:

> HOLY SPIRIT—The activity of God in a universal sense. The moving force in the universe as a whole. The Spirit is the infinite "breath" of God, the life essence of Being...To be "filled with the Holy Spirit" is to realize the activities of Spirit in individual consciousness. The quickening of a man by the Holy Spirit is peculiar to each individual and must be experienced to be understood.[21]

Could it be that Charles Fillmore, too, recognized the Holy Spirit as active both outside and inside the individual? God in the world contacts God in the consciousness to become "God with us." Both *Harper's* and Fillmore agree that the Holy Spirit is a power of God and cannot be understood as separate from divinity.

There is a going-forth and a calling-forth aspect to the work of the Spirit, each roughly paralleling one side of the controversy. God goes forth into the world and actively seeks humanity. When we discover God, it is as though we are finding a long-lost relative Who calls forth something from within our deepest selves. For metaphysical Christianity, it is this activity which we define as the Holy Spirit. In a very real way, *the Holy Spirit is kinetic divinity—God in action in the world and within ourselves.* This is a working definition and certainly not an all-encompassing one. But at least it allows us to proceed to our second question.

2. WHAT DOES THE HOLY SPIRIT DO?

We have already discussed the answer in scattered bits. God sends His Holy Spirit—God comes to us as the Holy Spirit—and encounters us at whatever level of spiritual/emotional growth we presently struggle. The Holy Spirit nurtures us, comforts us, encourages us. It is that still, small voice of calm. It is God in action, and its activities are indicated by the lifestyle of Jesus Christ.

Thus we can affirm with the great creeds of the Western Church that the Holy Spirit proceeds from both the Father and the Son... because the Son (i.e., the Christ, the Buddha consciousness, or whatever the Indwelling Divinity may be called) provides us with a perfect example of the Divine by which the Son-within-us (or Daughter-within-us) is able to recognize its own kinship to Divinity. Without this indwelling divinity, the activities of the Holy Spirit would remain inscrutable. If we haven't known love personally, we may be skeptical about love when it appears in our lives. The same could be said about any gift of God. Since we have the Wayshower, Jesus Christ, we are able to look at that one solitary life and learn what God is like. It is much easier to recognize our own in-dwelling divinity when we can see it in Jesus.

NOT JUST A CHEERLEADER

Can the Holy Spirit do anything in the real world, or is Spirit just inspirational? Let us say at this time that a God Who is incapable of acting in the real world is next to no god at all. Spirit has the primary job of quickening awareness, which sets us in motion and causes us to release powers of the divine-human nature within every person. That alone would be enough.

But God's activity is more than just moral example and encouragement; God is not a great Cheerleader in the sky. In this world there are natural ways that God manifests Himself: pointing us to discoveries that empower us to greater good, giving us assurances when we feel weak, alone, making connections that somehow work things out for the best, and standing beside us to strengthen us when disaster happens as it most certainly does, even to the most spiritual person alive.

Christian faith points to a different kind of power than the world normally understands. We want our heroes to conquer the bad guys and emerge rich and famous. But the New Testament shows us a model of nonresistance in the face of suffering and death. Jesus failed miserably by Hollywood's standards. The bad guys killed Him, scattered His friends, and then gambled for His clothing. He died penniless, friendless, and defeated.

And yet that is just the beginning of the story.

Christmas shows us hope; Good Friday seems to dash that hope at the foot of a blood-soaked cross. But Easter breaks the hold of death and shows us that nonresistance is the only power which truly lasts. Conventional models of power—armies, physical prowess, wealth, political clout—are shadows passing in the night. Nonresistance to the flow of God's goodness is the only real power, the only lasting power.

It is the Holy Spirit Who prompts us to look for the footsteps of Divinity in the disasters of human existence. The power of God protects us, not from pain and suffering, but from the most terrible fate of all—futility. If we own the whole world but fail to learn our lessons well, life lends to repeat the process again and again until we get it right.

The Holy Spirit is the Great Educator, the Counselor promised by Isaiah, the Guide Who continuously points us toward the best, most expeditious path up the mountain to Christ-consciousness. God is able to do this so subtly that it has been going on for eons and yet many people still wonder if there is a divine power at all.

MIRACLES?

Does God intervene in time-and-space to perform miracles? Miracles, as they are understood by the pre-scientific worldview of the biblical authors, are interventions in time and space to violate the laws of science by Divine Power. Good prior planning makes zap-crash-boom activities unnecessarily crude. God doesn't need to break the rules if He made them carefully enough. Events which seem miraculous to us show God working in a natural way which we do not yet comprehend. Magic and science are indistinguishable to the prescientific mind. Yet the Christian Truth movement has believed from its inception that God's activities are orderly. We only need to understand things properly.

THE COMFORTER

The Holy Spirit is also the Comforter, the One Who nudges us toward wholeness/holiness. Our future lies with God. Whenever we realize that in deeper, more meaningful ways, the Holy Spirit has been at work in our lives. It is interesting that this is the manifestation of the Spirit which Jesus explcitly promises to send—the Comforter, God's Presence and Power, to walk with us regardless of the circumstance.

BENEFITS OF THE SPIRIT: FRUIT & GIFTS

The Apostle Paul listed two different kinds of spiritual qualities which we'll call Benefits of the Spirit. The first category can be found in the fifth chapter of Galatians and is usually designated Fruit of the Spirit. Paul liked to draw up lists of good and bad qualities to emphasize his teaching points; perhaps the most famous is his "Hymn to Love" in I Corinthians.[13]

His zeal often seems greater when listing the no-no's. In the Galatians passage Paul can only think of nine "fruits" to contrast with his laundry list of fifteen "works of the flesh," which he ended with the koine Greek equivalent of *"etc."*! Like all moralists, Paul relished the gossipy, Jerry Springer side of human nature, which he could castigate and constrain with a list of no-no's.

Fortunately, he did not dwell exclusively on the negatives but moved to accentuate the positive. Here is Paul's list of good qualities which he called "Fruit of the Spirit": Love, Joy, Peace, Patience, Kindness, Goodness, Faithfulness, Gentleness, Self-Control.

Fruit of the Spirit differ from *Gifts of the Spirit* in that every Christian is expected to harvest spiritual "fruit," but the "gifts" are special talents awarded to various persons in varying degrees. Paul was not as certain about how many gifts there were; he listed four different groups of special talents. Some scholars suggest that since the lists are not identical they are not intended to exhaust the possibilities for other gifts.[22] The lists may be found at Ro. 12:6, I Cor. 12:8-10, 12:28, and 12:29-30.

SPEAKING IN TONGUES

A word must be said about the well-known and highly divisive phenomenon of *glossolalia* or "speaking in tongues", as it is popularly called. People who experience this say they were taken over by the Holy Spirit and began uttering strange languages which must be interpreted. Charsmatic utterances are not strictly a Christian phenomenon. There is scriptural evidence that praying or chanting in unknown sounds was practiced as early as the time of the Judges (I Samuel 10:9-13).

Cross-cultural studies show that various kinds of ecstatic awakening are practiced in nearly every human society. These may include chanting, dancing, possession by good or bad spirits, vision quests, or rituals of sympathetic magic. Doubtless those within Christian pentecostal circles would be outraged by listing the "gift of tongues" with these other practices, but anthropologists of religion rightly study human behavior and categorize religious acts according to functional similarities. It is not within the charter of the social sciences to pass judgment on the appropriateness of a particular religious practice, just to study the behavior as a phenomenon. For the anthropologist, ecstatic experiences of charismatic Christians and tribal rituals of pre-industrial societies fall under the same scrutiny.

The problem with "speaking in tongues" is that it has usually resulted in a kind of charismatic elitism within the church. Those who have the "gift" frequently express doubts about the salvation of those who do not. If one reads chapters 12 to 14 of I Corinthians in sequence, it is almost impossible to draw any other conclusion than to recognize that the Apostle Paul wrote that sequence—including the "Hymn To Love"— to deal with this kind of divisive elitism within the first century church.

His solution is to say that there are many different gifts, but they are given to each as a "manifestation of the Spirit for the common good." And therefore, "If I speak with the tongues of men and of angels, but have not love, I am a noisy gong or a clanging cymbal."

ACTIVE MEDITATION: A MIDDLE GROUND

Is the "gift of tongues" valid? Do people really become possessed by the Holy Spirit and "speak with the tongues of men and of angels"? Studies are not conclusive, since so much subjectivity is involved. Some religionists say glossolalia was a gift of the apostolic church only; some say that it is valid today. The phenomenon cuts across theological lines to involve believers from churches as diverse as the predominantly black Church of God in Christ to the multi-cultural, multi-ethnic Roman Catholic church, which has a significant plurality of "charismatic Catholics" within the ranks of laity and clergy alike.

Since no definitive study has established either the validity or the frivolity of glossolalia, we step into the realm of metaphysical speculation when discussing its point of origin. This is risky but unavoidable for a theologian to do.

Therefore, let us suggest a view of this "gift" and see if the idea works for meta-physical Christianity. It is my contention that glossolalia is a form of vocal prayer which detaches the cognitive processes of the mind from the act of praise, much like chanting a mantra. "Speaking in tongues," by this definition, is a form of active medi-tation, not a possession of the worshipper by a benign supernatural entity.

The advantages of this view are many. First, it complies with the evidence of studies that seem to show glossolalia as a series of unconnected sounds rather than an organized language. Second, it does not belittle the gift, because great spiritual bene-fit can come from such active, non-intellectual prayer. Also, this view offers a middle ground between those who insist that tongues is a gift from God and others who flat-ly reject the notion that it is a language of men and/or angels. This middle view says it can be a gift of the Spirit without being an angelic tongue. Finally, the idea that tongues is a form of active meditation removes the gift from the fringes of the occult so people who fear loss of control or some other negative impact on their spiritual life are more likely to try nonverbal sounds in prayer. Ancient traditions of chanting or singing to prevent the intellect from interfering with our feeling faculties show there is nothing to fear. King Saul did it with the explicit, prophetic blessings of Samuel, so it can't be all that bad.

We have not solved the old problems, but perhaps this approach offers a compro-mise that points us in the proper direction. Christian Truth students note that many possible avenues of spiritual growth are open before us. Marcus Bach, describing his own "Holy Spirit baptism" in the book *Questions on the Quest*, wrote: "It was, as I recall, a pure exclamation of adoration, and I am willing to let it go at that." [23]

Amen, Brother Bach. Amen.

MYSTERY AND WORSHIP

We have seen that the Holy Spirit is an exciting concept which provides vast possibilities for theological inquiry and metaphysical speculation. However, religious thinkers throughout the centuries have insisted that the deepest insights into the Spirit come not from academic studies but from a life lived in prayerful communion with God-within and God-in-the-world at large. In a sense the anamatists are correct when they see divine power pulsating through all Creation. Those who want to open them-selves to this spiritual power (the "let Him in" party) are also correct when they yearn for God's grace to come upon them and raise them to new life in Christ-conscious-ness. But those who have discovered God in the world could scarcely have done so if God had not first stood within them to point the way, and in this respect those who teach "prevenient grace" also have a piece of the Truth. When we realize the mystery of life and intelligence originates from a Holy Spirit both within/without, we shall begin to see the underlying unity of all things and begin to glean a hint of God the Good, omnipotent.

Ruth Furbee caught the sense of this eternal mystery in a poem called, simply,

WORSHIP

God made my cathedral
Under the stars;
He gave my cathedral
Trees for spires;
He hewed me an altar
In the depth of a hill;
He gave me a hymnal
A rock-bedded rill;
He voiced me a sermon
Of heavenly light
In the beauty around me—
The calmness of night;
And I felt as I knelt
On the velvet-like sod
I had supped of the Spirit
In the Temple of God.[24]

CHECK YOUR KNOWLEDGE

1. Explain the following: *Glossolalia, Holiness, Anamatism, Pantheism, Monism, Pneuma.*

2. How do the *"Fruit of the Spirit"* differ from *"Gifts of the Spirit"* in St. Paul's writings?

3. If someone broke a serious taboo in ancient Israel, what had to happen in order for the "blood-curse" to be lifted? How did this memory affect New Testament authors' imagery when they wrote about Jesus Christ?

4. What is the *"Let Him Out/Let Him In"* controversy?

5. Why is it essential to understand Spirit first when studying the Trinity?

6. The author suggests Glossolalia is a form of *Active Meditation.* What does this mean, and how is it another "middle way" between two extremes?

QUESTIONS FOR DISCUSSION

1. The author suggests that Greco-Roman polytheism might have grown into a Hindu-like faith. How did Christianity prevent that? What would Western culture be like today if Jesus Christ had not come?

2. Is "speaking in tongues" a valid Gift of the Spirit today?

3. Which side of the *Let Him Out/Let Him In* controversy do you favor? Why?

4. What is *Purity* and how can it be achieved in a secular age? Should we strive for purity?

5. Is the *Holy Spirit* a meaningful term, or should we abandon it as a vestige of medieval thinking?

6. How have you seen evidences of the Holy Spirit in your own life?

NOTES

1. Emmet Fox in Emmet *Fox's Golden Keys to Successful Living* by Herman Wolhorn (NY: Harper & Row, 1977), p. 51.

2. Acts 19:1-2 (RSV).

3. John 4:24 (RSV).

4. Macquarrie, *Twentieth Century,* p. 75.

5. Immanuel Kant in *Runes' Treasury,* p. 645.

6. Harris, p. 531.

7. John B. Noss, *Man's Religions* (NY: Macmillan, 1974), p. 98.

8. Paul L. Achtemeier, ed., *Harper's Bible Dictionary* (NY: Harper & Row, 1985), p. 401.

9. Maltbie D. Babcock (1858-1901), lyricist, "This is My Father's World." from *The Book of Worship for United States Forces* (Washington: US Government Printing Office, 1974), p. 76.

10. *Harper's Bible Dictionary,* p. 401.

11. Galatians 4:6-7.

12. *HBD,* p. 400.

13. Charles Fillmore, *The Revealing Word* (Unity Village: Unity Books, 1979), p. 97.

14. Nels M. Bailkey, ed., *Readings in Ancient History* (Lexington, MA: D.C. Heath and Company, 1969), pp. 54-55.

15. John 1:29 (RSV).

16. I Corinthians 6:19 (RSV).

17. Van A. Harvey, *A Handbook of Theological Terms* (NY: Harper & Row, 1978d), p. 112.

18. Meister Eckhart in *Silent Fire: An Invitation to Western Mysticism,* Walter Holden Capps & Wendy M. Wright, ed. (NY: Harper & Row, 1978), p. 114.

19. *HBD,* p. 401.

20. *MBD,* p. 629.

21. Fillmore, *Revealing Word,* p. 98.

22. *HBD,* p. 990.

23. Marcus Bach, *Questions on the Quest* (San Francisco: Harper & Row, 1978), p. 138.

24. Ruth Furbee, "Worship," in *Masterpieces of Religious Verse.* James Dalton Morrison, ed. (NY: Harper & Brothers, 1948). pp. 117-118

THE FATHER

Chapter Seven

One Presence/One Power: Divine Mind

Ineffable is the union of man and God in every act of the soul. The simplest person who in his integrity worships God, becomes God; yet for ever and ever the influx of this better and universal self is new and unsearchable. It inspires awe and astonishment. How dear, how soothing to man, arises the idea of God, peopling the lonely place, effacing the scars of our mistakes and disappointments. When we have broken our god of tradition and ceased from our god of rhetoric, then may God fire the heart with his presence.[1]
—Ralph Waldo Emerson

We began our study of the Trinity by looking at the Holy Spirit because metaphysical Christianity believes Spirit is the basic category by which we understand all things divine. Now we turn to the "first person" of the Trinity, *God the Father.*

INTERLOCKING CONCEPTS

What must be apparent very quickly is that the Trinity consists of three interlocking concepts which cannot be understood without each other. When we looked at *Spirit* (Chapter 6), we frequently needed to refer to Jesus Christ and to God the Father. This chapter, dealing ostensibly with the Father, will make repeated references to the *Son* and *Spirit,* and the following chapter (Chapter 8) discusses the Son (Christology) but will often touch on *Spirit* and *Creator-Father* to understand Sonship.

NEEDED: A GOOD THEOLOGICAL MAINTENANCE PROGRAM

The Trinity, as we have said, is a chosen viewpoint not necessarily identical with absolute reality. We simply have no tools to comprehend God in His/Her/Its vastness, so anything we say about God must necessarily be symbolic. The Trinity is just this: an effective way of representing symbolically that which is impossible to comprehend completely. Other ways of looking at God may be equally valid, but for Christians the time-proven symbol for Omnipotent/Omnipresent God is Father, Son, and Holy Spirit. We prefer to remain within the Christian heritage whenever a concept proves itself as useful as the Trinity.

Unfortunately, no religious idea works forever. Even long lasting ones need continual tune-ups lest they slip into pious superstitions that no longer speak to real human needs in the language of today. Accordingly, we have been reinterpreting the concept of the Trinity and will continue to do so as we examine the "Father" or the *Creative Principle* behind all that exists.

QUESTIONS DEMANDING ANSWERS

What do we mean when we speak of God the Father? In what way is God our Father, as Jesus called Him in the Lord's prayer? If God is in fact our Father, what does that suggest about our relationship to Jesus Christ? And what does divine parentage mean for us, if anything, as we struggle to adapt harmoniously to a world changing at warp-speed? These questions demand answers, but traditionalist Christianity does not even possess the tools to acknowledge the questions, let alone follow the implications of God's Parenthood through to its logical conclusions. If we're bold enough to try describing what God must be like, we'd better plan on falling far short of a perfect answer.

Failure in such a grand enterprise is no cause for regret. As Harvard Divinity School Professor Gordon Kaufman has pointed out, any God worthy of worship must certainly be far greater than any God we could domesticate in our theologies.

PROOF OF GOD'S EXISTENCE

No attempt will be made to prove that God exists. It cannot be done. But this is nothing to lament. God's existence cannot be disproved, either. In fact, most of the important truths of human existence cannot be proved or disproved:

Love is superior to hate.
Peace is better than war.
All human lives are of equal worth.

Enlightened people universally believe these principles, yet none of them can be proved. We can demonstrate their overwhelming good sense, but we cannot prove these ideas because they are *opinions* and not *facts*. Only scientifically testable facts can be absolutely proved or disproved, and even in the realm of science there must be a vast body of supporting evidence replicated many times before a fact is established.

Some ideas are just so basic that we find ourselves grasped by them. God's existence is one of those ideas which takes hold of us and provides us with a better way of looking at the world and its people. Great attempts have been made in the past to "prove" God exists, the most famous of these by medieval scholastic Thomas Aquinas. Some have been convinced, others have not. We shall not duplicate that effort. If you don't believe in God, we cannot change your mind with words. God is a working hypothesis to explain the meaning of life; we believe in God because that hypothesis works for us. Our goal is to show what God is like, not to validate His existence.

Perhaps we shall be accused of begging the question since we have assumed God exists and offered no proof; we plead guilty to all charges. God is part of our world-view and requires no more proof than love or peace or human equality require. We would not find a world without those qualities—or without God—a very happy place in which to live.

THE CENTRAL CONCEPT

God, Spirit, is the only presence in the universe, and is the only power. He is in, through, and around all creation as its life and its sustaining power.[2]

—Charles Fillmore, *The Revealing Word*

Looking at life from such a cosmic perspective is perhaps a bit foolhardy. We know so very little about this Universe. How can we speak with any kind of certainty about God, Who is even greater than the Cosmos?

In Chapter 2 we looked at the need for a way of organizing our thinking about life. We saw that everyone has some concept about how the Universe hangs together. The choice is not between empirical agnosticism and faith; the choice is, simply, what kind of faith shall we have? Human beings are irrevocably religious. They will deal with the great questions and find answers which permit them to live in a stable mental/emotional worldview. We can't speak with absolute certainty about meta-physical subjects; we can only share what works for us.

For metaphysical Christianity, we have said that the concept which best explains where life is headed and what is happening along the way is One Presence/One Power. Although we have discussed it previously, OP^2 is such an important concept for Christian theology that we have come nowhere near exhausting its possibilities nor plumbing its depths.

THREE WAYS OF LOOKING AT ONE GOD

Metaphysically, we can look at a God-concept three ways. Here we are using the word metaphysically in its common way, i.e., to indicate theories of what 1) lies beyond the realm of the physical sciences and 2) to explain how reality itself is constituted. Those three positions are *Atheism, Dualism, and Monism.*

NO PRESENCE / NO POWER: ATHEISM

Without embracing the loneliness and despair true atheism must bring, we must frankly admit this view at least argues its points consistently and makes a plausible case for itself. We need not agree with the conclusions of nontheists to learn from their better arguments.

Everybody is an atheist about something. No one believes the ancient Roman deities have any metaphysical reality. Jupiter, Venus, and Neptune are planets, not gods. Very few people reading this book would agree that the angry god of Christian fundamentalism actually exists. But our conservative brothers and sisters hotly deny that the Divine Mind of metaphysical Christianity has any reality. We are all selective atheists—believing in some religious ideas and dismissing others.

The possibility looms before us that no god exists anywhere; that is why belief in a Divine Power is called Faith as opposed to knowledge. But the atheist is in exactly the same position as we believers. His disbelief is, at best, an argument from silence. Atheism, too, is faith—faith that no god exists.

TWO PRESENCES, TWO POWERS (OR MORE): DUALISM

Dualism is the belief that two spheres of influence exist. One is the good, the other evil. Usually, things of the mind and spirit are good, and things of the senses and material world are evil. Plato fell into this trench warfare between material/spiritual realms, and since his thinking influenced early Christian theology, much of orthodoxy took the same plunge.

Actually, Dualism means there is more than one power. When the polytheist worships the sun god and the rain god and the moon goddess, he affirms that Spirit is broken into many pieces, power manifests from many sources. This provokes some difficulties theologically: If there is power other than God-power, where did that power originate? Further, if there is any power whatsoever that stands apart from God-power, how can God be said to be "All-powerful"?

Dualism assumes some power is good and other power is evil. Dualistic religion personifies that power into evil, supernatural beings: Satan, the Devil, Loki, Lucifer, Ahriman, Eblis, Apollyon, Satyr, Mephistopheles, Beelzebub, the "Dark Side of the Force." Mildly dualistic religions emphasize the good power while barely acknowledging the presence of the other option. Mainline Protestantism and American Catholicism are examples of minimally dualistic religious faiths today. The important point is that Dualism proceeds from a philosophical premise which says that there is more than one power behind the Universe, whereas atheism began with the proposition that there is no spiritual power at all. Only one more option is possible.

ONE PRESENCE / ONE POWER: MONISM

Monism says that there is only one power and one presence. If any power exists outside of God, He is not omnipotent. Theologian Charles Hartshorne suggests that God can do all the things He needs to do. Hartshorne would substitute adequacy for omnipotence, putting forth a model of God that is omni-competent, able to do all things He needs to do.[3]

Harsthorne's clever sophistry fails to solve the problem for dualistic theologies. If there is *any* other power, God cannot be said to be the Omnipotent Good we have worshipped. Monism, which asserts that there is only God-power and its absence just as there is only light and shadow, is the only true Monotheism.

Monism is quite ancient but has become popular in the West only in the last few centuries, chiefly through the medieval mystics like Meister Eckhart and nineteenth century Transcendentalists like Ralph Waldo Emerson, who wrote:

> Once men thought Spirit divine, and matter diabolic; one Ormuzd, the other Ahriman. Now science and philosophy recognize the parallelism, the approximation, the unity of the two: how each reflects the other as face answers to face in a glass: nay, how the laws of both are one, or how one is the realization.[4]

Today science and philosophy no longer support any kind of metaphysic, so Emerson's cheery confidence was short lived. In the closing years of the nineteenth century—about the time *New Thought* was born—philosophy was moving away from metaphysical studies. *"Who can know for certain such cosmic answers?"* they asked. By the middle of the twentieth century, existentialism with its emphasis on here-and-now, demonstrable and empirical evidence, had carried the day.

And since God is neither empirical nor demonstrable in the manner that scientists can control laboratory experiments, God-talk fell to death-of-God talk. Atheism, since it seeks to prove nothing metaphysical, became the most respectable religious philosophy for religious philosophers. So called " neo-orthodox theology" retreated to regroup behind walls of special revelation, biblical exclusivism, and dualism thinly disguised as Christian existentialism.

FRENCH CONNECTION: TEILHARD DE CHARDIN

Then came a brilliant Jesuit from France who had the temerity to step back and look at the great sweep of cosmic history and say:

> Where are the roots of our being? In the first place, they plunge down into the unfathomable past. How great is the mystery of the first cells which were one day animated by the breath of our souls!...In each of us, through matter, the whole history of the World is in part reflected...the human soul, however independently created our philosophy represents it as being, is inseparable, in its birth and in its growth, from the Universe into which it is born.[5]

His full name was Marie-Joseph-Pierre Teilhard de Chardin and he was born on May Day, 1881, at the Chateau of Sarcenat near Clermont-en-Auvergne. His family was of the nobility, so young Pierre received a fine education from his learned father and a Christian upbringing from a deeply pious mother. His sister became a nun, and he quite naturally entered the Jesuit Order at age eighteen.

From early childhood, Teilhard was fascinated with rocks and the earth. He followed this interest as a man and became a world renown scholar in the discipline of paleontology. But his work as a scientist, as important as it was, would be overshadowed by his meditations on the ultimate nature of reality. He was a passionate, gentle soul who was ill-equipped to weather the storms of controversy which his theological adventuring would generate. His superiors ruled that none of Teilhard's religious writings could be published during his life, and he obeyed without rebellion.[6]

What Pierre Teilhard de Chardin accomplished was to show how intimately human consciousness is bound up with the physical universe and to point down the corridors of time at the ultimate goal of evolution, union with God. It was a profound, cogent, disturbing theory.

Scientists cried that he had abandoned empiricism; theologians shouted that he had abandoned the Church. Teilhard saw it as simply following Truth wherever it led him. He could not weave a comprehensive theory of consciousness—of life itself—without a spiritual dimension. He knew there is at work a Presence and Power which keeps nudging, beckoning, urging sentient beings to grow and mature. God stands at both ends of history as the Source and Destination, Alpha and Omega. More importantly, God stands beneath, in and through history as its propelling energy, the One Presence/Power we know as consciousness itself:

> The entire problem, all my attention, the total attraction of my spiritual life, have been focused on this point and continue to be focused there: how to connect within my person the forces of both these centers—God and the world—or, more exactly, how to make them coincide. [7]

Teilhard went on to teach that all reality is moving toward Christ-consciousness, the *Omega Point* he called it. The whole process of cosmic evolution is under God's guidance, but God allows freedom of choice for each individual. We shall all reach Omega, but the course of instruction is self-paced. Christianity has just begun to discover the footsteps of this giant who walked among us. But radical ideas have an old heritage in the Christian faith.

"FATHERHOOD OF GOD": WHAT DOES THIS IMPLY?

One of the most revolutionary concepts was brought by Jesus Himself. He taught that the God of Israel—Yahweh, the fearsome, vengeful tribal deity who smote the firstborn of Egypt—is actually a loving, forgiving Father of all people. Certainly, the idea of God as a Father was not a new notion. Although it was not as dominant a motif as, say, the steadfast love of Yahweh for the fickle Hebrews, God's parenthood of the children of Israel can be found in many OT references. The concept is implied or stated outright in places as diverse as Exodus 4:22; Deuteronomy 14:1, 32:6; Hosea 11:1; Jeremiah 3:4, 19, and 31:9; and Psalm 103:13.[8]

What Jesus brought was an intimacy which is so profound that no English-language translator has yet had the courage to render the word used by the Master ("Abba!") into its closest modern equivalent: "Daddy." Jesus also taught His disciples to claim the same relationship with the Father for themselves. His greatest prayer does not begin "My Father" but draws a great circle, including all humanity: "Our Father, who art in heaven..."

Intimacy with God and universalism go hand-in-hand in the pictures of Jesus drawn by gospel authors, even though at least one of them, Matthew, was no universalist. What this suggests to scholars is that the Jesus of history, lost in the mists behind the curtains of written and oral traditions, stands firmly behind the New Testament church's confession of our childhood under God.[9]

PROBLEMS OF ETHICAL MONOTHEISM

Such intimacy with the Deity is absolutely unique in monotheistic religion. Islam regards God as Wholly Other—an awesome, completely transcendent, fearsome Being. Jewish mysticism and "charismatic" movements like Hassidic Judaism speak of God as an all-consuming flame, a love that drenches the soul and whirls it to ecstasy. But no one has dared to claim personal kinship with God but Jesus of Nazareth.

We noted in the previous chapter that simpler concepts of anamatism (spirit-force) may have yielded to animism (worship of distinct spirits or powers of nature) which in turn gave rise to polytheism (personification of those powers into gods and goddesses). In at least one instance (Hinduism), polytheism gave way to some expressions of higher monotheism (belief in just one God) when the gods and goddesses merged into one Supreme Being.

Monotheism has its problems, too. First, if it is an *Ethical Monotheism* (the Divine cares about right and wrong, rewarding right and punishing wrong), then it will be *inherently intolerant*. After all, if there is only one God and He cares enough about what people do/think/believe to reward the good folk and punish the nonsubscribers, then it is absolutely necessary for everyone to follow the same religion, the faith of the One True God.

If you disagree with the religious or ethical teachings of the church—which are, really, the religious/ethical opinions of the church's leadership—you are wrong. In fact, since there is only one Truth and God will punish those who do not affirm it, those who disbelieve are not merely wrong, they are evil.

Ethical Monotheism has a far worse record of abuses than polytheism, which tends to be lenient toward those who worship another deity. In our study of world religions we quoted sociologists Horton and Hunt who said that when religious leaders tortured nonbelievers to accept their faith and then killed them to save their souls (i.e., during the Spanish Inquisition), it is entirely possible they were operating from a sense of moral duty. Only an Ethical Monotheist could consistently argue in favor of suppressing dissent so violently because only believers in a single supernatural being who punishes wrong and rewards right have the One-Way premise explicit in their theologies.

A CLEAN SHADOW

Though some may be surprised, Ethical Monotheism is not the only Christian option. At various times during Church history ideas like *Deism, Naturalistic Theism,* and *Pantheism* have had their heydays. The best we can get from any god-concept is a clean shadow of the Unknowable. But sometimes we learn things from the odd-looking shapes of other god-images which are denied to us because of the very familiarity of our own theological shadow-pictures.

We do not need to rehearse the history of God-concepts at this time, but the three images mentioned above are significant enough for our study to demand at least brief treatment.

GOD AS SLUM-LORD: DEISM

Deism can vary from the sublime to the ludicrous. It reached its zenith during the late eighteenth century and served as the dominant God-model for the prime movers of the period known as the Enlightenment. Quite a few founding fathers of the United States of America—George Washington included—advocated an intellectual deism.

This model says that God created the Universe and set it in motion but does not interfere with its daily operations. Its best feature is Deism's ability to deal with the problem of evil; if God is not involved with the mechanics of everyday life He can hardly be held accountable for suffering, disease, and war.

However, Deism falls short because its god-concept is so remote as to make the Divine an absentee landlord ruling over his struggling tenants from the safety of the spiritual suburbs. Such a god, while intellectually satisfying, stands accused of apathy, ambivalence, and impotence. The god of deism is next to no god at all.

NATURE IS GOD: NATURALISTIC THEISM

Essentially, the adherents of *Naturalistic Theism* push beyond deism and arrive at no-god. Nature is god for them, and there is no need to postulate any kind of intelligence behind the operations of scientific principles. Albert Einstein and Carl Sagan are two of the best modern examples. There is a reverence for life in some of the writings of naturalistic theists, a sense of awe at the mystery of the Cosmos, but no Divine Mind at work. We are star-stuff, Sagan said, but nothing more.

This kind of secular thinking found theological expression during the *"God is dead"* debate of the 1960s, especially in the writings of Thomas J. Altizer and William Hamilton. Altizer and Hamilton went so far as to insist that God must be denied for humanity to be liberated. For Altizer, God has incarnated himself in the world and given up his distinct otherness, freeing us from dependence upon a power outside ourselves. However, "Christian atheism", as it was called by its proponents, proved unsatisfying to a majority of both Christians and atheists. It was too void of spirituality for most Christians and too biblical for most atheists. People want a God to love or, in the case of atheism, to reject. Altinger have us neither, preferring instead a philosopher's argument to the presentation of a dynamic theology from within the Circle of Faith. The best that can be said about *"Death of God"* theology today is that it died a swift, natural death.[10]

An obvious advantage to Naturalistic Theism is its sense of harmony with the Universe. Humanity is not some alien entity plopped down within time-and-space for three-score-and-ten years and then transplanted to heaven or hell for all eternity. We have a right to be here. This provides a much more reverent way of looking at ecology, human misery, and the responsibility of science to make the world a better place than does classical theism with its dualistic destinations and transient status for humanity.

An obvious disadvantage to Naturalistic Theism is that it speaks of mystery without allowing things to be genuinely mysterious. For life and consciousness to evolve from dead matter and energy makes no more sense than postulating a Divine Mind pushing the whole process along.

Atheistic and yet still optimistic, Naturalistic Theism has no basis for hope other than a blind euphoria about the ability of science to overcome all our difficulties. Listening to the fascinating yarns of Carl Sagan during his epic "Cosmos" series on the PBS television network, one could almost begin to believe that all we need to achieve the Kingdom of Heaven is better research.

Human history discloses otherwise. Unless there is some kind of spiritual growth, smarter folks just make smarter weapons. And if there is "spiritual growth," what standard does the Naturalistic Theist hold up as a model for humanity to emulate? Usually, it is an unconsciously religious model, a mixture of pop-psychology and the parables of Jesus. In any other enterprise, that would be called plagiarism. In theology, it's acute myopia compounded by intellectual elitism. Naturalistic Theism will never work as a Christian system because it is essentially unnatural and nontheistic.

GOD IS THE WORLD: PANTHEISM

If Naturalistic Theism goes overboard by reading God out of the Cosmos, *Pantheism* errs in the opposite extreme. For the pantheist, God is the Cosmos. Everything is God. This means every act, thought, being, and thing in the Universe can be added up and the grand total equals what God is. God is coextensive with the Cosmos, therefore He could not have created it or we land in the contradictory conclusion that God created Himself. God and the Universe must be eternal, since He is that Universe.

Pantheism finds expression in the philosophies of Spinoza, Hegel, and Royce and in the theologies of great Christian mystics like Dionysius the Aeropagite, John Scotus Erigena, and Meister Eckhart. Eastern religions are almost unanimously pantheistic, but ethical monotheists within Judaism, Christianity, and Islam have energetically suppressed *God-is-All* as a doctrine smelling of universalism. Certainly, a consistent pantheism does not allow any dichotomy between the saved and the damned. If God-is-All, then heaven and hell are at worst adjoining chambers in God's consciousness.

Pantheism's one major advantage is its grasp of the all-pervasive Presence of God. The Divine is not remote but totally immanent. God works in everything, not just a few spectacular moments of Divine intervention. God is impersonal, because the energy of the Cosmos is not geared to redeem the individual soul but rather to express the Divine in many forms.

The problem of pure pantheism is that it cannot explain why there are imperfections in the world, therefore it tends to deny that suffering, pain, and discord exist. This puts the pantheist in the very unenviable position of denying that his neighbor really hurts.

It is no accident that some of the most callous philosophies of life have been developed by Eastern religions and that the value of individual human life is not taken too seriously in cultures where pantheism holds sway. Ironically, pantheists are among the most pacifistic people on earth, many refusing to eat animal products and others watching where they step for fear of causing the death of insects underfoot. Pantheism fails because it cannot live in the real world, a requirement laid upon us by Jesus of Nazareth. In its extreme form pantheism falls short when God-the-All becomes God-the-Author-of-Horrors, like Hitler's genocide against the Jews and Ayatollah Khomeni's murder of Iranian Baha'is.

A simpler way of stating the problem comes to us from William and Mabel Sahakian's *Ideas of the Great Philosophers:*

> Since every person is part of God, it follows that if a child (also part of God) believes erroneously that 2+2=5, while at the same time his teacher (part of God as well) knows that 2+2=4 and that the child is mistaken, the entire situation is one in which God must be assumed to be simultaneously aware and not aware that he is in error. Thus, Pantheism injects contradiction in the mind of God, an inconceivable impossibility.[11]

WHAT'S LEFT?

So far we have looked at these God-concepts: *Ethical Monotheism, Deism, Naturalistic Theism, and Pantheism.* We have not exhausted all the possibilities; there are many options yet unexplored. To name a few: *Deistic Supernaturalism, Religious Humanism, Impersonal Idealism,* and *Agnostic Realism.* Although each view offers insights which may provide still another piece to the infinite puzzle, they are pretty much blind alleys for Christians.

We are seeking a God-concept which holds in dynamic tension the disruptive experiences of everyday life and the faithful assurance that God has everything under control; a way of looking at the Infinite God as Infinite Good that does not undermine God's role in the real world; a model which helps explain the personal, caring nature of God while still acknowledging that people can suffer; a method of understanding how God can be in-and-through everyone while we are still capable of atrocious error-beliefs and flagrant attempts to rip ourselves free from the good that God wants to give us.

A tall order, but it can be done. Several excellent thinkers have pointed the way. We shall make one brief stopover at a halfway house and then press on to our final destination.

wrote Ideas of the Great Philosophers

CREATION IMPLIES RISK: PANENTHEISM

Panentheism is not pantheism, although it borrows some of its best elements. Whereas pantheism said God is the world, panentheism says God immanently interpenetrates the Cosmos but is still distinct from it. The Sahakians explain:

> God possess self-identity and is independent of the particular objects of nature, though immanent in them. Panentheism differs from Deism which posits only a transcendent God; it also differs from Pantheism which identifies God with nature. That is to say, it agrees with Pantheism that the being of God includes nature, but adds the belief that God surpasses and embraces more than nature.[12]

Albert Schweitzer, Alfred North Whitehead, and Charles Hartshorne are among modern panentheists, although the term was coined by K. F. C. Krause (1781-1832) early in the nineteenth century. Panentheism says that God is in the world, inhabiting the very atoms of the physical universe, but is beyond the world as well. God incarnates Himself in and through the world but, contrary to the *Death of God* theologians, He is not exhausted by this going forth in creation.[13]

A key point in panentheism is that God perceives the world through creating His sentient creatures and therefore is gaining new experiences as we live and grow. In that case, we are adding to the sum of God's being by our choices. God cannot be complete in Himself because He does not have our choices as actual events until we choose.

Much like a parent who knows his child will go off to school, suffer scraped knees, and get in fights until the child learns how to live with others, God "knows" generally what we shall experience but does not know exactly which possibility we shall choose. If He did, there is no real choice involved, because billions of eons ago God knew what choices would be made today and therefore created us to make those choices.

By giving us the gift of freedom, God blinded Himself as to the specific options we select. As we make those selections God "grows" with us. According to Hartshorne, God needs us as much as we need Him, because His nature is creative expression and we are the fulfillment of that nature. Hartshorne wrote:

> A new era in religion may be predicted as soon as men grasp the idea that it is just as true that God is the supreme beneficiary or recipient of achievement, as he is the supreme benefactor or Source of achievement.[14]

Creation also implies risk. To send forth creative expressions of Himself, God must free those expressions to act in ways contrary to His will. Sentient beings must be able to choose dastardly, cruel behavior in order to freely choose to walk the paths of peace and love. Freedom cuts both ways or not at all. Believing that God the Good is behind everything does not guarantee happy outcomes in all instances, because God's greatest gift to us is freedom, and freedom means risk.

As the popular proverb goes: "A ship in a harbor is safe, but that is not what ships are created for." John Macquarrie agrees:

> It is by no means obvious that "in everything God works for good," but then this was not obvious to St. Paul who wrote these words. It has to be insisted again that this doctrine begins as an act of faith and hope, an attitude to life; it does not begin as a speculation about the world, and certainly not a speculation that can be thought up in the study away from the actual conflicts and decisions of life.[15]

CREATION AND THE BIG BANG

Panentheism avoids the contradiction of pantheism's self-creating God by asserting that God is not exhausted by the act of creation. Plenty of divine substance remains after all the matter-and-energy Cosmos springs forth from that primordial act of creation/organization.

This is metaphysical speculation of the highest order. But if Carl Sagan can step back fifteen billion years to the explosion which gave rise to our physical Universe and call it science, we can certainly tiptoe into the primeval dark before the Big Bang to peek at what was happening in the name of theology. Science cites the expanding Universe as evidence for the Big Bang; theology cites the existing Universe as evidence for God-substance. The two theories are wholly compatible when properly understood. When we look at Eschatology (Chapter 10) we shall discuss Creation and cosmology in greater depth.

ONE PRESENCE / ONE POWER

We have said the wellsprings of metaphysical Christianity flow from its cardinal principle. We have also frankly admitted that this pivotal concept, on which all theologies of Christian Truth churches turn, is neither explicitly biblical nor traditional but results from experience and reason. In that respect *One Presence/One Power (OP^2)* falls under the same heading as other nonbiblical doctrines (like the Trinity) and represents a minority view in the history of Christian thought (like universalism).

It is worth noting that although the Trinity and Christian universalism are nonbiblical and non-traditional respectively, both positions are staunchly defended by churchmen as orthodox as John Macquarrie (who was Lady Margaret Professor of Divinity at Oxford University), and a host of other high-visibility theologians of both Catholic and Protestant persuasions.

Christian mysticism has hinted the OP^2 concept for centuries, but so far there have been few attempts to state theologically what this idea means and to show how it relates to the totality of Christian theology. With apologies to those who know how complicated the task is, we shall now attempt in the remaining pages of this chapter to do just that. Proper treatment of subjects this vast requires an unhurried investigation of the biblical, traditional, and experiential factors leading us to conclude reasonably that God the Father is One Presence and Power. We shall have to settle for a whirlwind tour along the major routes of thought which might serve as pathmarkings for deeper study in later volumes specifically dedicated to this topic.

KENOSIS: EMPTYING OF DIVINITY

We shall call our concept *Incarnational Monism* and shall find the last piece to the puzzle in Paul's Letter to the Philippians:

> Have this mind among yourselves, which is yours in Christ Jesus, who, though he was in the form of God, did not count equality with God a thing to be grasped, but emptied himself, taking on the form of a servant, being born in the likeness of men. And being found in human form he humbled himself and became obedient unto death, even death on a cross. Therefore God has highly exalted him and bestowed on him the name which is above every name, that at the name of Jesus every knee should bow, in heaven and on earth and under the earth, and every tongue confess that Jesus Christ is Lord, to the glory of God the Father.[16]

Kenosis is the Greek word Paul used to describe the origin of Jesus Christ. He said Jesus *"emptied himself"* of preexistent *"equality with God"* when he was born into this world. But while Paul probably believed this act of kenosis was the unique prerogative of Jesus as the only Son of God, mystical Christian thought has often seen divinity as the essential ingredient in all consciousness. Medieval churchman Meister Eckhart:

> I have read many writings of both Pagan masters and the Prophets of the old and new Covenant (Testament), and have investigated seriously and with great zeal which would be the best and highest virtue by which Man could resemble again the archetype such as he was in God when there was no difference between him and God until God made the creatures.[17]

Eckhart goes on to suggest that kenosis separates us from that state of oneness, so we need "seclusion" to renew our relationship with God, which we hear echoed in pastoral theologian Henri Nouwen, who wants us to find a "desert" place in the city, in the hustle of everyday life, to commune with the Father.

Of course, both ideas are present in the well-known meditation experiences of Charles Fillmore when he began his own spiritual questing. Fillmore wrote:

> I noticed, however, that all the teachers and writers talked a great deal about the omnipresent, omniscient God, who is Spirit and accessible to everyone. I said to myself, "In this babel I will go to headquarters. If I am Spirit and this God they talk so much about is Spirit, we can somehow communicate, or the whole thing is a fraud."[18]

Meister Eckhart had asserted as far back as the thirteenth century that such dogged determination, when coupled with love, will flush God from His lofty state to transcendence and bring Him down to us whereby we become united with God and resume some degree of oneness with Him. Eckhart was absolutely convinced that God must come "down" to our level:

> But it is much more important that I force God down to me than that I force myself up to God. For my eternal bliss rests upon my being united with God. For God is more able to penetrate into me and become united with me, than I with Him.[19]

To the untrained ear, that sounds blasphemous. We seldom think of prayer as a way to "force God down" to us. The passage makes better sense when we note that Eckhart believed God could not resist a heart turned toward Him in sincere prayer. God's nature is loving-giving, an inseparable whole expressed by another New Testament Greek word, *agape*.

As hearts reach for Him, God can no more refuse to express His loving-giving nature than the sun could refuse to shine once the rainclouds are swept aside after a storm. "God cannot help abandoning Himself to a secluded heart," Eckhart wrote.[20] As the First Letter of John had said: "God is Agape." *Selfless love.*

KENOSIS AS NORMATIVE

If kenosis, God's self-emptying, is a one-time phenomenon manifested exclusively in Jesus of Nazareth, we can find no help in this concept for the vision of Oneness with God glimpsed by mystics like Eckhart and Fillmore. Then God's Fatherhood of the human race is a mere figure of speech, much like all Americans having the same "Uncle Sam."

However, if kenosis is the norm for all sentient beings— if we are all bits of divinity flung to the far corners of the Cosmos where we're to grope/grow back to full awareness of our Oneness with God—then the best of panentheism and incarnational theology merges in the concept of God as One Presence and Power. Even the problems of ethical monotheism are mitigated by kenosis. Certainly, God "cares" about right and wrong, but if God is acting in and through us then it makes no sense for one part of God to interfere with the operation of another part. If you are God expressing as you and I am God expressing as me, each "emptied" of full divinity by the primordial act of creation/expression, we must learn to see the divinity in each other without some outside force compelling us to act in a responsible, God-conscious manner.

If we are all incarnations of God, the notion of reward-and-punishment becomes ludicrous. Would God send a bit of Himself to hell? (Would any parent condemn his/her child for all eternity?) There might be built-in "rewards" for choosing the best path and less satisfactory responses from life if we choose otherwise, but no permanent damage would be experienced unless our model includes a God who enjoys self-inflicted wounds.

Kenosis also answers the objection about contradictions in the mind of God. If both child (thinking 2+2=5) and teacher (knowing 2+2=4) are kenotic incarnations of God (i.e., slices of divinity which have been emptied of full awareness), then the apparent contradiction is resolved. As those "slices of divinity" grow spiritually, finding harmony with their true nature by choosing the path of loving-giving walked by Jesus Christ, they become more Christ-like until they become so convinced of their identity in God they can say with complete confidence, "I and the Father are one." (John 10:30)

THEODICY: HOW GOOD IS GOD OMNIPOTENT?

We are nearly prepared to erect our God-concept from these hastily sketched notes. OP^2 forms the cornerstone. From this foundation we see that no power can exist outside of God, so we seem forced to make one of two choices about the nature of suffering.

Either the suffering and misery we humans experience is merely an illusion which must be denied, or the failures and pain of humanity come from our state as incomplete manifestations of God's Presence and Power. In other words, either 1) *bad things really don't happen* (which life experience shouts down as absurd) or 2) *God is somehow involved in the pain and failures* to which we are heir as human beings. This lands us in the old problem of *theodicy*, which is theology's attempt to square the idea of a loving, all-powerful God with the suffering of the world.

Formally stated, the dilemma is this: *If God knows about pain and misery but will not prevent it, He is not good. If He cannot prevent it, He is not all-powerful, hence He is not God.* If a quick answer occurs to you, re-read the problem; you aren't thinking deeply enough. Theodicy has given us theologians nightmares for untold centuries.

How does metaphysical Christianity answer its challenge? Let's review: We have insisted that God is the only Power and Presence in the Universe, and He is Good Omnipotent. Therefore, the problem must evaporate within Incarnational Monism, as we shall see it does.

If each sentient being is an incarnation of God, theodicy dissolves into growth-experiences. God sends His children off to learn and grow, knowing they will experience pain and suffering. This sending forth is not an act of Deism's absentee God or Ethical Theism's Supreme Judge. God goes forth in you and me to experience, to learn, to grow.

Knowing that creation implies risk, God is willing to risk disaster because growth is worth the danger. The Word becomes flesh because until God expresses Himself as the children of the Universe, He is not yet a Father. Listen to Meister Eckhart:

> The word "Father" implies a Son and the phrase "Father of Lights" implies an immaculate birth and a universal principle. The Father begets the Son in the eternal mind and also begets the Son in the

soul as if in his own nature...Thus we are all in the Son and are the Son. [21]

He wrote that in the thirteenth century—*Wow!*

God does not cause earthquakes, wars or diseases. He is Omnipotent Good, wanting nothing but the best for His children. He operates in a free Cosmos where earthquakes, wars, and disasters can occur. He begets Himself as you and me in such a Universe for the sake of creative growth, creative expression, loving-giving. He has provided ways for us to learn and grow in the most adverse situations, and has organized Reality itself to be supportive and health-giving. Because there is a loving-giving Father behind the curtain of the Cosmos, this is a basically friendly Universe. We affirm *One Presence / One Power* even in the face of apparent evidence to the contrary because we know our Daddy loves us.

INCARNATIONAL MONISM: THEOLOGY'S HIGHEST EXPRESSION

Christian Incarnational Monism is a better term to describe this unity-in-diversity brought about through kenosis and summarized for all time in the life and person of Jesus Christ. Once more, we have explored the Divine-Human paradox and have found the apparent contradictions of theodicy, pantheism, and ethical theism resolve in the principle of Christ-consciousness.

Incarnational Monism, if true, would explain the origins of intelligence, consciousness, and evolution. If the part of God that is Jesus Christ was "emptied" (kenosis) of its full divinity when He took *"the form of a servant, being born in the likeness of men,"* and if Jesus regarded humanity as His brothers/sisters, calling us to recognize our Abba-Father "in Heaven," then each sentient being can be regarded as an incarnation of that same God with the same potential as Jesus Christ demonstrated.

Great mystics of the Church have glimpsed this Truth, but it is so startling—so "too good to be true"—that few theologians have given it serious consideration. Everyday experience seems to contradict pantheism—we simply don't behave like God, unless we want our God to be a bank robber, a drug pusher, or a terrorist. But God in His/Her/Its fullness is not what we're talking about. Kenotic theology says that God "emptied" Himself of that fullness when He came to earth in Jesus Christ. The spark of divinity was there, but not the All-powerful, All-knowing, All-present Creator/Ruler of the Cosmos.

And yet, Jesus born at Bethlehem shows us God Almighty in a unique way. So powerful is Jesus Christ in our culture one could argue we have a Jesus-model for God, not a God-model for Jesus. Jesus Christ is not God-like; God is Jesus-like. Jesus is the window through which the Light of God shines, and the window determines the shape of that light.

CORNERSTONE FOR THE HOUSE OF TOMORROW

Incarnational Monism gives us a way to understand how God can be born in a stable, grow up an apprentice carpenter, and bleed to death on a Roman cross. Like panentheism, Incarnational Monism shows us a God Who is in and through all and yet beyond all. It is a flexible, biblical model to understand God as the OP^2 behind all that is, while still affirming the reality of suffering and human freedom without implicating God in the snares of theodicy.

As Metaphysical Christianity begins to develop theologians who will provide leadership for the twenty-first century, this idea of *Christian Incarnational Monism* could become the rallying-point for the Church of the future. It also gives us yet another bridge of light to our heritage as part of the mainline/liberal Protestant movement in the Western world. I believe that *Incarnational Monism* is an idea whose day has not yet come, a cornerstone laid in waiting for the house of tomorrow.

ONWARD TO CHRISTOLOGY

Christian theology cannot address the question of God without taking as its starting point the best example of God-with-us. Jesus Christ, we have said, was absolutely unique because He gives us a window through which God's light can shine and by which we can see what we are truly meant to be. In Jesus Christ we have a summary of all the good that God wants for His children. As the Apostle Paul wrote in his second letter to the Church at Corinth:

"For all the promises of God find their 'Yes' in him." [22]

We turn now to the unqualified *yes* of all those Divine promises—Jesus Christ— as we look at the final person of the Trinity, the Son of God.

CHECK YOUR KNOWLEDGE

1. What does the word "Abba" really mean, and how did Jesus use it?

2. What is the central concept of all mystical/metaphysical Christianity? How does this interface with the idea of God as a loving Father?

3. What are the advantages/disadvantages of: *Ethical Monotheism, Atheism, Deism, Naturalistic Theism, Pantheism, Dualism, Monism, Theodicy, Agape?*

4. What is *Panentheism?* Explain what the author means when he says: *"Creation implies risk."*

5. How does *Kenosis* (emptying) help to understand God as Father of us all?

6. Explain *Incarnational Monism* and show why the author feels it is Christian theology's highest expression.

QUESTIONS FOR DISCUSSION

1. If everybody an atheist about something, what are you an atheist about?

2. Does *Incarnational Monism* work within the One Presence/One Power framework and the basic categories of Christian theology? Does it work for you?

3. If God is all good, why is there evil and suffering in the world?

4. What does the author mean when he says *"the best we can get from any god-concept is a clean shadow of the Unknowable"*? Do you agree? What shape is your God-shadow?

5. The author said Jesus isn't God-like, God is Jesus like. What does that mean; do you agree?

6. If each sentient being is an incarnation of God, why do we feel so lost sometimes? (How can *Kenosis* apply here?)

NOTES

1. Ralph Waldo Emerson in *Gospel of Emerson*, Newton Dillaway, ed. (Unity Village: Unity Books, 1980), p. 114.

2. Fillmore, *RW*, p. 142.

3. Charles Hartshorne, *The Divine Relativity* (New Haven: Yale University Press, 1974), p. 34.

4. Emerson, p. 58.

5. Pierre Teilhard de Chardin, *Christ and the Universe* (Chicago: Franciscan Herald Press, 1973), p. 15.

6. For more information see the chapter on Teilhard in my book *Friends in High Places* (Unity Village: Unity Books, 1985).

7. Teilhard, p. 21.

8. *HBD*, p. 305.

9. *IOVC* p. 689.

10. Macquarrie, *Twentieth Century*, p. 386.

11. Sahakian, p. 88.

12. IBID, pp. 91-92

13. Macquarrie, *Twentieth Century*, pp. 273-27

14. Hartshorne, p. 134.

15. Macquarrie, op cit.

16. Philippians 2:5-11 (RSV).

17. Eckhart in *Runes' Treasury*, p. 348.

18. Charles Fillmore in *Freeman's Story of Unity*, p. 52.

19. Eckhart in Treasury, p. 343.

20. IBID.

21. Eckhart in Holden & Capps, p. 116.

22. II Corinthians 1:20 (RSV).

THE SON

Chapter Eight

Perfect Example of The Divine-Human Paradox

Once I was asked what the Father is doing in heaven. I replied that he begets his Son and that this activity is so pleasant to him and suits him so well that he never does anything else and that from the two there blossoms forth the Holy Spirit. When the Father begets his Son in me, I am that Son and no other. "If we are sons, then we are true heirs." He who knows the truth knows very well that the word "Father" implies the immaculate birth and the having of sons. Thus we are all in the Son and are the Son.[1]

—Meister Eckhart (1260-1327)

Metaphysical Christianity is Trinitarian, but just barely. The classical doctrine of the triune God—one substance, three "persons" or modes of expression, proceeding from each other and uniquely Divine—is plainly too limited for Christian Incarnational Monism to accept literally.

Literal trinitarianism provokes more questions than it answers: If only the persons of the Trinity are Divine, what about the rest of us? Is there more than one kind of consciousness, some Divine and some not-divine? If God is not our true "Abba!" the way Jesus taught He is, what commerce could finite beings have with a Supreme Being so holy, pure, and distant? If Jesus alone is the Second Person (Son) of the trinity, what possible relationship could we have to the Master other than as admiring followers who wonder how He did it? How can God be three, and yet one, without tritheism or contradiction?

GOT ANY ROOM IN YOUR PANTHENON?

Many trinitarians have a much larger concept of spiritual realities than orthodox theology allows, albeit unconsciously. Monotheism, we have said, insists there is only one God. This concept is interpreted in so many ways that some interesting variations occur within orthodoxy.

Insisting on only one God, most Christians nonetheless believe in a host of other supernatural entities which coexist in the divine realm. Anthropologist Anthony F. C. Wallace observes that Roman Catholicism's official system of supernatural beings— saints, demons, angels, etc.—pales into simplicity when compared with the multiple religious entities actually recognized by people in his own hometown. Writes Wallace:

> Even the so-called "monotheistic" religions invariably include an elaborate pantheon. Thus in the small Christian community in which I grew up, "the religion" (in the summative sense) included at least the following categories of supernatural beings in its pantheon:
>
> 1. God (the high god)
> 2. Jesus
> 3. The Virgin Mary
> 4. The saints
> 5. The Devil
> 6. Ghosts (souls of the dead on earth found in old houses and around cemeteries)
> 7. Souls in heaven, hell, or purgatory
> 8. The souls of normal living human being
> 9. Witches, who could take on the form of animals and harm people
> 10. Santa Claus (believed in only by children)
> 11. The Easter rabbit (also believed in only by children)
> 12. Souls of animals
> 13. Fairies (who bring quarters when teeth fall out, and live in closets or in woodsy places)
> 14. Superstition: beliefs concerning good or bad luck [2]

Wallace notes that not everyone believed in the whole list and there was always pressure to reduce the numbers. Who hasn't heard a sermon on Easter or Christmas bemoaning the "secularization" or "commercialization" of those high holy days? Presumably, the Santa Claus cult or the Easter Rabbit cult would be purged from the list if some preachers had their way.

We are not accustomed to thinking of religion in such broad terms. Wallace, a cultural anthropologist studying the phenomena of existing religions, has no qualms about listing all the supernatural beings people acknowledged in his hometown. If we step back and look at the larger picture, we can plainly see that belief systems which pass themselves off as monotheistic are really thinly veiled polytheism (belief in more than one god) or, at best, henotheism (belief in one overwhelmingly powerful god among many supernatural beings and gods).

RUDOLF BULTMANN: DE-MYTHOLOGIZING

This leaves us with a rather disturbing picture of mythologies intertwined with theologies, a fact pointed out by theologian and New Testament scholar Rudolf

Bultmann in his shattering essay, "The New Testament and Mythology." Published in 1941 in German, the work is now readily available in English and should be read by every serious Christian Truth student. Bultmann showed how the New Testament could be "de-mythologized", stripped of its pre-scientific worldview, while still preserving the "kerygma" (kernel of Truth) wrapped in its archaic thought-forms:

> If the truth (kerygma) of the New Testament proclamation is to be preserved, the only way is to demythologize it...The real purpose of myth is not to present an objective picture of the world as it is, but to express man's understanding of himself in the world in which he lives.[3]

We look out at a world we did not create and attempt to arrange life into a coherent whole, so that we can go grocery shopping without worrying about evil powers cursing our homes while we're gone or supernatural beings striking us dead on the freeway. Those religious systems which picture a plethora of gods and demi-gods vying for custody of the human soul will invariably give rise to a complex mythology and a ritual system designed to insure safe passage down the corridor of life and eternal reward at our final destination.

Simpler systems do not necessarily mean simpler mythologies, as anthropologists like Anthony Wallace have shown. Every worldview will contain some mythological elements because human consciousness cannot fully comprehend the Cosmos. Today's secret mythologies hide behind more appropriate socio-cultural fashions: Salvation through romantic love leading to marriage; science will solve all our problems; life evolved from the primordial soup to sentient human beings by accident of nature; the better educated a person is the less problems he/she will have in life.

MYTH, NOT FALSEHOOD

We must be very careful when using the word *myth* that it does not degenerate into a synonym for *falsehood*. The above list of modern myths is essentially a negative one because we can more readily see the mythical elements in ideas based on half-truths. There are other myths to explain life that are not so easily recognized: Democracy is better than dictatorship; chastity until marriage is the best way; all people are created equal. None of these are provable, yet millions of people—the author included—will organize their lives according to "myths" which explain how the world operates and how good people behave.

The parables of Jesus may not reflect historical incidents. There may not have been a "good Samaritan" or a "prodigal son." Nevertheless, those stories teach some profound insights about effective living. They are, in the larger sense of the word, myths.

Rudolf Bultmann and other biblical scholars want us to recognize the prescientific elements in New Testament writing while preserving the kernel of truth contained within the mythological husk. As we delve deeper into our study of Christology, we need to remember we are, in effect, constructing a new mythology around the central truths which mystical/metaphysical Christianity proclaims. If we do this self-consciously, there is no need to regret the process of world-building, required of all religious thought. This is our next step toward a new Christology.

QUICK REVIEW: MONISM

Incarnational Monism, which proclaims that there is only One Presence and Power in the Cosmos, is the only true monotheism, because Monism alone disallows any power outside of God-power. As we saw in our study of the Father (Chapter 7), Christian Monism is not crudely pantheistic but is kenotic and incarnational: God goes forth into creation, expressing Himself as matter-energy and as consciousness which has been emptied (kenosis) of its awareness of full divinity. He "begets" Himself as you and me, the "only begotten Son."

We cannot prove that this has occurred as an historical event. But Incarnational Monism is an appropriate "myth" to explain consciousness and free will while preserving the integrity of the biblical witness to humanity's incompleteness and tendency to sin. Incarnational Monism gives us the Divine wrapped in a self-chosen robe of fallible flesh, facing the stars. Only if God is within can we expect with confidence eventual victory over sin and death. Only if Jesus Christ is normative does humanity have a future.

With this formulation we have given theological expression to the faith-experiences of mystics throughout the ages. Now we shall see if these insights apply to *Christology*.

MONISTIC CHRISTOLOGY: IS IT POSSIBLE?

What would a monistic Christology look like? Is it possible 1) to believe in Jesus Christ as the Second Person of the Trinity while 2) remaining faithful to One Power/One Presence and 3) to the biblical witness?

The answer to all three questions is a qualified "Yes."

1) *Jesus is the Second Person of the trinity,* but only if we see Him as representative of the divinity-in-us. When we move Jesus of Nazareth to the right hand of God and make Him uniquely divine, He loses all value to us mortals. No longer can He represent anything to be attained or emulated, for if we are merely human we have no claim to anything divine.

As long ago as 1910, Harvard Professor of Church History Ephraim Emerton took issue with those who wanted to make the historical Jesus the only God-man to walk the earth:

> No, it is belief in the perfect humanity of Jesus that alone commends him to us as an attainable example. Without that he remains a mere abstraction, a shadowy image of humanity, a divine apparition clothed with the semblance, but lacking in the reality, of a man.[4]

Fortunately, Metaphysical Christianity solves the problem by seeing Jesus Christ as typical rather than unique. He is the Second Person of the trinity because all sentient beings are that Second Person, the "Son" of Divinity. Jesus is typical because He became what we shall all become, i.e., Christ-consciousness incarnate. Charles Fillmore wrote:

> God, the Father, Divine Mind, had an idea of man, and this idea is his Son, the perfect-man idea, the off- spring of God-Mind. This Son is the Christ, the only begotten of the Father...Manifest man should be as the ideal. He will be when the individual identifies himself with the Christ. When he is identified with anything less than perfection he manifests some degree of imperfection.[5]

2) This gives us a way to look at Jesus Christ and the Christ-in-us that interfaces nicely with *One Presence / One Power* yet stresses the importance of Jesus. A favorite motif for Jesus-models in Christian Truth circles is Wayshower. Quoting Charles Fillmore once more:

> Jesus is the Way-Shower. He came that we might have life more abundantly. He came to awaken man to the possibilities of his own nature. He came to bear witness to Truth. He used the one true way to the realization of eternal life and universal consciousness, therefore His influence on the (human) race cannot be measured. It is infinite and eternal.[6]

Rather than a sacrificial victim proffering his bloody body to appease an angry god, Jesus as Wayshower gives us a map of the unknown road up ahead. A story told to me by a Catholic priest a few years ago provides a good illustration.

> There was a Catholic layperson whose best friend and school-days chum was a Jewish Rabbi. While having lunch one day the Catholic excitedly told the Rabbi that his son was entering a seminary to become a priest.
>
> "So?" the Rabbi said nonchalantly as he stirred his coffee.
> "Don't you understand?" said the Catholic. "He could become a bishop!"
> Unimpressed, the Rabbi said, "So what?"
> At this the Catholic became even more adamant, "Do you realize he could one day become a Cardinal! Or even the first American Pope!"
> The Rabbi yawned, "So?"
> Finally the father said in exasperation, "Goodness! What do you want him to be—Jesus Christ?"
> The Rabbi smiled. "Well, one of our boys made it."

Exactly the point. "One of *our* boys made it." A human being was able to achieve such unity with the Divine-within that He could say with complete conviction, *"I and the Father are one."* (Jn 10:30) To declare that Jesus was human in no way diminishes his divinity. The greatest creeds of Christian orthodoxy have affirmed consistently that Jesus Christ was fully God and fully man. Two examples, drawn from the folio of unimpeachable orthodoxy:

Nicene Creed:

> We believe in one Lord, Jesus Christ, the only Son of God, eternally begotten of the Father, God from God, Light from Light, true God from true God, begotten, not made, one Being with the Father. Through him all things were made. For us men and for our salvation he came down from heaven: by the power of the Holy Spirit he was born of the Virgin Mary, and became man.[7]

Luther's *Small Catechism:*

> 125. Who is Jesus Christ?
> Jesus Christ is true God, begotten of the Father from eternity, and also true man, born of the Virgin Mary.
>
> 128. What two natures, then, are united in Christ?
> The divine and the human natures are united in Christ, both natures together forming one undivided and indivisible person (personal union).[8]

Christian Truth students can affirm the above historic doctrines about the nature of Jesus Christ without reservation. We differ with the theological mainstream in our anthropology—i.e., beliefs about the true nature of humanity—not about the essential Divine-human nature of Jesus Christ. Orthodoxy wants to make the Jesus-event absolutely unique. We see it as normative. Our Christology is highly orthodox otherwise, but it is an "otherwise" that makes all the difference in the Cosmos for mystical Christianity. As we study Christology, we study anthropology as well. Whatever we can say about Jesus we can say potentially about all sentient beings.

So investigation of the nature of Jesus Christ is really peeking into the future for all of us. This makes Christology extremely important and an understanding of Jesus' divine-human nature tantamount to knowing our true selves.

WE STAND WITH ORTHODOXY—IS THAT OK?

Early in Christian history, the Church fathers steered a middle course between the two extremes of *Adoptionism* and *Docetism*. These two tendencies must be understood before we proceed because they are still with us today.

1. Adoptionists said that Jesus was only human, that He had been "adopted" into special supernatural status when God chose Him as His Son. Nineteenth Century Unitarianism was almost wholly adoptionist, as shown by the passage quoted above from Professor Ephraim Emerton's book, *Unitarian Thought*. This view is more popular among educated people today than it was when the Unitarian thinkers of the early-modern era were struggling with Christology.

2. Docetism, on the other hand, has always been more popular with the masses of ordinary Christians. Docetism is the general term used to describe any Christology which says that Jesus was exclusively Divine, bearing no relationship to humanity other than physical resemblance.

Gnosticism usually took this position when it infiltrated Christian thinking. Some docetists went so far as to say Jesus, being God Omnipotent, could not really have been born, grown up, gotten hungry, suffered, and died. He certainly could not have felt angry, sexually aroused, or in need of bodily elimination, docetists insist.

Docetism is much more popular than Adoptionism. While studying at a Protestant seminary, the author was told by a professor that the Divinity of Jesus always preaches better than His humanity. A clearly docetic sermon could be preached from almost any pulpit, but a sermon stressing the human nature of Jesus Christ will raise eyebrows and provoke midnight sessions of the governing board. People want a Savior, not a fellow-servant.

Yet, orthodox Christian theology has always steered a hard, middle course between the rocky shore of adoptionism and the whirlpool of Docetism. Jesus Christ was and is "true God...and also true man." On this point we stand firm with the historic creeds and wizened scholars of the ancient church: Jesus was fully divine and fully human. Where we differ is on the point of unique divinity, as mentioned before.

QUANTITATIVE, NOT QUALITATIVE

To believe in the One Power/One Presence, we must infer that Jesus represents normative humanity. If there truly is only One Power and Presence in the Cosmos, God-power, then the consciousness of Jesus Christ cannot differ qualitatively from the consciousness of any sentient being. Any difference must be purely *quantitative*; He was able to achieve more and understand more than we because He reflected more of the Divine light than we presently do.

This brings us to the third and final question. We are now prepared to look at our model for a Monistic Christology from a biblical perspective.

3. Monistic Christology **is faithful to the biblical record.** In the end, Jesus reflected so much light the world could not hold Him. The New Testament authors were not certain how it happened, but the crucified man Jesus became the risen Lord. And that faith was at first little more than proclamation of the resurrection of Jesus. Studying the preaching of the first century church, as preserved in the letters of Paul, the synoptic gospels, and the book of Acts, we see the main thrust of their mission was to tell the world that Jesus Christ had risen from death.

How seriously can we take such claims?

Many modern biblical scholars have taken a position that is shockingly radical. Some argue that Jesus had little self-consciousness of any role as Messiah, let alone as the Divine Son of God. Several others flatly reject the resurrection as a historical event. Rather, it is a good myth which gives us insights into the nature of life but cannot actually have occurred. These are not rabble-rousers from the fringes of academic cultism; these opinions are held by some of the top biblical scholars of our time.

Of course, being a world-class scholar is no guarantee of accuracy, and there are just as many first-rate professors of biblical studies who believe the resurrection is an historical event. What we can say for certain is this: Whether they could explain it or not, the early Christian community believed in the fact of Jesus' resurrection so completely they were willing to die for the new faith.

BY FAITH ARE WE SAVED

In our discussion of God the Father (Chapter 7), we suggested a way to look at Jesus that sees Him as kin to all humanity. We called the concept by its biblical name, kenosis, and said the idea is based on the description of the Christ-event found in Philippians 2:5-13. Paul declares that Jesus the Christ left His creative union with God—a union in diversity—to empty Himself (Greek, *kenosis*) of that Oneness and take on the form of a "servant."

Kenotic theology is in general disrepute today because it causes severe problems for any theology built upon the Gospel of John. In the fourth gospel Jesus is painted as a God-man possessing supernatural powers and knowledge not available to a mortal. Presumably, that precludes an "emptying" of the kind described by Paul.[9]

However, the Johnnine materials are the latest and least historical of the gospel narratives. Written after 90 A.D., John's Gospel comes at least thirty years after Paul wrote his letter to the church at Philippi. That means the kenotic idea pre-dated John's Christology by several decades and represents one of the earliest Christological formulations in the Bible.

We noted earlier that modern biblical scholarship sees the Jesus pictured in each New Testament source as a literary character through whom the author is trying to explain his own theological viewpoint. This distinction is so important, and so seldom recognized by casual students of the Bible, that it almost cannot be over-emphasized: *When you read the words of Jesus in Matthew, Mark, Luke, and John you are not necessarily reading the words of Jesus. You are reading the words of a literary character created by the authors of Matthew, Mark, Luke, and John to carry the torch of their religious views.*

John's gospel is the easiest to identify as blatantly re-worked theology. At several places the author departs on long, intricate theological discourses which are thinly disguised as sermons, admonitions and even prayers by his Jesus. Johnnine literature knows nothing of the fear shown by the Jesus-character drawn by Mark. John's Jesus is a being of light who has access to supernatural knowledge and whose theology reflects late first-century thinking influenced by Greek ideas such as the Logos.

But we needn't be so hard on John, whomever he was. If you sat down to pen a gospel based on the Jesus stories learned from others, Jesus would speak with your colloquialisms, too. First century Christians had no precedent other than the Hebrew Bible and no information other than oral tradition and a few second-hand, written accounts. This becomes undeniably clear upon reading the introduction to Luke's gospel (Lk. 1:1-4).

Sifting the limited data available, gospel writers told us a story. Their efforts gave us priceless information about Jesus and valuable insights into what the various schools of thought within the first century church were saying about Him. We owe to the gospel writers our deepest appreciation and respect; it is through them alone we learn about the life and ministry of Jesus. In an age before electronic news media, they can perhaps be forgiven if the image they present to us is colored by the passion of their faith. But although they are our sole authentic source for stories about Jesus's life, there is a still better source to learn about Jesus' faith.

PAULINE CHRISTOLOGY TO THE RESCUE

Paul ever wrote all his letters at least ten years before the first gospel—presumably Mark—was written. That means Paul's Christology is older, closer to the events, than any other extant source. In fact, we get better information about the apostolic church from Paul's letters than from the books specifically about that first generation (such as the gospels and Acts). Since the post-Paul books were written forty to sixty years after the ministry of Jesus (His ministry began around 30 A.D.; the gospels and Acts come to us from the period 70-90 A.D.), the Jesus stories and tales of the apostles found in the New Testament actually reflect the issues and ideas of the second generation church and not the problems faced by the founding apostles.

This is obscured by the general misconception about who wrote the gospels. They were not written by the first generation apostles, as Luke clearly testifies in the preamble to his gospel, but by second- or third-hand authors who conceived to write "an orderly account" of the events "just as they were delivered to us by those who from the beginning were eyewitnesses and ministers of the word." When we read Paul's authentic letters, however, we are not reading about the first generation church; we are peeking over Timothy's shoulder as he takes down the rambling, feisty dictation pouring from the mind of the first theological giant of the Christian church, Paul of Tarsus. Paul's Christology is, not surprisingly, quite amiable to metaphysical interpretation.

Keying on Paul, whose Christ-figure is a pre-existent entity subservient to the Divine[10], we can draw a generalization based on the mystical tradition and experience: If Jesus descended from union with God, emptying Himself of Divine Mind, and if we are His brothers and sisters, then we did, too. As we have said, the cornerstone of metaphysical Christology rests on the deep conviction that Jesus was what we shall be; He is the Wayshower. If He were uniquely Divine, His deeds and words would be utterly useless to us. How can sinful, alienated humanity emulate the Divine? Only as a sacrificial lamb to be slaughtered in our place to rescue us from an angry God would Jesus Christ have value. And frankly, that kind of God would be no bargain.

But if Jesus the Christ is one of us, then everything we can say about Him can also be said about ourselves. This is such a radical, startling concept to many Christians that it sounds outrageous. It requires a whole new orientation toward the historic Jesus. Instead of a different spiritual being, He becomes the pattern of our own unfoldment. Instead of a distant demi-god who walked among us out of compassion for our ineptitude, Jesus emerges from our ranks. Instead of showing how far beneath the Divine we humans are, Jesus shows us how high we can go. In the words of a popular song, the Jesus event "lifts us up where we belong."[11]

BRIDGING THE GAP

For metaphysical Christians, Jesus-the-Christ is a bridge-concept which opens the way to our true nature as incarnations of God. Like Him, we emptied ourselves of that divinity and took on the form of a servant. Like Him, we shall return to the Father/Mother God after we fully realize our potential, learn our lessons, and graduate from this level of existence to whatever awaits us.

The process is more open to us now that we have seen His example. One of our number has achieved union with God; a hometown boy has made the big time. If we believe He did it—and that He is our older brother—then we must believe in our own potential as well. Belief in the possibility of unity with God empowers us to make greater strides in spiritual growth. By faith are we saved from futility, meaninglessness, and despair.

ON TO SOTERIOLOGY...

In the last three chapters we looked at the Trinity. We began with *Spirit*, because the mystic believes Spirit undergirds everything, supplying the very Cosmos with the Power to be. *Father* is the term used by Christians to describe their relationship with that Presence/Power. Neither raw energy nor uncaring mechanics stand beneath Reality, spinning galaxies on their mindless journey to oblivion. At the heart of the Cosmos we hear the voice of Jesus crying, *"Abba! Father!"* Life itself cares, because God-power is love. Jesus, as our Wayshower pointing to the *Son*, is both unique and normative. He is unique because, in the words of Emerson:

> Alone in history he estimated the greatness of man. One man was true to what is in you and in me. He saw that God incarnates himself in man, and evermore goes forth anew to take possession of his World.[12]

Jesus is *normative* because He is the pattern all sentient beings must eventually achieve. As Dietrich Bonhoeffer pointed out, no one will "become like Jesus;" that was his distinct identity. Everyone will become the Christ, fully attuned to his/her Divine spirit.

This kind of trinitarian theology is both orthodox and radical, biblical and existential. It is orthodox because these views are based on the middle ground walked by Church thinkers between the two extremes of *Adoptionism* (which said Jesus was strictly human, chosen by God for a special task) and *Docetism* (which held Jesus was pure Divinity with no humanity whatsoever); it is radical because such a Christology makes Jesus a universal example of the divine-human paradox instead of the one and only God-man of dualistic theologies.

It is biblical because we make use of concepts like *kenosis* (emptying of divine nature to become human) and yet existential because, after *de-mythologizing* the message of its pre-scientific worldview, it allows us to find God in our own consciousness and in the community of believers as well as hanging from the cross.

We have noted that Christology becomes *anthropology* because Jesus Christ is true man, the image of God written in large print for even the spiritually nearsighted to see. But we cannot stop here, for Jesus was more than a good example. His incarnation, life, teaching, crucifixion, and resurrection accomplished something for the sake of the human race. Biblically, this has often been likened to a sacrificial lamb offered for the sins of others. Such bloodthirsty imagery we utterly reject as unworthy of the God Who would be called *"Abba! Father!"*

Tough questions still remain as we struggle to make sense of the Jesus Christ event in the light of mystical awareness of the God-within. How are we to understand the work of Jesus Christ? How did one man's obscure life and senseless death fling open the prison doors and set free the spirit of humanity? In what way did He overcome sin and death, making eternal life readily available to all? Can we speak meaningfully of *sin, guilt, atonement, and redemption* without sacrificing the high insights of Incarnational Monism?

We turn next to this most important topic, the study of salvation itself, *Soteriology.*

CHECK YOUR KNOWLEDGE

1. Explain the following: *Tritheism, Henotheism, Kerygma, De-Mythologizing, Wayshower, Anthropology, Adoptionism, Docetism, Unitarianism, Logos.*

2. How does *monotheism* differ from *monism*?

3. Which concept is more "popular" among the rank-and-file of mainline Christianity, Docetism or Adoptionism? Why?

4. Does Metaphysical Christianity agree or disagree with orthodoxy on the full humanity/full divinity of Jesus? What is the difference?

5. How does Pauline Christology help mystical/metaphysical theology? Is Paul in agreement with the Johnnine materials?

6. How are we like Jesus? How is Jesus absolutely unique?

QUESTIONS FOR DISCUSSION

1. Isn't it blasphemous to suggest that we are sons and daughters of God? What gives us the right to make such an audacious claim?

2. List and discuss the supernatural beings in your childhood pantheon. In what ways are you still dualistic?

3. How does *myth* differ from falsehood? Can myth be truer than an historical event? How?

4. In what respect is Jesus the Wayshower for Christians? Is His role as Wayshower closer to a *docetic* or *adoptionist* Christology?

5. Mystical/metaphysical Christianity differs with the historic creeds inasmuch as they assert the *unique* divinity of Jesus. What do we believe about His Divinity, and why? Is it biblical, traditional, experiential, or rational?

6. Write a one-page summary of you personal creed, covering at least your "doctrine of the Trinity" and theological anthropology (i.e., what you believe about human-ity). Read and discuss these in a group of Truth students. (Any surprises?)

NOTES

1. Eckhart in Holden & Capps, p. 116.

2. Anthony F. C. Wallace, *Religion: An Anthropological View* (NY: Random House, 1966), pp. 72-73.

3. Rudolf Bultmann, *Kerygma and Myth*. Hans Werner Bartsch, ed. (NY: Harper Torchbooks, 1961), p. 10.

4. Ephraim Emerton, *Unitarian Thought* (London: The Lindsey Press, 1913), p. 164.

5. Fillmore, *Dynamics*, pp. 43-44.

6. *IBID.*, p. 285.

7. Nicene Creed, *Book of Worship for U. S. Forces*, p. 718.

8. Martin Luther, pp. 102-105.

9. George Arthur Buttrick, series ed., *The Interpreter's Dictionary of the Bible*, Vol. 3 (Nashville, TN: Abingdon, 1962), p. 7.

10. Cf. Philippians 2:6-7; I Corinthians 15:25-28.

11. "Up Where We Belong" from the Paramount Motion Picture *An Officer and a Gentleman,* lyrics by Will Jennings, 1981.

12. Emerson, p. 100.

SOTERIOLOGY

Chapter Nine

Sin, Atonement and the Work of Jesus Christ

Therefore, if any one is in Christ, he is a new creation; the old has passed away, behold, the new has come. All this is from God, who through Christ reconciled us to himself and gave us the ministry of reconciliation; that is, in Christ God was reconciling the world to himself, not counting their trespasses against them, and entrusting to us the message of reconciliation.

II Corinthians 5:17-19 (REV)

In the fourth century before Christ, Plato wrote a series of running debates between his mentor, Socrates, and various other Greeks. Most of these discussions, fortunately, have come down to us in whole segments called *Dialogues.* Although Socrates acts as the main character in the *Dialogues* just as Jesus holds center stage in the gospels, in both instances we are dealing with literary characters whose words are influenced by the stage business given them by the authors.

Let's listen to a few key exchanges between Socrates, our hero, and Euthyphro, a young man who is on his way to testify against his own father for impiety. Remembering that Socrates would be forced to drink hemlock for the same offense, we can see why Plato raises the central issue of this dialogue.

EUTHYPHRO: Yes, I should say that what all the gods love is pious and holy, and the opposite which they all hate, impious.

SOCRATES: Ought we to enquire to the truth of this, Euthyphro, or simply to accept the mere statement on our own authority and that of others? What do you say?

EUTHYPHRO: We should enquire; and I believe that the statement will stand the test of enquiry.

SOCRATES: We shall know better, my good friend, in a little while. The point which I should first wish to understand is *whether the pious or holy is beloved of the gods because it is holy, or holy because it is beloved of the gods.*

EUTHYPHRO: I do not understand your meaning, Socrates.[1]

No one worries about whether Plato put the words into Socrates' mouth when they read the *Dialogues*. Even though it is highly unlikely that young Plato was standing behind a pillar of the temple, quill in hand, copying the words in shorthand while Socrates twisted poor, egotistical Euthyphro into an Athenian mental pretzel. It is also highly unlikely that eye-witnesses transcribed the Sermon on the Mount or its parallel version in Luke's Sermon on the Plain (Lk 6:17-49). But when biblical scholars show us the secondary sources and conflicting testimony within New Testament documents, some people find their faith threatened. Why?

One reason is that Jesus Christ defines reality for many people in a way that a mere philosopher never could. Jesus has *Authority* in the minds of millions, and when our authorities waver it is as though the four corners of the universe tremble at the thought.

This is the first question Socrates asks at the beginning of the passage quoted above. How much authority should we give to Authority? Shall we accept all traditional ideas because questioning key beliefs sends us groping in the dark? The more profound our respect for the authority, the greater our terror if it should prove unstable. Most folks like to live in a world where the rules stay constant; questioning minds like Socrates' would challenge us to examine our deepest assumptions.

Euthyphro doesn't realize what he's admitted when Socrates gets him to agree that inquiry is better than authority, but we do. Ideas must be tested, we said in Chapter 3, both by critical analysis and practical application, and once we accept that premise all external authorities have fallen.

After wringing this concession from unsuspecting Euthyphro, Socrates (or is it Plato?) next asks the most profound theological question found in classical Greek philosophy. Properly understood, the answer to this question divides people into two camps and creates a nearly irreconcilable rift between those opposing forces. One view or the other must be true. Everything in theology depends on how we answer.

Socrates asks Euthyphro *"whether the pious or holy is (1) beloved of the gods because it is holy, or (2) holy because it is beloved of the gods?"*

Euthyphro frankly confesses Socrates has lost him there. He needn't feel alone. Most people need to read the formula several times to grasp its importance. The distinction is not trivial, but absolutely definitive in religious thought. Socrates' question is not mere sophistry. Its implications for theology are enormous, because before any religion can speak of *Sin* it must understand what makes an act *good* or *evil*. Appeal to authority won't do. We must look at the question and decide for ourselves what constitutes the holy and the unholy. To further compound the gravity of this question for Christian theology, Socrates rightly shows that, when viewed from theocentric perspective, there are only two possible answers.

1) AN ACT OR BELIEF IS GOOD/HOLY BECAUSE GOD APPROVES OF IT.

While at first glance this may seem a highly admirable view, stressing loyalty in God, there are some profound difficulties with a theology which says goodness is determined by God's Will. (See Fig. 9-1)

$$\frac{\text{ACTION/BELIEF}}{\text{GOD'S WILL}} = \text{GOOD}$$

Fig. 9-1 *"GOOD"* depends on whether or not God approves. There is no *GOOD* except those acts, beliefs, events, practices which God has blessed with His endorsement.

If an action is good because God approves of it, then God can operate by complete whimsy. While we might be inclined to allow God to act whimsically, the danger becomes apparent when we realize that various religious zealots have used this argument to justify all manner of heinous misdeeds. If we are convinced God approves, any act of greed or violence can be called an act of God, hence made morally acceptable. People can feel justified in their racism, sexism, and religious prejudices as long as they can find a proof-text from their favorite source of authority (Bible, Koran, Marx/Lenin, etc.) Shakespeare saw how dangerous unchecked reliance on proof-texting could be. One of his characters in *The Merchant of Venice* grumbles:

> In religion,
> What damned error, but some sober brow
> Will bless it, and approve it with a text?

With the first option Socrates gave Euthyphro, there is no standard of good or bad, right or wrong, except Divine fiat. God could declare black is white and night is day; both would be correct if our theology is predicated on God's authority and not some sort of eternal principle undergirding all Reality. This brings us to the other option.

2) AN ACT OR BELIEF IS BELOVED BY GOD BECAUSE IT IS GOOD.

Reversing the equation (Fig. 9-2), we see that God's approval comes because an act or belief is inherently good. This model suggests there is a standard of good which is so lofty that even the Divine must conform to it.

$$\frac{\text{ACTION/BELIEF}}{\text{GOOD}} = \text{GOD'S WILL}$$

Fig. 9-2 God's approval depends on whether or not the *ACTION / BELIEF* is *GOOD*. Goodness is self-validating, because it is a Standard (Principle) to which God *must conform*, because It is not in His nature to do otherwise.

Of course, this means the true Divinity is that Standard. Nothing can be higher than God, so if there is a principle of goodness to which God must conform then that Principle must be God. This, of course, describes Platonic idealism. There is no doubt which answer he wanted us to choose. for Plato, the Beautiful and the Good are eternal categories what have inherent value. God cannot be less than the Beautiful and the Good, nor can God change the Beautiful and the Good by Divine decree. Good is good because it possesses inherent goodness, not because God validates its goodness with His approval.

Which is exactly what mystical/metaphysical Christianity, in its modern expression as the Christian Truth movement, has been saying for over a century. God is Principle. God is the very Standard of goodness Itself. Either we live in a Universe governed by law and principle—albeit complex and apparently erratic at times—or we live under chaos, subject to Divine whimsy. We shall have much more to say later about the random factors which God seems to have programmed into the super-structure of Reality (Chapter 14, Divine Order), but for now let's just affirm that God must function in a consistent, orderly way which still allows for human response and freedom.

CHOOSE TODAY WHOM YE SHALL SERVE

Plato forces us to choose between a God who stands above goodness, validating it with His will, and a God who is the Goodness-principle Itself. The biblical record is inconsistent on this subject, with the OT generally in favor of whimsy (e.g., Joshua, I & II Kings) the NT usually supporting God-as-Goodness (e.g., synoptic gospels, John's gospel, I John, James, most of Paul). Christian tradition, too, is divided on the matter. Mysticism, however, has refused to see God apart from Goodness, often insisting (as with Meister Eckhart) that God is compelled by His nature to be loving, good, kind, and responsive to the receptive soul. With this background we are now able to consider the nature of sin and its consequences.

Unless we agree what constitutes *good*, we cannot hope to construct a meaningful theology of *sin* and *atonement*. If sin is the absence of good, we need to know what we're missing. So we must focus our discussion on *good* and its lack, which we call *sin*.

AND NOW A WORD ABOUT "SIN"

"Sin" is a dirty word for a lot of mystical/metaphysical Christians. We don't like to talk about sin, partly because many Truth students have come from religious traditions which tend to over-emphasize human frailty and guilt, but also because we have seldom taken time to think through the implications of sin and guilt. Early in this work we decided that no corner of the Christian world-window would escape our scrutiny if there were even a hint of Divine light seeping through the stained-glass designs shaped by hands who came before us. An understanding of sin would give us a glimpse at the problems within the divine-human power of will, because an act of will is certainly required for any sort of behavior to be called sin under any definition imaginable to us. Hence, we need to unpack the symbolism of sin and make it intelligible to modern minds.

Another function of theology is to "establish dialogue within the theological circle," and that purpose is served whenever mystical/metaphysical Christians tear down walls of thought separating us from the mainstream of the Faith. If Christian Truth churches are ever going to dialogue across denominational lines with other liberals, such as Protestants and like-minded mystics of other communions, Truth students will need to learn what excites their near-neighbors on the Christian family tree and how to incorporate some of that excitement into the emergent metaphysical theologies while remaining true to the premises already discussed in this study.

And *sin* is an exciting subject. It has kept preachers in business for almost two thousand years. We noted in our discussion of *Gifts/Fruit of the Spirit* (Chapter 6) that the Apostle Paul seemed to relish trotting out long lists of no-no's to this observation let us add that the popularity of daytime soap-operas and prime-time series which show the seamy side of human nature show that the public has always agreed with Paul. Gossip, the soap-opera of everyday life, unfortunately continues to be a favorite pastime among church people and brings a whole new meaning to the word *sin.*

A complete discussion of sin would move us into the realm of *theological ethics,* also known as *moral theology.* We want to focus our attention on the remedies and not the dis-ease, so our emphasis here will be appropriately directed toward *at-one-ment* and ways to affect a healing consciousness when sin has wounded the individual. However, we must at least briefly discuss the nature of sin in order that we can meaningfully speak about ways to overcome sinfulness. As we said earlier, this means we must decide what constitutes *good,* because sin is the absence of that goodness. Since that which is *ultimately good* is synonymous with God, our discussion must begin with God's nature itself.

HEBREW CONSCIOUSNESS

The biblical library is no place to look for harmony, but on this point there is a surprising degree of agreement. God is *Goodness* itself, and His goodness is described in the Old Testament as 1) Steadfast Love (Hebrew: *Hesed*), 2) Justice tempered by 3) Mercy or Kindness. This formula is expressed frequently throughout the OT, but perhaps the finest statement of God's character is reflected by the prophet Micah:

> "With what shall I come before the Lord,
>   and bow myself before God on high?
> Shall I come before him with burnt offerings,
>   with calves a year old?
> Will the Lord be pleased with thousands of rams,
>   with ten thousands of rivers of oil?
> Shall I give my first-born for my transgression,
>   the fruit of my body for the sin of my soul?

> He has showed you. O man, what is good;
> and what does the Lord require of you
> but to do justice, and to love kindness,
> and to walk humbly with your God?[2]

The quality of *Justice* is an interesting concept which alone could be the subject of a whole volume; it has inspired quite a few works on theological ethics. From a metaphysical point of view, Justice can be seen as combination of the four divine-human powers studies thus far: *Understanding, Wisdom, and Power* as enacted into being by the *Will*. Some theologians have said that *Steadfast Love* is not likely in society at large, but *Justice* is possible.

Steadfast love (*Hesed*) means loyalty, the kind of devotion a good king could reasonably expect from his subjects. Implied in the term is a contract between two parties, called the *Covenant* or *Testament* in biblical terms. The ruler treats his subjects with justice and they respond with steadfast love, i.e., dutiful service and faithfulness. Of course, this exactly describes the Hebrew idea of a covenantal relationship between Yahweh, the God of Israel, and His chosen people.

But even divine justice must be mitigated by an even greater divine *Mercy*, often translated *Kindness*. Jewish thought has usually held, contrary to widespread belief in Christian circles, that people are capable of keeping the Law, all of the Law. However, Jewish pragmatism surfaced when ancient writers stressed the merciful kindness of Yahweh. Knowing that humans could keep the Law was no guarantee they would readily do it. God must be merciful with us, they reasoned, because few could stand before the King and Judge in a state of righteousness under the Law. In fact, the entire body of the Law and the sacrificial system for forgiveness of sin was another example of God's merciful kindness. He could have just as easily abandoned all humanity to drift aimlessly in lawlessness and sin, which to the Jew are one and the same.

The OT concept of divine goodness, then, describes loyal love, supreme justice, and even greater mercy. Life, too, must reflect that steadfast love, justice and mercy, or the whole system is a contradiction. therefore, to the Hebrew, the world was a system which operated according to divine principles.

Sin, to the ancient Hebrew, was any attempt to negate that orderly flow by stepping outside of the Law. Law-less-ness, in its many forms, was sin. The greatest sin for the ancient Hebrew was idolatry, worship of something other than Yahweh. If God is One, any attempt to move beyond Oneness to worship god in the plural was a threat to the whole system of divine Law and Order. There could be no other gods beside Yahweh, because on His steadfast love/justice/merciful kindness rested the hope of fallible humans for reconciliation with their neighbors and with the orderly flow of life itself.

OT writers generally gave Yahweh credit for personal authority above any abstract standard of good, but none would be so rash to suggest that He ever acted in any manner contrary to His nature, which was steadfast love/justice/merciful kindness. He simply could not be unloving, unjust, unkind, or merciless. Conversely, humans could be. And that formed the basis for the cry of the prophets to national repentance for the whole people of Israel. Sin, therefore, was an attempt to negate the Law, which was summarized so aptly by Micah: "Do justice, love kindness, and walk humbly with your God."

NEW TESTAMENT CONSCIOUSNESS

Christian writers, heeding the words of Jesus, saw their task as fulfilling the Law rather than setting it aside. Even so, Christian thinkers began the work of re-thinking the ancient faith almost immediately after the resurrection in the light of that world-changing occurrence. No longer was justice enough, even when softened by merciful kindness. No longer did they owe dutiful love to God and neighbor, because Jesus had introduced the radical new concept of *Selfless Love (Agape)* to squander recklessly on even the most unloveable. God's nature was now understood by reference to the life, teachings, and character of Jesus Christ. Not a benign despot who doles out mercy, God was now seen as a loving Father Who longs for His children to return unto Him even when they are in full rebellion and have raced off to attempt to overturn every divine law.

In the New Testament we meet a different God concept, a God Who comes to us in worldly weakness and Whose power is set free through utter defeat: Not Caesar on a throne but Jesus on a cross. In the paradox of this central Christian image—Jesus Christ crucified—we find a key to understand the absolute goodness of God, i.e., His self-giving love which breaks the power of even the most terrible circumstances.

The crucifixion has always been a problem for Christians. Even though some branches of the faith have chosen to emphasize the suffering of Jesus almost to the point of morbidity, the early Church agreed with Paul that the cross was a "scandal" and a "stumbling-block" (my irreverent paraphrase: *banana peel*).

The cross was not used as a symbol for the faith of Jesus until several centuries had passed, partly because it was still the Roman government's treatment of choice for criminal conduct and partly because the Church had to answer a lot of questions within its ranks about what sense it made for Jesus to die such an ignoble death. Christians began to see the paradox of the Cross as a powerful symbol which speaks to something deep inside of us: It is the very absurdity of Calvary which makes the crucifixion of Jesus Christ so real.

Could Jesus have avoided this nasty fate? Certainly. He had several escape routes open, including simply leaving Jerusalem before they arrested Him. Instead, He chose to embrace the cross, showing us that even in the midst of scandalous defeat and apparently utter failure, God's One Power/One Presence is at work. The symbol of defeat becomes the central image of Christian triumph. Good Friday gives way to Easter morning. All bets are off. We can't expect disaster any more, because God empowers us to break through to health, happiness, and prosperity even if we seem utterly ruined by worldly standards. We can look at the cross and see it as a mystical symbol of the One Power/One Presence, God the Good, Omnipotent. We'll say more about its symbolism later.

UNDERSTANDING SIN: RABEL'S RECIPE

To talk about Sin and Atonement, we first need to define sin. That is a tough task. Modern life suggests that one person's sin is another person's freedom. Yet, life is full of heroism and horror, and we could not live in a world which provided no clues to decide between good and un-good. For our working definition we'll turn to Ed Rabel, an original thinker and teacher at the Unity School of Christianity. He blended biblical concepts with modern Christian mystical thought by this simple recipe: *Sin is an attempt to negate Divine Ideas.*

OT consciousness held that sin is an attempt to negate the Divine Ideas of loyal love, justice, and merciful kindness (Micah 6:8). NT writers viewed sin as an attempt to negate the Divine Ideas of love, life, prosperity, health, and forgiveness. Thus Rabel's recipe, which is both comprehensive and easy to apply, bridges OT and NT views of sin.

It works for theology, too. Virtually everything which today's theologians would call sin are anti-human deeds and unhealthy attitudes: murder, racism, sexism, homophobia, drug abuse, irresponsible use of resources, stealing, inflicting emotional or physical pain. All these can be understood as attempts to negate Divine Ideas. Murder is an attempt to negate the Divine Idea of Life. Theft is an attempt to overturn the orderly flow of Divine Prosperity. Racism, sexism and nationalism are attempts to violate the Divine Idea of Love. Mr. Rabel would probably agree with Paul Tillich's dictum that *sin is separation.* By choosing sin instead of wholeness, we separate ourselves from what God intends us to be.

PROCESS THEOLOGY

Plato was right, too. Good is good because of its inherent goodness, not because God wills it. Divine Ideas are Spiritual Law under which God's Holy Spirit functions. But rather than a set of rules governing Divine action, Divine Ideas are kinetic law, God-in-expression. *God the Father* is the same as *God the active Spirit*, both are the same as *God the Son*, or Christ-consciousness.

In recent years it has become fashionable for theologians to speak of God as a Process. We might say that Christian Truth students see the God-Process as a Totality, a Unity. God is the goodness-principle in action, the process of goodness unfolding in the real world.

CHARTING THE SIN-RECONCILIATION CYCLE

Any attempt to negate Divine Ideas—to work against the good which God is always trying to manifest in our lives—is bound to have an unhealthy effect on the individual. Theology, borrowing a term from anthropology, might call such behavior Maladaptive. We can chart how its mischief operates in our lives until we learn to overcome sin through faith in Christ, which is the most adaptive behavior for the human situation (Fig. 9-3). Faith in Christ-within is not only good theology, Christians believe it is the healthiest growth-pattern available to humanity. We shall see if that contention holds under closer investigation of the Sin-Reconciliation Cycle.

Fig. 9-3 **THE SIN-RECONCILIATION CYCLE.**

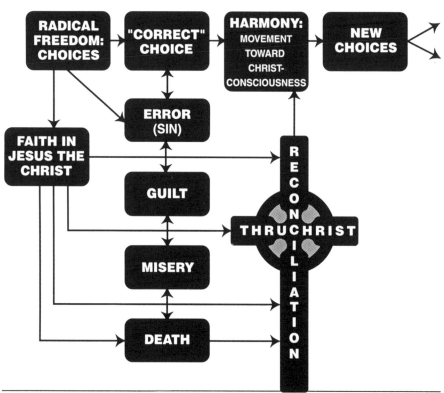

Fig. 9-3: The downward arrows through *Sin-Guilt-Misery-Death* also have upward-pointing tips, indicating it is possible to climb up from these lower states of consciousness by individual effort. *Faith in Jesus the Christ* interrupts the downward movement in consciousness, breaking the cycle at all levels and ushering the individual into harmony by *Reconciliation thru Christ,* which means bringing the person to a renewed awareness of the in-dwelling Christ. This moves him/her into position to make new choices and repeat the cycle, always returning to affirm the in-dwelling Christ whenever *Sin* (error) results from wrong *Choices.* At the lowest level (*Death*), we have dropped to stagnation by an act of will, and therefore another act of will, i.e., reaffirming our Oneness with the Christ, comes and gets us. When someone has sunk this low and rises again to new life, it is a true resurrection-experience.

1. RADICAL FREEDOM. Implicit in the human condition is freedom. Not all Christian thinkers have agreed, notably Reformationist John Calvin, but modern theology is fairly unanimous in affirming that we humans are free to behave as outrageously as we can imagine. To wander as far from the optimum path as error beliefs can carry us. We have a divine right to be wrong.

But this also means we have the power to choose good. Without the ability to choose un-good (evil), there is no freedom to choose good. Radical freedom gives us the tools to follow the rules. Without the power of Will operating in a totally free person, no growth is possible. Thus the interaction of Will and freedom kicks open the first door leading from Sin to Christ- consciousness. Next we must consider freedom's consequences, the price we must pay to achieve saving faith in Christ-within.

2. ERROR (Sin). Wrong choices are part of learning. Children cannot master solid geometry before stumbling around in simple arithmetic, floundering before the dragons of multiplication, subtraction, addition, division. Every step of the way, errors show us where the road is by marking its edges, showing where the road-is-not. In snow country, tall sticks mark the outside edges of the highway for snowplows. Errors give us that sort of information, steering us down a clear path by showing the drifts of snow or tangle of weeds along life's highway.

However, we must not make the mistake of romanticizing misdeeds; some errors are more painful and less innocuous than a slip in math or science. There is a vast difference between arriving at an incorrect quotient in long division and arriving at a supermarket to commit armed robbery. Thankfully, for most of us behaviors so blatantly harmful as armed robbery have been fenced off our life-highways by moral standards (mores) built into us through life experience. If someone seriously argued in favor of armed robbery as a morally correct action, we might question that person's sincerity or sanity.

Humans live very closely with other humans, so we must have codes of behavior which facilitate cooperation and harmony while allowing for healthy competition. Codes will vary quite profoundly from culture to culture, but the key element in each is that the approved behavior will contribute to the health and well-being of the society at large, hence will be *adaptive*. To rob a grocery store is an act which is harmful to the good of the greater society, hence stealing in that context is an *error*, a *sin*. It is also an *attempt to negate the Divine Idea of Prosperity* and therefore qualifies metaphysically as sin.

However, stealing horses from another tribe was an act of bravery for the Lakotah Sioux. Young men proved their courage and enhanced the tribe's wealth/prestige by raiding other tribes, which by the definition we have been applying would make such behavior adaptive and therefore not sinful. Stealing horses from a brother Lakotah in the next lodge was just plain horse-theft and an act of disloyalty totally repugnant to their value system, a cardinal sin. Why? Because the greater good of the larger society was not served by intra-tribal theft. If a man could not lie down at night without worrying that his cousin in the next lodge might cut the ropes and make off with his prize ponies, no one would band together and mutual defense, corporate food gathering, and cross-family marriage would all become impossible.

Does horse theft under those conditions meet the metaphysical definition for Sin? Was it an attempt to negate a Divine Idea? Right the contrary. Raiding other tribes for horses, which was seldom violent in the days before the white man, was a method of opening the tribe to increased prosperity and redistributing that wealth throughout the society. No one tribe could hoard horses, because at some point the herd became too large to defend from stealthy raiders.

In a way, raiding for horses was a kind of primitive reverse-income tax, the poorer groups receiving compensation from their richer neighbors and thus leveling wealth in Native American culture. Raiding also provided rites of passage for young braves to leave childhood and become full adults, an important function in any social system. Today, we hand young people the keys to the car and, eventually, a high school diploma. In the society of the Plains Indians, becoming a man meant earning your own transportation by raiding another tribe for a horse. The only diploma was the right to "dance" the deed by the fire once the young man returned from his exploits. To be consistent with what we have said so far about human behavior and religious teaching, we cannot call horse theft among the Lakotah, *Sin*.

Anthropology comes to the rescue of theology at this point. Murder, in-group theft, adultery, and incest are outlawed because they are *maladaptive*. These prevent group cohesion, growth, happiness, and well-being. Societies which have allowed murder, unrestricted theft, open adultery, and incest may have existed in human history, but these behaviors are so destructive that any social order which mistakenly calls them "good" will not last long. There is an objective quality to sinful behavior which outpictures both in the life of the individual and in society at large.

3. GUILT: OBJECTIVE AND SUBJECTIVE. Although no known society has openly advocated such maladaptive behavior as murder or adultery, every group of humans has had its murderers and adulterers. Sin defines the road, but there are those who stray so far afield they have great difficulty finding the path again. Human nature seems to work against us just when we need clear thinking the most. Studies show that people tend either to 1) rationalize their errors by blaming them on people or circumstances, or 2) assume responsibility for events over which they had no control. Psychologists call these two tendencies *under-responsible* and *over-responsible* behavior.

UNDER-RESPONSIBLE BEHAVIOR: *"IT AIN'T MY FAULT!"*

An *under-responsible* person refuses to admit she could ever be wrong; it is always the other person's mistake, or events forced them to act that way. The slogan for under-responsible people is, "It ain't my fault!"

Al Capone earns the prize as history's most under-responsible gangster. When he was finally brought to justice, did the great mobster confess his sin before the nation? Did he say, "OK—you got me. I was wrong!"? No way. Listen to what Al Capone actually said:

> I have spent the best years of my life giving people the lighter pleasures, helping them have a good time, and all I get is abuse, the existence of a hunted man."[3]

OVER-RESPONSIBLE BEHAVIOR: *"I'M THE GUILTY ONE—I DID IT!"*

If under-responsible folks refuse to admit their errors, *over-responsible* ones take the blame for everything. If you had a flat while driving him to the hospital for an emergency appendectomy, the over-responsible person apologizes and feels he has caused your mishap. These folks mistakenly believe they have the power to work havoc on a wide-scale just by coming in contact with people, place and things. "If I had not asked Uncle Chester to eat Christmas dinner with us, he would never have slipped on the ice in front of his house late that night and broken his hip," they moan. They feel guilty if someone else mistreats them; returning a badly burned steak at a restaurant is impossible. They even feel guilty if the weather is bad on a day they planned a trip, because if they had not planned to go the bad weather might not have arrived to punish them and spoil the day for everyone else.

OBJECTIVE GUILT

What we have been discussing is guilt, and we have been looking at its effects on human consciousness. As suggested above, there is an *objective* quality to sin. If we act contrary to God's design for a healthy person—e.g., express personal power at the expense of others for greed or twisted pleasure—we have cut ourselves off from both our humanity and our divine nature as well.

Sentient beings are best understood as a divine-human paradox, a complex of spiritual and physical energy brought into existence through Divinity's emptying Itself of fullness so that a bit of itself can know creativity and growth. When we do things which run us afoul of that process—when we try to void out the divine idea stamped in our spiritual nature—we stray into sin. There is little doubt that we suffer real, actual disadvantages by sinning, much like a person butting his head against a stone wall. God, however, does not need to punish sin any more than society needs to jail people who butt into stone walls.

If we hurt anything by sin it is ourselves. Hence, we can speak of objective guilt, which is another way of saying self-chosen spiritual harm. This model speaks to the idea captured recently by those who say that *S-I-N* stands for *Self Inflicted Nonsense.* Under-responsible people. i.e., those who will not face their culpability for maladaptive behavior, still suffer by sinning, just as the person beating his head against the wall will experience pain whether or not he acknowledges its source.

Sometimes objective guilt results from things we do, but other times we harm ourselves by choosing not to act. Refusing to help someone in genuine need, the sin of the priest and the Levite in the Good Samaritan parable, causes us to miss an opportunity for growth. Laziness in our devotional life keeps our spiritual batteries discharged and less able to meet those daily mini-crises with Divine Ideas. Falling into a rut in marriage causes even the brightest love to fade. Those failures have traditionally been called *sins of omission*, and there is no good reason for abandoning the term.

Conversely, those acts which we willfully perpetrate against our higher, divine nature are *sins of commission*. Both generate objective guilt because both stunt the perpetrator's spiritual growth.

SUBJECTIVE GUILT

If *under-responsible* people harm themselves objectively, *over-responsible* behavior results in *subjective guilt*, which is the anxiety we feel when knowing we've done something we should have avoided or avoided something we should have done. Often subjective guilt can be too self-critical, as with an *over-responsible* person, but it can also be right on target. When caught in a self-protecting lie, the moral person rightly feels guilty.

This kind of guilt, held in balance by a healthy ego, generates the energy needed to take corrective actions in our attitudes and behavior. If getting caught in a lie were not painful for most of us, human society would be a network of falsehoods. Sometimes, one wonders if a little more subjective guilt-work isn't needed to tone up our sagging truth muscles, especially for our political leaders.

Here again we have an example of the middle path, this time between the dichotomy formed by *under-responsible/over-responsible* behaviors. Too little responsibility for maladaptive actions and the person suffers objective guilt with scant opportunity to correct the problem because he experiences no anxiety to energize his quest for improvement. Too much responsibility for actions, taking the blame when he is a bystander, and the person's self-confidence is paralyzed by anxiety so that no growth is possible. In both instances, unresolved guilt generates stagnation. We fail to grow. This state we shall call by its real name:

4. MISERY. Locked in a sin-guilt downward spiral, the sinner experiences misery, which is the outpicturing of wrong choices and the resulting stress those errors bring on the emotional/spiritual health of the person. Obviously, this can happen whether or not the person consciously realizes his misery. An under-responsible person will blame everyone else but suffer nonetheless. Misery also knows no distinction between objective and subjective guilt: whether a person feels guilty or not, sin works its mischief by de-humanizing the sinner, robbing him/her of opportunities to grow in Christ-consciousness. Racism, sexism, and religious prejudices can be unspoken assumptions—sins of omission, never acted upon—but will nevertheless keep the bigot from understanding the universality of God's spirit in all sentient beings.

Some of life's most miserable circumstances can masquerade as success and happiness, so we can never judge by external appearances how spiritually advanced a person might be. Too many outwardly happy marriages show the first signs of distress only after one or the other files for divorce. Too many seemingly successful men and women end their lives by suicide.

The price paid for objective and subjective sins of omission or commission is a poor quality of life. Billionaires like the late Howard Hughes, living in fear of disease and becoming a virtual prisoner of his own wealth, cannot be said to be prosperous. Athletes who pump their bodies full of drugs cannot be called healthy. Misery is the outpicturing of bad choices and error-beliefs, but the Apostle Paul had the best commentary on where sin finally leads if unchecked: *"The wages of sin is death..."*[4]

5. DEATH: UTTER STAGNATION. Some early metaphysical teachers, notably Charles Fillmore, believed that we need not die. They saw death resulting from error-beliefs, not some natural process begun by birth. Other Truth teachers have said physical death is not the issue; Spiritual death looms as the only danger of any consequence when we relentlessly pursue paths leading away from mystical awareness of God-within. Those who believe our bodies can regenerate and never know physical death say sin, as error-belief, drags us down to die. Death, they insist, is not necessarily part of the human condition. We expect to grow old, weaken, and die, and so our belief in that process actually causes aging and death.

PROBLEMS WITH LITERAL "REGENERATION"

As appealing as this teaching may be, we can find no analog to such a fantastic doctrine in biblical writings, the history of mystical Christian theology, or life experience. Jesus of Nazareth died, and if anyone could claim Christ-consciousness in its fullest human expression surely it was He. His resurrection is a victory over death, not a denial of death's reality. If a spiritual state exists in which there is no aging, no weakening, and no physical death, as all Christians believe there is, it must certainly exist beyond the physical world in a psychic/spiritual realm where the Energy of God lives forever, and we are one with that loving Energy.

Besides its obvious philosophical problems, *regeneration* in the here-and-now flies in the face of everyday experience. All nature moves from energy to expression to fulfillment to expiration of that energy. Scientists say the very Cosmos itself is heading either for burn-out or re-birth billions of years from now, depending on some highly complex questions astrophysics has yet to answer. Increased God-consciousness may invigorate and give us long-lasting health, perhaps enough to live many times longer than our current lifespan. However, life on this plane is certainly no prize worthy of eternity.

Whatever happens after physical death, the resurrection of Jesus Christ shows us that life does not end in the grave. That is the Christian hope which spurred the apostles onward when all the world seemed to stand against them.

Both ideas—physical death and spiritual death—agree that sin as we have defined it inhibits growth and promotes stagnation. For this reason, the diagram (Fig.9-3) shows death as the "On Hold" stage of existence. We do not mean that everyone who dies is automatically plopped into a holding pattern; the illustration shows what the *Sin-Redemption cycle* looks like for living, struggling persons. Those are the only sort of spiritual entities about which we can speak with any kind of certainty.

BRIEF SUMMARY

So far we have seen that *Radical Freedom*, through freedom of *choice*, leads inevitably to *Error (Sin)*, which can be an act we have chosen *(commission)* or a growth we have avoided *(omission)*. In either case, sin brings *objective guilt* because following less than the optimum path will arrest our spiritual progress. Error also results in *subjective guilt* as we experience anxiety. Persons who refuse to acknowledge their part in the choices of non-choices leading to sin are said to exhibit *under-responsible behavior*, while people who feel they are at fault when they could not have possibly been the cause of an action are *over-responsible*. In any case, uncorrected error continues to alienate the person from his/her spiritual identity in Christ, producing first *misery* and finally *death*, which are the out-picturing of error-beliefs resulting in *suffering/stagnation* (misery), and the holding pattern which a person has chosen when locked into error-belief (death).

FIND BEDROCK OR COLLAPSE

Our study has been diagnostic thus far. We have discussed sin and its effects on the person, charting those effects in a downward fall from the path which God wants us to find and walk. But how shall we regain the road once we are lost in the tangle? Will better information do the trick? Hardly. Merely listing the requirements for God-consciousness is like telling a drowning man how to swim.

New Testament writers were adamant that mere knowledge is not enough. It takes action to bring wandering humanity back on course again. We must want to follow the Christ-within, decide to turn our lives over to the Omnipotent Presence and Power, and begin "to walk humbly" with our God. Such an act of sheer trust would be unthinkable if Someone had not come and showed us the way.

To discuss this idea we must grapple with concepts which are wholly alien to metaphysical Christianity, although they form the mainstay of traditional Christian theology. This brings us to the critical point in bridge building, the moment at which we drive into the mucky bottom and search for bedrock to support the final span linking our metaphysical Christian archipelago with the Christ's Church on the mainland.

There is no avoiding this messy task. Either we find our foundation here or the bridge comes tumbling down.

ATONEMENT: CHRIST DIED FOR YOUR SINS

The New Testament is unequivocal on this point: Jesus Christ came to save humanity from bondage to the law of sin and death. This idea can be found in all four gospels, the Pauline and deutero-Pauline letters, Acts, and the general epistles. It is implicit everywhere else. NT thought builds upon a foundational belief that Jesus of Nazareth somehow gave humanity access to eternity, ways to throw off the burden of sin, and power for effective living. Paul said it boldly, simply, and no allegorical gamesmanship can siphon the power away from these words:

> While we were still weak, at the right time Christ died for the ungodly. Why, one will hardly die for a righteous man—though perhaps for a good man one will dare even to die. But God shows his love for us in that while we were yet sinners Christ died for us.[5]

Surprisingly, there is no clear NT explanation as to how the death of Jesus saves the "ungodly." Looking back through two thousand years of interpretation, it is difficult for us to factor out the shades of meaning which Christian theology has given to the work of Jesus Christ.

We are so familiar with orthodox interpretations of the Jesus-event that something must be said about these various Atonement theories before moving on to consider a restatement of Jesus' mission in metaphysical Christian language. Our primary source for this brief foray into the history of Christian doctrine is Dr. Georgia Harkness' book *Understanding the Christian Faith*.

There are, of course, many possible ways to contemplate the work of Jesus Christ. Some explanations contain elements which most modern theologians—and all Truth students—reject outright, but looking at these solutions to the Easter problem will give us better insight into the whole spectrum of historic Christian thought and will provide a springboard for leaping beyond those limited concepts to a higher, more worthy interpretation of Atonement.

Before we begin, it is worth noting that the crucifixion, not the resurrection, caused a problem for early Christians. Jewish followers of the Nazarene expected a resurrection at the end of time. What they did not expect was their messiah to be publicly crucified. Almost immediately after the Easter appearances, Christians began trying to interpret the crucifixion in the light of their historic faith and their firm belief that Jesus had risen from the dead. Soon, they fell back upon Temple imagery. By the end of the first century, John's gospel was proclaiming that Jesus was the "lamb of God, who takes away the sin of the world."[6]

Far from an act of violence ending the career of their messiah, the crucifixion was now an integral part of the plan for the salvation of the world. Biblical authors never quite got around to explaining *how* the death of Jesus "takes away the sin of the world." That effort, which began in writings of the early Church, goes on today in the volume you are reading. Here, then, are some of the more well-known theories of Atonement.

APPEASEMENT THEORY

Dr. Harkness prefers the word *propitiation*, from the King James translation of I John 2:2—*"...he is the propitiation for our sins; and not for ours only, but for the whole world."*

A better translation comes from the *Today's English Version*: "*...And Christ himself is the means by which our sins are forgiven, and not only our own sins, but also the sins of all men.*"

However, the *Appeasement Theory* follows the older, King James wording. God is an All-Holy, All-Righteous Supreme Being who cannot stand the sight of sin. Life in this world implicates human beings in free choices which result in errors, therefore people invariably break God's rules and sin. This makes God angry because He doesn't like sin and cannot seem to separate His dislike for sin from his alleged love for the sinner. God is between a rock and a hard place.

Enter Jesus Christ. Appeasement Theory says the only way to placate God is for Jesus to die as a sacrificial offering, much like the blood sacrifices offered by pre-Christian religions to mollify angry gods. God accepts the blood of Jesus and His wrath is soothed by this eternal sacrifice. Besides the comic figure of a God whose own temper gets the best of Him, there are some serious theological problems with Appeasement Theory. John Macquarrie points to the most serious defect:

> It is necessary indeed that some particular historical event should bring to light in a signal way the "mystery hidden for ages and generations," but no historical event changes God's attitude, or makes him from a wrathful God into a gracious God, or allows his reconciling work to get started—such thoughts are utterly to be rejected.[7]

To which Harkness adds her critique:

> When this (propitiation) is taken to mean, as it too often has been, that an angry God has to be appeased, the modern Christian rightly rebels. It sounds like primitive religion, and clearly is not the kind of God that Jesus worshipped and served! Jesus' God of fatherly love for all men, even sinners, needs no sin offering to propitiate his wrath.[8]

There are some passages in Paul which could support Appeasement/Propitiation theory, but Macquarrie shows these verses can be read differently depending on the context. Further, he insists the idea is so abhorrent that it fails other tests such as *reason* and *experience*.

> Even if it could claim support from the Bible or the history of theology, (Appeasement theory) would have to be rejected because of the affront which it offers to reason and conscience.[9]

As abhorrent as Appeasement/Propitiation is, there are ideas even more outrageous which have been taught and believed by Christian theologians.

RANSOM THEORY: SUCKER-PUNCHING THE DEVIL

This may be the oldest official doctrine of the Atonement, dating back to the early centuries of Church history. According to *Ransom Theory*, humanity is enslaved to evil powers, especially the Devil, and must be purchased from Satanic influence like a slave bought at the auction block. There are a number of Pauline passages which lend proof-text support to this clearly incredible notion, most notably these remarks in Paul's First Letter to the Corinthians:

> You are not your own; you were bought with a price... You were bought with a price; do not become slaves of men.[10]

Besides the inability of proof-texting to "prove" any doctrine in the eyes of modern theologians, these passages could be interpreted as merely emphasizing the costliness of Jesus' self-sacrifice, much the way we might say that we bought a much-wanted item but it cost us "a King's ransom." No sensible person would ask, "To whom did you pay the ransom to get this?" We understand figures of speech for what they are and never take them literally in everyday conversation. (Has anyone ever "dropped you at the corner"?)

If we add the gospel references (Mk 10:45 and Mt 20:2) to Paul's comments in I Corinthians and the mention of "the man Christ Jesus, who gave himself as a ransom for all" in the pseudo-Pauline First Letter to Timothy (I Tim 2:6), we still fall far short of a biblical theory of the Atonement as a payoff to the forces of evil.

The Ransom Theory is helpful because it points to the high cost of the Atonement, but, since it presupposes evil powers who hold title to the world and the souls of humanity, such mythological dualism marks the Ransom Theory as more akin to the Gnostic heresies than to mainline Christian thought.

Ironically, however, one of the "friends" of Christian Truth teaching, Origen of Alexandria, firmly believed that God paid Satan with the death of Jesus for the souls of all humanity which the Devil held in captivity. Satan was duped, however. He did not realize he would not be able to hold a mere Jewish carpenter in bondage as he held other mortals; in effect, Christ had sucker-punched Old Scratch. According to Origen, when Jesus rose from the grave He threw off the shackles of satanic control and led humanity out of bondage like Moses departing from Pharaoh with Israel.

Even adding the impressive name of Origen to its pedigree, the Ransom theory doesn't work for metaphysical Christianity, which builds its theology on the unshakable rock of One Presence/One Power. Recently a more sophisticated version of the Ransom Theory has resurfaced, chiefly through the views presented by Swedish theologian Gustaf Aulen in his book *Christus Victor*. Aulen is no crude fundamentalist and numbers people like John Macquarrie in his camp of admirers, but his conclusions still require a low theology of dualism which Christian Truth thinking rejects as totally inconsistent with God's nature. To his credit, Aulen frankly admits the problem:

...the classic idea of the Atonement is dualistic and dramatic: it depicts the drama of the Atonement against a dualistic background. If Dualism is eliminated, it is impossible to go on thinking of the existence of powers hostile to God, and the basis of the classic view has been dissolved away.[11]

Here is a teacher at war with his own errors, certain that some unseen force must lurk in the shadows causing frail humanity to slip. He tries to clean up his mythological foundations with footnotes explaining that he is speaking of neither "metaphysical Dualism between the Infinite and the finite" nor "absolute Dualism between Good and Evil typical of Zoroastrian and Manichaean teaching..." but rather means "the opposition between God and that which in His own created world resists His will; between the Divine Love and the rebellion of created wills against Him."[12]

But his very punctuation gives Aulen away. *Good* and *Evil, Dualism, Infinite*—all receive capitalization, suggesting they have ultimate meaning for him, or at least A. G. Herbert, his translator, believed so. It makes no sense philosophically or theologically to dispense with *"metaphysical Dualism"* and then insist that dualism really exists in some other form, i.e., as the opposition to God's Will by our created, finite wills. Either there is One Presence and Power in the Cosmos or there is not. If not, then what we have is not true dualism but multifarious powers and presences, returning us to the age of polytheisms.

Unless, of course, there are *two equal and opposite dualistic powers*—God and Satan—at war for eternity. No one, not even the Zoroastrians, has been hardy enough to claim that kind of split-apple Universe, because two equal and opposite powers cannot be said to possess Omnipotence, unless held in some kind of unity such as seeing them as two ends of the same process, which would make nonsense of the whole concept of goodness.

Macquarrie rightly faults Aulen for failing to demythologize the biblical sources of his Soteriology, but a greater problem lies at the heart of any theology built on dualism, namely, locating the source of those "principalities and powers" which hold humanity prisoner. If everything comes from God, there can be no "power" of evil. If everything does not come from God, he is no god. In eternity as in the created Cosmos, the only available resource is God-power. The only logically consistent answer to the dilemma is *Incarnational Monism* tempered by an understanding of kenotic emptying as normative for all sentient beings. This necessarily precludes any evil power gripping at human souls. Shadows have no talons.[13]

PENAL SUBSTITUTION THEORY

Also called *Vicarious Atonement*, this is the best-known theory because it is currently preached by our fundamentalist brothers and sisters. Interestingly, *Penal Substitution Theory* is not an ancient doctrine of the Church, like *Ransom Theory*, but a rather new development. The idea was formulated in the Middle Ages by an English theologian and Archbishop of Canterbury named Anselm. Georgia Harkness wrote:

> As Anselm propounded it, man's sin before God is a debt so great that no mere man, but only the God-man, could pay it; and he could make atonement, not by any act of duty that was required of him, but only by something not required—the giving of his life.[14]

The idea springs from the legal system and has its antecedents in the writing of Tertullian (second century A.D.) who was well versed in Roman law, hence one of the names used to describe vicarious atonement is *Penal Substitution*.

Here's how it works: God is the Judge. We stand before the bar, guilty as charged, awaiting our sentence of eternal damnation, which is demanded by God's justice and righteousness.

But, wait!

Here comes Jesus Christ, offering to take the penalty for our sins by suffering on the cross in our place. God accepts Jesus as our substitute. (How much we are involved in the deal gets theologians hopelessly entangled in arguments about "subjective" and "objective" views of vicarious atonement; we shall avoid that jungle.) Guilty sinners are set free from the curse of the sin-death cycle by Jesus' willingness to suffer in our place.

Beyond its philosophical difficulties, three main objections to *Penal Substitution* leap out at modern Christians.

1. The whole idea is morally untenable. Who could ethically allow another to be punished in his place? Suggesting that Jesus willingly went to Calvary still fails to remove the act of cowardice on the part of humans who are not willing to face the consequences of their actions. If another person goes to prison for a crime committed by someone else, how do we feel about the person who allows his substitute to suffer in his place? To accept this kind of replacement is an act of selfish cruelty, which is one of the definitions of sin. Hence, vicarious atonement only works if by sin we are saved from the curse of sin.

2. It negates grace. More profound are the difficulties *Penal Substitution* places upon the concept of *grace* as it interacts with the process of spiritual *growth.* As it is usually defined, *grace is God's goodness which floods our lives whether we deserve it or not.* Certainly, God wants us to have all the good He can get us to accept—but that is the very problem with vicarious atonement. If God wants good for His children, eternal punishment is not necessary. Justice demands righteousness, but *grace* offers mercy. Why should God be encumbered with a legal system, which He ostensibly created, that He must circumvent by bribing Himself?

3. Finally, the result of Penal Substitution is an unchanged sinner set loose on heaven. No growth is required, no spiritual development. Just forgiveness slopped out to creatures who have no need to reach for the stars because heaven has been lowered to their level, handed to them *gratis*. Charles Manson goes to Disney World. In fact, those who advocate vicarious atonement most strenuously insist that any effort on the part of sinful humanity to improve itself amounts to a denial of God's free gift of salvation. "Works righteousness" or "salvation by works" earns the label of heresy for these people because it suggests we can do something for ourselves beyond humbly accepting the slot in heaven reserved for us by the death of Jesus on the cross. Small wonder Deitrich Bonhoeffer pronounced such an easy-to-afford, no-money-down ticket to heaven "cheap grace."

The valuable element in Vicarious Atonement Theory is, of course, its emphasis on the free flow of good to humanity from a gracious God. Essentially, Penal Substitutionists are correct when they say we cannot earn salvation, if by salvation we mean merely avoiding hell and achieving heaven, because no such places have ever existed. God's forgiveness need not be earned because, as Unity minister Eric Butterworth likes to say with his penchant for turning truisms inside out, God cannot forgive us. Why? Because He was never angry with us in the first place.

FOSDICK & THE PRODIGAL

In the parable of the Prodigal Son (Luke 15:11-32) the father never lets his spend-thrift child provoke him to anger. Harry Emerson Fosdick was senior pastor of New York's Riverside Baptist Church, author of a stack of books, a popular radio minister and one of the great preachers of the twentieth century when he wrote this analysis of vicarious atonement as contrasted with the teaching explicit in the parable:

> The Prodigal has sinned against his father, and the father—not a feudal lord but an honest-to-goodness father—sees the returning son, penitent and ashamed, coming home from the far country. According to Anselm and his kind, can the father run and fall on the prodigal's neck and kiss him? Oh, no! A legal reparation must first of all be made. There must be an elder brother, of another sort alto-gether from the one described in Jesus' parable, who will volunteer to let himself be flogged to death, crucified, or what you will, after seeing which the father, his legal honor satisfied, can welcome the returning son. Can you imagine Jesus thinking in such terms as that? These legalistic theories of the atonement are in my judgment a theological disgrace.[15]

If God demanded such a blood-guilt sacrifice He would be unworthy of worship. Fortunately for the whole of creation, there is no need for *Substitution Atonement* to justify sinners. In the courtroom language of that legalistic theory, we need not be acquitted because no charges have been filed.

MORAL INFLUENCE THEORY

This idea, popular in some liberal churches today, sees Jesus Christ as the One Whose life and death point to the perfect pattern for humanity to emulate. Georgia Harkness finds much in this model to commend itself. It has the advantage of linking Jesus' death to His life and teachings, which gives us reason to study His words and try to follow Him. It also counters the tendency to see the cross as somehow magically changing God's mind about humanity.

However, Dr. Harkness raises certain objections to any theology of Atonement built strictly on the *Moral Influence Theory*, and we must admit her points are well taken. If Jesus died as a martyr to his own teachings, how does His death differ from the death of any other human—Socrates, Lincoln, Dietrich Bonhoeffer—who was faithful to high principles to the end? Furthermore, other theologians have noted that the high standards set by Jesus often lead to frustration rather than inspiration. If Jesus is uniquely divine, as orthodoxy claims, any standard He sets will be necessarily unattainable, hence useless. *Moral Influence* is better than any other theory yet discussed but still not a complete explanation of the Atonement and the work of Jesus Christ which Christian Truth students can affirm.

RECONCILIATION THEORY

As mentioned earlier, the key to Easter is Christmas. We cannot say God is present in some ultimate way in the incarnation of Jesus Christ—since all sentient beings are incarnations of the Divine Presence and Power—but because God's radiance floods through that one solitary life, Jesus Christ is our window to see what is present in every sentient being. "If one wishes to speak about God," writes T. A. Kantonen in his analysis of Karl Barth, "he must say Jesus Christ over and over again."[16] Whereas Barth saw Jesus as ultimately unique, we have seen the opposite. The man of Nazareth shows us God-within because Jesus is ultimately typical.

Christmas provides the entry-point where Jesus Christ breaks through walls of darkness built by ignorance and to let the light of Divine goodness shine through. Jesus so perfectly reflected that Divinity that our whole God-concept in the Western world is really a Jesus-concept. We fully agree with Karl Barth: He who would see God must look first to Jesus Christ. Easter confirms that decision.

PROCESS THEOLOGY STRIKES AGAIN

Yet, here we encounter another thorny problem. Generations of Christians looked at Jesus and still found no problem in owning human slaves, beating their wives, waging wars of territorial conquest, and approving child labor. As numerous modern authors have shown, Jesus has been characterized by each successive generation in the terms of their own consciousness. To put another way, we have made Jesus in our image and will probably continue to do so. There simply is no transcendent vantage point where we can shuck our ethnocentrisms and see Jesus with the eye of complete objectivity. We are part of the process, and our interaction with Jesus throughout history has been a constant struggle to reinterpret, re-evaluate, re-make, re-work both the Christ-concept and the Soteriology which stems from that model. Taking this as a given—that Jesus-models are all in transition—we can see positive strengths flowing from a dynamic, ever-changing Christology/Soteriology.

First, a Process Theory of Atonement gives us another form of dialogue in our spiritual growth. As the Jesus-model/ salvation-model interacts with our life-experience, both are changed. If God works through Jesus Christ to affect our "salvation," this means the process of *dialogue-change-growth-dialogue* is the actual means for grace to flow to us.

Rather than bemoaning the fact that we have altered the Jesus model so profoundly throughout history, we could see those changes as the clearest evidence that God is at work in Christ Jesus, in the words of the Apostle Paul, "...reconciling the world unto Himself." A static Jesus-model would be another millstone around the neck of future generations, but since we have seen new things in the Jesus-model throughout history we can conclude that God will continue to prompt us to look even deeper in the future as circumstances warrant. God really does come to us in Jesus, not as a once-and-for-all-time revelation but through a process of continuous discovery by which we find the Good who seeks us.

RECONCILIATION: A WORKING MODEL

When Paul wrote, "God was in Christ reconciling the world unto Himself," he gave us a clue to understand Atonement as an unfolding, continuous process. This is exactly what happens when we look at the life-death-resurrection of Jesus. The model works on us, and we on it, so that we see God at work reconciling the world to His perfect model through the model of Jesus Christ. In Jesus we see what is happening in microcosm.

God is an Eternal Father. For Him to be a father takes children—"For we are indeed his offspring," Luke's Paul reminds the Athenians (Acts 17:28). Taken seriously, this means all people are God's children; He is the forgiving father of the Prodigal Son story (also found uniquely in Luke). We are being "reconciled" to God by moving back home to Him.

To reconcile the world unto God the Father means according to this interpretation to assist all sentient beings on their journey to spiritual union with God, a union which does not blur our individualities but makes us more fully unique as an irreplaceable piece of God's Omnipotent Presence.

God's reconciling acts could not be realized if not for two factors: Christ-indwelling each sentient being, and some method to grasp the destination, to show the way. Not as a moral influence, although that is important, but as a Wayshower to stake out the road up ahead. We are not fully convinced of this indwelling divinity because human freedom means the right to be wrong, so we fail and fall short of our aspirations. In the long history of humanity, very few people have achieved any kind of high-order spirituality which would suggest indwelling divinity.

Enter Jesus of Nazareth, fully human, yet pointing like an arrow at the Divine-within. If He did it, we can do it, too. By freely embracing the cross, Jesus chose to be a road sign for the rest of us. But more than a road sign, He is the Map, the Path, the Way, and Destination.

We look to Christmas and say, "He was born, one of us." We listen to His stories and study His life and say, "He struggled against the same kind of negative-thinking all people face." We look at the cross and say, "That's the worst that would happen to us. We could die shamefully, alone, innocent, and undeserving of punishment." We look at the empty tomb and say, "This event cancels the worst possible fate, because it confirms God's power over death and the presence of Divine Order even in the face of apparent disaster."

Putting the four revelatory events together—*Christmas, His life/teachings, Good Friday, and Easter*—we can say, "Life brings hope of growth toward Christ-consciousness. We are all incarnations of God, struggling to know as Jesus knew that we are One with the Father. Life brings challenges and suffering because we are truly free. But even in the face of the worst that could happen, God is working through it all to bring His perfect, long-term results. There really is only One Presence/Power, and the birth, life, teachings, death, and resurrection of Jesus show that God's goodness will triumph."

PRESERVING THE BEST

This model for the Atonement gathers up in itself the positive elements of all the others discussed in this chapter. The costliness of Jesus' sacrifice cannot be underestimated, as the *Ransom Theory* holds. He had to endure, for love of humanity, a cruel and wholly undeserved fate. As the *Substitution Theory* insists, we know we cannot earn God's approval, but we disagree with Substitutionists because we say that God's approval has never been withdrawn from humanity. He certainly does not want us to harm ourselves by sinning, but He never lapses in relentless love for even the nastiest, most negative person. A house divided cannot stand.

We will also find some agreement with the Appeasement Theory, because Sin (error-beliefs which outpicture in the life of an individual as attempts to negate Divine Ideas) must be taken seriously. Sin may be Self-Inflicted Nonsense, but we feel the sting of it nonetheless. If continued unchecked, sin leads to misery and death, i.e., spiritual stagnation. Reconciliation Theory shows that we cannot rest on the merits of the Savior because we are called to become what He is. We shall never become Jesus Christ, for He, like all sentient beings, is absolutely unique. We shall become fully aware of our Oneness with God, and so represent Christhood in our diverse forms. We are reconciled to God when the whole process culminates in Christ-consciousness; until then, reconciliation is an ongoing process.

Because it is only through faith (i.e., consciousness) that we are "saved" from the Sin cycle, we can appropriate the solution to the human predicament only through a free act of Will; we must accept what we are and let the model of Jesus Christ work in and through our lives. This provides the avenue of escape (Fig. 9-3), breaking the power of sin and death and releasing us to our full Divine Potential.

Earlier we said we want to hold in dynamic tension the realism which forces us to admit that there is sin/suffering in the world and the optimism which sees God's goodness triumphing in our lives. We called the solution to the realism-optimism paradox *Mystical Realism*. A theory of Atonement based on this model of ongoing reconciliation gives us a good look at Mystical Realism in action.

SYMBOLISM OF THE CROSS

The best symbol for God's One Power/One Presence in the midst of apparent evil and evident suffering is the cross. The horizontal bar represents the Omnipresence of God in everyday life; the vertical bar shows the downpouring Power of God into our world, His willingness to shower goodness on us if we turn our lives to Him.

Placing a circle around the junction of those two bars gives us a *Celtic Cross*, which the author believes is the best symbol for the insights of Metaphysical Christianity. (Fig. 9-4)

Fig. 9-4 A Celtic Cross. The circle stands for eternity and oneness, which, when added to OP^2, gives us the cornerstone affirmation of the Christian Truth in visual form: One Presence/One Power, God the Good, Omnipotent. In the cross God truly was "reconciling the world unto Himself;" the process goes on today and will continue until we all are One in Him.

Though the future is always in doubt, the outcome of life is assured for the Christian. Jesus Christ is the Alpha and Omega, the first and the last. From God-consciousness we came, and to reunion with God we go. With this certainty, we turn next to *Eschatology*, last things.

CHECK YOUR KNOWLEDGE

1. Identify the following: *Steadfast Love (Hesed), Merciful Kindness, Agape, Divine Ideas, Sin-Reconciliation Cycle, Over-Responsible /Under-Responsible Behavior, Radical Freedom, Propitiation, Ransom Theory, Dualism, Penal Substitution Theory, Moral Influence Theory, Reconciliation.*

2. What, according to the text, is *Sin*? Give your critique of the author's definition/evaluation.

3. Would stealing a horse from another Indian people be the same as stealing a horse from a kinsman for the Plains Indians? Which was *"sin"* and why?

4. NT authors added what dimension to the OT understanding of *sin* and its remedy?

5. How does faith in Jesus Christ break the cycle of Sin-Death, so that we can now call it the *Sin-Reconciliation Cycle*?

6. List the positive elements of the other four theories of *Atonement* mentioned in the text and show how the good points are taken up into *Reconciliation Theory*.

QUESTIONS FOR DISCUSSION

1. How do you deal with both subjective and objective guilt in your life? Should we even be discussing *sin* and *guilt*?

2. Compare and contrast the OT concept of *Hesed* with the NT's *Agape*. Do any differences resolve themselves in Reconciliation Theory? How?

3. Do you tend to be an "Over-responsible" or an "Under-responsible" person? Which is healthier? What alternatives are there to these two?

4. How do you interpret these words from Paul?—"But God shows his love for us in that while we were yet sinners Christ died for us." How did the death of Jesus Christ save us? Or did it?

5. In what respect is Jesus the Wayshower in your life?

6. Do you agree with the author's statement that the Celtic Cross (Fig. 9-4) is "the best symbol for the insights of mystical/metaphysical Christianity?" What other symbols would you like to see displayed by churches?

NOTES

1. Plato's "Euthyphro," Benjamin Jowett, trans., Dialogues of Plato in *Great Books of the Western World,* Vol. 7 (Chicago: University of Chicago Press: 1952), p. 195.

2. Micah 6:6-8.

3. Dale Carnegie, *How To Win Friends and Influence People* (NY: Simon and Schuster, 1936), p. 20.

4. Romans 6:23.

5. Romans 5:6-8.

6. John 1:29.

7. Macquarrie, *Principles,* p. 314.

8. Georgia Harkness, *Understanding the Christian Faith* (Nashville, TN: Abingdon, 1981), p. 78.

9. Macquarrie, *Principles,* p. 314.

10. I Corinthians 6:19b-20.

11. Gustaf Aulen, *Christus Victor* (NY: Macmillan, 1969), p. 11.

12. IBID., pp. 4-5n.

13. Macquarrie, *Principles,* pp. 318-321.

14. Harkness, p. 81.

15. Harry Emerson Fosdick, *Dear Mr. Brown* (NY: Harper & Brothers, 1961),p. 134.

16. Kantonen, p. 32.

ESCHATOLOGY

Chapter Ten

Where Do We Go From Here?

ESCHATOLOGY - that area of theology which is directly concerned with the "study of the last thing(s)"...death, particular judgment, heaven, hell, purgatory, Second Coming of Christ, resurrection of the body, general judgment, consummation of all things in the perfection of the Kingdom of God.[1]

On the wall of the student center at the seminary I attended, some wag had scribbled these two lines:

Repent, accursed sinners, for the End is near!
(If you've already repented, please disregard this notice.)

As much as we'd like to know, we really don't. No one knows what destiny, if any, awaits the soul of individuals and humanity at large. People have been born and died for countless generations, yet we still don't know for certain where human consciousness comes from and whether it continues beyond mortal existence or evaporates with the last brain waves at death.

Many people have claimed such firsthand knowledge throughout history. As long ago as the days of King Saul, literature has reported instances of contact between the living and the dead (I Samuel 28:3-25). But these are necessarily second-hand reports at best, unconvincing to those who have not themselves experienced ghostly appearances. There is no guarantee that we would believe our senses even should an apparition materialize before us, as Jesus shows in his parable of the Rich Man and Lazarus:

And he (deceased Rich Man) said, "No, father Abraham; but if some one goes to them from the dead, they will repent." He said to him, "If they do not hear Moses and the prophets, neither will they be convinced if some one should rise from the dead." [2]

Neither can the subjective element in all reported sightings of spiritual life-forms cannot be overlooked. Hindus seldom encounter departed Muslim saints; Jews are rarely visited by the Virgin Mary. Ethnocentric expectations color what we see when these visions occur.

When Native Americans living on the Great Plains went on vision-quests, they received their goal only after sensory deprivation, starvation, and sleeplessness. What they saw took its shape from the symbolism of the religion of the Plains tribes. They did not see Jesus on the Mount of Transfiguration or Mohammed arriving triumphant at Mecca. As we noted earlier, *There are no tiger-gods where there are no tigers.*

While individual experiences cannot be cited as proof of life after death, they cannot be discounted purely on intellectual grounds by those who have not experienced such dramatic encounters. It is their very subjective nature which makes these "contacts" so powerful for those who experience them.

The power of such an encounter can be so profound in the life of an individual that quite a few religions, the Judeao-Christian among them, have absolutely forbidden any activity involving contact with the dead or the use of spirit-mediums. We shall explore this subject more deeply in Chapter 19, where we discuss the dangers of "special revelations," but for now let's just say that such experiences, though perhaps individually valid, cannot form the basis for a   comprehensive theology of last things and therefore can be of no help to us in studying Eschatology.

Indeed, many religions offer deep insights about life after death, but those insights may not properly be called knowledge. Organized beliefs comprising any Eschatology must come from creative thought and not from first-hand experience or scientific evidence. As we look at Last Things, we must continually remind ourselves that any examination of eternal destinies must necessarily be a study in faith, not fact.

VALIDITY OF FAITH

Of course, there is nothing wrong with beliefs based on faith rather than verifiable evidence. Earlier in this book we said that religious insights are subject to personal validity, not scientific validity. Those beliefs must then be tested in the larger arena of theological dialogue—either formally, in the case of academic discourses between theologians, or informally over a cup of coffee after the Sunday sermon.

Love is probably the most important human attribute, yet it is more closely related to faith, hope, and charity than cold logic. What would you say if asked why you love your spouse? You might reply with a litany of his/her good qualities: kindness, generosity, sense of humor, sexual attractiveness, sensitivity, altruism, etc. But those are just attributes, not facts proving love.

Most of us know any number of kind, generous, humorous, sexy, sensitive, altruistic people. Yet we love only one person with the kind of lasting intensity and depth that brings two people together as mates for life. Marriage is based on faith, not fact, but good marriages begin with faith which has its eyes open, has done its homework, and has made a loving, careful decision. Faith need not be synonymous with ignorance, like the schoolboy adage which describes faith: "When you believe somethin' you know ain't true."

METAPHYSICAL SPECULATION & POPULAR ESCHATOLOGIES

Because of the nature of Eschatology, this chapter will deal in thought-forms which are much more speculative and metaphysical than almost any other section of the book. It is unavoidable. Eschatology is inherently speculative, which is one of the reasons that talk about "the end of the world" has remained so popular throughout the ages.

A word must be said about those "popular eschatologies" before we plunge into the topic from the perspective of legitimate theology. If we rule out the brief flash of hippie-Eastern apocalypticism which sent droves of long-haired, blue-jeaned college dropouts scurrying to form communes in remote areas before the End, virtually all other pop-eschatological movements in Western society have been based on flagrant misunderstandings of the book of Revelation. To read the Apocalypse of St. John as a program for the end of the world is to overlook two important points about that feisty, first century treatise.

1) Every generation since the ink dried on the original autograph has found signs and evidences that their age was the time of the End.

Biblical authors themselves unanimously believed theirs was the last generation. So passionate was this belief that II Peter was written around 150 A.D. expressly to deal with the growing restlessness because the End had not yet come. Listen to the author, obviously not the Apostle Peter, as he deals with these serious objections to the dwindling Christian hope of a rapid Parousia, or second coming of Christ, and Final Judgment of the living and the dead:

> First of all you must understand this, that scoffers will come in the last days with scoffing, following their own passions and saying, "Where is the promise of his coming? For ever since the fathers fell asleep [died], all things have continued as they were from the beginning of creation." ... The Lord is not slow about his promise as some count slowness, but is forbearing toward you, not wishing that anyone should perish, but that all should reach repentance. But the day of the Lord will come...[3]

New Testament authors had written at white-hot speed, certain that the Parousia would occur before the writer could scribble his manuscript. When Jesus says of the little children *"to such belong he kingdom of heaven,"* He may be expressing senti-mental thoughts about the openness of childhood, or He may be expressing Matthew's belief that those children—which would be Matthew's own generation—will live to see the kingdom come.[4]

Matthew's hopes have been shared by millennialists ever since. Read about the nineteenth century revivalist movements and see how the End was predicted time after time. Those predictions will continue far into the future because John's Apocalypse was written and preserved by ancient people who expected the Last Things to happen to them. As we read Revelation their excitement leaps centuries to infect us, and we expect these things today.

2) The book of Revelation is written as underground literature of an oppressed community to encourage the faithful. Promises of the End are more cheerleading than prophecy. The central message of the work seems to be "don't worship the beast," which means don't abandon your faith in the face of worldly pressures and persecutions. The "beast" of course, was the Roman emperor whose loyalty oath included offering wine and incense to an image of the reigning Caesar, an affront to both Christian and Jew.

"OUR NOMINEES FOR THE BEAST ARE..."

Today the beast can be any material object or person or intellectual pursuit which seduces the Christian away from following the Christ. But our fundamentalist brothers and sisters continue to insist that the beast has a real identity and will show himself soon. Like their pop-religion predecessors of earlier generations, some modern fundamentalists believe they have definitely understood the symbolism of John's Revelation and that the Russians, Chinese, and Common Market are clearly foretold as harbingers of the End. Napoleon, Kaiser Wilhelm, Hitler, and Stalin—all earlier candidates for beasthood according to previous interpreters—are tactfully omitted in the mountains of brightly jacketed drivel which those ultra-conservative presses keep churning out for an eager readership. Eschatology is good business for publishers, provided they are willing to ignore the towering evidence against such frivolous interpretations.

We have probably spent enough time on pop-eschatology. If further study is desired, many good sources are readily available. An excellent introduction to the book of Revelation is the chapter on that subject in William E. Cameron's *Great Dramas of the Bible* (Unity Books). Also, the *Interpreter's One-Volume Commentary* (Abingdon, 1971) has several excellent monographs on biblical apocalypticism and the Revelation to John, especially the fine introductory remarks by the commentator on that book, the late Dr. S. MacLean Gilmour.

The real message of Revelation is timeless and will continue to inspire generations to come as they struggle with the "beasts" which threaten their faith. Hopefully, more intelligent biblical teaching will be normative and fewer diagrams will be printed ticking off the countdown.

ENDS AND BEGINNINGS

Eschatology comes from the koine Greek word *eschaton*, meaning literally "the end." Eschatology, therefore, is a study of endings, of last things. Since an ending presupposes a beginning, Eschatology is an idea wholly alien to several schools of Greek philosophy, notably the Eleatics, who held that Ultimate Reality is changeless Being. If there was no creation, there can be no end.

Also, if all life is cyclical, as other Greek thinkers surmised, then talk about an end is meaningless. Of course, not all Greek philosophers agreed, but it is fair to say the central thrust of Hellenistic philosophy was toward a cyclical view of time that allowed little room for a doctrine of last things.

Hebrew thought, however, has always been linear, not circular. Genesis leaves no doubt about the progressives of time directly from God's primordial act: "In the beginning God created the heavens and the earth." (Gen. 1:1) Both the Hebrew Bible and the New Testament end with notes of prophecy about the future, suggesting that our founding fathers in the Judaeo-Christian faith never lost sight of the linear dimension to life and the responsibility which an onward-and-upward flow brings to mortals.

Isn't there a way to hold the obvious forward-motion of time in harmony with the obviously cyclical nature of life itself? Later in this chapter, we shall see if both could be true.

CATEGORIES TO EXPLORE, CONTROVERSY EXPECTED

Eschatology is usually divided into two general categories, individual and corporate human destinies. A further subdivision might be made between the destiny of a given group, such as Israel or the Church, and the destiny of humanity at large. Or we could opt to explore the grandest question of all and ask, *"What shall happen to the Cosmos at the end of time?"* Although our space is limited, we shall attempt to address the wide range of related subjects by focusing on three categories:

1) Individual destinies

2) The ultimate fate of the human race

3) The Universe—will it end?

Such a controversial subject is bound to stir up disagreement, but we cannot skip a topic as important as individual and corporate destinies of humanity and the Cosmos simply because controversy makes some folks uncomfortable. Controversy, we have said, is not in itself bad. Some of religion's finest insights have come only after the clash of contravailing ideas. Let's attack the problems of Eschatology with this kind of hopeful anticipation of healthy disagreement, remembering that these are not the last words on the last things, just the way one theologian sees how Eschatology fits into modern Christian thought.

1) INDIVIDUAL DESTINIES

What happens when we die? No religious question evokes greater interest than this. In fact, doctrine and discussion about life after death comprises perhaps the largest sub-category in the world's religious scriptures. Christianity owes its existence to a particular life-after-death experience recorded in history, and the New Testament can be thought of as a discussion of the resurrection from both sides of that event, before and after, since the post-resurrection appearances of the Risen Lord powerfully shaped everything the primitive Christian community thought, taught, and wrote.

A WORLD-WIDE QUESTION

Discussions about life-after-death are by no means limited to Western tradition. Islam holds before its followers the vision of paradise for the faithful and perdition for the infidel; Hinduism teaches various forms of reincarnation leading to absorption into the One. Great religions of antiquity devoted vast energies to projects that would insure eternity for believers—albeit only high-ranking ones like the king or the nobility. Priest-craft has included funerary rites, magic, and necromancy in order that the soul of the believer may pass into the spirit world. Volumes like the Tibetan Book of the Dead were written to give the dying person guidelines as he departed this life, a practice which survives in the form of rites for the dying such as Extreme Unction, the "last rites" of the Catholic Church (see Chapter 12).

Of the major religious teachers of humanity, only Buddha remained silent on the question of individual survival after death, preferring to let his disciples dwell on right living and following the Eightfold Path, in the belief that such a well-ordered life would prepare a person for whatever awaits her beyond life's boundaries. Of course, his disciples could not allow such a burning question to go unanswered. Various schools of modern Buddhism have developed complex theologies of last things.

IS HOPE UNIVERSAL?

John Macquarrie calls the belief that life will somehow make sense in the end "the universal presence of hope in mankind."[5] But eternal life has also been called a wishful projection (Feuerbach), a consolation for the oppressed (Marx), a denial of the eternal return of the same (Nietzsche), an un-realistic regression of the psychologically immature (Freud).[6]

Hans Küng counters: "If I believe in eternal life, then it is always possible to endow my life and that of others with meaning."[7]

Without the possibility of eternity, life falls into meaninglessness, the Cosmos is empty space punctuated with energy-sources which are burning themselves out; sentient beings are chemistry accidents. Eschatology, therefore, either validates or voids the whole theological enterprise. No wonder the New Testament is a thoroughly eschatological collection of remembrances pointing to Christian hope in life eternal.

As even a brief survey of the literature of legitimate theology shows, there are a great variety of ideas about individual destinies across the Christian theological spectrum. These various beliefs are reflected quite profoundly in the thinking of laypeople, as the author has learned. Sometimes, when conducting multi-denominational religious retreats, I have asked people to write down what they believe awaits us after death. These responses are then solicited and written on a big sheet of white paper with a thick, felt-tip pen so everyone can see the growing list. Here are some of the notes from one session, which was from a mixed group of Protestants (no avowed Metaphysical Christians):

Q: WHAT HAPPENS AFTER DEATH?

Heaven or Hell immediately.
Heaven or Hell or Purgatory.
Sleep until judgment, then Heaven or Hell.
Sleep until judgment, then life in paradise for, "little flock" and
extinction for non-believers in Jehovah.
Oneness with God if ready, otherwise reincarnation.
I don't know. I don't like to think about death.
Nothing happens—when you're dead, you're dead.
Heaven for everybody.
Heaven for good people; everyone else goes to Enid,
Oklahoma.

Some of the responses are admittedly facetious, but there are some painfully honest answers in this short list. One person professed belief in reincarnation while another said death is the end of consciousness. Remember, this exercise took place on a religious retreat and the replies came from active church members, not unchurched agnostics. Maybe the most honest response of all was the simple remark, "I don't know."

If we're honest with ourselves, we may find the bedrock of our belief system honeycombed with doubts about personal survival after death. It could scarcely be otherwise. Living requires us to take this life seriously, and if we were absolutely certain that a better life awaits us in the hereafter who wouldn't elect a quick death? Doubt keeps us on the job, working at the spiritual growth we need to achieve in this world. Hamlet struggled with this very question and arrived at a similar solution in Shakespeare's greatest tragedy. It is that "unseen country" standing in the shadows beyond life which beckons and frightens us.

If we could see it more clearly, we might be tempted to abandon spaceship earth or, if the vision were not a happy one, despair could crush our ability to live the best possible life in the here-and-now. Some doubts are healthier than certain knowledge. Life after death must remain in the realm of possible-but-uncertain because our lack of absolute knowledge in this instance is good for us. However, religious thinkers will continue to speculate about personal survival because it is such an important ques-tion. Remembering that all eschatologies are educated guesswork, we shall take a look at some of the commonly held beliefs about life after death in Western traditions.

A) Extinction. Belief that death ends consciousness is the oldest personal eschatol-ogy in the Judaeo-Christian heritage. This may surprise some, but there is ample evidence in the Old Testament that extinctionist eschatologies predated any form of survivalism in ancient Hebrew thought. Some examples of extinctionism in the Old Testament are Jeremiah 51:39, 57; II Samuel 14:14; Job 7:21; Psalm 39:13. By the time of Ecclesiastes the Hebrew community was pondering this issue, reflected in the brooding soliloquy by the unknown author of that book:

For the fate of the sons of men and the fate of beasts the same; as
one dies, so dies the other. They all have the same breath, and man

has no advantage over the beasts; for all is vanity. All go to one place; all are from the dust, and all turn to dust again. Who knows whether the spirit of man goes upward and the spirit of the beast goes down to the earth?

(Ecclesiastes 3:19-21)

By the time of Jesus, Jewish theology was divided on the question of personal survival after death. Newer ideas about life after death were needed if the scales of the Cosmos were to balance in favor of Divine justice. Too many times people of God had suffered defeat at the hands of pagan conquerors. Although the prophets kept calling Israel to repent, promising Divine Retribution if she did not, most people simply did not believe they were bad enough to suffer that kind of brutality from the hand of Yahweh.

When the Maccabean revolt produced martyrs who died after offering sacrifice, hence in a state of ritual purity or sinlessness, many Jewish thinkers decided that there must be life after death and a final judgment at which God's justice prevails. The old idea that all suffering comes from sin no longer met their actual life experiences since the martyrs were technically sinless at the time of their deaths. Something had to give ground to accommodate this event within Jewish theology. God's goodness and justice was unimpeachable; therefore the balance must occur after life at a last Judgment.

It was not entirely a new idea, but it was new enough for ancient Judaism. A rift in Jewish thought had occurred which prevailed through New Testament times between those liberals who believed in life after death and those who clung to the ancient teaching of extinction. The "liberals" were known as the Pharisees, and the old guard conservatives were the Sadducees (see Mark 12:18-27; Acts 23:6-10 for some interesting biblical anecdotes about their split).

Modern extinctionist eschatologies of the Western world fall into three broad categories: 1) Absolute, 2) Conditional, and 3) Redemptionist.

1) Absolute extinctionists believe some philosophical variation of the popular pessimism represented by the member of the retreat group who said, "Nothing happens—when you're dead, you're dead." Death ends consciousness permanently for all sentient beings. Modern religious humanism leans in this direction; it is also the philosophy of all true atheists.

2) Conditional extinctionists believe that *some* people will cease to exist, usually wicked ones or those who fail to affirm some particular belief system deemed absolutely essential by the Conditionalist. Jehovah's Witnesses believe that everyone who fails to worship Jehovah will cease to exist after the resurrection to come. The "condition" required for extinction of consciousness is lack of faith.

3) Redemptionist eschatologies of extinction are quite modern and sophisticated. They try hard not to be extinctionist but fail at last because they hold that we do cease to exist. Some current theologians believe death ends consciousness (extinctionism) but that God still "remembers" us and therefore, somehow, we are preserved in the Mind of God; we are redeemed, although we'll never know it.

This should not be confused with the mystical union with God, through which the individual overcomes the *I-Thou* dichotomy to identify with the Divine. Redemptionist eschatologies of extinction believe the human consciousness actually ends—we die and live no more. Yet, because God "remembers" us, our essence is somehow preserved.

All forms of extinctionism fail to address the central question which provokes men and women to look beyond life to a continued existence: If death ends consciousness, what is the purpose of achieving consciousness at all? Is the high intellectual/spiritual awareness represented by the human mind simply a tool to gather more food, to defend the human creature in a hostile world, to outwit his enemies? If death ends it all, then life itself is the ultimate absurdity in a wasteful, scandalously cruel universe. This, of course, is the old Jewish dilemma written anew. God's justice requires that consciousness continues.

B) Heaven or Hell. Perhaps the most widely held eschatological belief in Christian theology until modern times was that there are only two possible spiritual destinies for every soul: heaven or hell. Heaven was a place of unlimited happiness, hell a place of endless misery. Medieval artists gave us a picture of wailing souls in fiery agony and blissed-out semi-angelic beings reclining on pillowy clouds. But in his *Letters from the Earth* Mark Twain satirized the fantasy of the classical "paradise" and showed that no one in his right mind would want to live in such a heaven. We pick up the action as Twain's Satan—a member of the heavenly court temporarily exiled to earth—is describing the human concept of heaven:

> Now then, in the earth these people cannot stand much church—an hour and a quarter is the limit, and they draw the line at once a week. That is to say, Sunday. One day in seven; and even then they do not look forward to it with longing. And so—consider what their heaven provides for them: "church" that lasts forever, and a Sabbath that has no end![8]

Another place Satan tells what happens in "heaven":

> Meanwhile, every person is playing on a harp—those millions and millions!—whereas not more than twenty in the thousand play an instrument in the earth, or ever wanted to. Consider the deafening hurricane of sound—millions and millions of voices screaming at once and millions and millions of harps gritting their teeth at the same time! I ask you: is it hideous, is it odious, is it horrible?[9]

Admittedly a piece of dated satire, Twain still gives us pause to think about the fantasies we have accepted about heaven: Would we really want to live there?

HELL, NO?

Hell is another image that artists have enjoyed painting, perhaps because through representing souls enroute eternal damnation they could get away with portraying the naked human form in an age when women's ankles had to be covered. Heaven and hell are biblical categories, to be sure. Yet, the Bible's descriptions of heaven and hell are not the source of our mental imagery. The true source is probably medieval mythology which had its culmination in the greatest eschatological farce ever written, Dante's *Inferno*.

Reading New Testament accounts of hell it is clear, for example, that Satan is not the overlord of hellfire and the divinely appointed jailer of damned humanity as he is shown to be in the art imagery of Renaissance Europe. That comes from Dante; it is thoroughly un-biblical. Satan, who represented the ultimate evil of the Roman empire in the minds of First century Christians, is cast into a fiery lake in John's Apocalypse, not put in charge of the place. Evil, like death, is done.

But beyond the biblical problems churned up by eternal hellfire presided over by Satan, there are even greater difficulties in maintaining a belief in any kind of an eternal punishment when such a horrendous concept is considered from an ethical/moral perspective. No less a distinguished churchman than theologian John Macquarrie can speak freely against what he calls "the barbarous doctrine of an eternal hell." Macquarrie writes:

> Needless to say, we utterly reject the idea of a hell where God everlastingly punishes the wicked, without hope of deliverance. Even earthly penologists are more enlightened nowadays. Rather we must believe that God will never cease from his quest for universal reconciliation, and we can firmly hope for his victory in this quest, through recognizing that this victory can only come when at last there is the free cooperation of every responsible creature.[10]

Lutheran theologian T. A. Kantonen adds:

> Every sincere Christian shudders at the idea of eternal perdition as the fate of anyone, and if we err in rusting that God's infinite resources will provide a happy ending for all, we may hope to be forgiven.[11]

Belief in an eternal hell, although popular with some rank-and-file churchgoers, is simply not the concept taught to students preparing to enter the Christian ministry at mainline Protestant theological seminaries—one United Methodist, the other United Church of Christ. The author attended two Protestant schools of theology and recalls that *virtually no one on the faculties spoke in favor of belief in hell.* Very few members of the student body reflected this outdated, sub-Christian notion in their personal belief systems. Certainly, the fundamentalists threaten their flocks with eternal damnation while holding up a vision of bliss in paradise, but those churches represent a flight from the complexities of modern, pluralistic society. Those outdated theologies are destined to go the way of other maladaptive religious beliefs of the past.

Those laypeople who believe in some kind of hell—and there are quite a few even in the mainline churches—most often have never reflected on the ghastly character of such a belief. Punishment of any kind is only justified when the end result is improved character or prevention of future offenses. Today any parent who beats his child simply because the little one has erred would rightly be considered a child-abuser. Enlightened parenting sets the example and lovingly corrects the child's natural mistakes rather than dishing out merciless punishment. Even criminals are imprisoned in the hope of rehabilitating them or, at the very least, preventing them from committing other crimes.

Yet, why do the tortured masses suffer in hell? To learn some lesson? Hardly. To prevent further sin? Not at all. The plain fact is that hell, as it is brewed up by our premodern, un-Christian fantasies by way of Dante, exists just to hurt and inflict pain on those unlucky souls who did not get their spiritual act together during their brief span of life on earth. Could any concept be more monstrous? If some want to argue that Jesus taught an eternal hell and therefore the concept must be good, listen to Dr. Kantonen:

> It is inconsistent with all we know about God to suppose that he is more vindictive towards his children than we are toward our own worst enemies. This position (nonexistence of eternal punishment) has been supported by appealing to various passages in the teaching of Jesus and the apostles. *'I,'* says Jesus, *'when I am lifted up from the earth, will draw all men to myself'* (John 12:32). He pictures the shepherd-love of God as persistently seeking the lost one 'until he finds it' (Luke 15:4)...Many of Paul's sayings seem to point to the same conclusion. (E.g., Phil. 2:10-11, Rom. 11:32, I Cor. 15:28.)[12]

Perhaps gospel authors or subsequent editors added threats of hell to the words of Jesus, but we shall never know. What is most important is that the undisputed message of Jesus Christ was a message of forgiveness and universal membership in the Kingdom of God. Perhaps Jesus did employ existing imagery about hell from the Greco-Roman worldview when He taught. In His lifestyle and personal faith, Jesus went far beyond such limited concepts. He spoke about hell, but He acted like a universalist.

Heaven is the other extreme, but it too has met with criticism in the modern world. What kind of existence would provide no challenge to grow, no new learning, no creative work to be accomplished? If the classical heaven and hell are the only two possible choices, eternity offers bleak prospects, indeed.

C) Reincarnation. Contrary to general belief among the metaphysical churches, reincarnation was never widely popular in Christian theology. Belief in the return of human consciousness in another human body has always smacked of Far Eastern religious thought, something imported from India by way of sea trade routes and overland caravans. *Metempsychosis*, as the early Church fathers called reincarnation, occupied only peripheral importance in their speculations. An idea as explosive and, in the classical definition of the word, as heretical as metempsychosis would have been refuted at great length by the highly combative apologists for orthodoxy. The fact that no such body of refutations exists suggests that either very few people knew about the concept of reincarnation or, more likely, it was seen as so foreign that no responsible churchman gave it any serious credibility. There are some points, however, where familiar biblical passages could be reinterpreted to support reincarnation. When Jesus asked his disciples a profound question, their answer could easily mean the apostles believed in reincarnation:

> And Jesus went on with his disciples, to the villages of Caesarea Philippi; and on the way he asked his disciples, 'Who do men say that I am?' And they told him, 'John the Baptist; and others say, Elijah; and others one of the prophets.' (Mark 8:27-28)

Jesus seldom hesitated to correct his disciples when they committed major thought-blunders, yet according to all three synoptic gospel writers (Matthew, Mark, and Luke) he stepped right over an opportunity to express disapproval of a reply which seemed to favor reincarnation. Some commentators have concluded, Jesus tacitly approved of reincarnation, since the apostles' suggestion that he might be a reborn prophet met no rebuke from their master. It is an argument from silence, and there is another problem as well.

Are the disciples really suggesting reincarnation here?

Elijah, the one prophet mentioned by name, was believed to have been taken up into heaven bodily in a fiery chariot. Other prophets might have done likewise. Hence, Jesus could be the original Elijah or the original nonspecific prophet, not a reincarnated one.

Perhaps the line about "John the Baptist" suggests that some people, in that age before the electronic news media, had not heard or not believed that the prophet of the Jordan was dead. Jesus could scarcely be John unless He was John's ghost or John resurrected, neither of which would have been impossible for ancient minds to conceive. However, these two conclusions seem unlikely from the context.

BORN AGAIN?

A far more interesting possibility exists for reincarnationist eschatologies when considering the mystical statements in the fourth gospel, especially those famous words Jesus addressed to Nicodemus: "You must be born again."

Traditionally this passage has been spiritually interpreted to mean a renewal of the person when he/she accepts the Lord Jesus Christ as personal savior. However, there is nothing in the context which prohibits a reincarnationist interpretation. Reincarnationism isn't eschatologically invalid from a Christian perspective, just that it is relatively alien to Western thought.

D) Universalism. The belief in universal salvation is ancient within Christianity. As mentioned above, there are clear indications of germinal stage universalism in the writings of Paul and in the gospel stories told by and about Jesus. Perhaps, through the parables of Jesus, some of the Master's own universalist theology slips past the editors who had a vested interest in seeing the wicked punished by the time of the great persecutions at the end of the first century. By the late second and early third centuries, great churchmen like Origen were openly proclaiming that God would not allow anyone to be lost. This meant some kind of eternal life for everyone and eternal punishment for no one.

Universalism, however, is not without its problems. If everyone goes to the same place (i.e., heaven), what is the purpose of life on earth and why did Jesus Christ come? If the mass-murderer is to be rewarded alongside his victims, how can we speak at all about God's justice? And what happens to those who refused to learn, refused to grow? Are they forced to don angel wings, one-size-fits-all?

A FRESH LOOK AT PURGATORY

Some theologians believe that growth must continue even after physical death and that dying accomplishes nothing other than changing the locale of our education. John Macquarrie wants to resurrect the old High Church idea of Purgatory, which he sees as an ideal concept to fill the gap between incomplete spiritual growth and diversity-in-union with God:

> Heaven, purgatory, and hell are not sharply separated, but form a kind of continuum through which the soul may move, perhaps from the near-annihilation of sin to the closest union with God. Indeed, the concept of purgatory served the valuable purpose of introducing the dynamic, moving element into the traditional scheme, where heaven and hell could easily be mistaken for fixed immutable states.[13]

Macquarrie's purgatory fits our category of universalist eschatologies because he flatly rejects any eternal punishment and believes everyone will eventually "be saved." However, his use of a word which has such a medieval sound to the modern ear does little to reach those who want the Church to address itself to the present and future.

A far better word-picture might be the old term *Sanctification* or its modern equivalent, *Spiritual Growth*. In any event, those of us who claim the mystical tradition have little quarrel with Professor Macquarrie's basic idea that growth continues after this life and can be seen as a matter of degrees rather than some arbitrary line which must be crossed to enter heaven and avoid hellfire.

COLECTIVE ESCHATOLOGIES: WHAT'S UP FOR THE COSMOS

Individual destinies are only part of the problem facing us, albeit the most important part for every individual. The other two metaphysical questions which eschatology asks are, "What will be the fate of the human race?" and "Will the Universe come to an end?" Although we are not as personally involved with these questions as we are when contemplating our survival after death, nevertheless we have an investment in this Universe and are naturally curious about how the currents of time will treat our heirs and our world. Of all our speculations, this will doubtless be the most speculative, but science does offer some possible answers which can help theology at this point. We move now from Personal to Collective Eschatologies.

2) THE HUMAN RACE AND ITS ULTIMATE FATE

If history is any indicator, we are a wandering race. From our African Genesis we drifted northward and learned how to survive in the snows of Eurasia, still farther and we adapted to warm waters of the Indian Ocean where we learned to build rafts that carried our seed to tiny specks of rock in a vast, uncharted sea. It is no accident that some of our greatest works of literature tell of travel to strange, new lands. There is something in the human consciousness that beckons us onward, away from the security of old ways and into the open sea where all things are possible to those who believe.

Earlier in this work we quoted the popular proverb, "A ship in a harbor is safe, but that is not what ships are built for." We are a race of shipbuilders, adventurers, and explorers. And the greatest years of human exploration lie ahead of us as we begin to dip a toe into the ocean of galaxies that comprises our Cosmos. If science can find a way to circumvent the Light Barrier— which at this writing is still believed to be the absolute speed limit of the Universe—then our descendants shall surely take their needlecrafts, Bibles, and candy bars aboard starships to other worlds. Perhaps the destiny of the human race lies beyond Earth. Perhaps not. But if God has created a Cosmos in which starflight is possible in a reasonable amount of time, doubtless our descendants shall discover its secrets and take the treasures of the mystical Christian heritage with them as they embark on the greatest adventure of all time.

Even Macquarrie agrees that this is no longer the stuff of fantasy but must be seriously addressed by responsible theologians. He quotes Alice Meynell's futurist poem in a visionary passage from his own book, *Principles of Christian Theology*:

> The overwhelming probability is that countless billions of "histories" have been enacted in the cosmos, and a space-age cosmology calls for a vastly enlarged understanding of divine grace and revelation. Now that man is reaching out into space, Alice Meynell's prediction is not so improbable:

> > Doubtless we shall compare together, hear
> > A million alien gospels, in what guise
> > He trod the Pleiades, the Lyre, the Bear.[14]

If we abandon the Earth before our sun explodes in the far, far distant future, humanity might endure in some form to the very end of the Cosmos—if there is to be such an end.

3) THE UNIVERSE—WILL IT END?

There are only two possible answers to this question and both of them are scientifically based. Either we live in a continuously re-creating Universe or the Cosmos is a one-time phenomenon which is headed for oblivion. Biblical images of the end seem to represent only one possibility. If we divest the mythological trappings from NT accounts of "the End" we find a totally re-created heaven and earth, no hint of an all-encompassing death appears in the wildly optimistic words of John's Apocalypse:

> Then I saw a new heaven and a new earth; for the first heaven and the first earth had passed away, and the sea was no more. And I saw the holy city, new Jerusalem, coming down out of heaven from God, prepared as a bride adorned for her husband; and I heard a loud voice from the throne saying, "Behold, the dwelling of God is with men. He will dwell with them, and they shall be his people, and God himself will be with them; he will wipe away every tear from their eyes, and death shall be no more..."

> (Revelation 21:1-4)

Although written in a prescientific age, the New Testament's complete trust in Divine Order transcends the limitations of a flat-earth cosmology, providing insights which apply to the space age and beyond. Yet, there is no promise that this Cosmos will survive eternally. A new heaven and a new earth are indicated; the old one passes away.

Scientists are divided about the fate of the Universe. While most agree that the present Cosmos began after a Big Bang some fifteen-plus billion years ago, some believe that the Universe will continue to expand outward from that explosion until the last star burns out, and others believe an implosion will occur which will eventually result another Big Bang. The latter group, in effect, sees the Universe as a kind of cosmic accordion which exploded outward and collapsed inward any number of times—perhaps an infinite process without beginning or end.

Still another possibility comes from Einstein. Space is curved, so that one can theoretically continue in a straight line and end up at the point of origin without turning from the original course. If that is true, some scientists say that all matter could have exploded outward fifteen billion years ago only to reconvene at some moment in the far future.

These are scientific ideas about the future of the Cosmos. Although the question does have profound theological implications, it remains a scientific question and not a metaphysical one. Science and religion have a working partnership as long as science continues to look for new information about the physical Universe and religion offers its insights about ways to live more effectively in the Cosmos. When science starts making pronouncements about spiritual Truth or religion begins to publish decrees about the origin or fate of the Universe, both are out of their areas of expertise. Religion must accept the discoveries of science as gifts from the God Who created/organized the Cosmos; science must turn to religion to learn how to love our neighbor in a dangerous, weapon-ridden world.

SECOND COMING, REVISITED

Unfortunately, some religious groups make noise about an end of the world by a supernatural intervention of God in time and space. With all due respect to our brothers and sisters in churches which specialize in end-of-time theologies, that is simply not how God operates, nor is it faithful to the message of the New Testament when that message is removed from its mythological packaging.

Jesus Christ taught a kingdom that was "not of this world," but he proceeded to give men and women teachings that would enable them to live at peace in a world without end. Most of all he showed people a natural way of life, a practical faith. There were no magical, superhuman powers in his healing miracles—he told his disciples they could do these things, too. He saw himself as the Son of God, but told men and women they had power to become likewise. His answer to the criticism from the religious leaders who accused him of making himself God was to quote Psalm 82:6, *"I said, you are gods."*

This admittedly represents late first century thinking, since it comes from John's gospel, but even the synoptics show a Jesus who marveled when men marveled at his works. Johnnine theology might represent a few decades of mulling this over in the minds of first century Christians, but it might also represent strains of tradition originating with Jesus Himself. It is unlikely that a person who believed other humans could attain His degree of spirituality would also believe only supernatural intervention by God in time and space at the Last Judgment will right the wrongs of this world and usher in the Kingdom of Heaven for an elect few.

How better to see the "Second Coming" as a continuous process whereby Jesus the Christ "comes" to men and women of succeeding generations with a freshness that speaks to each new situation in words of Christian hope? For Jesus, the Kingdom of Heaven is always in our midst, always within us. If that is true, the natural order shall roll on and God's kingdom shall find ways to manifest itself in and through the Cosmos as we know it. Supernaturalism is not required in a well-planned Universe. *Divine Order* will do nicely.

FAITH THE KEY

Any discussion of eschatology can only be an exercise in shortcomings, but Christian Theology in all its diversity is our topic and we shall pursue the broad course of studies as we continue our survey. People have wondered about what lies after death, what stands at the far end of time, from the earliest days of human life.

Archeologists find that even prehistoric peoples like the Neanderthal buried their dead with tools and artifacts as though they wanted to send their loved one into the next world with the proper equipment to live well.

Books by pop-religious authors warn people that *The End Is Near*, that we are approaching Armageddon. Intelligent, well-educated people spend vast sums of money on psychics, fortunetellers, and various self-designated seers because we want to know what lies ahead.

But we don't know. And that's why they call it "faith."

A PERSONAL VIEW

A few years ago the author was pondering Life, Death, and Eternity over a chef's salad when a sudden realization became clearer than ever before. Like many of the great riddles of life, we can't know for certain what fate awaits the Cosmos in general ourselves in particular.

It was not a terribly original thought, but the realization which followed sounded new to me: We can't know for sure, and that's OK. It makes for a better life of service to believe rather than to know, to hope rather than to be certain.

Taking a pen and notebook, these words flowed easily. They are not the last words on last things, but they say what one person sees when he stands looking into the face of sprawling, lovely, incomprehensible mystery.

A WORTHY SACRIFICE

If I offer my whole life as a Sacrifice
on the altar of Thy service,

If I provoke people to ask spiritual questions
and love them into greener pastures of mind
and soul,

If I expend my life-energies in ceaseless striving
for World Unity and individual Christ-consciousness,

If I give my talents and strength so long as
I have breath and awareness
To help others walk the path of peace
in the footsteps of our Lord Jesus Christ,

Then whatever awaits after the life-force has flowed
from my body—
Be it eternal progress,
eternal bliss,
or eternal oblivion—

Will do just fine,

And my life will have been worthily lived.[15]

CHECK YOUR KNOWLEDGE

1. Identify/explain the following: *Eschatology, "Popular" Eschatoligies, Parousia, Eschaton, Apocalypse, Extinctionism, Universalism, Purgatory, Metempsychosis, Second Coming.*

2. What was the general difference between Hebrew and Greek conceptions of time? How did this affect the theology of each?

3. List and explain the three kinds of extinctionist eschatologies mentioned in the text.

4. What position do most modern theologians take on the existence of hell?

5. Did the early Church believe in reincarnation? Based on what evidence?

6. What three possible fates await the physical universe?

QUESTIONS FOR DISCUSSION

1. Could "purgatory" be a useful concept for Truth churches? How would you interpret it?

2. What happens to consciousness after physical death? How do you know?

3. Do you believe in reincarnation? Defend your answer by citing evidence and arguments from the four sources of theological information—*Scripture, Tradition, Experience, and Reason.*

4. Christian Truth Churches and all Mystical/Metaphysical Christians tend to be universalists. If so, what kind of eternal destiny awaits people like Adolf Hitler?

5. Do you agree with the author's contention that humans will explore the stars? What might happen to Christian theology if Alice Meynell's poetic vision comes true?

6. What does the *"Second Coming of Christ"* mean in your belief system?

NOTES

1. Richard P. McBrien, *Catholicism* (Oak Grove, MN: Winston Press, 1981), p. 1101.

2. Luke 16:30-31 (RSV).

3. II Peter 3:3-4, 9-10a.

4. Matthew 19:14b.

5. John Macquarrie, *Christian Hope* (NY: Harper & Row, 1978), Preface.

6. Hans Küng, *Eternal Life?* (NY: Doubleday, 1934). p. xiii.

7. IBID., p. 11.

8. Mark Twain, *Letters from the Earth* (NY: Harper & Row, 1962), p. 12.

9. IBID., p. 232.

10. Macquarrie, *Principles*, p. 367.

11. T.A. Kantonen, *Life After Death* (Philadelphia: Muhlenberg Press, 1962), p. 47.

12. IBID.

13. Macquarrie, *Principles*, p. 367.

14. IBID., p. 172.

15. Thomas W. Shepherd, "A Worthy Sacrifice," unpublished poem, 1977.

SACRAMENTAL THEOLOGY: A NEW LOOK

Chapter Eleven

Martin Luther and Ulrich Zwingli had a lot in common. Both were German-speaking leaders of the Protestant Reformation: Zwingli (1484-1531) helped the Germanic Swiss provinces break with Roman Catholicism, while the anti-establishment escapades of Luther (1483-1546) made him undisputed leader of the religio-political rebellion in Germany proper.

Both agreed on all major points, save one: the Sacraments. They decided to meet at Marburg in the autumn of 1529 to discuss unity in the struggle to establish a free church in Europe. Possibly, the two great reformers could close ranks and join forces against a powerful and, at that time in history, inimical central church in Rome. A United Protestant Church was visible on the horizon as they met. Roland H. Bainton comments on that meeting in his book *The Reformation of the Sixteenth Century:*

> A truly surprising measure of agreement was attained. On only one point was accord impossible, and that was the Supper of the Lord. The great rite of Christian love had become the ground of contention.[1]

And what was their difference of opinion? Like the testimony of an American president hundreds of years later, their contention centered on the meaning of the word *is*. When celebrating the first Eucharist Jesus had said: *"This is my body."* To understand the importance of this we must quickly review some theologies of the Lord's Supper.

CRASH COURSE IN CATHOLIC SACRAMENTAL THOUGHT

Catholic theology, along with Eastern Orthodoxy, has always maintained that the elements of bread and wine are miraculously changed into the substance" of the body and blood of Jesus Christ after they are consecrated by an ordained priest. The bread and wine remain physically the same, but their essence is now changed so that they are literally Christ Himself.

For Catholics, the celebration of the Mass is in fact a re-enactment of Calvary; Christ's body is sacrificed anew upon the altar by the priest. Since Jesus Christ is seen as uniquely God, those who hold such a "high" theology of the Eucharist often vener-ate the bread and wine once the act of priestly celebration transubstantiates it into the body and blood of the Savior. The next time you visit of a church with such a "high" sacramental theology, look for a small flickering flame at the front of the sanctuary; this indicates a portion of the sacrament has been held "in reserve" and is present for adoration. For those communions with this theological stance, that bit of consecrated bread is literally a chunk of God Almighty.[2]

AND THE REFORMERS SAID...?

Two different interpretations. Zwingli thought Jesus really meant, *"This signi-fies my body,"* or, *"Let this bread represent my body when you do this in remem-brance of me."* The Swiss position was a radical break with ancient tradition. For Zwingli, the *Eucharist* (Greek, *"to give thanks"*) is merely a commemorative meal. In his *Seventy-Seven Articles*, the Swiss reformer wrote:

> Christ, having sacrificed Himself once, is to eternity a certain and valid sacrifice for the sins of all faithful, wherefrom it follows that the mass is not a sacrifice, but is a remembrance of the sacrifice and assurance of the salvation which God has given us...Christ is the only mediator between God and us.[3]

No two positions could be further apart than the Zwinglian idea of symbolic remembrance and the Catholic doctrine of transubstantiation.

Luther, however, disagreed with both. In Zwingli we find rationalism, a faith that appeals directly to the mind. In Martin Luther there is a strain of mysticism which gave him the tendency to look deeper into things of the spirit. Luther developed a remarkable theology of the Lord's Supper which said, in effect, that Christ is present in everything.

Theologian Paul Tillich summarized Luther's teaching:

> Christ is present in everything, in stone and fire and tree, but for us he is present only when he speaks to us. But he can speak to us through everything ... In a Lutheran service during the Sundays in spring, you always find a tremendous amount of flowers and things of nature brought into the church, because of this symbol of the participation of the body of Christ in the world.[4]

Christ is in "stone, fire, and tree." Christ is in the light of the farthest galaxy. Christ is in the lily pad, the cactus, and the dung heap. But in some places the pres-ence of Christ (i.e., God's presence) is more discernible than others. Events in time-and-space where God's presence becomes elevated, so that we become aware of Spirit which pervades everything, are quite special and mysterious. They are points at which we see through the dark glass of human limitations and glimpse the true nature of the Divine-human paradox.

How can finite human minds contact the infinite God?

Upon what common ground may we stand when communing with our Creator? Where do we find God in the world? Or, as some might ask, how do we reach upward, to take part in the life that God can offer us, when all we can build is a Tower of Babel? These questions must be answered prior to any meaningful discussion on regular encounters with the Divine through the Sacraments.

HOW IS GOD KNOWN?

Until this point in our ongoing study we have assumed God can be known by finite human beings. Yet, we have offered no theological reflection on how such contact is possible, or whether the Divine or human side must initiate the encounter, or what form this contact might take. The differences for Christian thought are profound, depending on the options we select.

For example, if we say *"God can be known to us through prayer,"* does that mean we approach God, or God approaches us? Are we able to build a modern, more effective "Tower of Babel" to ascend to God through higher spiritual enlightenment, or must God descend to our level and lift us up? In other words, does God come "down" to us through His act of revelation, or do we climb "up" to Him by our act of discovery?

Does a quick reply comes to mind? Be careful. Questions like this are often religious icebergs ready to gouge unsuspecting theological pleasure-ships that sail too glibly into their wake. Although theologians can rightly be accused of occasionally making mountains out of molehills, undisciplined religious talk tries to leap molehills which prove to be alpine cliffs for the unwary. We cannot simply dismiss major theological problems like this one with a frown and an exclamation, *"But everyone knows...!"* Everyone knew the earth was flat, too.

REVELATION OR DISCOVERY?

Once we allow that such interaction happens we are left with the question, "Who does what?" There are two usual ways to consider the problem of human traffic with the Divine. 1) God comes to humanity, revealing unto us that which we never would have otherwise known. 2) We search for God until we find His footprints, then piece together the story and discover His Truth. We shall consider these separately.

1) REVELATION: GOD COMES TO US

One of the best contemporary descriptions of revelation comes from John Macquarrie, whose work we continue to consult as we work through the categories of Christian thought: ...essential to the idea of revelation is that what we come to know through revelation has a gift-like character. If, in general terms, we say that what is disclosed in revelation is the dimension of the holy, then, in the revelatory experience, it is as if the holy "breaks in" and the movement is from beyond man toward man.[5]

Revelation means the movement is downward from God to woman/man. Macquarrie says that religious communities are built around a primordial revelation given to the founder by the Divine. But communication between God and human does not stop with the initial downpour of information, after which everyone is reduced to shuffling through accounts of that initial experience like Supreme Court Justices arguing the precedents of Constitutional law. There must be continuous contact with the Divine, or the founding revelation will deteriorate into antiquated meaninglessness. We look at Macquarrie's comments on present-day manifestations of Divine Truth, note the careful tone he sets when dealing with extracurricular, personal instruction received directly from God by individual believers. Macquarrie writes:

> We do not normally dignify our day-to-day experiences of the holy by the name of "revelation," and no theology properly called so could be founded on private revelations, for, as has been stressed already, theology expresses the faith of a community. Yet on the other hand we would never have believed that anyone had been the recipient of a revelation unless we ourselves had some experience of the holy. Indeed, the very notion of revelation would be completely unintelligible to us unless we knew first hand some experience that bears some analogy to revelation.[6]

There is the problem in a nutshell. These points will surface again when we examine critically the dangers of "special revelations" in our chapter on Pop-Fad Spirituality (Chapter 19), but for now let's consider how to determine if an idea authentically represents "revelation" or is just someone's fantasy. In many ways, this is the problem we faced when discussing epistemology (Chapter 3), however here we are testing a single source of religious information—i.e., revelation—rather than scanning the various ways to know Truth.

If God comes to us by revelation, we still need to apply the tests of epistemology to that input. We must first ask whether such God-to-humanity communications even exist. Macquarrie thinks so. He also believes, and we would agree, that the community of faith provides the best testing ground for religious ideas, even ideas coming from alleged Divine revelations, but hastens to add that the testing works both ways.

> It is present experience within a community of faith that gives rise to theology and that enables us to recognize the primordial revelation as revelation; but if theology is to be saved from the dangers of subjectivism, the varieties of experience within the community must be submitted to the relatively objective content of the classic revelation on which the community is founded.[7]

When we discussed epistemology we focused on this kind of dialectical model of knowledge. Seek Truth and be fearless, but bring all to the yardstick of Jesus Christ as present to us in Scripture, mediated through Tradition, and examined by Reason.

Only this give-and-take keeps the ancient teachings from becoming fossilized, which Macquarrie agrees would provide us no revelation at all. Dialogue and critical analysis permit us to evaluate new ideas and practices encountered in everyday life-experience.[8]

NATURAL THEOLOGY VS REVELATION

If we find God in such a community experience or through the primordial revelation, we still face the same question: Did God come to us or did we discover Him? Macquarrie is far gentler with humanity that some recent theologians like Karl Barth (pronounced *Bart.*)

In 1937-38 Barth was invited to present the Gifford Lectures which, according to the will left by the late Lord Gifford, were supposed to present Natural Theology, today an archaic term, which meant Barth was to discuss religious philosophies based on reason rather than divine revelation. Barth accepted the commission, but he totally disregarded its stipulations:

> I certainly see—with astonishment—that such a science as Lord Gifford had in mind does exist...I am convinced that so far as it has existed and still exists, it owes its existence to a radical error.[9]

Kantonen says that in Barth's theology:

> Man's ultimate need is God but his attempt to think or to find God is futile. God is not the object of man's rational apprehension, moral striving, or religious feeling. The God who is set up as the object of human religiosity is only a man-made idol. The true God is always subject, not object, one who stands over against man, one who takes the initiative, one who speaks to man by his own sovereign word, one who in Christ reveals himself and acts to restore man into personal fellowship with himself.[10]

Neo-orthodox thinkers like Barth, Brunner, and Bultmann insisted that the impetus must come from God, not humanity. If there were no revelation from God, we would know nothing about Him. In His greatest self-disclosure, God comes to us as Jesus Christ. We do not come to Him. That would be as impossible as the Tower of Babel. We cannot reach God because we are part of the problem, the giants of neo-orthodoxy said. Our spiritual science is flawed.

2) DISCOVERY: MATH & MYSTICISM

A radically different opinion holds that all knowledge is discovered. Even if God lowers instructions from heaven in a golden basket, someone will have to find the basket and interpret those instructions. Discovery is the basic procedure for all information, spiritual subjects included.

Charles Hartshorne, Unitarian-Universalist layperson and professor emeritus, leaned in the direction of discovery in his weighty little book *The Divine Relativity*. Hartshorne believed certain religious ideas (i.e., God's existence) can be logically demonstrated, and he had no patience with those who say God is just too mysterious to understand:

The very people who choose the soft words, paradox and mystery, for what, so far as they have shown, are simply contradictions in their own thinking, resort to the harsher terms, absurdity or contradiction, do they not, when they meet with difficulties not essentially different in systems which they oppose? ... an illogical position is hardly strengthened by the apparent logic with which it furnishes reasons for its own illogicality.[11]

Hartshorne's point is well taken. We need not embrace absurdity in order to pledge our loyalty to Jesus Christ. However, faith is more than logic. One possible critique of Professor Hartshorne is that he relies too heavily on pure logic, since the rational mind represents only half of the formative factor of *Reason, i.e., Intellectual Reason*; the other half is *Intuitive Reason*. Add to this *Experience*, mediated by dialogue with a larger community of believers, which can be measured against the standards of *Tradition* and compared with the record of the "primordial revelation" (*Scripture*). This four-fold interaction gives us the total expression which we call Christian Faith.

Yet, Christian theology is really not a group effort but an individual encounter between the believer and his/her Lord. The individual does the work, experiences faith, dialogues with other Christians, and compares the result with the Jesus Christ yardstick as He is known both in the life of the community and through the primordial, scriptural revelation. Because everyone's spiritual growth is an individual learning plan, God does not make our faith-decisions for us. Jesus Christ acted as though He believed every person He encountered had the divine power to choose the best path. Jesus presented alternatives from which His listeners had to choose, and He told an assortment of stories to reach a variety of learning styles.

Discovery says that we find God; Revelation insists that God finds us. There is yet a third alternative heretofore unmentioned.

3) WE SEEK GOD UNTIL HE FINDS US

Perhaps the seeking is two-sided. In the parable of the Prodigal Son, the Father sees his wayward progeny approaching from a great distance and rushes out to meet him. If this parable represents the model of Divine-human interaction favored by Jesus, as many scholars believe, then we can see initiative is required on both sides.

To preserve human freedom, God cannot force goodness and Truth upon us. He must patiently wait until we move in His direction. That is Discovery. However, as soon as a person comes to his senses and heads homeward to the Father, God comes rushing to greet us with blessings unanticipated.

Other parables suggest God does not loaf around in heaven while His children are wandering in the wilderness. The Good Shepherd goes after the lost sheep; the woman lights her lamp and sweeps her house until she finds that misplaced coin. In Jesus Christ we find Discovery and Revelation perfectly integrated. To paraphrase

Eric Butterworth, Jesus was a human like us Who discovered the power within Him, and by that great discovery He reveals something of our indwelling Divine Spirit.

With this two-fold, dialectical understanding, we can now turn to the study of those places in life where God's presence is revealed/discovered for us.

SACRAMENTUM

Luther believed the points of contact were the Sacraments of the Christian church. Before we can reconsider sacramental theology we must first look at some traditional views of these time-and-space happenings which are celebrated in some form by every congregation that calls itself Christian.

First, a word-study of the term seems to be in order. Our English word *sacrament* comes into the language by way of dual misunderstandings, one linguistic and the other theological.

The Latin word *sacramentum* was a common term in pre-Christian times to describe a bonding procedure of the Roman judicial system. When two adversaries went to court, each was required to deposit a sum of money—a *sacramentum*—which the loser would then contribute to religious charity. The word *sacramentum* also referred to the oath of allegiance a new recruit took when entering the army. Consequently, the term gradually became a synonym for an oath or covenant.

#1 - THEOLOGICAL MISTAKE

By the second century the church father Tertullian equated conversion to the Christian faith with this oath of allegiance, calling the process *sacramentum*. But it was Pliny the Younger (ca. 112 A. D.) who reported the outlaw activities of this new religion, explaining that Christians bound themselves together to commit crimes. Pliny told the emperor that he wasn't certain what kind of crimes Christians were committing, but anyone so completely dedicated to a secret society must be up to no good and should be punished. As a pagan, he could scarcely understand the significance of the Christian *sacramentum* even though he rightly saw that joining the faith required a commitment on the part of the convert. That was the theological misunderstanding.

We can forgive Pliny for his ignorance; few people understood Christian theology in its early days. Some would say the situation has changed little throughout the ages. Go beyond the ranks of the professional religious thinkers and you encounter an amazing variety of ignorance as to what the Church has really taught. Perhaps this is the way it must be. Theology is like any other profession: specialized vocabulary, technology (tools + knowledge), and procedures. Laypeople seldom care about the ideas which excite us theologians, but that is probably a blessing masquerading as a deficiency.[12]

However, the linguistic mistake was, ironically, made by a professional theologian, Tertullian, and the greatest linguist of the early church.

#2 - LINGUISTIC MISTAKE

In the fourth century Pope Damascus commissioned St. Jerome to translate the Bible into the common language of their day, Latin Vulgate. To accomplish this Herculean feat, Jerome moved his desk to Jerusalem where he studied, conversed, and debated with the preeminent rabbis who still lived in the land which gave birth to both testaments. The result was a superb translation, based on ancient texts, which could be studied by anyone who read Latin vernacular.

A secondary purpose, but one which was even more important for the still-young Church, was that Roman Catholic priests reading the Sunday text during worship in the Western church were reading in the language of the common people. Peasants, tradesmen, wives, young children—all heard the gospel in their language. Jerome's Bible did for the fourth century Latin-speaking churchgoers what the modern translations of Scripture have done for twentieth century Christians.

However, Jerome's translation was not without flaws. When he rendered the passage "Repent, for the kingdom of Heaven is at hand," into Latin, it came out, "Do penance, for the kingdom of Heaven is at hand." He also translated the New Testament Greek word *mysterion*, which biblical authors used to describe church practices such as baptism and the Eucharist, into Latin as *sacramentum*. Instead of mysteries, these occasions would be seen by the Western Church as oaths of allegiance sealing the recipient to the faith.[13]

St. Augustine (A. D. 354-430) defined a Sacrament as a "visible sign of an invisible reality," which is often described in modern churches as a visible sign of invisible "grace."[14] To investigate properly what that short phrase means we would have to discuss *grace, signs,* and the distinction between the *visible* and *invisible* activity of God.

Instead of wallowing into that thicket, let's just invoke artistic license and paraphrase Augustine's definition with a little help from Luther: *A Sacrament is any place at which God's normally mysterious, unknowable Presence breaks through and makes itself known to seeking souls.*

People who grew up in traditional churches might be surprised at a sacramental theology which begins with such a broad brush stroke. Since the Council of Trent in 1545, Catholic thought has tended to limit the sacraments to seven: *baptism, confirmation, the Eucharist, penance, extreme unction* (last rites), *ordination,* and *matrimony.*

Protestant reformers took issue with this list and defined a sacrament even more narrowly. Not only did the act have to be a way for God's grace (goodness in action) to manifest itself, a genuine sacrament must have been inaugurated by Jesus and explicitly commanded by Him. According to the earliest account of the Last Supper (I Corinthians 11:23-25), Jesus did this only in regard to the Eucharist. Only baptism, ordained by the risen Lord in Matthew 28:19, also qualifies as a legitimate sacrament for most Protestants.

In general, Protestants also differ from Catholics by insisting, in John Calvin's words, that the sacraments "communicate no grace from themselves, but announce and show, and, as earnests and pledges, ratify, the things which are given to us by the goodness of God."[15]

Protestant sacraments are not a "medicine of immortality," as Ignatius of Antioch called them in the second century. They do not give the recipient something which he/she did not have before the sacramental act. Baptism and the Lord's Supper play a part in Protestant theology roughly equivalent to the Bible: they are places where the believer can receive inspiration but are not funnels through which God pours Himself out to people regardless of their receptivity.[16]

The ancient church defined the mysterion/sacramentum much more broadly than either Protestant or Roman Catholic doctrines presently allow. According to Dr. George Wesley Buchanan, writing in *Harper's Dictionary of the Bible*, early Christians accepted almost any evidence of God's activity as a sacramental event:

> Although baptism and the Eucharist were considered the primary sacraments, the term "sacrament" was used in the early church to describe many kinds of religious ceremonies and practices. By the twelfth century Hugo of St. Victor listed some thirty sacraments. This was probably the result of Augustine's definition of sacraments as signs pertaining to things divine, or visible forms of invisible grace. Since there is no limit to the number of ways God's grace can be expressed, the number of sacraments increased with Christian sensitivity and imagination. Therefore the Council of Trent (A.D. 1545) decreed that not all signs of sacred things had sacramental value. Visible signs become sacraments only if they represent an invisible grace and become its channels.[17]

NO ONE COMES UNTO THE FATHER EXCEPT BY US

Sacramental theology has always intrigued mystics, mainly because it says that God deals One-to-one with His people. Yet, some mystical thinkers have been suspicious of church-administered, liturgical sacraments. These "visible signs" have been clutched by professional clergy, who controlled access to the "invisible grace" the sacraments offered. If you can't get to heaven without the sacraments, and if the clergy are empowered to withhold those rites from communicant believers—guess who's really in charge of heaven?

In medieval times the Church was able to bludgeon kings and lesser rulers into submission by threat or actual imposition of the Interdict which meant every church in the region affected would close its doors. That was serious business. No weddings, funerals, baptisms, or Eucharist. No forgiveness of sins. When the whole Western world worshipped as one universal catholic Church, the Interdict was the equivalent of a spiritual nuclear bomb. Interdicts were effectively laid upon France in 998, Germany in 1102, the city of Rome in 1155, and England in 1208.

The events surrounding an Interdict were so overwhelming to the medieval mind that people behaved as though the culprits named by the Church were carriers of the plague. Will Durant describes an episode in his massive, multi-volume *Story of Civilization:*

> When King Robert of France was excommunicated (which led to the interdict of 998 against the whole country) for marrying his cousin he was abandoned by all his courtiers and nearly all his servants; two domestics who remained threw into the fire the victuals left by him at his meals, lest they be contaminated by them.[18]

Later, the Interdict would be ignored or laughed off by rulers and large segments of the Christian world, especially after the Reformation. Today, even personal excommunication seems like a medieval anachronism, and the idea of putting a whole nation on a spiritual starvation diet is, hopefully, an idea whose time has passed.[19]

If we bring ancient thought into dialogue with modern experience, we may be able to see many places where God's presence is discernible. Some of these will be experiences of corporate worship in a very traditional sense, such as the Lord's Supper rightly understood by the recipient, but others will be private, personal moments when God is able to catch our attention.

Who has not stood under the *mysterion/sacramentum* of the night sky and breathed the awe-inspiring Presence? What is more evocative of the Divine than deep meditation, heights of prayer, or episodes of love?

It may be helpful to discuss some of these life-events as sacramental encounters, especially if we are serious about constructing a systematic theology that is thoroughly mystical and touches base with the great themes of Christian thought. As we look at sacramental theology from this wide, inclusive viewpoint it is important to remember that Metaphysical Christians are members of the Church universal, heirs to all that has gone before us, and not as curious spectators watching a religious procession. We may even differ with some of our ancestors in the central premises of the Ancient Faith, but we do so as participants in the body of Christ. The Sacraments, more than anything else, provide a potential bridge to link the archipelago of the Christian family with itself.

THE FRAMEWORK: TWELVE TIME-SPACE EVENTS

We said that our operating definition of a *sacrament* will be *any place where God's normally mysterious, unknowable presence breaks through and makes itself known to us.* This means sacraments are existential events—they happen in the course of daily life. Under this definition a sacrament is less like a novel and more like a stage play, a drama in which we are players, not mere spectators. You experience, interact with, a true sacrament; you don't watch it like a television show.

Any number of space-time events could be sacraments, but for the sake of economy let's consider a limited number of occasions at which God's presence can become discernible to the receptive person. Thirty, suggested by Hugo of St. Victor in the twelfth century, is too many to treat even lightly in a single chapter. Two, insisted upon by the Protestant Reformers, seems unnecessarily restrictive.

Since Christians discover God consistently in their spiritual lives, one could argue that any number is arbitrary and therefore equally valid/invalid depending on who's scoring the list. For our purposes, we shall limit the discussion to twelve points. There is an unconcealed artificial structure in this system, but any attempt to describe mystical points of contact will necessarily involve some kind of flimsy framework at best. Jesus Christ spoke in parables, not systems, perhaps because systematic thinking limits the subject matter to the shape of the pigeonholes provided by the systematizer.

To provide cohesion and structure, each sacramental event will be linked to one of Charles Fillmore's *Twelve Powers*, so a few brief comments on that work are required before venturing further. There are many other possibilities, many ways to approach sacramental theology depending on the angle of attack desired. We could have chosen a classical religious theme like the fruits of the Spirit listed by the Apostle Paul (Galatians 5:22) or the Beatitudes of Matthew's Gospel. Psychology could have given us a working framework, like Abraham Maslow's Pyramid of Human Needs or the behaviorism of B. F. Skinner.

However, since this work represents an attempt to do systematic theology from within the Metaphysical Christian circle of faith, Charles Fillmore's book, *Twelve Powers,* provides us a flexible yet comprehensive way to achieve that starting point while standing fully within the wider circle of modern Christian thought. Mr. Fillmore struggled with the problem of how to organize his thinking about the Divine-human paradox. What ingredients do human beings have within them that come from the original recipe cooked up by the Creator? For a while he thought he would use seven powers; extant notes show that "Papa Charley" tried several combinations of categories before settling on twelve. He liked twelve, a good biblical number, because it provided him with twelve New Testament characters who could represent these human-Divine powers. Just as the church had created "patron saints" to represent various professions or activities, this master mystic linked the disciples with the *Twelve Powers.*

As we have already admitted, there is a certain artificiality to any theological system. Fillmore's twelve categories suffer if we push the model too far. Still, there is something intriguing about the way these twelve interact and interface. Although some of his ideas are controversial—few moderns will agree with Fillmore's views on human sexuality in the chapter on Life in Twelve Powers—the reasonable reader must concede that every human being needs traces of each "power" to be a whole person before God and in community with other people. Fillmore's system is neither psychology nor yet theology but a wise old man's overview of the human condition as it could be under God's guidance. We shall use these twelve categories to provide a framework for investigating the Sacraments from a wider, more inclusive perspective.

WHITHER COMES *SACRAMENTUM / MYSTERION?*

Sometimes the door to mystical awareness will open during a highly liturgical event, such as the Eucharist; other times it may be a lonely encounter or even an experience not usually considered religious in a traditional sense. The key turns when any event presents people with a heightened awareness of the Divine Presence.

Since we stand within the theological circle of Christianity, we shall pass without comment, in this context at least, those extrasensory/spiritualist encounters persons have claimed which reflect a magical, supernaturalistic, or occult origin. Christian faith is not a game of peek-a-boo with discorporate spirits, nor an attempt to manipulate magically the Cosmos to squeeze blessings from an impersonal, uncaring supernatural realm. Christianity is a relationship to God through Jesus Christ. All the sacramental experiences to be described are valid for the Christian only if approached, ultimately, as paths leading to the God revealed in Jesus.

With that caveat in mind, we move on to discuss twelve points at which God's presence can be known to modern mystical Christians. We'll call these the *Twelve Sacraments of Life.*

CHECK YOUR KNOWLEDGE

1. Explain/identify the following: Eucharist, Transubstantiate, Ulrich Zwingli, Revelation, Discovery, Primordial Revelation, Sacramentum/Mysterion, Latin Vulgate, St. Jerome, Interdict, Twelve Powers.

2. Why were Zwingli and Luther unable to agree?

3. What was Karl Barth's objection to "Natural Theology"?

4. Does the author believe God is known through Revelation or Discovery?

5. What is the definition of a "Sacrament" given by the text?

6. What "linguistic mistake" did St. Jerome make and how has it affected the way the Church views the sacraments?

QUESTIONS FOR DISCUSSION

1. In what way, if any, is Christ present in the Holy Communion, according to your view?

2. Does God "reveal" Himself, or do we "discover" Him?

3. How does the "primordial revelation" of the Christian faith keep from becoming "fossilized"?

4. Are there places when/where God's presence becomes more discernible to you? Are those your "sacraments"?

5. What do you think life would be like in a medieval town that was placed under the Interdict?

6. Do you like a church service rich in symbolism and ritual, or do you prefer the low-church "hymn sandwich" liturgy with a bare minimum of ceremony? How could different worship needs be met by the same church?

NOTES

1. Roland H. Bainton, *The Reformation of the Sixteenth Century* (Boston, Beacon Press, 1956), p. 92.

2. Harvey, p. 88.

3. Ulrich Zwingli in *The Protestant Reformation*, Lewis W. Spitz, ed. (Englewood Cliffs, NJ: Prentice-Hall. 1966), p. 84.

4. Tillich, *History*, p. 261.

5. Macquarrie, *Principles*, p. 7

6. IBID., p. 8.

7. IBID., p. 9.

8. IBID.

9. Karl Barth in Kantonen, *Christian Faith Today*, p. 32.

10. Kantonen, p. 31.

11. Hartshorne, pp. 4-5.

12. HBD, p. 890.

13. IBID.

14. Harvey, p. 211.

15. IBID., p. 213.

16. HBD, p. 577.

17. HBD. pp. 890-891.

18. Will Durant, *The Story of Civilization, Vol. IV, The Age of Faith* (NY: Simon & Schuster, 1950), pp. 755-756.

19. IBID., p. 755.

THE TWELVE SACRAMENTS OF LIFE

Chapter Twelve

Twelve Places Where God Gets Our Attention

The first seven categories roughly correspond to the classical sacraments of the ancient church:

FAITH - High Worship (Eucharist, Lord's Supper, Inspirational Music)

LIFE - Parental Love (Infant Baptism/Christening)

ZEAL - Dedication (Adult Baptism, Ordination)

LOVE - Experience of Selfless Love (Marriage)

POWER - Inspired Teaching/Preaching (Confirmation)

RENUNCIATION - Assurance, Forgiveness (Penance)

STRENGTH - Healing Prayer, Memorial Service (Extreme Unction or Last Rites)

The first two sacraments are agreed upon by nearly all Christian churches—*Lord's Supper* and *Baptism*. Note that "agreed upon" does not mean all Christians agree about what these practices mean or who should officiate or participate. Right the contrary! More than one Protestant denomination has splintered specifically because the people breaking away did not agree on sacramental theology. Luther and Zwingli had many children.

Some churches substitute *Adult Baptism* (sometimes called "Believer's Baptism") in place of *Infant Baptism*. For the purposes of our system, we shall call Adult Baptism the sacrament of Zeal. Various conservative Protestant churches have a problem with infant "baptism," but they find no difficulty in "Christening" new babies in a ceremony that closely resembles a waterless baptism. (Sometimes, water is used!) We'll explore the differences between Infant/Adult Baptism when we look at the two sacraments, *Life* and *Zeal*.

The last five sacraments go beyond even a distant relationship to sacraments usually discussed and bring us to a far more comprehensive position on the nature of sacramental experiences:

ORDER - "Starry Night" Experience, Nature-Communion

UNDERSTANDING - The "Ah-Ha!" Experience when grasping a spiritual truth intellectually

WISDOM - Meditation, Moments of Non-Cognitive Guidance

IMAGINATION - Creative Outpouring, "The Muse"

WILL - Prayer Moments When We "Know" God is Listening

Each category represents a valid sacramental experience under the operational definition we have established for what constitutes a sacrament. To do justice to this complex, important topic would require an entire volume devoted to nothing but mystical sacramental theology. We have nevertheless begun the work by staking out the boundaries and inviting others to dig deeper into this rich but neglected field of mystical study. Yet, once begun, we cannot abandon the bare marking posts that plot the outlines of sacramental theology from a mystical Christian perspective. We must seize the opportunity to break a little ground before we go on to the next topic in our whirlwind survey of systematic theology.

However, lest anyone expect a catechistic recitation of orthodox beliefs, we must point out that the entire thrust of this book has been and continues to be a survey of systematic theology from the perspective of Christian metaphysics. If readers plunge into this chapter expecting to find confirmation for childhood teachings in mainline Christianity about the Sacraments, doubtless some disappointment will result. Nor shall the anti-orthodox reader find this treatment of sacramental theology entirely satisfying, because we shall mention those points at which normally orthodox ideas interface with viewpoints popular in Metaphysical Christianity. Obviously, some serious differences with traditional theology will occur, but in the spirit of diversity and theological boldness entrusted to us as heirs to the Protestant heritage, we offer no apology when our pursuit of Truth takes us beyond the conventional into new thoughts, new ways of looking at the Ancient Faith. When we fail to satisfy those iconoclasts who want all the old ideas overturned, we offer the same lack of sympathy. The test of Truth must be that it stands alone, supported by our continuing review of its central principles against the standards of Scripture/Tradition/ Experience/ Reason interpreted through the central, Metaphysical Christian principle of One Presence/One Power. To do less would abrogate our responsibility as followers of Him who said, *"You shall know the Truth, and the Truth shall set you free."*

With apologies for its scanty nature and full awareness there will be much left unsaid, we turn now to a deeper study of these twelve categories.

SEVEN TRADITIONAL IDEAS REVISITED

Continuing our exploration of sacramental theology, we now consider twelve general ways in which God's presence can be discerned by us. These are just samples of the many ways that a loving and gracious God makes Himself known to His people. It is not our intent to inaugurate new rituals or overturn long established practices, but rather to offer some observations on the experiences of God which everyday living can bring.

1. THE SACRAMENT OF FAITH

EVENT: High moments of worship when a person "feels" God's presence through prayer, music, spoken words, or other elements in a worship experience.

SPIRITUAL ACTIVITY: Any element of corporate worship or moment of mystical communion, such as inspirational music, but especially the *Eucharist* (*Lord's Supper*).

Following Luther's lead, we see that Christ's "body" (i.e., his spiritual presence) could theoretically be discerned in everything and every place, but the Divine Presence is best experienced in those high moments of worship when the God-within-us is elevated within range of our powers of perception.

Of course, Luther wanted this to apply only to the Eucharist, but once he had opened the door to mystical awareness there was no stopping those who would come after him from finding God in other places. Indeed, our whole sacramental theology is built on Luther's assertion that the Christ is everywhere if we only would discern Him. There is good, biblical evidence supporting this as the viewpoint of the ancient church.

In last chapter of the Gospel of Luke we find recorded a remarkable story, known popularly as the Walk to Emmaus. Two of Jesus' followers—one called Cleopas, the other unnamed by Luke—are walking toward Emmaus late in the afternoon on the original Easter day. They are discussing the events of Holy Week when Jesus appears to them. Significantly, at first they fail to recognize their Master as He walks with them and explains the Hebrew prophecies about how the Messiah must suffer, die, and rise again on the third day—today! Only when they stop for the night do these intimate followers of Jesus realize who He is, then only in conjunction with an action He performs. Luke reports:

> He sat down to eat with them, took the bread, and said the blessing; then he broke the bread and gave it to them. Then their eyes were opened and they recognized him, but he disappeared from their sight. (Luke 24:30-31, TEV)

Luke wants his point hammered home, so he repeats the key elements four verses later:

> The two explained to them [other disciples] what had happened on the road, and how *they had recognized the Lord when he broke the bread.* (24:35) (Italics added)

This is precisely Luther's theology of the Eucharist. The presence of the living Christ becomes discernible in the communion meal. Jesus was Jesus all the way along the road to Emmaus, but only after He "said the blessing...broke the bread and gave it to them..." Luke reports, "...their eyes were opened and they recognized him."

In a sacramental encounter, God's omnipresence is elevated into view, like a card labeled "Look here!" popping up from a file box. We behold the Christ, then realize He was strolling beside us all the way to Emmaus.

This all makes perfect sense metaphysically. We can affirm, with the higher Christologies and ancient traditions, that the Real Presence of Christ's body is found in the bread and wine of the Lord's Supper. After all, if the Christ-spirit is in the stone, the fire, the air we breathe, it certainly must be in the bread and wine of Holy Communion.

What can this mean for innovative worship? What examples of new ways to celebrate the Eucharistic meal have been attempted by Christian churches? Not surprisingly, quite a few varieties exist and have met with success.

A number of churches offer "spiritual communion," where the minister leads the congregation in a guided meditation which seeks to honor the command to "remember" Jesus. William L. Fischer advocates this practice in his slim book, *Alternatives:*

> Let's consider the sacraments, in a deep sense. Wine represents blood, and blood represents life. Therefore, wine is symbolic of the Life of God coursing through our bodies. Bread represents the body of Christ, and this in turn is representative of divine substance. If the flesh profits nothing and the words are the important thing, why not observe communion by using our words in prayer?[1]

Indeed, why not? In our working definition of a sacrament as any place where the authentic presence of God/Christ can be discerned, wouldn't a commemorative meditation in remembrance of Him qualify as a Eucharist of the spirit? The only drawback is that people who find value in physically celebrating the Lord's Supper and actually eating bread/drinking wine may find the practice too abstract for their religious tastes. Since this form of communion uses no physical elements at all, it seems to work best in churches with strongly non-traditional leanings.

Other groups celebrate the Lord's Supper by substituting water/bread instead of wine/bread or grape juice/bread; this is the form of the sacrament offered by the Mormon Church. A possible way to introduce this variation might be to read the story of Jesus at the Marriage at Canaan where He turned the water into wine. Still other varieties include a common meal, often a "first century" dinner at which Mediterranean foods are served, followed by the Eucharist in traditional or alternative form; a "cookies and milk" communion for children; a "flower communion" in the spring during which people bring garden blossoms to the church and exchange their gifts for the flowers grown by another; or a Lord's Supper offered traditionally but in some variant format such as at a home prayer circle, choir practice, or youth worship service. In the super-cold of Alaskan winters, the author frequently offered the Lord's Supper to soldiers at field locations. Sometimes the wine would freeze solid, so we took the liberty of replacing unleavened wafers with C-ration crackers changing the wine into non-freezing brandy. Not surprisingly, attendance skyrocketed.

All these variations have been tried and proven successful in the right context. Sensitivity and common sense are the key to any worship experience: One is more likely to succeed at substituting a flower communion in an informal, less traditional church setting than in a heavily liturgical program such as a Catholic Mass or Lutheran Sunday Worship. However, the movement toward experimentation has permeated all sectors of the church. Even our more "liturgical" brothers and sisters are finding they have freedom to try innovative approaches to sacramental ministry, especially if the event is in a non-traditional location away from the main worship service.

Do we not trivialize the sacrament by making it just another theophany in a universe teeming with God-Stuff? If we were to assert that God's presence is conspicuous—i.e., always perceptible to everyone, everywhere—then this critique would be valid. That is not what everyday experience shows us. Instead we find, in the numbness of daily living, points at which God's presence breaks through us. Like a supernova making us aware of what was an ordinary star, God manifests Himself in those instances when we allow ourselves to perceive Him. Other high moments of corporate or private worship also fall into this category. When we perceive God is here, the commonplace becomes holy ground, and a *mysterion/sacramentum* takes place.

MUSIC: A FORM OF WORSHIP

A special word must be said about music as worship and its power to bring a person to awareness of God's reality. Music is often employed by worship leaders as background sounds for movement—offertories to move the offerings, processionals/recessionals to move the worship leaders or the choir into position and back again at the close of the service.

However, properly understood, music is a form of worship and not an interlude. To sing unto the Lord is to pray: It is no accident of preservation that gave us musical directions found between the verses of several psalms. Music can sometimes lift heart and mind when words fall like tin raindrops on shuttered ears. Some of the finest spiritual experiences occur during corporate worship through music. People often report that their highest worship experiences occur when listening to great religious classics like Handel's *Messiah* or when singing *The Lord's Prayer* as a congregation. Music can be a sacramental experience.

2. THE SACRAMENT OF LIFE

EVENT: Experience of parental love.
SPIRITUAL ACTIVITY: Christening, infant baptism.

What parents have not felt God's wondrous presence when gazing into the eyes of a child, especially their own child? The Christian community ceremonializes this love by the first rite of passage administered to new members of the religious family, infant baptism. Yet it is the impetus behind this ceremony which constitutes the genuine sacramental encounter.

The love we feel for children—that sense of continuity with our Creator and with life itself—is the real *Sacrament of Life*. Bringing forth new life from old, establishing a new generation to serve God and humanity, is what we celebrate when we gather to welcome a new child into the Ancient Faith as a member of the covenant community. Because of the awe-inspiring power of such love as exists between parent and child, those moments when we recognize and feel that love constitute genuine sacramental encounters.

3. THE SACRAMENT OF ZEAL

EVENT: The "God is with me" feeling when acting in His service.

SPIRITUAL ACTIVITY: Dedication, Adult Baptism, Ordination, Consecration of person or place; also the "conversion experience," when a person accepts Christ as Lord of their life.

Biblical authors frequently take time to narrate in great detail the dedication of some great shrine, like the Temple at Jerusalem, or consecration of a new leader like Samuel, David, or Jesus. Something special happens when people decide on a new spiritual venture; walking with God is always easiest the first few paces. At those high moments when we make a conscious decision to follow God's guidance, often we can feel the Divine Presence in a unique way.

Under our special definition, those experiences of new beginnings, when we feel that God is with us, are sacraments in the truest sense. Adult Baptism, certainly, would fall under this category. So would ordination of a new minister, dedication of a church officer, or consecration of a new religious facility such as a worship center or Sunday school building.

Another sacramental encounter which falls under this category is the "conversion-experience." More will be said about this highly controversial topic when we look at *Evangelism: Shall We Do It?* in Chapter 16. Briefly, we might say that persons who make a conscious decision to follow Jesus Christ have experienced God in a unique way. There was no less God present before the person decided to recognize God-in-Christ, but after the decision to follow Jesus, there is much more God-presence discernible. A conversion-experience fits our description of a sacramental encounter.

BAPTISM: KIDS OR GROWN-UPS?

Something should be said about baptism of adults in this context. A raging controversy has split church after church on this subject, even though some Metaphysical Christians find it difficult to understand what all the shouting is about.

Before the sixteenth century there was no real controversy about baptism; the Church baptized its babies and its adult converts. With the Reformation, Protestants began to question to validity of infant baptism. If *baptism* means joining the church, how can an infant choose to follow Christ? A sacrament that gives the believer a measure of God's grace? How can anyone but a full, consenting adult receive it?

Furthermore, do we follow the example of Jesus by offering infant baptism? He waited until He was thirty years old to accept baptism, and the New Testament knows nothing of babes in arms receiving the blessings of a priest at a water baptism. Some Protestants considered this such an important point that they broke with mainline Protestant thinkers like Luther, Zwingli, and Calvin to form newer, more radical denominations that practiced only believer's baptism. Since these groups insisted that all adults must be baptized, even though many had received infant baptism, they were known as Anabaptists. Nearly all modern Baptist churches descended from those radical thinkers.

MIDDLE WAY

A more moderate position is an inclusive, both/and theology rather than the either/or positions of earlier times. Certainly, adults who feel they have had a significant renewal of belief or have professed their Christian faith for the first time should be invited to celebrate this encounter by receiving baptism as part of a corporate worship experience. Baptism, like the Eucharist, is not a private affair but is a welcoming of the Christ-spirit by the whole community. It should ideally be part of a regular worship service at which the candidate for baptism and the congregation of faith both covenant together to help the new member grow spiritually.

However, infant baptism is also perfectly logical and biblically defensible when related to the circumcision rituals of ancient Israel. A Jewish boychild was circumcised on the eighth day as a sign that he was part of the covenant community of Israel. Christians naturally substituted infant baptism—a rite practiced widely in the ancient world and not specifically Jewish nor exclusively Christian—for the painful experience of circumcision.

Taking their cue from John the Baptist (who seems to have begun the practice for Christians) and St. Paul (who argued against being circumcised of the flesh because it frightened too many gentiles away from the new Faith), early Christians baptized both babies and adults as they joined the ranks of the Church. After Christianity became the universal religion of the Western world, only babies provided new members, therefore adult baptism was seldom required.

Thus we could argue from *Scripture, Tradition,* or *Reason* for either adult or infant baptism. The deciding factor for most Christians today will doubtless be the fourth source of religious values, *Experience.* If we grew up with infant baptism, the practice seems natural and acceptable. If only "believer's baptism" was allowed in our home churches, more than likely this will appeal to our grown-up religious tastes.

Theologically, the "best" form of baptism is the one which works within our comfort zone. From a Metaphysical Christian perspective, any tasteful practice will do. It is worth noting that several major denominations—among them the United Methodist Church—allow for virtually any form of baptism: adult or infant, immersion, pouring, or sprinkling. And there are, again, other options available to those in the more experimental communions under our expanded definition of Sacramental Theology.

OTHER OPTIONS

One alternative is to substitute some other medium for water in baptism. Some churches "christen" their babies with a name-giving ceremony that ends with the minister sprinkling rose petals on the head of the infant. This delightful variety preserves the form of baptism but incorporates a new element through the colored petals in lieu of water.

Another alternative is no baptism at all but to substitute "christening" for infants and a worship service to welcome new adult members. This is quite popular among churches founded since the nineteenth century, especially some New-Thought Christian churches. While there is nothing wrong with this practice, the same effect could be obtained by offering "infant baptism" and adult welcoming. The result would be to gain wider credibility in the Christian community for those churches involved.

THE CREDIBILITY ISSUE: BOTTOM-LINE SACRAMENTS

Baptism and the Lord's Supper, in some form, seem to be the bottom line for most Christians. Any church which discards these two entirely does so at great peril to its historic connection to the Church Universal. Those movements which specialize in seeing themselves as non-Christian "churches" may not be troubled by cutting themselves off from their heritage, but a Christian movement can step only so far beyond the Circle of Faith before it ceases belonging to the family of Christ Jesus.

Great Metaphysical Christian teachers—from pioneers like Ernest Holmes, Charles Fillmore, and Nona Brooks to James Dillet Freeman, Eric Butterworth, and Johnnie Colemon—have always steered the New Thought movement away from more radical expressions of religiosity that wanted occult/esoteric studies or paranormal experiences to supplant the leadership of Jesus Christ. All religious thought, for the Christian, must ultimately be measured against the God-with-us we have met in Jesus Christ. Christian churches, to be worthy of their heritage, must come to terms with at least with the two sacraments practiced by the Church Universal, the Lord's Supper and Baptism. Many variations are possible; some variation is necessary unless the church wishes to leave the Christian family in pursuit of other circles of faith.

4. THE SACRAMENT OF LOVE.

EVENT: An experience of agape, selfless love; "true love," when a person realizes he/she has found the one with whom he/she wants to spend forever; love on many levels of such as deep friendship that brings one to selflessness and joy, love of a group or a nation, love of humanity as a whole; supremely, love of God.

SPIRITUAL ACTIVITY: Marriage.

The *Sacrament of Love* is not limited to marriage, but no other institution better demonstrates the potential for joy and disaster that love represents. At present, too much emphasis is placed on the romantic/passionate aspect of love and not enough on camaraderie, cooperation, and friendship.

As a pastor of a local church, I often felt that someone ought to tell all newly-weds that the wild, giddy feeling they have will last six to twenty-four months, after which they will begin to discover what they really have in common and whether they like each other enough to stay wedded. Passion is terribly important; no good marriage ever began without that throbbing, over-powering urge to make love. However, the intensity that one feels initially is the entry-level of relationships and will not last. Passion will come and go in the months and years ahead, like the tide. What you have left after the tide goes out will determine whether or not you will enjoy low tide enough to wait for the flood.

Marriages based only on passion are like tent-cities set up at a gold rush. When the ore is gone, nothing is left to hold the people to the location and they pack up and leave for newer claims. The problem with this pack-and-move lifestyle is that it is operating out of a mythology. There is no eternal vein of gold that will never run dry.

There is no eternal, passionate relationship that will never cool down. Human beings aren't made like that.

THREE GREEK WORDS

If relationships are based solely (or even primarily) on *eros*, i.e., the passionate nature, they are doomed from the start. If they are based on *philia*, friendship, they have a much better chance to survive. However, if they are based on *agape*, selfless love that puts the other person first, then the moments of *eros* and *philia* will rein-force an already solid foundation of caring and commitment.

In fact, all relationships would fare better if they were grounded in *agape*. Friendships often break down when one party says or does something reprehensible to the other. Jesus knew this would happen, so He told a bushel of parables about forgiveness. But His greatest teaching about friendship—the parable of the Good Samaritan—explores the nature of *agape* and stands as a radical statement about our responsibilities to help other people regardless of how different, alien, or foreign they may seem to us.

Those times when we reach the fringes of our potential, those infrequent moments when we feel/sense love as it could be if we truly lived *agape*, are the expe-riences we have grouped under this heading as the *Sacrament of Love*.

5. THE SACRAMENT OF POWER.

EVENT: Inspiration from the words of scripture or a teacher; ministry of the Word that touches mind and heart to bring awareness of God's presence.

SPIRITUAL ACTIVITY: Confirmation, Scripture Reading, Sermon, teaching, any form of exhortation or instruction in a spiritual context.

Most of us belong to the Christian family because Christ came to us through others. Someone spoke words of Truth. We heard those words and became confronted, convinced, converted, and confirmed in the faith. Perhaps the "conversion" came so slowly that we cannot look back in a date book and find a notation which reads, *"March 15—accepted Christ today. Tuna fish for lunch."* Perhaps there actually is a date when we felt seized, grasped by God's power for the first time. Both experiences—gradual growth and dramatic decision—have been reported by faithful Christians for nearly two thousand years now.

A common element in Christian proclamation and teaching is the use of language to convey ideas and Truths too complex and too exhaled to box up in mere words. Sometime around twenty years after the crucifixion/resurrection of Jesus Christ, a teacher took time to dictate a letter that began like this:

> Paul, Silvanus, and Timothy,

> To the church of the Thessalonians in God the Father and the Lord Jesus Christ: Grace to you and peace.

> We give thanks to God always for you all, constantly mentioning you in our prayers, remembering before our God and Father your work of faith and labor of love and steadfastness of hope in our Lord Jesus Christ...[2]

The Apostle Paul was taking a few moments to respond to some questions and problems that he heard the Christian community at Thessolonika was encountering in their spiritual growth. Paul had no idea he was writing the first lines of the New Testament. First Thessalonians is probably the oldest piece of writing in the Christian canon and represents an attempt to instruct people in the faith by the written word. It was an effort which has been repeated by countless writers throughout Christian history, including the author of this work.

But, if we are honest, we must admit that this effort is doomed to failure unless it is backed by a living community of faith where people can see the Truth in action. Emerson wrote:

> The spirit only can teach. Not any profane man, not any liar, not any slave can teach, but only he can give, who has; he only can create, who is. The man on whom the soul descends, through whom the soul speaks, alone can teach. Courage, piety, love, wisdom, can teach; and every man can open his door to these angels, and they shall bring him the gift of tongues.[3]

Another paradox emerges here. We cannot truly learn from mere words such lofty concepts as reconciliation, love, wisdom, peace. Yet, without words we could not communicate even our failing efforts to reach the edges of Divine Goodness. Words are, as Paul Tillich would say, symbols pointing to a reality that far transcends their limitations. Without those symbols, handles by which we grasp the utterly ungraspable, all spiritual effort would be futile because no one could share the insights he has gained. Jesus could not have taught us so much about Truth; the Bible could not have been written, and its light in the darkness would be quenched. Words capture only the faintest hint of Divine Goodness, but they are the best tool we have of sharing those hints with our sisters and brothers in this world.

Perhaps that is why the inspiration which comes from words—read or spoken—must always be checked out by: 1) applying the new insights to everyday life and 2) discussing new ideas with other members of the covenant community.

The first effort is what we call *Practical Christianity*; the second is *Christian Theology*. When the voice of God breaks through to us via the spoken/written word, we experience another sacramental encounter. We call this the *Sacrament of Power* because it can be a life-changing, empowering event.

Some ways we can experience God through the spoken/written word include: Listening to or reading Scripture; hearing a gifted teacher, especially a powerful preacher; group study of Christian Truth; hearing the words of a spoken prayer or guided meditation; watching a dramatic presentation on stage, television or at the movies (this can be the most powerful teaching tool of all); and hearing Christian ideas in songs.

This is, of course, only a partial list. There are many more opportunities for God's presence to be made known to us through the spoken or written word; you can doubtless add to this list from your own experiences.

A continuously popular method of spiritual instruction for young people is the ancient practice of giving special classes to young candidates for church membership which leads to a worship service celebrating their joining the Christian fellowship. This has traditionally been known as the sacrament of *Confirmation*. Generally, the more ceremonial the regular church service is on Sunday morning, the more likely it will offer a formal Confirmation program for young people. Churches as diverse as the very liberal United Church of Christ and the solidly conservative Wisconsin Synod of the Lutheran Church both practice Confirmation.

Dr. James Glasse, former president of Lancaster Theological Seminary of the United Church of Christ, told a story that the author recalls from seminary days which sheds some interesting light on the function of Confirmation. Jim Glasse, himself a Presbyterian, spent several years as a young pastor fresh from a northern seminary but assigned to rural parishes in the South. When he tried to follow the northern Presbyterian practice of offering Confirmation classes to the young people of his southern Presbyterian church, the new pastor was greeted by polite refusals.

Mystified, Glasse sought out a likely candidate for Confirmation and invited her to join the new class he was intent on offering. She said, "No, thank you." When the young Reverend Glasse pressed the younger parishioner to explain why she didn't want to join the church she told him she was going to Christian Camp that summer and would "get saved" there, so she didn't need to attend Confirmation class to become a church member!

A wiser-and-older Dr. Jim Glasse explained to us, his seminary students, that *"getting saved"* was the way young people joined the church in that rural southern area. The experience of Christian Camp provided the same opportunity to hear teaching, study scripture, and respond with a commitment to Jesus Christ as Confirmation classes. Whatever the process, the end result is achieved when a person responds to the *Sacrament of Power*, an epiphany of God through the medium of the spoken/written word.

6. THE SACRAMENT OF RENUNCIATION.

EVENT: Experiencing the release of forgiveness; letting go and letting God; releasing any hindrance to spiritual growth or any belief/practice that is keeping us from following Jesus in newness of life.

SPIRITUAL ACTIVITY: Traditionally, the acts involved in the rite of penance, i.e., confession of one's shortcomings and assurance of pardon; alternatively, any technique which brings one to awareness of the forgiveness/acceptance that God always showers upon His children.

Guilt and guilty feelings are not a popular topic in liberal religious circles in general and Christian Truth churches in particular. We are supposed to be people who have left all the guilt-trips behind us when we discovered liberal Christianity. "If God is love, how can we be guilty in His sight?" we ask.

But that is exactly the point: We know better, and yet guilt feelings still claw at us. In our discussion of Sin (Chapter 9) we noted that radical freedom implicit in human existence leads to mistakes (*sin*) which result in guilt, misery, and death, either spiritual or physical. We saw that guilt has both a *subjective* and an *objective* side to it, since we do incur unhappy consequences from unchecked wrong choices (*objective guilt*) and often punish ourselves emotionally for real or imagined transgressions (*subjective guilt*).

OFF-LOADING THE BURDEN

A natural question flows from this sin-guilt cycle: *"How do I free myself from guilt and guilty feelings?"*

The answer, of course, is Christ-consciousness: making Jesus Christ Lord of our lives leads the way to becoming sons and daughters of God as truly as was the Nazarene. However, the actual process begins not with a spiritual fill-up but with a purge of the soul through the *Sacrament of Renunciation*.

Charles Fillmore spoke of this process in his chapter on "Renunciation" in *The Twelve Powers*:

> All Christians who have had experiences variously described as "change of heart," "salvation," "conversion," and "sanctification" will admit that, before they experienced the great change of consciousness represented by these names, they had been "convicted of sin" or had determined to give up the ways of the world and do the will of God...If the system has been burdened with congestion of any kind, a higher life energy will set it into universal freedom. But there must be a renunciation or letting go of old thoughts before the new can find place in the consciousness.[4]

Before we can be filled with God-stuff, we must off-load the junk. Of course, God-stuff permeates everything, even the junk of life. But the polar star of our new Sacramental Theology has been the idea that a true *mysterion/sacramentum* occurs only when we recognize the presence of God. True, we are not guilty before God for our petty failures, or even our great sins. Jesus the Christ shows us the forgiving love of an *Abba-Father* who wipes away our tears and greets our confessions with an unconditional embrace. But sometimes we need forgiveness, even though it is unnecessary in the sight of God.

Such forgiveness can only come when we have bled the poisons of self-hate from our souls. This is the true purpose of Renunciation: To open the door of our hearts so we are able to accept forgiveness. Renunciation is the first step the Prodigal Son took when he came to his senses and decided to go back to the place he belonged.

Renunciation is the front porch of the greatest Christian concept of all, *Reconciliation*. Without Renunciation, there can be no release from the cycle of sin-guilt-misery-death. Renunciation means to let go of the evil, to renounce it. It means to bless and release self-hatred, putting faith in the Christ-in-you.

Roman Catholic and Eastern Orthodox Christians have practiced the Sacrament of Penance continuously since the early days of the church. While this has led to some abuses—the most notorious was the selling of "indulgences" as exit-visas from purgatory during pre-Reformation days—the actual, day-by-day effect of this process is of great psychological and spiritual benefit for those who practice it in genuine faith. Protestant theologian John MacQuarrie testifies to the effectiveness of such a soul-cleansing:

> Perhaps we should not pay too much attention to pragmatic considerations, but we can hardly ignore the fact, attested by Jung and other psychoanalysts, that Protestants are much more likely to end up on the psychiatrist's couch than Catholics who practice the sacrament of penance.[5]

The idea of "confessing" to a professional religious leader is not likely to catch on in Protestant churches because of our strongly individualistic streak. Although we feel, as children of the Reformation, that confession is a private matter between the believer and God, we shall be spiritual wastrels if we omit this step in our prayer life because of some vague notion that we "shouldn't feel guilty."

Confession of one's shortcomings to another human being is so vital to a mental/spiritual healing process that it is an imprint step in the Alcoholics' Anonymous program. AA and all its offshoot groups (Gamblers, Parents, Overeaters-Anonymous, Etc.) insist that to properly get one's life back under control a person must confess to God and to another person those things which are burdensome from the old way of doing business. People who have gone through the 10-Step Program have told the author this step was at once the hardest and most meaningful to accomplish in their recovery program.

If Reconciliation begins with Renunciation, Renunciation begins with emptying. When we pray about things that we feel guilty, we are draining the foreign matter from our spiritual engines before filling up with pure God-fuel.

At the point where we feel the release of forgiveness, we have   encountered a genuine Sacrament.

7. THE SACRAMENT OF STRENGTH

EVENT: Life-experience that demonstrates God's presence, e.g., a prosperity demonstration, healing, or "coincidence" that speaks to us; also, when becoming aware of finitude and death such as the transition of a loved one.

SPIRITUAL ACTIVITY: Healing prayer, memorial service; traditionally, Extreme Unction (Last Rites) and the anointing of the sick.

"God is in the world," said philosopher Alfred North Whitehead, "or He is no where."[6] Former US Army Chief of Chaplains Kermit Johnson once told a prayer breakfast the author attended at Fort Wainwright, Alaska, that the chief heresy of modern life is the inability to believe God can do anything in the real world.

Yet, as Carl Sagan has pointed out, the modern world is necessarily secular, humanistic. We emerged from a cloud of superstition and magic, for such was the world of our ancestors. Romanticize the golden ages gone by as we may, the reality is that until the last few decades the vast majority of humanity believed their lives were threatened by evil spirits and controlled by dark forces from realms beyond the physical universe. Sociologists Paul B. Horton and Chester L. Hunt describe an existing culture, the Dobuans of Melanesia, in their widely-acclaimed college textbook *Sociology*:

> The Dobuan child soon learns that he lives in a world ruled by magic. Nothing happens from natural causes; all phenomena are controlled by witchcraft and sorcery. Illness, accident, and death are evidence that witchcraft has been used against one and call for vengeance from one's kinsmen. Nightmares are interpreted as witchcraft episodes in which the spirit of the sleeper has narrow escapes from hostile spirits. All legendary heroes and villains are still alive as active supernaturals, capable of aid or injury. Crops grow only if one's long hours of magical chants are successful in

enticing the yams away from another's garden. Even sexual desire does not arise except in response to another's love magic...[7]

The New Testament shows us an ancient cosmology, crudely controlled by supernatural powers and totally lacking any concept of natural laws. In fact, more people have lived in this kind of superstitious world than have lived in the modern, scientific age. Today the pendulum has swung to the opposite extreme. We live in a world that no longer looks for any supernatural causes whatsoever. When the Challenger space shuttle exploded killing seven astronauts, no one seriously proposed that witchcraft was involved. A Dobuan investigator would have insisted that someone was brewing black magic.

Thankfully, we have come a long way from fears about evil spirits and witchcraft. Yet, the danger facing modern humanity is not that they will attribute all events to the Divine, but that they will forget the Divine still exists and is actively involved in the world. When God breaks through our no-God programming of modern life and gets our attention, we have experienced the *Sacrament of Strength*.

Charles Fillmore called this power by three names: *Strength, Stability*, and *Steadfastness*. Although the result of this sacramental encounter is renewed strength, such strength is not brute force but a renewed equilibrium, a balance of harmony in the center of life. The experience which provokes renewed faith is as difficult to explain as the faith itself.

Those places in life when God speaks to us through coincidence, for example, give us mini-spiritual experiences that do not translate into anyone's understanding but our own. When a person has such a moment—an old friend pops into our life and tells us something that gives us just what we've needed to hear—there is no doubt that God is speaking through mundane circumstances, yet there is no possible way we can relate such a subjective encounter in objective terms so that someone else can feel their faith renewed as well.

These encounters are solitary, tailor-made for the person receiving them and non-transferable. When you have experienced a faith-strengthening, mini-theophany, you will know what it is, but you will be as helpless as anyone else in describing the event in logical language for another person. It is a *mysterion* and a *sacramentum* that knows your name but vanishes like morning mist when you try to embrace it mentally or explain it rationally.

PERSONAL EXAMPLE: *"GOOD"*

Here is one personal example. Do not expect Mount Sinai or some other dramatic event. I find spiritual insights often come through reflection upon coincidences. One day I assisted in a funeral of a church member, a difficult task for any minister. Standing by the grave I wondered how we could talk of good in a world where there is so much suffering and death. As I pondered, my eyes drifted down to an old tombstone on the ground beside the fresh grave. It was carved with a single name: *Good.*

Later that afternoon while driving home and thinking about this coincidence, I happened to notice the New Testament Greek flashcard ring hanging from my mirror—a way of keeping up with my Greek vocabulary by flipping to a new "Word of the Day" each morning. The word hanging there in front of my eyes was *agathos*, which means—you guessed it—*good*.

Did this mean God was gently reminding me that good is all around us, even in the midst of tragedy? I took it that way. It was an ephemeral encounter, yet it gave me renewed strength. Driving along the front range of the Colorado Rocky Mountains, that Greek flashcard dangling in the red light of sunset, I experienced the *mysterion/sacramentum* of *Strength*.

Traditional religious practices to celebrate this encounter are found in the ceremony of Last Rites (Extreme Unction, i.e., anointing with oil and commending into God's hands for healing or transition to the next phase of existence); healing prayer of many kinds; and the funeral/memorial service. Properly administered, even unchanging ritual can provide a meeting place for believers to encounter God through the Sacrament of Strength, although more frequently the sacrament occurs in quiet moments and solitude. Early in the history of the church, souls in search of solitude went off to the desert where they could be alone with God. Well-known Catholic spiritual writer and pastoral theologian Henri Nouwen believes solitude is terribly important in this rush-rush world and that we have far too little time for spiritual pursuits. Writing in his book *The Way of the Heart: Desert Spirituality and Contemporary Ministry*, Nouwen sounds a warning for busy clergy that is equally applicable to over-committed laypeople:

> Precisely because our secular milleu offers us so few spiritual disciplines, we have to develop our own. We have, indeed, to fashion our own desert where we can withdraw every day, shake off our compulsions, and dwell in the gentle healing presence of our Lord. Without such a desert we will lose our own soul while preaching the gospel to others. But with such a spiritual abode, we will become increasingly conformed to him in whose Name we minister.[8]

We have seen the seven sacramental encounters recognized by the traditional church from a new perspective. But we do not stop here. Next, we move beyond historical categories to find the other five places known to human experience where God makes Himself/Herself manifest.

FIVE NEW THOUGHTS

All experiences discussed so far have been, at least peripherally, related to the seven traditional sacraments. Now we go beyond, to explore five additional points of contact between the individual and the Divine. Some of these require very little elaboration; they are common experiences that every human being knows well. Others will need more explanation. Nevertheless, in each we are stepping out into no-man's land between established theological ideas (like the Lord's Supper) and practices not normally regarded as religious in a Christian sense (like *satori*). We turn to these new ideas about what constitutes a sacrament with the measuring-stick of Scripture/Tradition/Experience/Reason in hand, mindful that in all things spiritual our final Authority is the Christ.

8. THE SACRAMENT OF ORDER.

EVENT: The "starry night" experience; awareness of Divine omnipresence and majesty; feeling the Awesome, the greatness of the Cosmos.

SPIRITUAL ACTIVITY: Nature communion; prayer-walk; "satori."

Countless volumes have been written on this topic; doubtless many more will appear. For our purposes we shall allow a brief space to discuss the *Sacrament of Order* because it is such a common human experience that few words are necessary to introduce it. Who has not walked under the starry night sky and sensed the Presence of God? The Psalmist wrote long ago:

> *The heavens are telling the glory of God;*
> *and the firmament proclaims his handiwork.*
> *Day to day pours forth speech,*
> *and night to night declares knowledge.*[9]

When the "starry night" sense of wonder is coupled with an awareness of God's presence in all things, so that the believer catches a glimpse of Divine Oneness, this is the Sacrament of Order. In the East it is called, among other things, *satori*. A full-blown experience of satori can be world-shattering, life-changing. Listen to these words, culled from pages of description written by the westernized Eastern mystic Paramahansa Yogananda, as he describes an encounter with and evanescent union in the transcendence of God:

> An oceanic joy broke upon calm endless shores of my soul. The Spirit of God, I realized, is exhaustless Bliss; His body is countless tissues of light. A swelling glory within me began to envelop towns, continents, the earth, solar and stellar systems, tenuous nebulae, and floating universes. The entire cosmos, gently luminous, like a city seen afar at night, glimmered within the infinitude of my being...[10]

It could not last, of course. Even a mystic completely devoted to pursuing the Divine, as Yogananda was, had to come down to earth again.

> Suddenly the breath returned to my lungs. With a disappointment almost unbearable, I realized that my infinite immensity was lost. Once more I was limited to the humiliating cage of a body, not easily accommodative to the Spirit.[11]

What was the reaction of Yogananda's teacher to this momentous experience? He brought the young mystic back to earth where he belonged:

> My guru was standing motionless before me...He held me upright and said quietly: *"You must not get overdrunk with ecstasy. Much*

> *work yet remains for you in the world. Come, let us sweep the*
> *balcony floor; then we shall walk by the Ganges.*"[12]

Most people in Western society find this kind of spiritual experience, frankly, difficult to accept. If a *satori*-like encounter of omnipotent/omnipresence described by Yogananda is too much to believe, then let it describe the upper limits of the Sacrament of Order, and let those quiet moments when we can feel God's presence in nature provide the more attainable lower end of the spectrum.

Any contemplative exercise which takes aspiring mystics to higher realms must bring that same person back to earth again. The objective of a spiritually disciplined life is not visions and ecstasy; it's to sweep the balcony and know God is with you while the dust clouds engulf your feet.

9. THE SACRAMENT OF UNDERSTANDING.

EVENT: The "Ah-ha!" experience when intellectually grasping a spiritual truth.

SPIRITUAL ACTIVITY: Studying, reflecting or discussing spiritual ideas.

Even more common in everyday life is that moment when something clicks and a new spiritual understanding drops into place in our minds. At that moment, we have grasped something—or perhaps we are grasped by something—which gives us new insight. Clarity of thought gives us a sense of God working in and through us. Hence, it is a sacramental encounter.

10. THE SACRAMENT OF WISDOM.

EVENT: Moments of Divine Guidance.

SPIRITUAL ACTIVITY: Meditation.

Prayer is talking to God; meditation is listening. When we "hear" an answer, we have experienced the *Sacrament of Wisdom*. This encounter differs from the *Sacrament of Understanding* because the latter is an intellectual insight which seems to drop in from a higher consciousness. Wisdom is more than knowledge or intellectual comprehension; wisdom encompasses all levels of thought and feeling. Wisdom is more than knowing how, it's knowing when, where, and why, too. Wisdom is closely related to faith and love because it breathes as a whole-person experience and not just a sniffing creature of the intellect. Those instances when we feel divinely guided—especially those encounters of the Divine we experience by meditation—may be classified under this Sacrament.

For example: A young woman faces a choice of whether to accept a proposal of marriage from a certain young man or postpone marriage until she completes her college education. Intellectually, she knows all the facts. She can answer the how questions easily. When she applies herself to prayer and meditation about this question, she will be seeking *Wisdom* to make the right choice. For this reason, Charles Fillmore also called this Divine-human attribute the *Power of Judgment.* "*Wisdom, justice, judgment, are grouped under one head in spiritual consciousness,*" he wrote.[13]

Cora Dedrick Fillmore carried the idea even further in her book *Christ Enthroned in Man*:

Every soul has free access to the source of wisdom within. As we approach the divine source of wisdom and begin to realize our oneness with it, we find that we are evolving a higher intelligence than that of the intellect and that we are learning the greatest of all sciences, the science of mind...Divine wisdom, divine judgment, has in it the essence of goodness.[14]

When we feel that guidance overtaking us, we are experiencing the *Sacrament of Wisdom*.

11. THE SACRAMENT OF IMAGINATION.

EVENT: Moments of creative insight when "the muse" works for us.

SPIRITUAL ACTIVITY: Creative arts, dance.

This Sacrament is better known to creative artists—writers, poets, painters, and people who work with their hands and minds to create something that did not exist before. When Divine Guidance breaks through our walls of unwillingness, we experience the *Sacrament of Imagination.*

Although self-consciously artistic people will recognize this encounter most readily, everyone has experienced the power of creative imagination in their lives. Some form of creativity is present in every conscious mind. Perhaps it's just looking for a new way to walk home or discovering a new recipe, but part of the job-description for *Homo sapiens* is to be a creative thinker.

Adaptability made human beings the dominant lifeform on this world. Our hunger for tools grew hand-in-hand with our thirst for objects of beauty to revere. So archeologists find, buried in the graves of our ancient ancestors, not only cooking utensils and digging stones but shaped images of buffalo, deer, and people. Creativity is as natural to humans as walking upright. Only modern humanity, with its pre-packaged lifestyle, has restricted creative expression to an elite handful of professional artists. The rest of us get coloring books.

When we open ourselves to the Sacrament of Imagination, a rainbow of creative energy will pour from us. We may not be Rembrandt, but each human soul has the power to create ideas and things of beauty brought about by those ideas. Everyone has a right to experience the God-given flow of Imagination.

12. THE SACRAMENT OF WILL.

EVENT: Moments of Prayer when we "know the Truth."

SPIRITUAL ACTIVITY: Affirmations and Denials; entering the Silence.

Our last sacrament to consider is, in many ways, the key to them all. According to Cora Fillmore, only through an act of Will can we avail ourselves of the many blessings which God is trying to shower upon us. She wrote:

"Divine will is the mediator between God and us. It operates between the inner realms of mind and the outer manifestation."[15]

We experience God when we establish a prayer-relationship with the Divine through an act of Will. One good pattern for prayer is the widely practiced method of Affirmation and Denial. We shall discuss a Theology of Prayer in Chapter 17, but for now let's look at this prayer-form in action without analyzing it too deeply.

AFFIRMATION/DENIAL

In conventional prayer the worshippers "talk" to God. Affirmation/Denial means people really talk to themselves by repeating words of Truth. As a kind of centering prayer, it puts people in touch with ideas about God they already believe with their heads but are unable to feel confident about. We can find a good example in the Twenty Third Psalm:

> *The Lord is my shepherd,* (Affirmation)
>
> *I shall not want.* (Denial)

Affirmation tells us what God is capable of doing; Denial reminds us not to worry because everything is in His hands. Both are acts of Will. When we feel overshadowed by the Presence of God, reassuring us that all is well, we have experienced the *Sacrament of Will.* Only an act of Will on our part makes the all-pervasive Presence and Power of God available to us. God does not force Himself on people. Faith begins when we choose to respond to the nudging, whispering, "still small voice" within each conscious being.

ENTERING THE SILENCE: AN ACT OF WILL

One final point about this sacrament: The strange paradox is that, when we seek to pursue God with our minds, the Divine Infinity sprawls before us, unfathomable to our finite intelligence. When we give up trying to comprehend God and enter into a relationship with Him, we discover how near He always has been. It requires an act of Will to turn ourselves over to God and become non-resistant. We must willfully give up willing; we must have control enough to relinquish control. Knowing God is not unlike falling in love. It is a matter of the heart, which resists all efforts to organize the experience into language intelligible to anyone who does not love as deeply as we do.

Great mystics speak of *"The Silence"* beyond speech where we know God's presence as certainly as we know who we are. It is not reached through intellectual pursuits, although good thinking can clear away much of the mental underbrush that clogs our path to Christ-consciousness; this is the task of the theologian. *The Silence,* however, can be reached only by moving beyond words to adoration, quiet communion, and openness to "hear" the unspoken Presence of God.

Entering *The Silence* requires an act of Will which moves us beyond willing to a place of utter receptivity. It is losing ourselves to gain ourselves, releasing the world in order to gain a new way of dealing with the world.

ST. FRANCIS' SUMMARY

Hundreds of years ago one of the greatest mystics who ever lived gave us the finest summary of the life spent in service to God and humanity. It still reads as crisply as if some enlightened pastor just jotted it down as a closing prayer for next Sunday's worship service.

Perhaps the best way to understand the Sacraments is to read the famous *Prayer of St. Francis of Assisi* every day of our lives. In this blank-verse hymn, the mystical mixes with the practical, the paradox of giving-to-receive finds one of its highest expression in the Christian faith. The result is a life bathed in the continuous light of the Divine Presence, a life that is itself a sacrament for all the world:

> Lord, make me an instrument of Thy peace;
> Where there is hatred, let me sow love;
> Where there is injury, pardon;
> Where there is doubt, faith;
> Where there is despair, hope;
> Where there is darkness, light;
> And where there is sadness, joy.
> O Divine Master,
> Grant that I may not so much seek
> To be consoled as to console;
> To be understood as to understand;
> To be loved, as to love;
> For it is in giving that we receive,
> It is in pardoning that we are pardoned,
> And it is in dying that we are born to eternal life.[16]

CHECK YOUR KNOWLEDGE

Match the *"Power"* to its corresponding *"Sacrament"*:

DIVINE-HUMAN POWER	SACRAMENT OF
1. FAITH	PRAYER MOMENTS
2. LIFE	MARRIAGE/SELFLESS LOVE
3. ZEAL	ASSURANCE/FORGIVENESS
4. LOVE	"AH-HA!" EXPERIENCE
5. POWER	INSPIRED TEACHING/PREACHING
6. RENUNCIATION	HEALING PRAYER
7. STRENGTH	DEDICATION/ADULT BAPTISM
8. ORDER	MEDITATION
9. UNDERSTANDING	"STARRY NIGHT" EXPERIENCE
10. WISDOM	HIGH WORSHIP/EUCHARIST
11. IMAGINATION	PARENTAL LOVE/INFANT BAPTISM
12. WILL	CREATIVE OUTPOURING

QUESTIONS FOR DISCUSSION

1. The author strongly asserts that at least *baptism* and the *Lord's Supper* must be observed in some form or a church severs *"its historic connection to the Church Universal."* What do you think?

2. How would you change the list of Powers/Sacraments? What would you delete? Add? Modify?

3. Isn't all this sacramental heritage part of the baggage we must discard in order to free ourselves from seeking God in the outer and concentrate on the inner where Christ indwells? Can we do both? Should we?

4. Can symbolism and ritual bring us closer to God? Explain.

5. Is there any value in "confessing" to another human being as practiced by Roman Catholicism and various "anonymous" groups?

6. Describe your personal moments of Sacramentum/Mysterion.

NOTES

1. William L. Fischer, *Alternatives* (Unity Village: Unity Books, 1980), p. 56.

2. I Thessalonians 1:1-3 (RSV).

3. Emerson, pp. 55-56.

4. Charles Fillmore, *The Twelve Powers of Man* (Unity Village: Unity Books, undated), pp. 142-143.

5. Macquarrie, *Principles*, p. 484.

6. Alfred North Whitehead's importance for theology is discussed with reasonable clarity in Kantonen, *Christian Faith Today*, pp. 94-107. Tackling Whitehead undiluted is for none but the hardy.

7. Horton & Hunt, p. 93.

8. Henri J. M. Nouwen, *The Way of the Heart: Desert Spirituality and Contemporary Ministry* (NY: Seabury Press, 1981), pp. 30-31.

9. Psalm 19:1-2 (RSV).

10. Paramahansa Yogananda, *Autobiography of a Yogi* (Los Angeles: Self- Realization Fellowship, 1979), p. 168.

11. IBID., p. 169.

12. IBID.

13. Fillmore, *Twelve Powers*, p. 46.

14. Cora Dedrick Fillmore, *Christ Enthroned in Man* (Unity Village: Unity Books, 1981), p. 70.

15. IBID.

16. St. Francis of Assisi. "Prayer of St. Francis."

ECCLESIOLOGY: CHURCH AND MINISTRY

Chapter Thirteen

One...minister who fascinated me and who had an extraordinary following used none of the old techniques that ministers in the historic churches commonly subscribe to. He made no parish calls; he had no use for membership drives. He shunned financial campaigns and carried on no special social relationship with the members of his congregation. In fact, there were any number of people on his church roll who scarcely knew him. To analyze his success was impossible for those who did not understand...They knew nothing of his intuitive power or the fact that he carried his church in his heart.[1]   —Marcus Bach

WHO SPEAKS FOR THE CHURCH?

During the author's years as an Army chaplain, two facts became clear about the state of religious consciousness among American Protestants.

1) Young men and women in uniform generally did not know what a "Protestant" was and which church groups fit into that broad category.

2) When discussing American Christianity, virtually everyone had a stereotype of what a Christian was, and that model was distinctly conservative.

And if few people had any notion of the actual pluralism within Protestant thought, almost no one knew anything about the churches which are decidedly liberal in thought and lifestyle. What this says above all is that ultra-conservative churches have been much more successful in publicizing their viewpoint than moderate and liberal denominations, even though these liberal-to-moderate groups are numerically greater than their right-wing counterparts.[2]

Traditional Christian values and thinking have taken a backseat to the more vociferous, more energetic public presence of fundamentalism. Some may wonder that a distinction may be drawn between the ultra-conservative theologies and more traditional views of mainline Protestantism. The same kind of confusion existed among young soldiers. A strong tendency exists within mystical/metaphysical circles to lump all other churches into the same kettle as fundamentalism.

To understand properly the contribution of mystical Christianity and to fulfill its obligation of dialogue with other communions of faith, we need to push beyond such simplistic generalizations and grasp the truly pluralistic nature of Christian thought. Even a casual study shows that fundamentalism is not "traditional Christian theology" either in a biblical or Reformation sense. These new-right theologies can be traced to the anti-modernist movements which rose in reaction to scientific discoveries and biblical scholarship which took place during the last century.

In his book *The Christian Faith Today*, which we have quoted earlier in this study, T. A. Kantonen lists three main reasons why mainline Christianity rejects fundamentalism. After praising the ultra-conservatives for their zeal and loyalty to the Bible, Dr. Kantonen delivers a devastating critique of their theologies:

> First, fundamentalism is incompatible with the Bible's own method of self-authentication. Heaping extravagant praise on the book and claiming miraculous origin for it places the Bible in the same category as the Koran and the Book of Mormon. Mere appeal to the authority of the Bible proves nothing, for every sectarian and fanatic quotes Scripture to prove his own position. The Bible provides its own vindication when we appeal with Luther from the letter of the Bible to Christ, its living center.[3]

Merely claiming to *"follow the Bible"* is to proclaim that a person has no need of Tradition, life Experience, or Reason. We have already seen that this is simplistic and untenable. All people are influenced by their world, so no one goes to the Bible without formulated ideas. The best we can hope for is active dialogue to establish a working understanding of what God is trying to do in our lives and in the lives of all His people. Kantonen continues:

> Second, fundamentalism is incompatible with the method of divine revelation in general. God's revelation of himself is marked throughout by a bipolarity of the human and the divine. This is true of Christ, of the church, of the sacraments, and also of the Word. The deification of a book into something divinely inerrant is a form of the docetic heresy, a denial of the human nature of the Word.[4]

The Divine-human paradox is central to an understanding of God's actions in the world. If the Bible represents a clear stream of pure divinity, then it stands alone in all Creation, occupying a place of perfection Jesus Christ did not even claim for Himself. On the other hand, if the Bible represents God speaking through human minds—with all the typical, healthy misunderstandings and limitations to which human minds are subject—then the message of the Scripture can talk to us in our language because its authors have walked our path and caught a glimpse of Truth that transcends human limitations.

The Bible can be freely interpreted because it was freely given; it is more poetry than science, more love letter than law book. This leads us to Kantonen's final point:

Third, fundamentalism is incompatible with the mission of the Holy Spirit to teach new truth. It freezes revelation to a fixed period in past history and transforms the Bible into a collection of proof-texts for corroborating doctrinal preconceptions. The Bible is the living Word when the Holy Spirit uses it to create faith and provide vital new insights into divine truth.[5]

If fundamentalism does not speak for the Church, it certainly speaks to the minds of many people. Notwithstanding their fall from grace due to sex scandals among their ranks, radio and television "electronic evangelists," many of whom represent ultra-conservative theologies, have been highly successful in selling their message to the public. To the vast majority of people in English-speaking, Protestant America, fundamentalism equals "the church" and a narrow Biblicism is the only possible Christian theology.

This acquiescence to fundamentalist ideology is even more remarkable when we consider that poll after poll shows the public at large growing theologically more "liberal" all the time! Even among seminary students of the more conservative denominations, studies have shown a marked tendency toward such typically liberal ideas as Universalism, full emancipation of women, and freedom of choice in personal ethics and lifestyle.

What's going on in American Protestantism?

Now we have a puzzle before us. Studies show that people tend to identify Protestant Christianity with ultra-right theologies, but other studies indicate that greater numbers of people are becoming more liberal in thought and lifestyle even while becoming more conservative in their "official" religious beliefs. It's almost as though the Protestant movement in the United States has splintered three ways:

1) Vocal fundamentalist minority who think they're the only true church,

2) Confused majority of people who claim they're conservative on Sundays but who follow liberal lifestyles the rest of the week, and

3) Quiet minority of religious liberals who have allowed conservatives to define what is and is not American Protestant Christianity.

What a mess!

And not only Protestantism. We noted earlier in this work that Roman Catholics in the United States and Canada show an even greater rift between what they do and what they're supposed to do as communicant members of their church. As this chapter was originally drafted, the current issue of *U. S. News & World Reports* featured a cover article on the recent crackdown ordered by Pope John Paul II against American Catholic leaders because of liberalism in the ranks. Targeted for Papal rebuke were people like Seattle's Archbishop Raymond Hunthausen, who teaches freedom of conscience in birth control, premarital sex, and divorce.

More sobering for the leadership of that church are studies cited by the same article which show 41 percent of American Catholics favor free choice in abortion, 51 percent would allow homosexual relations between consenting adults, and 73 percent believe Catholics should be allowed to divorce and remarry. Birth control, which is still outlawed by Papal decree, was favored by over two-thirds of the American Catholic population. The article notes:

> U. S. Catholic leaders fear the result—not that the laity will desert the church altogether, but that they will simply turn their backs on the hierarchy, ignore its teachings and dismiss the "universal" church as irrelevant to their fate.[6]

HOW CRAZY IS THAT?

Two possibilities occur immediately. First, people may be tuning religion out when it speaks about modern life, much the same way they have learned to tune out commercials. Perhaps the lively music, energetic people, or beauty of the church still meets the worshipping public's religious needs. But, if we have grown accustomed to hearing nothing significant from church leaders, sooner or later we stop listening entirely, one wonders how many members of conservative, liberal, or moderate churches don't have the slightest idea what their branch of the faith teaches or believes?

The other possible answer is even less comforting. Perhaps large numbers of people have developed two worlds in which they live. One world is the everyday, Monday-to-Friday, work/home/place of recreation. In this "normal" world we find things scientifically arranged and subject to the laws of nature. Rain falls because of the westerly drift of weather patterns. The price of gasoline rises because of international politics and economic pressures. Sickness comes because of diseases; food comes from the supermarket or the farmers' fields. Good seems to be suffering a lot of setbacks.

Then Sunday arrives, and these folks slip into Church World, the realm of religion. God sends rain; prices waver because they are a sign of the End; death comes from sin's curse which God pronounced upon humanity; science is of the devil; the earth is seven thousand years old and the center of the Universe. We can almost hear the television *Tonight Show*'s host, Jay Leno, chirping: "How crazy is that?"

This dichotomy has been noted many times by theologians. Admittedly, it is a crude caricature, but represents the problem stretched so that we can see it more clearly. If people are convinced that religious faith is nothing but fantasy, it should surprise no one that multitudes are bowing before altars on Sundays and living like agnostics the rest of the week.

Because the image of Protestant Christianity has been so tainted by the powerful, wealthy influence of fundamentalism, we needed to begin our study of the Church with an examination of that influence. Too often, people come to the liberal churches with yards of baggage dragging behind them that has *"Turn or Burn"* stamped on every suitcase. Too often, liberal Christians have been willing to let fundamentalism define what is or is not "Christian." Too often, we have failed to assert our right to the Christian heritage in terms that are both faithful to the Gospel and meaningful to us.

It has been a central thesis of this survey of Christian theology that the faith of Jesus Christ is a diverse family under His lordship, and that within the Christian family there is plenty of room for half-cousins and in-laws. Our critique of fundamentalism, like any critical analysis, is only justified as it helps define whom we are and what we are trying to accomplish. Otherwise, it would be destructive to the body of Christ, which is the whole family of the Faith.

THE CHURCH: *EKKLESIA* AND *KOINONIA*

Now that we have reiterated the right and obligation of Metaphysical Christianity to speak for the Church, we must look at that institution, the community of faith. Our starting point for investigating the Church is the first of our formative factors, *Scripture*.

New Testament authors chose two words to describe their community of faith: *ekklesia* and *koinonia*. The first term (*ekklesia*) is generally translated with the modern English word *church*. From the Greek root word we form the word *ecclesiastic* which means clergyperson. *Ecclesiology* is the study of the Church and her ministries.

Ekklesia has an English equivalent word, *ecclesia*, used by historians to describe the popular assembly of ancient Athens; the word can also mean any assembly. From this archaic meaning we find the idea of the Church as the first century Christians saw it. They were the *Ekklesia*, the assembled congregation. There is a sense of the word which also means *called-out*, a gathered community of those called to serve, much like a state legislature. Christians saw the Church could be the popular assembly of all humanity, a great town-meeting of all humankind. There is no trace of elitism in the word.

Koinonia is a term which has become widely favored by liberal/moderate theologians to describe the fellowship of Christians. Van A. Harvey defines it in his *Handbook of Theological Terms*:

> Koinonia is a word frequently used in the New Testament to refer to the peculiar kind of communion Christians have with God and with one another in Christ...The word is frequently used in contemporary theological literature to refer to the kind of community that should characterize the churches instead of the undisciplined occasional gathering of individuals for worship, on the one hand, or a kind of superficial friendliness characteristic of the fraternity or lodge on the other.[7]

In theological circles, *koinonia* means the fellowship of believers as it ought to be. The word suggests selfless love, disciplined study, sharing and commitment to Truth. It is an excellent word for Metaphysical Christians because it so clearly reflects the kind of energy and love that usually characterizes a New Thought church.

Beyond defining the words, a student of New Testament Christianity finds that the early Church saw herself as a movement with a destiny unprecedented in world history. Christians were to carry the Good News to the ends of the earth. Because of this mandate to teach Truth, every believer was a deputy town crier. Every Christian was expected to tell others about the Good News of Jesus the Christ. Not everyone was a teacher, as Paul pointed out in I Corinthians 12, but everyone was able to live the Christian life and show others how Truth works.

Another key point is that the Church was not a building. Even when permanent "churches" were raised and great cathedral towers pointed skyward, the Church was not the structure at which the people met. The Church was—and is—the people.

CHURCH BECOMES CATHEDRAL

Sometime between those early days and the modern era we lost that concept. *Ekklesia* became *basilica*; the gathered community became identified with the stone-and-stained-glass gathering place. Today, most Christians say they *go to church,* when in New Testament times the believers *were the church.* In a biblical sense, this was a grievous error, equivalent to idolatry. To build permanent structures for Christians to meet and carry on he work of study, teaching, and proclaiming the Truth was not a mistake; organization and institutionalization is both inevitable and desirable. Nor is there anything wrong with beautiful buildings and great works of art, like statuary or stained glass windows. The problem would be the same if the people met at St. John's Storefront Church or St. John's Mighty Fortress Church at Fifth and Main. When we begin to confuse the place we meet with the institution which meets there, we have taken a step backward from a biblical understanding of what the Church is.

When "the Church" is located at First and Main, we can come and go, leaving our faith in the vestibule and returning to the "real world" where science and reason rule. Next Sunday, we can return to "the Church" and pick up our religious mindset again. For one-hour plus-or-minus we can pay our respects to morality, goodness, and decency, then drop our Sunday-go-to-meeting mentality in the vestibule again when we sally forth into the nonreligious world.

But if we *are* the Church, no such dichotomy is possible.

Biblically, there is no question that the believers in Jesus Christ lived their faith. When Paul wrote his letters to the churches at Thessolonika, Corinth, Ephesus, Galatia, Colossae, and Rome he was not writing to a building on the corner of Forum Street and Gladiator Square. He was writing to people who knew themselves as the Church.[8]

Early Christianity gave way to the medieval Church, and the gulf between individual believer and the larger fellowship widened into a grand canyon, as we shall see as we look at the Church from our next perspective, Tradition.

"TRADITION" IN THE CHURCH

As theologies hardened during the infighting which characterized the first few centuries of the faith, the Church at large (i.e., the Catholic or *Universal* Church) began to see itself as a world apart from the common experience of humans. Men and women retreated from a plague-ridden, war-torn society to shut themselves behind monastery walls where they could pursue spiritual and intellectual pastimes without interruption from the unhappy outside world. So complete was the withdrawal that some churchmen wondered if anyone could be saved outside a monastery's stern disciplines.

Those who reflected on the Church during the Middle Ages often saw her as an ark bobbing on a troubled sea. Little thought was given to the possibility that the poor peasants scratching the soil to coax forth crops year after year were full members of the body of Christ and were, in fact, the Church itself. It was a time of aristocracy when minor nobles ruled great districts, often with life-and-death power over citizens. Absolute monarchies controlled the nobles, and the Church exerted power over the monarchs from time to time (see our discussion of the Interdict, Chapter 11).

But now the Church was no longer the people, nor was it yet the stone walls of the cathedral. That would come much later with the development of free denominations after the Protestant Reformation. In medieval Europe, the Church was the political/ecclesiastical system which supervised Western Christianity, from parish priest to Pope.

All over Europe, there was one Church only. If a man were not baptized into it, he was not a member of society. Anyone excommunicated by the Church lost his political rights as well. At the same time, it was the Church which provided sanctuary for those endangered souls who took refuge within its walls. It was the Church which insisted that the poor did not have to fast as much as the rich, and which forbade servile work on Sunday. It was the Church which provided the poor with social services—free food and free hospitalization. For a long while, the Church was the sole source of education and scholarship. Its hold on people's affairs, no less than their minds, was enormous.[9]

CHURCH SCREENS OUT PEOPLE

Politically, the medieval Church was organized along feudal lines. The basic local unit was called a diocese, which was supervised by a Bishop with his headquarters in the largest town. Deacons assisted him, and in rural communities the duties of visiting the sick and caring for the poor were carried out by the lowest-level clergyman, a *Presbyter* as he was sometimes called, which meant *Elder*. All these officials were ordained priests, of course.

Above them developed a complex hierarchy of regional bishops, known as *Archbishops* and *Patriarchs* or, in the Western Church, *Cardinals*. Above this whole superstructure sat the Pope, whose power grew through the centuries until reaching its apex in pre-Reformation times.[10] Monastic communities had their own hierarchy, generally related to but separate from the power structure of the locality in which the monastery stood.

A peasant attending Mass in a high-vaulted church would feel as though he were entering another world, the world of the Holy. His thoughts about "the Church" probably centered on his relationship with the local priest and the ceremonies and feasts of the Christian year. If medieval Europe was more "religious" than our time, it was a religiosity which kept the worshipper locked into the role of the consumer with the Church as the supplier of salvation.

The priestly hierarchy held the keys to heaven. Only through obedience and proper attendance to his duties as a Christian could a medieval layperson dream of fellowship with God. The rift between the people and their Lord became so complete during this time that the ceremonial portion of the Mass—where the priest raises the elements and transforms them into the body and blood of Christ—was consider too sacred for the profane eyes of the multitudes to behold. Priests erected screens to keep the ritual invisible to the masses at the Mass, although the nobility sat in special boxes to the left and right of the altar in the cross-shaped sanctuaries. There they could watch the Mass without sharing the holy event with the unwashed rabble.

With the Protestant Reformation of the sixteenth century, the screens began to fall. Luther overturned centuries of elitism when he proclaimed the "Priesthood of all believers." He meant that, quite literally, every believer in Christ has the same obligations and shares the same rights before God. No one stands as an intermediary between the person and God according to Luther. The Church became once more the people.

But this new populism would give way to new elitism as the developing Protestant denominations evolved their systems of training, placing, and depending upon ordained clergy. Some Protestant ministers grasped at authoritarian heights unknown even to the medieval Catholic priest, for they sought to establish theocracies ruled jointly by cadre-clergy and laypeople who held the proper beliefs. Experiments in church-states were tried in Geneva under John Calvin and in several new world locations. Americans often forget that, although founded to provide religious freedom for this or that group, more than one of the original thirteen colonies proceeded to deny those freedoms to anyone who failed to subscribe to their interpretation of what religion ought to be. And, of course, everyone discriminated against the Jew.

To be fair, we must admit that American and Canadian political thought has fiercely defended the rights of religious minorities. Most Protestants and Catholics have enjoyed freedom of thought since the days of the American revolution, and Jews soon established their political presence by emigrating from crowded, anti-Semitic European cities to new towns growing up along the Eastern seaboard. By the middle of the nineteenth century, Jews had gained the unquestioned right to practice their religion in English-speaking North America, even though much anti-Semitism continued to exist and discrimination in education, hiring practices and housing was rampant. The Jewish presence may not have been popular in frontier America, but it was legal. Most people growing up in North America encounter a cultural mix consisting of a multitude of Protestant denominations (256 at last count), Roman Catholicism, Eastern Orthodoxies, Judaism, and a smattering of non-Western faiths.

How does this heterodox cultural landscape affect our way of looking at the Christian Church and the ministry? To answer this we must turn to the next Formative Factor, *Experience*.

EXPERIENCE: HOW DOES CULTURE AFFECT RELIGIOUS THOUGHT?

What is your idea of what constitutes "the Church"? If you were a young girl growing up in the Bible belt of Kentucky, you probably would have a highly developed idea of the Church. It would be rural, evangelical, fundamentalistic and lively. As Dr. Jim Glasse discovered (Chapter 11), you would expect to join the Church by "getting saved," which for you would mean an emotional/intellectual decision to accept Jesus Christ as your Lord and to acknowledge the Bible as literally true.

However, if you were a boy growing up in a downtown Boston Catholic parish, the Church would mean priests and nuns, midnight Mass and CCD classes, confession, and penance. Your method of joining the Church would be to make First Communion by the time you are seven years old and Confirmation in your early teens. The Bible would be a holy book, but the clergy would be your real source of authority and their view of what the Scripture means would influence your thinking greatly.

Anyone growing up in a culture must be influenced by that culture. As we have noted: *There are no tiger gods where there are no tigers.* Even those who rebel against their upbringing are paying homage to their background by opposing its cherished values; one cannot be dead set against confessing sins to another person unless there were those who taught that this is the proper way to achieve forgiveness. Expending vast energies in a life-long battle against a system of belief shows as much dependence upon that system as rigidly following its most minute dictates. If the cornerstone of our faith is rejection of any viewpoint, we have not a positive religious faith but the shadow of someone else's religion. Too many people come to liberal churches in a spirit of rebellion, never taking the time to find out what they believe. Metaphysical Christian churches house many fine ex-Catholics, ex-Baptists, and ex-Methodists who continue to define themselves by what they reject rather than what they accept.

Experience plays a huge role in shaping who we are as religious persons. Cultural influences are so pervasive that the very way we look at the world is determined to a large extent on how our culture sees reality. In Chapter 12 we looked at the Dobuans, a cultural group in Melanesia which trains its children to be suspicious because of the dark forces which they believe stand behind everyday life. As a contrast, take the Zuni Indians of New Mexico whose worldview is the polar opposite of the Dobuans.

Zuni supernatural entities are all benign and frequently helpful. Magic is practiced through long, careful ceremonies, but there is no trace of frenzy or orgiastic elements. The Zuni lives in a happy world of moderation where children are welcomed and cooperation is a cardinal virtue. Individual Zuni seek no power or leadership; tribal headmen have their duties forced upon them against their wishes. But listen to Horton and Hunt describe the ethical system they live by if you want a picture of a culture radically different from the Dobuans and us:

> The Zuni have no sense of sin. They have no picture of the universe as a conflict between good and evil, nor any concept of themselves as disgusting or unworthy. Sex is not a series of temptations but part of a happy life. Adultery is mildly disapproved, but is largely a private matter and a probable prelude to a change of husbands. Divorce is simple; the wife simply piles her husband's things outside the pueblo, where he finds them, cries a little, and goes home to his mother. Since the family is matrilineal (descent follows the mother's family line, and family residence is with the mother's family), a divorce and the disappearance of the father do not seriously disrupt the life of the children. Yet divorce is not very common, and serious misconduct is very rare.[11]

Is our way right and theirs wrong? That really depends on whether you are a Zuni or not. Life experience shapes our religious values so profoundly that we are not even aware of how culturally dependent we are. It is obvious that a planet which could produce social systems and worldviews as vastly different as the Dobuans and Zuni necessarily has room for many variations in theology among its higher religions.

A THEOLOGY OF THE CHURCH AND MINISTRY

Taking seriously all the problems mentioned above, we move toward a view of the Church that fits the life-experience of modern mystical Christians that is biblical and that preserves the best elements of traditional Ecclesiology. So far, we have heard that many voices have been raised in the name of "the Church," quite often in an attempt to silence others who see the mission of the Christian faith differently. We have noted that Mystical/Metaphysical Christianity has an important contribution to make and cannot allow extremists or hyper-orthodox opponents to shut down those who speak as the Church from the liberal view. Accepting that culture plays an important role in shaping our worldview, we nevertheless must be ourselves and speak the Truth as we see it while allowing for diversity within the Christian family.

What, then, is the Church for Metaphysical Christianity? We suggest three elements: 1) Ideas, 2) Heritage, 3) People. All are equally important and cannot exist without each other.

1. THE CHURCH IS IDEAS.

Christianity is not a system of doctrines but a living relationship with God through the Lordship of Jesus Christ. Theologians have said this before, yet the statement is itself an idea, a concept, a way to organize life and faith.

First and foremost, the Church is the storehouse of those great ideas about God which spoke to our ancestors in the ancient faith and continue to speak to us today. Protestants gather not for ceremonies but for the Word of God, which is not limited to the written words of a book but comes alive when two or more gather in His name. More than a storehouse, the Church is workshop, marketplace, and hothouse for growing, shaping, and exchanging ideas. No system can capture the Truth of God so perfectly that it will stand forever without need of revision. Rethinking the faith in each generation is the continual task of theology and the continuing challenge for every serious Christian. The Church is both the product of that thinking/rethinking process and the location where our theologizing gets done.

2. THE CHURCH IS HERITAGE.

Beyond the ideas which define who we are as a people, the rich heritage of the Christian faith constitutes another element making up the Church. We are not just head-stuff; we are art and music and ceremony, too.

The Church is candlelight services on Christmas Eve, white lilies on the altar at Easter. Defining the Church without bringing into the picture our religious symbols and customs is like explaining San Francisco without mentioning hills, cable cars or the Golden Gate Bridge. Metaphysical Christianity has its own special story and its own impressive heritage to add to the Church Universal. From Centering Prayer discovered in the medieval monasteries to congregations joining hands and singing "The Peace Song"[12], Christian Truth churches have a distinctive flavor which no other movement within Christianity duplicates.

A sense of history helps a religious community define itself and understand what its people are doing when they gather on the first day of each week as a community of faith. The *ekklesia* becomes *koinonia* when we become aware of our history and the direction we are traveling.

3. THE CHURCH IS PEOPLE.

Most of all, the Church is people. It is the "gathered community" (*ekklesia*) which joins in fellowship and love (*koinonia*) under the lordship of Jesus Christ. Most people know the Christian faith through association with other people. We have been have taught by their words and, more importantly, by their lives what it means to be a follower of Jesus.

From its earliest days, the Christian Church was characterized as a body of committed, caring people. "See how these Christians love one another," a Roman pagan wrote in the opening years of church history. If that had remained true, perhaps humankind would not have suffered so much through the subsequent centuries.

Certainly, the atrocities visited upon humanity by churchmen in the name of God would not have occurred if we had kept our covenant to be the *ekklesia* and *koinonia*, the gathered community of loving fellowship. But for all our faults, the Church is still the people. About that original fellowship Wayne A. Meeks writes:

> One cannot read far in the letters of Paul and his disciples without discovering that it was concern about the internal life of the Christian groups in each city that prompted most of the correspondence. The letters also reveal that those groups enjoyed an unusual degree of intimacy, high levels of interaction among members, and a very strong sense of internal cohesion and of distinction from both outsiders and from 'the world.'[13]

If the metaphysical churches do anything well it must certainly be to reflect, on our better occasions, some of this original spirit. A strong sense of group identity vibrates in and among Christian Truth churches, an almost Richter-scale-measurable level of excitement tingling in an atmosphere of dynamic, loving fellowship seldom found elsewhere.

While there are dangers in maintaining one's distinction from members of other groups and from the world at large—especially when arrogance replaces charity in dealing with communicants of other Christian fellowships—most people join a Metaphysical Christian Church because of the excellent caliber of her people as much as anything in the theological flavor of our congregations. As one wag said, "We joined here because of the people, and we stay in spite of them."

THEOLOGY OF MINISTRY

No discussion of the Church would be complete without a look at ministry, the other major category under the general heading of Ecclesiology. We briefly discussed the "priesthood of all believers" taught by Protestants in general and Martin Luther in particular. Instead of a special status conferred by supernatural authority of the Church, Protestants tend to look at ministry in terms of function.

When a Christian does something which fulfills a task of ministry—i.e., preaches a sermon, visits the sick, teaches Christian Truth to another person—he/she is exercising a function of ministry and therefore is a "minister" of Jesus Christ. Since anyone can perform acts of kindness or convey the Truth to another, anyone can *minister*.

That is what Luther meant by the "priesthood of all believers." Biblically, the concept harks back to these words from the New Testament:

> But you are a chosen race, a royal priesthood, a holy nation, God's own people, that you may declare the wonderful deeds of him who called you out of darkness into his marvelous light... Live as free men, yet without using your freedom as a pretext for evil; but live as servants of God. Honor all men. Love the brotherhood. Fear God.[14]

The emphasis is not upon *election* but upon *service*. There can be no trace of superiority in the true Christian, because we are called to serve others in utter humility. When Jesus walked among His disciples, He set the highest example—touching, feeding, healing, washing, and loving everyone who would avail themselves of His ministry.

We are called to do likewise.

However, there must be those persons whose task it is, according to the unknown author of Ephesians:

> ...that some should be...pastors and teachers, for the equipment of the saints (believers), for the work of ministry, for building up the body of Christ, until we all attain the unity of the faith and knowledge of the Son of God.[15]

A *"pastor and teacher"* is an ordinary Christian with special gifts in the area of speaking, administration, teaching, and other necessary functions to keep the Church in business. Some pastors are talented in a multitude of ways. Others, the author among them, squeak by with a nimble tongue and manage a friendly smile. Some are candidates for sainthood; some are villains who should be driven from office. Most of us are somewhere betwixt the two extremes, just like most of our parishioners.

Dr. James Glasse makes an important point in his book *Profession: Minister* when he reminds us that a pastor is called because of skills and not necessarily because he/she is the most spiritual person in the congregation. "Professional ministry" is just that: a profession requiring skills and education. If the minister is also a highly developed person spiritually, that is an added benefit.

Certainly, the professional pastor should not be a knave whose morality and character is highly suspect, but saintly standards should not be held for the religious professional, either. The tendency to put our clergy on pedestals, the role Sinclair Lewis called the "professional good man," can only result in disappointment and disillusionment for the parishioners. Enjoying this exalted status without protest is trifling with a fate worthy of Humpty-Dumpty.[16]

If the clergyperson is seen as someone who has already achieved Christ-consciousness—or even as someone who is well on the way—his/her opportunities for growth experiences will be severely limited. One clergyperson told me he did not want to attend a workshop on biblical studies that I was conducting at his church because he didn't want the church members to know that he, too, had much to learn about the Bible.

Ministers of many denominations sneak into liquor stores to buy a bottle of spirits even though their churches may allow them to drink alcohol. The best story comes from rural Pennsylvania during my days as a graduate student at Lancaster Theological Seminary. I served as a student-assistant to a young minister whose parish stretched along the backbone of the Allegheny mountains in central Pennsylvania. He told me that he and his wife were eating dinner on their anniversary, drinking wine, when a member of his congregation approached them and scolded, "I caught you!"

Although said with a twinkle in her eye, this church member thought it was a trifle naughty for her minister to be drinking in public regardless of whether their church allowed its people to drink. The ultimate absurdity of this situation was that the woman doing the scolding was also the owner of the restaurant!

Double standards are unhealthy for everyone, and since the clergy talks about subjects toward which we are all striving, necessarily the professional minister will always fail to practice everything he/she preaches. If we allow our professional clergy to be real people as well as spiritual leaders, Christian love and a sense of *ekklesia/koinonia* will prevail. We might remember that when Moses came down from the Mountain and found the people sinning, he flew into a rage and smashed the first draft of the Ten Commandments. Even high-level spiritual leaders blow it sometimes. Patience and prayer will always help clergy-laity relationships.

THE CHURCH AND MINISTRY

We have seen that the Church is ideas, heritage, and people. Furthermore, we considered that ministry is a task which everyone can carry out, although some persons have been set aside as specially trained leaders to help us all do ministry in Christ's name. The Church and her ministry go hand-in-hand, for neither could exist without the other. And by the word *ministry* we refer to the widest possible definition of those tasks which Christians of all vocations perform in service to humanity as commanded by Jesus the Christ.

It is the job of the Church to "minister" to a hurting, broken world. Our faith to do ministry in the face of such a world can sustain us only if we believe that, ultimately, God's plan for all sentient beings to be reunited with Him will be realized. The word for that movement toward unity-in-diversity-in-God is *Divine Order*, our next topic.

CHECK YOUR KNOWLEDGE

1. Identify/explain: *Ekklesia, Koinonia, Basilica, Diocese, Bishop, Deacon, Presbyter, Pastor, Laity/Layperson, Clergy, Ministry.*

2. What are the two worlds in which some religious people live?

3. Explain Luther's "priesthood of all believers."

4. What three elements does the text say constitutes "the Church"?

5. Is the Church a building? Give a historic example.

6. The text says, *"Protestants tend to look at ministry in terms of function."* Explain.

QUESTIONS FOR DISCUSSION

1. If ultra-conservative Christianity reflects neither the heritage nor current posture of legitimate theology, why do so many people think of fundamentalism as "the" Church? How could we change this misconception?

2. Do you know people who live in the "two worlds" mentioned in this chapter? Are Metaphysical Christians guilty of this dichotomy in their thinking?

3. How could a local church provide more opportunities for members to do ministry? List and discuss possibilities/problems with increased lay involvement in ministry.

4. How much did your religious upbringing affect who you are today? Do you have any strong memories or impressions of the Church or clergy from your youth?

5. Why are we here? What is the purpose for the Church?

6. Is the Church a special community? What makes it so?

NOTES

1. Marcus Bach, *The Unity Way of Life* (Unity Village: Unity Books), p. 174.

2. Although the conservative/fundamentalist churches are experiencing rapid growth, studies have indicated the general population is growing more "liberal" on religio-social issues. See the article "The Pope Gets Tough" by Merril McLoughlin, in November 17, 1986, *U.S. News & World Report*, for the Catholic statistics.

3. Kantonen, p. 24.

4. IBID., pp. 24-25.

5. IBID.

6. Merril McLoughlin, *U.S. News & World Report*, p. 65.

7. Harvey, p. 142.

8. For a deeper discussion of the early church see Wayne A. Meeks, *The First Urban Christians* (Yale, 1983), especially Chapter 3, "The Formation of the Ekklesia."

9. Anne Freemantle, *The Great Ages of Man: The Age of Faith* (Alexandria, VA: Time-Life Books, Inc., 1979), p. 12.

10. IBID., pp. 31-32.

11. Horton & Hunt, p. 94.

12. Sy Miller and Jill Jackson, "Let There Be Peace On Earth" in *Songs*, Yohanna Anderson, compiler (San Anselmo, CA: Songs and Creations, Inc., undated), p. 109. (This little booklet contains nearly 600 songs of all sorts, most with guitar chords; it is perfect for youth groups, retreats, informal worship, etc. The publisher's address given inside the jacket is *Songs and Creations*, P.O. Box 7, San Anselmo, CA 94960.)

13. Wayne A. Meeks, *The First Urban Christians* (New Haven: Yale, 1983), p. 74.

14. I Peter 2:9, 16-17 (RSV).

15. Ephesians 4:11-13 (RSV).

16. James D. Glasse, *Profession: Minister.*

DIVINE ORDER

Chapter Fourteen

In his dialogue *Timaeus*, Plato shows a debt to earlier Greek thought as he forms his own theory of spiritual growth. Drawing on ideas from the Pythagoreans and the Elusian mystery cult, Plato describes a pre-existent soul which lived among the stars until plummeting through various intervening planes of existence to crash land upon the earth where it was united with a body. During its fall from grace, the soul took on attributes and characteristics of the various lower levels enroute this material world. Like a high-flying bird somehow forced to earth, the task of the soul according to Plato is to learn how to fly and reclaim its rightful place in the realm of spiritual perfection.[1]

This, of course, is the antecedent of virtually all notions of soul-growth as a path to reunion with the Divine. In Hebrew thought, the story of Adam was simply a way of explaining how things got the way they are. When Christian thinkers looked back through the Christ-event to reinterpret the Adam-legend, Genesis became the entry point in human history for all sin and Adam's disobedience became "the Fall" which brought the curse of sin-death-judgment upon all humankind.

In doing so they brought Platonic imagery in synch with Hebrew mythology. The result was a Christianized Platonism (actually Neo-Platonism) which accepted the fall of humanity. The part about our exalted status in pre-existent communion with Divine Mind became a subject of controversy. Origen said yes; others were not so certain about pre-existence. Christian Platonism, like all theological "schools," had dissent within its ranks. However, most agreed that we fell from a higher state to our present condition of spiritual disrepair.

To make the scheme work, early Christian thinkers supposed that humanity was created in a kind of perfection and chose to reject God's companionship through an act of defiance in Eden. Although that is not what the biblical story actually says, it was close enough to make the case for Neo-Platonism plausible. That was important, because the fledgling Christian church desperately needed intellectual respectability if she were to reach beyond her natural constituency (lower classes, slaves, and women) and embrace educated members of Hellenistic society.

Plato had built no bridge to Hebrew thought; that task was relegated to the great Jewish thinker Philo and the subsequent Christian Platonists of the Alexandrian school.[2] But the chemistry of Hebrew thought and Platonism was a dangerous brew for the early Church. Too many wild, hedonistic cults also borrowed from Plato, and his strict dichotomy between spirit and matter gave pagan Platonists the intellectual grounds to dismiss as meaningless the historically grounded, God-with-us epics of the Jewish Bible.

Alexandrian Christians discovered allegory as a means of rescuing the Hebrew Scriptures from literalism and consequent absurdity in the eyes of the intellectual establishment of their day, but the scholars of Antioch took a hard line against pagan influences in biblical scholarship. If Alexandrian Christianity was born of gentile-thinking Platonism with its roots in the *gymnasium* (*community center*), Antiochan Christianity looked homeward to its Hebrew source, the *synagogue*. The Antiochan school emphasized literal meanings when interpreting the Bible, ruling out the speculative metaphysics of Alexandria.

Soon, Christian thinkers would deplore the drift toward Hellenistic ideas, so that by the second century Tertullian could cry, "What has Athens to do with Jerusalem?"

Myths about our first parents in the Garden of Eden were rebaptized as historical events. Ironically, the Platonic concept of a "fall," which has never been a central part of Jewish thought, survived the downfall of Christian Platonism. So did the dichotomy between matter and spirit, body and soul. While rejecting the Origenist tendencies toward Christian monism—which worked from a Platonist base but went far beyond crude dualisms into a vision of the underlying oneness—literalists managed to preserve some of the worst ingredients in the Neo-Platonist worldview.

They threw out the baby and drank the bathwater. Instead of moving toward unity with God, which was the goal of Alexandrian Christianity, the Western church adopted an eschatology which proclaimed our worthlessness and inability to approach the Divine. Instead the Wayshower, the archetype of what all people ought to be, Jesus became the pre-existent, only begotten Son sent to earth to repair the damage by giving us a ticket to heaven which we did not deserve.

Any number of ideas might have carried the day. Unfortunately for the Church, some of the less savory worldviews fused to form a far-reaching negativism about humanity and the world. Hebrew thought, with its emphasis on the health and wholeness of people before God, was abandoned in favor of a radical other-worldliness that made the Platonists look like speculative amateurs. Eventually, Original Sin became the official doctrine of the Church.

Things got worse.

EXCUSE ME—HOW DID SEX GET INVOLVED?

Many churchmen—monks and ascetics as they were—unhesitantly identified the Original Sin with sexuality, a conclusion which baffles Jewish scholars to this day. Apparently the celibates, who wanted to disparage even healthy sexuality, were not dismayed by the Hebrew propensity to see the Creation as good. Zealously negative thinking allowed some Church fathers to find sexual travesty in a story of simple disobedience. Where is the sexual crime in Eden? In the minds of medieval monks.

Of course, not everyone was swept along by the tidal wave of anti-Platonism, anti-intellectualism. My book, *Friends In High Places* (Unity Books, 1985), traces in the broadest possible terms the undercurrent of mysticism which has always been present in Christian theology. We shall not duplicate that effort here, however incomplete the study of our ancestors in the faith may be. We must not forget that melody humming in the wings just offstage, the mystical heritage which Christian Truth churches share.

Our purpose in reviewing the formative process of orthodox theology is to note that Christian thinking made a choice in its infancy. It rejected the promising Neo-Platonist worldview in favor of a hard-line literalism; it chose to see a humanity disconnected from God and incurably out of harmony with its neighbors. Most unfortunately, orthodoxy chose to see Jesus Christ as the unique Son of God whose blood-sacrifice paid the price of admission to an undeserved heaven. There were other options, all as thoroughly Christian as the one adopted by orthodoxy, but this package emerged as the majority view.

In this chapter, we look at one of those lost possibilities. Instead of struggling helplessly against our inherently sinful nature, the intervention of Jesus alone providing a vehicle for salvation, we return to the earlier concept of a descent from union with God. We contend that: this way of doing Christian theology is at least as, if not more, biblical as the one which eventually won the day in the ancient world; a mystical interpretation better explains the Christ-event; that Metaphysical Christianity holds the key to healthier theology for the future of the faith.

The pivotal concept on which all else turns is "the Fall" from unity with God. As we have said earlier, Creation-centered theology presents us with an attractive alternative to the non-biblical Creation/fall model. Unless we solely understand "creation" in its narrowest sense (i.e., a one-time event that happened fifteen billion years ago), then God's creative activity must be ongoing and evident today. The name of this process, by which we are slowly-but-surely growing back to awareness of our rightful place as Individualities within God's unified Presence and Power, is *Divine Order*.

WE GET TO CHOOSE

Divine Order is the term most often used when speaking of this onward rush toward Christ consciousness. It is an idea subtle and complicated, yet easily understood. Simply put, Divine Order means the "first law of the Universe."[3] And what is that "first law"? H. Emilie Cady explains:

> There is but one power in the universe, and that is God—good. God is good, and God is omnipresent. Apparent evils are not entities or things themselves. They are simply apparent absence of the good, just as darkness is an absence of light. But God, or good, is

omnipresent, so the apparent absence of good (evil) is unreal. It is only an appearance of evil.[4]

If any power exists outside of the Divine, then God is not all-powerful. As we have observed, only Christian Incarnational Monism is a true *mono*-theism. Yet, we experience sickness, suffering, and willful acts which any sane person would classify as evil. How can we deny that evil exists?

We can't and we don't. Christian Monists say that 1) evil and suffering are the absence of good and 2) good is the only true reality.

If we turn off the light and sit in the dark, it makes no sense to say, "There is no such thing as darkness." What makes better sense is to say, "I have no light by which to see because I've extinguished the source of light." Darkness owns no force which suppresses light; dark is the absence of light.

However, some Christian Truth teachers have emphasized the positive nature of goodness so completely that students of Metaphysical Christianity sometimes refuse to acknowledge that adverse circumstances can occur. This is unfortunate. No moral failure exists if a healing-oriented person gets sick; no lack of faith occurs when prosperity fails to demonstrate in every single instance. We need not rush to the friend who has suffered a terrible loss to assure them there is no such thing as loss for everything is *good, good, good!* That kind of metaphysical malpractice discloses not only impoverished thinking but a lack of sensitivity to the feelings of other persons.

The greatest mystics throughout the ages have not insisted that pain and suffering do not occur; they have taught that apparent evils have no power over us because we are essentially spiritual beings. Spiritual beings cannot get sick or suffer permanent damage. God really does have everything under control, although the present circumstances may argue to the contrary.

Bad things do happen to people. Some situations are so heart-breaking that we might even say there is no light in that given place at all—no goodness apparent to our human eyes. The Nazi death camps are certainly the classic example of places where the light of God's goodness grew terribly dim. For example, Jewish psychiatrist Viktor Frankl described what morning was like for him at Auschwitz:

> The most ghastly moment of the twenty-four hours of camp life was the awakening, when, at a still nocturnal hour, the three shrill blows of a whistle tore us pitilessly from our exhausted sleep and from the longings in our dreams. We then began the tussle with our wet shoes, into which we could scarcely force our feet, which were sore and swollen with edema. And there were the usual moans and groans about petty troubles, such as the snapping of wires which replaced shoelaces. One morning I heard someone, whom I knew to be brave and dignified, cry like a child because he finally had to go to the snowy marching grounds in his bare feet, as his shoes were too shrunken for him to wear.[5]

Even in those horrible places, people were sometimes able to offer each other loving help and reflect the faintest hint of God's goodness. Frankl wrote:

I remember how one day a foreman secretly gave me a piece of bread which I knew he must have saved from his breakfast ration. It was far more than the small piece of bread which moved me to tears at that time. It was the human "something" which this man also gave me—the word and look which accompanied the gift.[6]

Viktor Frankl discovered the death camps could strip human beings of every shred of dignity, except one. No one can take from us the power to choose the way we shall respond. This freedom to respond is humanity's greatest blessing and challenge. We choose, and everything depends on our choosing. We respond, and our response shapes the world.

KENOSIS AND DIVINE ORDER

What gives us the power to choose unspeakable cruelty or magnificent heroism? If all power comes from God, the answer is clear: God-power within us, struggling to grow. We have real choices to make. Sometimes we are twisted and bent by life's experiences and we choose the path away from goodness. Other times, we wander close to the route we should be following. As we move closer or further from the optimum pattern for our lives, we move quickly or slowly in our growth toward Christhood and reunion with God.

When we add the concept of *kenosis* to this process, the whole picture snaps into sharp focus. That bit of God-stuff which you represent has been "emptied" of its certainty and flung into your circumstances for the opportunity to learn and grow by freely selecting the good over the un-good. You have the power to elect utter chaos or Divine Order.

The Jesus Christ model shows us that even in the most adverse circumstances, the human-divine paradox within each of us has the capacity to transcend, to express forgiving love, and to move through defeat to resurrection. In fact, the Jesus-event shows us that every sentient being not only can achieve Christhood but shall achieve reunion with God.

NOT PREDESTINATION

However, Divine Order is not predestination, because we alone determine the how and when of our spiritual growth. The outcome is sure, but the course leading to that eventual Divine triumph is strictly in our hands. Every time we throw down the tools and abandon the growth process, God brings us back to the very spot we fled and gently presses the utensils of spiritual sculpturing back in our hands. Chip by chip, fleck by fleck, we shall eventually carve from the block of human existence the image of Christ, and it will be our image. Ralph Waldo Emerson gave us this moving tribute to the nature of the human-divine paradox within every person:

The day of days, the great day of the feat of life, is that in which the inward eye opens to the Unity in things, to the omnipresence of law:—see that what is must be and ought to be, or is the best. This beatitude dips from on high down on us and we see. It is not in us so much as we are in it. If the air come to our lungs, we breathe and live; if not, we die. If the light come to our eyes, we see; else not. And if truth come to our mind we suddenly expand to its dimensions, as if we grew to worlds. We are as lawgivers; we speak for Nature; we prophesy and divine.[7]

HEALTHY THEOLOGY REQUIRES CRITICAL ANALYSIS

So far we have been discussing the direction and goal of Divine Order, i.e., reaching for Christ-consciousness. Now we must look at the process by which this proceeds. To examine the underlying beliefs of any theology requires critical analysis; to do so in an attitude of respect for those who have given us so much good thinking requires Christian charity.

We have said that theology is *"organized reflection on God, the Divine and Ultimate Concerns,"* and have affirmed the obligation of the theologian to recognize no taboos when exploring the far corners of any belief system. In the spirit of healthy respect and great indebtedness to our recent ancestors in Metaphysical Christianity, we shall now consider whether one of the most fundamental premises agreed upon by most of the early-modern metaphysicians is in fact still a valid way to do business. From the careful tone set by this introductory paragraph, you have probably already guessed the answer.

IMMUTABLE LAW OR PROBABILITY/TENDENCY?

When the New Thought pioneers did their work, the dominant images they drew upon were from the physical sciences. Teachers like H. Emilie Cady, Emma Curtis Hopkins, Mary Baker Eddy, Ernest Holmes, and the Fillmores speak about Law and Science by which things of the Spirit function in an absolute cause-and-effect chain of events.

These ideas flow from a worldview which is essentially mechanical and which originated in the thinking of Sir Isaac Newton. Before Newton (1642-1727), science was an oddity among university studies. Men (not yet women) poured over ancient texts or engaged in lengthy verbal and written duels to find answers to their questions. As we saw in our study of Epistemology (Chapter 3), the experimental method to obtain data, which can be analyzed to determine scientific truth, was foreign to the medieval mind. Look at what happened to one of Newton's predecessors:

> ...when Roger Bacon (c. 1220-1292), the most celebrated European scientist of the Middle Ages, sought "to work out the nature and properties of things"—which included studying light and the rainbow and describing a process for making gunpowder—he was accused of black magic. He failed to persuade Pope Clement IV to admit experimental sciences to the university curriculum, he had to write his scientific treatises in secrecy, and was imprisoned for "suspected novelties."[8]

Like the Zuni and Dobouans, medieval people explained their world by unseen forces, some benign and some malicious. Rain came through divine action and sickness could be attributed to witchcraft or a broom closet full of other supernatural agencies, including the Supreme Being. God made the sun rise and set; He brought frost and thaw, drought and flood. It never occurred to the vast majority of human beings that there could be natural laws standing behind the observable phenomena of the world.

Not until Isaac Newton.

Newton popularized the scientific method. He didn't originate the principles of experimental science, but his contribution was so important that one scholar calls him "the first popular hero of modern science."[9]

What Newton did was to show that everything which happens in the world has a natural cause and can be expressed mathematically. He completely stripped the physical world of its supernatural premise. God did not turn the earth or crank up the curtain of night; such crude analogies were the product of human imagination. Rather than a comic figure racing about backstage to drop the night sky and roll the sun into place every morning, Newton's God was a Grand Designer Who planned the Universe according to Divine Law. Listen to the biblical cadence of Newton's laws:

> For every action there is an equal and opposite reaction.
> Gravity holds planets in their orbits and humans upon the earth.
> Objects in motion or at rest tend to remain in motion or at rest.
> Light is composed of colors which break down according to
> mathematical values.

On and on he went, pouring out scientific elixir which could be replicated by experiment, measured, and calculated by anyone. The world would never be the same again.

LAW RULES

All the great discoveries of the Age of Enlightenment can be summarized in a single phrase: *This is a Universe governed by laws.* Understand the law, fathom the mechanics of the Cosmos, and you can confidently predict the outcome. Just as 2+2=4, so does Newtonian physics show us a world that is ordered, precise, and mechanical.

When the great Metaphysical Christian thinkers of the modern era did their primary work, Newtonian physics still shaped human thought about the Cosmos. As Emerson's theories about God-in-us began to find practical expression in the healing work of Quimby, Eddy, the Fillmores, and others, these practitioners naturally sought to understand why and how their ideas worked. They knew what worked, but giving those practices a theoretical base was not easy. Some thinkers—Emilie Cady and even Charles Fillmore—sometimes recommended against too much study when it took the place of practice. Their point was well taken, but usually ignored.

Newtonian physics was the unspoken scientific model of the day, just as Hegelian idealism in its American Transcendentalist expression was the dominant philosophical system. Remember, we are talking about worldviews, which are often so pervasive and subtle that we are not aware of their existence.

Metaphysical Christians of the nineteenth and early twentieth centuries assumed Newton's mechanical Universe was identical to Reality, that everything could be reduced to absolute law and science. And since Truth is one, metaphysical Truth must be law and science, too. *"This is a Universe governed by laws."* All we need to do is understand the laws and apply them correctly to demonstrate a given result. Metaphysical absolutism was born a natural birth.

Then the elegant, orderly Universe of Isaac Newton—with its sublime mechanical principles that always apply everywhere, *world without end, Amen*—began to crack. Physical scientists, peering deep into the sub-atomic levels of matter, discovered that things just ain't what they seem.

For openers: There is no such thing as matter and energy. Everything is *matter-and-energy*. Just as water, ice, and steam are the same substance in different forms, so are energy and matter one and the same force/object. We can no longer speak of one without the other. But that's not all. A bigger shock was coming. At the heart of the Universe—in the sub-atomic microverse of which everything is composed—*there is no such thing as law*. There are only probabilities and tendencies. Instead of the absolute certainty of classical Newtonian physics, science now knows that random factors operate at the sub-atomic level.

This does *not* mean "when the relationships are understood by better theories, we'll be able to explain why certain sub-atomic particles behave a certain, unpredictable way." It means there is unpredictable behavior woven in the fabric of the Universe. The most basic level of the Cosmos operates in chaos, not order. Sub-atomic particles are ruled by tendencies, not law. This new approach is called *quantum mechanics*. We do not need to understand its complicated structures, but perhaps this brief passage from *Harper's Dictionary of Modern Thought* will help:

> Whereas in classical physics the state of a system is specified by a precise simultaneous determination of all relevant 'dynamic variables' (position, momentum, energy, etc.), the Uncertainty Principle asserts that this specification cannot be made for small-scale systems. Thus complete determinism is lost, and in quantum mechanics systems are specified by stating the probability of given values...[10]

PESKY MOLECULES, OBEDIENT CUPFULS

In the larger world around us, mechanical laws operate with predictable precision. Water boils at 100 degrees centigrade at sea level all over the earth. However, when we peer down into the atomic level, certainty becomes probability, because even a non-boiling cup of water contains a staggering number of molecules. One science teacher told the author that if one molecule per second had been removed from a cup of H_2O since the creation of the Universe, the water level in the cup would not be visibly different.

We know this vast pool of molecules in a cup of water will boil at a given combination of temperature and air pressure, but we don't know when *this* pesky water molecule will choose to boil. We can predict with absolute certainty things in the aggregate, but with no certainty whatsoever when talking of the particulars. Even more astonishingly, *the way we look at a given phenomenon can influence its behavior!* (Hang on; this is going to get weird.)

For example, light. Is it a wave or a particle? Well, that depends on how we look at it. Looking at it as a wave, certain principles and rules apply. Looking at it as a particle, other rules and conditions take over. Both sets are true, and yet they are mutually exclusive. There is no unitive theory to bring them together because light is wave-particle, neither and yet both.

Furthermore (I'm not making this up!), an observer who measures the spin of a subatomic particle at one location will force a twin particle miles away to spin in the opposite direction. Quantum physics has revealed a Cosmos that is unified yet peculiar, in which the observer creates the reality which is being measured.

BACK IN THE FUTURE?

Time is another fun topic for those who crave an orderly Cosmos. We now know that as an object's velocity begins to approach the speed of light, the flow of time slows down. It is even theoretically possible to reverse the process, to make time flow backwards. This is the stuff of science fiction, yet it could be playing at a physics laboratory near you in the near future.

The author has an acquaintance who is head of the physics department at a midwestern university. The professor said that students enter his discipline because they love the precision of Newtonian physics, which is taught at high school. "When students in the physical sciences reach college and graduate school," he chuckled, "they learn things aren't as well-behaved as they seem."

SOCIAL SCIENCE MODEL OF THE COSMOS

Social sciences contribute to our understanding of the probability principles of life, too. Listen to sociologists Horton and Hunt as they discuss the unpredictability of human behavior:

> ...most scientific prediction deals with collectives, not individuals. The agronomist predicts what proportion of seeds will grow, without telling which little seed will die. The chemist predicts the behavior of several billion hydrogen and oxygen atoms, without predicting the behavior of any single atom of hydrogen or oxygen. The sociologist (or any social scientist) can rarely predict what any one person will do, although he may be able to predict what most

of the members of a group will do. In other words, the sociologist may predict the probability of an action...[11]

When the Denver Broncos score a touchdown at Mile High Stadium in Denver, even an amateur sociologist can predict with 100 percent accuracy that the home crowd will cheer. At this writing, Mile High Stadium has been sold out for every Broncos game in the last twenty years. If the book in your hands becomes the classic the author envisions it will be, no doubt the Broncos will still be selling out the stadium as you read these words in the twenty-second century, and the home crowd will still be cheering whenever the home team scores a touchdown.

But no sociologist can predict whether Harvey Schmidlappe, sitting in seat Z-47, will cheer or not. Neither psychologist, psychiatrist, clergyperson nor seer can tell if an individual will respond a certain way with any kind of accuracy.

Why? Because the seat might be empty—there are always a few no-shows for NFL games, even at Mile High Stadium. Or the person sitting in seat Z-47 might be a visitor from another town, or he might not care about football; maybe he bet on the other team, or his mother died the night before.

Human beings are intricate, complex, matter-energy events who possess the same kind of randomness found at the sub-atomic level: They are free agents in the middle of a crowd. That's why medical science is an inexact enterprise. Give Mr. Jones a dose of medicine X, and he gets healthier. Administer the same drug to Mr. Smith and he suffers a violent allergic reaction and almost dies. Medicine is a participatory endeavor, relying as much on the response of the patient as the treatment of the doctor. We know that aspirin tends to relieve pain and inflammation, but will aspirin cure Mrs. Bonaducci's headache or relieve Mr. Tuttle's bursitis?

Spiritual science can help here. Ample evidence suggests that medicine works better when people believe in the treatment. In fact, a lot of people have gotten healthy while taking placebos, sugar pills which were given in place of strong drugs. Those people got well because their minds took over and did the job instead of depending on chemical healing.

Now, there is nothing wrong with medicine. I am not suggesting that everyone taking prescription drugs should flush their pills down the toilet and go cold turkey. However, medical treatment today might more frequently succeed if it incorporated a mental/spiritual dimension which recognizes that people who think healthy thoughts get healthier quicker and tend to stay that way longer. Does this suggest that all healing flows from the God-power within, whether released by mental or medical means?

This, of course, is the basic discovery which gave rise to all the Christian Truth churches. When that discovery occurred late in the nineteenth century, early experimenters in what was then called the "Christian sciences" looked to the physical sciences for a theoretical model that explained what was happening. Since all the world was Newtonian, classical physics with its mechanical laws provided the framework by which our founding mothers (later, founding fathers) described their new "spiritual science." It was thought to be a true science, because Truth teachings demonstrated results again and again.

Myrtle Fillmore was healed of tuberculosis, and then sitting at her kitchen table she taught others who came to her because they learned through the grapevine of Myrtle's healing. Others got healthy, too. These ideas spread like an infection of healing, and the movement which later came to be called "Unity" was off and running. Similar stories are told of Mary Baker Eddy and Nona Brooks, founders of the Christian Science and Divine Science churches, respectively. This was no abstract concept brewed up over tea at a gathering of academic theologians. These ideas brought healing, prosperity, and wholeness when applied by almost everyone. And so they were taught as law and science, based on the model of Newtonian physics, for so they were believed to be.

Early metaphysicians often insisted that, if we follow a given spiritual practice faithfully, we must demonstrate a positive result. Since they believed scientific laws were absolute and unvarying, it made perfect sense that spiritual law would follow the same pattern. It is no accident that New Thought teachings were at first called by the generic term "Christian Science", and that their science was based on a Newtonian premise. This presumption of spiritual mechanics ignored the fact that Truth teachings had to be applied by human beings, Homo sapiens, thinking/feeling persons. We are not interchangeable cogs in the wheel of the Cosmos. We are matter-energy events with a thinking/feeling nature. Humans are less like Newtonian physics and more like quantum physics, because if Mrs. Blavatsky affirms health with all her faith and energy and Mr. Tuttle does likewise, there is still no absolute guarantee they will be healed. As medicine is a participatory "sport", so is spiritual science.

If humanity at large applies Truth principles, we can predict with confidence that vast numbers will experience healing/prosperity demonstrations. But we cannot guarantee that you or I will get healthy or prosperous in a given circumstance because we are free to respond unpredictably. This in no wise negates the power of Divine Order any more than recognizing the human factor in medicine negates medical science.

But if the foregoing is an accurate description of reality, then Christian Truth churches have some major re-tooling to perform in their language and theological assumptions.

NO WHIMSICAL GODS ALLOWED

The great bulk of metaphysical writings speak of *law* and *science* when referring to Truth teachings. Those original metaphysicians rightly saw that God is not whimsical. Operating in an orthodox Christian milieu, early-modern Truth teachers had to combat the notion that God doles out favors according to His inscrutable emotional Nature.

Like Santa Claus in the sky, the god of classical theism nods here, frowns there. *"Yes, you may have a new car. No, your mother may not recover from her heart attack."* Small wonder people have turned aside from a god who could be so unpredictably arbitrary!

In place of the god of classical theism—which was really a projection of the oriental despots of biblical times—some modern mystical thinkers have suggested Deism's god of the grand scheme, the impersonal planner who draws His plans and never, never varies from precise, predictable operations. Unconsciously, they took us back to pre-Jobian Hebrew thinking where a balance mechanism governs the Universe: Right action (*thought*) produces right results absolutely; wrong action (*error-belief*) produces unfavorable results in an equally absolute manner. Of course, the problem with such a tally-sheet Cosmos is that it doesn't bear the scrutiny of personal experience. Good people suffer; bad guys win big. Right thinking powerfully affects the outcome, but happy endings don't happen 100 percent of the time, even for positive thinkers. We still need to grieve when we lose a friend. We must be free to hurt with someone who is walking the valley of the shadow.

OTHER PROBLEMS WITH THE LAW/SCIENCE MODEL

Carried to its ridiculous extreme, the concept of God as immutable Law means that suffering must come through some fault of the person. All we need do is affirm the right Truth idea and healing, prosperity, and wholeness must follow. That is simply not the way the Cosmos operates.

Certainly, there are numerous demonstrations of healing, prosperity, and wholeness, so many that we can generalize those practices which work best into a set of "laws" and "rules." However, when dealing with the free agency of human response, human freedom, no law or rule applies 100 percent of the time.

FOUR CHOICES FOR MODERN "JOB"

What happens to the people like Job among us, people who work at Truth principles with all their heart and yet experience no healing? There are four possible responses to this dilemma.

1) **You didn't do it right.** If the Law always works when properly applied, then failure to demonstrate means improper application. This is the most common reaction of faithful Truth students when they fail to demonstrate healing or prosperity, and it is usually correct. More times than not, something is missing and the demonstration will be forthcoming as soon as the person gets back on track.

But not always. Who doesn't know someone who has worked prosperity or healing principles with no apparent result? In the Old Testament, Job's friends urged him to repent and confess his sins because God would not send such calamities on a person who was living a righteous life. Job knew better, and his reaction brings us to the second possibility.

2) **God is welshing on His contract.** Sounds outrageous? Think about it. Job had the temerity to insist that God was cheating. Everyone knew that good was rewarded and evil punished, so why was he suffering? He knew in his heart that he was innocent, a

fact which God confirmed when the Lord asked Satan (the inspector general in this story):

> Have you considered my servant Job, that there is none like him on the earth, a blameless and upright man, who fears God and turns away from evil?[12]

If Job knows he is doing everything according to the Law of God and still suffering miserably, the one possible conclusion is that God has reneged on His promises. Much of the Book of Job contains the hero's complaints about the injustice of God. Not a very patient fellow, Job. At least he didn't succumb to the temptation of metaphysical agnosticism, which is the third and final reaction to unanswered prayer.

3) Truth is not true. This is frequently the conclusion of people who have been peripherally involved with the Metaphysical Christian movement, who float into our churches and try a few affirmations, succeeding for a while, but then march out the door in hot pursuit of the next religio-psychological fad when they meet a real challenge that doesn't go away as soon as it is denied three times. Sometimes it takes tenacity to break through the walls we have erected in consciousness.

So far, we have noted three possible responses when we fail to demonstrate successfully in the face of an unpleasant situation: 1) You didn't do it right; you're not applying Truth teachings properly; 2) God is welshing on His contract; 3) Truth is not true.

There is also a fourth possibility.

REALITY CHECK: DOES IT ALWAYS WORK FOR YOU?

4) Truth is not immutable law but probability. Why? Because people are involved. Teach a billion people to affirm health, prosperity, and wholeness. What will happen? There will be a lot of healthy, prosperous, whole people living long and productive lives. But will Harvey Schmidlappe get his demonstration? Will Mr. Tuttle's bursitis go away? Will Ms. Bonaducci find her soul mate? We simply don't know.

Now, if we contend that Truth is immutable law, an assumption unconsciously based on the now-defunct Newtonian worldview, then we have a real problem when a specific individual fails to demonstrate in a specific instance. We must say: 1) You didn't get it right; 2) God is welshing on His contract; or 3) Truth is not true. There are no other alternatives when our system operates from a Newtonian premise.

However, if we recognize the insights of quantum physics, then we have a perfectly logical, scientific explanation when Truth teachings fail to demonstrate. Namely, they are high-degree probability/tendencies and not changeless, mechanical laws.

God's grace is changeless; His will for us is always good.

Still, we must acknowledge theologically what we have all experienced privately: Sometimes a Truth procedure doesn't get us anywhere, regardless of how faithfully we apply Truth teachings. Sometimes a Metaphysical Christian dies while affirming Divine healing (even though death itself can be a kind of a healing, if we are serious about immortality and growth-potential throughout eternity). Sometimes prosperity does not demonstrate in our immediate circumstance, even while we are "knowing the truth" about our eternal prosperity in God-substance.

This stark fact of life: 1) in no way questions the faith or sincerity of the Truth student; 2) reflects that God never reneges on His promises or whimsically changes the rules because, 3) Truth teachings are absolutely true in all instances once we recognize they must 4) operate within the limitations of the Divine-Human paradox as Principles rather than grind on as inexorable law.

PRINCIPLES, NOT LAWS

Early-modern Truth teachers were absolutely correct when they attacked the notion of a whimsical god, but to counter this error-belief they fell back upon the Newtonian model of a mechanical Universe operating precisely within changeless law. What we are suggesting here is that these teachings are better understood by the quantum terminology: They are tendencies and probabilities rather than immutable law. Principles, rather than equations. Guidelines, not mechanics. More art than science. Less like the principles of mathematics, more like the principles of good writing.

An example from my years as a Little League coach will help here. I taught the boys and girls on my teams three rules when hitting:

1) Swing level

2) Keep your eyes on the ball

3) Try to make contact, not kill the ball

These were the *Principles of Batting*. Did they always work? Of course not! But the kids who applied these principles consistently hit the ball more often than they did when they allowed themselves to chop away, lose sight of the ball, and swing like a tornado.

Truth teachings may work so well that we can think of them as mechanical laws, but that model does no justice to the random factor which God has apparently programmed into the Cosmos under the rubric of freedom. If, however, Truth teachings are principles instead of laws, we have a much more flexible theoretical model to explain why some people have dramatic results and others experience frustrating failure to demonstrate healing, prosperity, or wholeness in their lives. Principles are not equations which always apply, like Plato's abstract world of perfection where geometrical forms float in an ethereal soup that could not spill into reality without contamination.

Although the word *principle* can mean *unchanging law*, it also can mean "a guiding sense of the requirements and obligations of right conduct: a man of principle."[13]

Charles Fillmore's definition of Principle in *The Revealing Word* seems to allow for such a loose interpretation, especially if we differentiate between Divine Principle and the application of those principles by faulty human consciousness:

> **Principle**—Fundamental Truth. Divine Principle is fundamental Truth in a universal sense, or as pertaining to God, the Divine. It is the underlying plan by which Spirit (God) moves in expressing itself ...God immanent in the universe is the great underlying cause of all manifestation; the source from which form proceeds. Although Principle is formless, it is that by which all form is produced.[14]

What we are proposing is a two-tiered definition of Principle. At the level of Divine Consciousness, *Principle* refers to Divine Order, which is the whole process of expression/creation, differentiation of God-energy into individual entities (you and me), involution/evolution toward higher consciousness which will culminate in Christ-consciousness, and Union-in-diversity with God. This is Divine Principle, and it cannot fail.

However, the divine-human paradox shows that perfect divinity must manifest itself through imperfect humanity. We have been "emptied" (kenosis) of full God-consciousness, and so has the very Universe. Science now knows, through quantum physics, that even time/space is a relatively imprecise, imperfect expression. So when we humans apply Truth teachings we are invoking *Applied Principle*, which must function in an imperfect Cosmos. When we use the word *Principle* in this study we are referring to Applied Principle, the imperfect application of Divine Ideas in a free Universe. It functions according to probability and tendency, not mechanically, because it must work in the lives of free, sentient beings.

THORN IN THE...

No Truth teacher can promise instant demonstrations. The best we can do is affirm that Truth teachings work and God is One Power/One Presence, regardless of circumstances. Certainly, Truth Principles do work in the vast majority of instances. But there is always that situation like St. Paul found himself in, described by the Apostle in his second letter to Corinth:

> And to keep me from being too elated by the abundance of revelations, a thorn was given me in the flesh, a messenger of Satan, to harass me, to keep me from being too elated. Three times I besought the Lord (Greek: *Kurios*) about this, that it should leave me; but he said to me, "My grace is sufficient for you, for my power is made perfect in weakness." I will all the more gladly boast of my weakness, that the power of Christ may rest upon me. For the sake of Christ, then, I am content with weakness, insults, hardships, persecutions, and calamities; for when I am weak, then I am strong.[15]

Very strange words for Metaphysical Christians to understand. First, we must de-mythologize the passage of its dualistic trappings ("messenger of Satan"), then shed our ethnocentrism to grasp what Paul is trying to say. He has been following Truth Principles but no healing has been forthcoming. His guidance from "the Lord" (prob-ably Jesus—Paul likes the Greek word *kurios* when referring to Him) is that he will receive no healing in this situation.

Paul's response is one of the high-water marks of New Testament mysticism. He affirms Divine Order even in the face of "weakness, insults, hardships, persecutions, and calamities." Pushing beyond mere acceptance of less than happy circumstances, claims spiritual benefits from apparent lack: "For when I am weak, then I am strong."

What does this mean, if not that God's goodness surrounds us even in the most adverse situations? When the outer world cannot come in line with our expecta-tions—when we suffer disappointing setbacks, sickness, or loss when a healing demonstration does not result—the best we can do is follow Paul's lead and affirm Divine Order in all appearances to the contrary.

What the Apostle to the Gentiles has done is focus our attention on the purpose behind demonstrations. If a Christian thinks following Jesus Christ means just the ability to manifest perfect health or demonstrate a new sports car every year, that person had better read the New Testament again.

We practice spiritual techniques for the spiritual benefit to be gained. Certainly, prosperity and health and good relationships are what God wants for us because they are our birthright as His Sons and Daughters. But not every journey leads to Treasure Island; some have gone into slavery, others to Auschwitz. We cannot dismiss those sufferings as irrelevant or see those who endured human inhumanity as merely lack-ing in the proper metaphysical training. Jesus Christ went to Calvary, and the heart of His teaching contains a profound understanding of the misery possible in this very real world. He knew suffering well.

Spirituality is the goal, not sports cars. But if God wants good things for us, as He must, then the sports cars of life will surely follow once we turn toward His Divine Order. That, by the way, is exactly what Jesus said: "But seek first his king-dom and his righteousness, and all these things shall be yours as well."[16]

CAN GOD BE TRUSTED?

God is either trustworthy or not. He sent us into a world where chaos sometimes reigns supreme, where nice people get cancer and bad guys are not always punished. In this Cosmos of billions and billions of sentient beings, natural events and freak accidents, God has set up Truth Principles as a response to the exigencies of life in a free Universe.

But they are *principles* rather than laws, because the Universe is truly free, even down to the sub-atomic level. Truth does not seem to function as immutable law but rather as high-probability tendencies.

SCIENTIFIC AND SPIRITUAL TRUTH EQUALLY TRUSTWORTHY

This does not invalidate Christian Truth principles any more than to understand the response of a patient's body invalidates medicine. If one patient receives an antibiotic and his infection gets worse, medical science doesn't throw away all the antibiotics and let infections run their course. Humans are highly individualized, bio-psychological entities whose response can be predicted only in large numbers. Most people will not go into shock when given a life-saving antibiotic, but some will. It is no concession to shamanism for the medical establishment to admit they cannot determine how our individual bodies will receive/reject treatment.

When the spiritual dimension is added, the situation becomes even more complex. Sometimes a person will fail to follow Truth Principles properly and, obviously, will fail to demonstrate. Other people seem to demonstrate so easily that they become lazy about learning more. Paul may have been one of those.

Still others follow Truth teachings faithfully but are not healed, receive no prosperity demonstration, gain no better toehold on healthy relationships. For those few people, the words of the Lord to the Apostle Paul, whom He loved dearly, most surely apply: "My grace is sufficient for you, for my power is made perfect in weakness."

SO TRY SOMETHING ELSE...

God's power working in and through the Cosmos cannot be limited just because a particular Truth strategy fails to demonstrate healing or prosperity. When medical treatment sees that a particular drug or therapy is not helping the patient, doctors back off and try a new approach. They don't discard the first treatment, knowing it may work perfectly well on another patient even though failing miserably this time.

"Treatments," as they are sometimes called, might work more effectively if we followed the same procedure. Some people give up too quickly. When demonstrations do not follow, veteran Truth teachers know, Divine Order must be affirmed. There is no better time to remind ourselves that there is a natural flow to life, a Divine Order behind the organized chaos of the Cosmos, which functions even when randomness and accident seem to rule the day. God's power comes to us most powerfully when we recognize that no matter what happens to us, we are His children and shall return unto Him.

Job's complaints about God not playing fair were finally answered in the fortieth chapter of that remarkable book. Speaking to Job from the whirlwind, the ancient author has God ask a question which both undermines and strengthens his faith:

Will you even put me in the wrong? Will you condemn me that you may be justified?[17]

It was Job's system that was wrong; his worldview put too many restrictions on God. In this life, good is not always rewarded, evil not always punished. Truth teachings apply, but in some instances demonstrations will not happen the way we expect.

At those times, we need to remember God's question to Job and his answer to Paul, for they fit together perfectly.

Divine Order is the whole system, not a portion of it. We saw in Chapter 10 (Eschatology) the ultimate goal of life is reunion with God. That goal shall be accomplished. But the process leading to Christ Consciousness is complicated, jagged, and sometimes messy. God could not have created a Universe with the precious gift of freedom if everything worked like Newton's mechanical Cosmos.

It is worth noting that although Newton labored mightily to stay within the fold of the Anglican church and succeeded—he wrote over 1.3 million words on biblical and theological topics alone—many of his successors found the idea of a self-perpetuating, orderly Universe luring them into deism, which is one short hop from nontheistic humanism.

Today, with a scientific worldview that accepts the unitive nature of matter-energy (scientifically, there really is only one kind of power-presence), and quantum theory which accepts tendencies and probabilities, God and the spiritual realm don't seem all that improbable anymore.[18]

Divine Order is the summary term we have chosen to describe this ongoing, tendency-probability process which will reach culmination in Teilhard's Omega Point, which is Christ-consciousness. Not everyone will cheer each time the home team scores, but by the time the game is over everyone will be on the same team and everyone will be cheering. Divine Order in all things means we know where we're going even while momentarily lost.

SCIENCE AND LAW: RETHINKING THE TERMS

Having said all this, we now return to some of the foundation statements which Metaphysical Christian churches shall doubtless continue to employ. We are returning for a fresh look, predicated upon a new understanding of the terms.

Christianity is science in every modern sense of the word, i.e., the Cosmos operates systematically based upon principles. God is not whimsical but orderly. We could scarcely imagine a Universe in which water boiled at different temperatures depending on the mood of the molecules. That doesn't happen. Even though a particular molecule may be "moody" and refuse to boil, the vast majority of the gazillions of molecules in a pot of water will boil on demand, expressing the "laws" of probability. God's power is released in this way, showing favoritism to none. God's One Presence/One Power is available everywhere in full measure.

Yet, we now know that human beings are amazingly complex, matter-energy-beings who respond differently under identical circumstances. So, although Principle is eternally true, results will vary depending on how the person interfaces with God's power.

God never overwhelms us, forcing us to accept His goodness. Spiritual health is always elective surgery. Even so, not everyone who affirms health and follows all known formulae for prosperity will always manifest healing and abundance. Both

Principle and person must resonate in harmony. As we have shown, the freedom-factor knit into the fabric of the Universe does not allow us to say that such-and-such will *always* produce this result.

Science, therefore, is an accurate description of God's operations, but only if we understand the post-Newtonian Universe. *God is Law*, if we use the word the way science now does. *Laws of science* are high-degree probability-tendencies which show the same results when applied in identical circumstances, in nearly every instance. Good science is forever skeptical, denying itself the luxury of words like "always" and "never" because it has been burned too many times. God is Law, but the Law must interact with free human beings. Perhaps that is why the great mystics have told us to relax and let God work through us regardless of the circumstances, always knowing that Divine Order is at work despite our inability to get desired results.

If we use these terms carefully, conventional metaphysical language can make sense theologically, biblically, and practically. We need always to remind ourselves that God's Truth is greater than any system, and a Universe without the possibility of surprises and mystery would be intolerably drab. As Charles Fillmore wrote:

> The Principle of Being is not only all good, but it is all intelligent. It is the fount of your intelligence. When you study it you will find yourself becoming one with the principle of all wisdom. To be one with the principle of All Intelligence is to know. When you know you will find yourself so broad in judgment and understanding that you will have charity for all who differ from you in religion, meta-physics, and even politics.[19]

ONE FINAL CAVEAT

The problems we have been addressing in the teachings of the founding mothers/fathers of modern Christian Truth churches are not of application but of explanation, not practice but theory. Many Truth students, the author included, find themselves totally agreeing with the early-modern New Thought teachers when they say *what works* and disagreeing with those august personages when they try to explain *why it works*.

Excited by their discoveries, these New Thought teachers rushed to explain these Truth teachings in the scientific language of the day. Thus we have Charles Fillmore describing the non-existent "ethers" which he believed surround earth and talking about "ganglionic centers" in the human body where none can be found.

Scientific language has the power to bestow credibility today, just as Greek philosophy brought respectability to a radical, new belief system taught by that stubborn band of Christians in the first century of the faith. Twenty centuries later, early-modern Christian Truth teachers continued seeking to explain why those Jesus Christ ideas work. Borrowing the respectable thought-language of their day, they never realized how dramatically science would reverse itself. That was their only real error.

Christian thought must never wed itself to a particular worldview or scientific orientation, or the "God of the gaps" will evaporate when better science crushes old models in favor of new ones. Even the quantum theory is not without its critics. Perhaps the next generation of Christian thinkers will wonder how we could have ever cast God's healing/prospering power in such limitations as either Newtonian Mechanical Law or Tendency-Probability of quantum theory. We send them our prayers across the gateway of time, hoping they will realize we are children of our own age as surely as were the founders of Metaphysical Christianity.

CONTROVERSIAL, BUT NECESSARY

Of all the topics discussed in this book, this will doubtless be one of the most controversial among Metaphysical Christian circles. The author is willing to take the risk because he believes strongly in theological dialogue. Perhaps in a future work the fruit of the discussion which will surely be generated by this chapter can be shared. In any event, the issue is stated clearly and no longer lingers in the twilight of topics too sensitive to explore and yet too important to ignore. Whether these conclusions are correct, of course, remains to be seen. With respect for the intelligence and keen insights abroad in the Christian Truth community, these observations are hereby released into your hands for consideration.

QUESTION OF PRIORITIES

If there is a natural course of life flowing toward Christ-consciousness, a goal which will be achieved eventually, what does this confidence mean in regard to our relationship with the world and with our fellow human beings? Do we find ourselves willing to ignore the pain of others because we can rest assured in their ultimate victory in Christ? Or do we feel compelled to rush about, saving the world? Of theological topics most frequently underrepresented in metaphysical thinking, *Social Ethics* must surely lead the list as the least discussed category of all. Into this vital, relatively unexplored region we must now venture in our survey of Christian thought and quest for a systematic theology from a Metaphysical perspective.

CHECK YOUR KNOWLEDGE

1. Explain/identify: *Christian Platonism, Alexandrian School, Antiochan School, Philo, Origen, Predestination, Sir Isaac Newton, Newtonian Physics, Quantum Theory, Immutable Law* vs. *Probability/Tendency, Divine Principles, Applied Principles.*

2. Which "school" won the argument in the early Church, Alexandria or Antioch?

3. What are the three logical possibilities, mentioned in the text, if a person believes Truth functions as immutable law and yet he/she does not receive a demonstration?

4. Compare/contrast Newtonian and quantum views of reality and show how they impact on mystical/metaphysical thought.

5. Why did early-modern Truth teachers describe their findings as *law*? What alternative does the text suggest?

6. What is the difference between *Divine Principle* and *Applied Principle*?

QUESTIONS FOR DISCUSSION

1. Do you agree with the author's contention that early-modern Christian Truth teachers made a mistake in aligning their discoveries with the Newtonian worldview? What are the arguments on both sides? Are there other options?

2. What does *Divine Order* mean to you? How is it different/similar to *predestination*?

3. If the author is correct in his analysis what effect, if any, will a switch from Immutable Law to Applied Principles have on the following: *Healing, Ministry, Prosperity Teachings, Prayer/Meditation, Bible Interpretation, Christology, One Presence/One Power, and the "Law Of Mind Action"*?

4. If we descended from union with God in order to return, what is the purpose of the whole exercise?

5. What part should dialogue and "healthy" controversy play in theology?

6. Is this chapter likely to provoke controversy, as the author anticipates? Why?

NOTES

1. Capps & Wright, p. 13.

2. Thomas Shepherd, *Friends in High Places* (Unity Village: Unity Books, 1985), pp. 4-5.

3. Fillmore, *Revealing Word*, p. 56.

4. H. Emilie Cady, *Lessons in Truth* (Unity Village: Unity Books, undated), pp. 44-45

5. Viktor E. Frankl, *Man's Search for Meaning* (Boston: Beacon Press, 1963), p. 31.

6. IBID., p. 86.

7. Emerson, p. 61-62.

8. Daniel J. Boorstin, *The Discoverers* (NY: Random House, 1983), pp. 401-402.

9. IBID.

10. Bullock and Stallybrass, *Harper Dictionary of Modern Thought*, p. 517.

11. Horton & Hunt, p. 33.

12. Job 1:3 (RSV).

13. Jess Stein, ed., *The Random House College Dictionary* (NY: Random House, 1980), p. 1053b.

14. Fillmore, *Revealing Word*, p. 156.

15. II Corinthians 12:7-10 (RSV).

16. Matthew 6:33 (RSV).

17. Job 40:8 (RSV).

18. Boorstin, p. 407.

19. Fillmore, *Dynamics*, p. 22.

SOCIAL ETHICS

Chapter Fifteen

I fairly sizzle with zeal and enthusiasm as I spring forth with a mighty faith to do the things that ought to be done by me.

—Charles Fillmore

What is the responsibility of the Christian toward the world and her peoples? Shall we seek only to save them by handing out bibles and teaching them to pray? If so, what sense can we make of the frequent commands of Jesus to heal the sick, clothe the naked, feed the poor, comfort the oppressed? The response of some Good Samaritans today is to look down at the battered victim in the ditch and say, "I'll pray for you...here's a good book on the subject."

What about the flip side of this question: Isn't it the business of religious groups to promote religious values and beliefs? Can't we reach more people by changing their hearts than by marching in the streets? Where does our responsibility end, or must we personally try to feed all the hungry and clothe all the naked? Even Jesus seemed to admit this was impossible when He told His disciples, *"The poor you will always have with you."* Am I my brother's keeper, or just his soup kitchen?

A NEGLECTED SUBJECT

There is no issue as neglected and as ready to be studied by Christian Truth churches as Christian Social Ethics. But before we begin to explore the thorny garden paths of today's issues, we need to back off and take a long look at what is meant by ethics in general and Christian Social Ethics in particular. Perhaps this review will be tautological for you; if so, feel free to skip forward to where we begin constructing a theory of social ethics for mystical/metaphysical Christians. Even if you have a solid background in moral theology, you might find this discussion of the four main types of ethical systems a good review.

THE WORD FOR TODAY IS — ETHICS

"Ethics" is a much misunderstood word today. Like many technical terms, it has acquired a popular meaning which makes the subject difficult to discuss without confusion. Commonly, we speak of a person behaving "ethically," or "unethically," which loosely means "properly" or "improperly." But when a theologian or philosopher launches into a discussion of ethics, no such neat dichotomy between good and evil presents itself.

Philosophically, *ethics* is the attempt to examine critically those questions which deal with what is *Right, Good,* and *Proper* in human values. Another term for ethics is *Moral Philosophy* (for religionists, *Moral Theology*).

Ethics is not so much a code of behavior as a way to make value decisions. Some people would never tell a lie or run a red light under normal circumstances, but might under other conditions: If a madman appears at the door, waving a loaded pistol and demanding to know if a certain person is having tea in the parlor, few people would feel compelled to answer truthfully. If they were driving a critically ill friend to the hospital at four o'clock in the morning, most people would run every red light they encountered on the deserted city streets.

What makes some behavior acceptable in one series of events and morally wrong in another? What changes our rules, standards, and mores? How do we behave in those many, many instances when no clear-cut answer emerges, nothing but gray areas where any choice may prove right or wrong? One learns quickly that where issues of right-and-wrong are concerned, there are as many possibilities as there are participants. Some are outrageous, some elegant beyond words.

Most lie in that vague hinterland where distinguishing *Good, Right,* and *Proper* is like picking a white thread from a gray in the dawnlight before sunrise. When we move beyond individual ethical considerations and look at the value-system of a group, society, or nation we are entering the domain of Social Ethics. Here the problem becomes far more complex because we are now dealing with systems of values that may be in conflict. The Mormon Church of the nineteenth century practiced polygyny, i.e., allowed men to marry more than one wife. That custom ran afoul of the community standards of the nation as a whole and precipitated a near-war between the United States and the Utah territory. In Islamic societies, a man's right to have four wives is unquestioned, but in North America another standard prevails. The Mormons changed their rules in the face of violent opposition by the rest of their country rather than risk further military confrontation with an overwhelmingly superior non-Mormon society.

What makes polygyny acceptable in Algeria but anathema in Alabama? The complex interaction of culture, human choice, and nature makes groups what they are. Individual ethics looks at moral standards and values by which the person lives his/her life; social ethics asks critical questions about group morality and standards of conduct. As the world grows smaller through technological advance, few topics will be as important for the well being of the human family as an intelligent approach to social ethics in the emerging global village.

ARGUMENTS AGAINST DOING THEOLOGICAL ETHICS

As with any controversial topic, attempts to forge a pattern for Christian Social Ethics from a mystical basis sometimes generates resistance within the community of faith. In all fairness, it must be admitted that some arguments against exploring this subject are well founded. However, no theology can be complete without addressing the problems of Moral Theology. Choosing not to speak to questions of social ethics is to make a statement which too often sinks us deep into apathy. Could a responsible Christian live through the slave era and not be an Abolitionist? Could a Christian watch the Civil Rights movement develop in the United States and not be moved to take a stand in favor of integration?

Certainly. Millions did just that.

Millions of slave-owning or slavery-condoning Christians spoke against the emancipation of blacks before and during the Civil War. Millions of God-fearing Americans prayed that they would not have to integrate their schools, that African-Americans would keep in their place and stop marching for freedom.

How is that possible, you ask?

Examine the questions, discover what motivated people to take moral positions which are now seen as clearly repugnant, and you are doing social ethics. It is not enough just to *feel* that your cause is right; every fanatic claims certitude. We must understand the process to ask critical, empirical questions. To make good choices, we must be able to handle prickly issues and apply techniques of valuing that flow from our Christian heritage and are as free from prejudice as possible. That is no easy proposition.

As we noted and discussed in Chapter 4, every culture is to some degree ethnocentric.[1] Ethnocentrism creeps into our religious thinking and affects the way we look at ethical/moral problems. Because of this tendency, theological ethics must always be in dialogue—within the community of faith as Christian thinkers discuss problems and cross verbal swords over solutions, and between Christian ethicists and non-Christians who explore moral questions. Only by listening to those who stand outside our house will we ever know what it looks like in its wholeness.

There is something of a feisty, controversial spirit to theological ethics which may require new religious behavior for Metaphysical Christians. We tend to want peace at any price, without realizing that the founding fathers and mothers of modern Metaphysical Christianity were far from milquetoasts when they gathered to discuss the faith. Charles Fillmore was known for his kindly spirit, but he was also unafraid of disagreement. James Dillet Freeman writes:

> Often in his classes, a student would be answering a question and Mr. Fillmore would ask, "Where did you get that idea?"
>
> The student would reply, "I read that in such-and-such a Unity book, Mr. Fillmore."
>
> "Are you sure?"

"Certainly, Mr. Fillmore, that is right out of page so and so."

"You know," he would say, "that is not exactly right," and then he would go on to explain the point in a way that clarified it.

Often in his classes, he would interrupt his students, when they were quoting him, with the question, "But what do *YOU* think about it?" The main aim of his teaching was to get his students to think Truth through for themselves.[2]

It is in this kind of free exchange that Truth emerges. The Christian community, we have said, works best when it is a marketplace and not a factory, where varieties of belief and practice lend color and vigor to our spiritual growth. Charles Fillmore knew he must not bottle up a formula and issue it wholesale to his students. One of his favorite affirmations was, "I reserve the right to change my mind."[3] He wrote:

> Beware of the circumscribed idea of God! Always provide for an increase in your concept. Don't write down any laws governing your conduct or your religious ideas. Be free to grow and expand. What you think today may not be the measure for your thought tomorrow.[4]

Through critical discussion of ethical issues, opportunities for change naturally arise. We learn quickly which ideas work and which are fantasy when we bring them to market. However, there are some legitimate arguments against an active involvement in Christian Social Ethics. In keeping with our aspiration to promote healthy discussion, we shall briefly explore five of these, attempting to set forth the objections to Christian Social Ethics in a fair manner and to answer those concerns with the response a Metaphysical Christian Ethicist might offer. You are certainly invited to disagree and encouraged to "reserve the right to change" your mind.

OBJECTION #1: Faith Should Be Strictly Oriented Toward Spiritual Growth.

Mysticism's highest goal is union with God. Those who object to discussing theological ethics often contend that involvement with the problems of this world might blunt our drive toward mystical Oneness with God by draining energies on concerns of this world. Too much passion for the problems of this world could bog us down and make us forget spiritual growth as the primary goal of life. Thus, our spirituality might suffer from confrontations with a world that does not yet understand Christian Truth teachings.

RESPONSE: It has always been a challenge for the religious person to live in the world without becoming "worldly" in the pejorative sense of the word. There are countless biblical injunctions to warn believers about the danger of becoming too closely associated with popular causes and fashions; in the mind of some New

Testament authors, "the world" is always a term of derision which is contrasted to the Kingdom of God.

Yet, even the author of John's Gospel—who rails against "the world" at every opportunity—could not help formulating the central mission of Jesus Christ in these words: "For God so loved the world that He gave His only begotten Son..."(John 3:16).

It was to help "the world" (i.e., all people) that Jesus taught His message of healing love. In fact, several places in the Gospels, Jesus explicitly commands His disciples to get involved in social action: clothe the naked, feed the hungry, visit the sick and imprisoned, bless the children, heal those facing health challenges, comfort those who mourn, teach all nations, love your neighbor, do the will of the Father, be a neighbor in deed as well as in belief—the list is practically endless.

The parables of Jesus overflow with good deeds and people who took action in the real world: the Good Samaritan, the Father of the Prodigal Son, the Good Shepherd. His teaching was reinforced by a life of compassion and involvement with others: cleansing lepers, healing paralytics, giving sight to the blind, feeding the multitudes, Zacchaeus, healing on the Sabbath, warning of the dangers of violent solutions, and many other instances of help or compassion extended by Jesus.

In fact, the only people against whom Jesus explodes in a stream of invective are the leaders of the religious community who have become so concerned about nit-picking at points of the Law that they forgot why the Law was given in the first place: to help people find fellowship with God and their neighbor. In perhaps the most powerful statement on the responsibility of Christians to other people found in the New Testament, Matthew's Jesus says:

> "Depart from me, you cursed, into the eternal fire prepared for the devil and his angels; for I was hungry and you gave me no food, I was thirsty and you gave me no drink. I was a stranger and you did not welcome me, naked and you did not clothe me, sick and in prison and you did not visit me." Then they also will answer, "Lord, when did we see thee hungry or thirsty or a stranger or naked or sick or in prison, and did not minister to thee?" Then he will answer them, "Truly, I say to you, as you did it not to one of the least of these, you did it not to me."[5]

When we de-mythologize this passage of its ancient eschatology, we still have a message of almost frightening admonition: Failure to help people in need is tantamount to turning one's back on the Christ. It will lock us into a pattern of no-growth until we learn this lesson. The author of the First Epistle of John wrote: "...he who does not love his brother whom he has seen, cannot love God whom he has not seen."[6]

Can we say that we love our neighbor if we duck our responsibility to help make this a better world? The Christian Social Ethicist would answer, *"No."* However, there are other arguments against doing social ethics, some pretty good ones.

OBJECTION #2: Others are Available to Do Social Action; our Task is to Teach Truth to the World. That is its Greatest Need.

This is a subtle variation on the first argument, but very popular in some religious circles and among the laypeople of many churches. Although many clergy people took an active part in the Civil Rights era and Anti-War protests, countless others refused to get involved because they felt it was their duty to save souls, not challenge the status quo. It is not a new problem.

The Reverend Theodore Parker, nineteenth century Unitarian minister and uncompromising Abolitionist, decried the complacency of even the liberal churches in his day. In the book and motion picture *The Hiding Place*, Corrie Ten Boom tells of her Dutch clergyman who refused to get involved in the secret program of sheltering Jewish families from the Nazi's because he felt his first obligation was to care for the souls of his people.

The Metaphysical Christian variation on this argument is that our calling is to teach individual spiritual growth, not become emmeshed in socio-political causes. If we teach people to turn within and find the Christ, they will grow enlightened enough to do good in the world on their own.

RESPONSE: Contained within this objection are two sub-points.

1) Social activism is not the business of churches because our job is to teach spirituality (or save souls, depending on the religious tradition).
2) If we get about our business and teach people about God, they will accomplish by themselves the good that should be done in the world.

We'll look at both arguments in order.

Sub-Point #1. Churches should stick to religion.

Jesus demolished this excuse when he scolded the Pharisees and Saducees for their superficial religiosity that took them away from justice and mercy. Any religion which exempts us from our obligations to real people in the real world is not a religion but an escape mechanism, a fantasy. How could a person follow the Christ within and yet refuse to feed the helpless hungry?

Buddhists tell the story of Gautama, the first Buddha, and His father's attempt to prevent Him from seeing the pain of the world. The father was told by a soothsayer that Gautama could become either a homeless monk or the emperor of all India. Knowing that exposure to suffering often turns people to religion, His father determined to blot out all traces of misery from Gautama's world. Only healthy, young people attended Him. Whenever the young prince went riding, His father cleared the highways of old, sick, and hungry people. His life contained no hint of suffering.

Then the gods intervened. Young Gautama saw an old man and learned about aging; He met a sick man and discovered disease; He watched a funeral procession and knew there was death. Overwhelmed by grief and anxiety about His own fate, Gautama finally encountered a mystic in a yellow robe whose calm, peaceful demeanor showed that it was possible to live in the real world and yet be a spiritual person. Thus began the quest which ended when He discovered the Noble Eightfold Path and attained Enlightenment. He became the Buddha, walking a path of moderation in all things.[7]

Certainly, religious movements must teach spiritual values and stand for personal growth before God. But all the great prophets of humankind have reiterated the necessity for involvement with the problems of society. Call any Divine Messenger to the stand and take testimony: read the writings of prophets and teachers from all the faiths of humanity and see if you can find one which tells us to run away from the world, ignore the cries of the hungry and the oppressed, and seek our own salvation exclusively? When Jesus told us to "seek first the Kingdom of God and its righteousness," He never said for do it to the exclusion of our responsibilities to our neighbor. Christianity is more than a call to higher consciousness—it is a summons to action, to commitment, to discipleship.

Sub-Point #2. Inspire others.

But what about the second sub-point? Can't we inspire people and not get involved ourselves? If we teach people about God, won't they change the world themselves?

Yes and no.

When everyone becomes enlightened—fully aware of the Christ within—the world will be a much happier place. The only question here is one of degrees: Shall we wait for enlightenment to descend upon all humanity? Or shall we try to help people live a better life here and now, during their struggle to achieve Christ-consciousness? Perhaps the real question ought to be, *"Can we truly be walking the path to Christhood if we ignore the cries of the poor, the hungry, the oppressed?"* What answer would Jesus Christ give to that question?

Those who say churches should teach religion and let the people go forth to live an enlightened life are following the "Leaven in the Loaf" model of social ethics. Sprinkle a little yeast into the batter and the whole mass rises to become light, fluffy bread. Sprinkle enlightened souls through the population and human consciousness will rise to higher levels without any apparent effort at reform.

The only problem with this theory is that it doesn't work.

History shows that some kind of organized effort is necessary to meet and overcome social evils. Were segregationists "bad" people who needed the example of "good" citizens who favored integration? Were those of us who served in the long, painful conflict in Southeast Asia "wrong" and those who fled to Canada or marched in the streets against that war "right"?

Often, *right* and *wrong* get sorted out later by historians. People like us live in the anxiety of a gray world where ethical decisions can usually go either way. It takes more than an enlightened person to raise consciousness; it takes dialogue among people who are struggling to learn God's will. The "Leaven in the Loaf" theory assumes that there is one correct way of living, and that all we have to do is find that path and live it in order to influence society in the right way. But what happens when we don't know the right way? What happens in those messy, sticky areas where even enlightened people are confused? If we deal with ethical problems by dialogue and intelligent analysis, we stand a better chance at reaching some kind of societal consensus.

OBJECTION #3: Too Many Hungry and Poor; How Can We Possibly Cope?
Even a quick look at the monumental problems of the Third World (hunger, disease, poverty, oppressive regimes, ignorance, overpopulation) or at our own society's blind spots (hungry people amid plenty; sexism, homophobia, lingering racism, poverty, drugs, violent crime, apathy, general intolerance) could paralyze a person by the enormity of the world's challenges. Even Jesus acknowledged that the poor are always with us. What can one person, even one church, do?

RESPONSE: A simple reply to this objection? *Do something!* What might happen if every follower of Jesus Christ decided to improve the world, even in some small way? We may not be able to save the planet single-handedly, but we can certainly affect the spaces surrounding our lives. What if a church member "adopted" a child through the Christian Children's Fund? [CCF is a marvelous, non-denominational, inter-faith foundation through which individuals and groups can sponsor children who live under some of the world's most desperate circumstances, bringing them food, clothing, and education so they may rise from childhood poverty to some degree of adult prosperity.] Or what if a church decides it will help to buy a new health clinic through another international service agency? Surely we can't save all the hungry and clothe all the naked ourselves, but we can feed some, clothe some. Laziness can masquerade as despair when confronted by problems of this magnitude. We don't have to solve all the problems of the world to get involved with social action. We must simply decide to act, now. Choosing a plan of attack may be the greatest obstacle facing a church that resolves itself to get started. That's our final objection.

OBJECTION #4: Social Action is Too Divisive. Too Many People Disagree on the Issues.
One of the great one-line folk proverbs of our culture is, *Never discuss religion or politics.* And what is Christian Social Ethics? Religious discussion of political topics! Just about every agenda item for consideration as an ethical concern has socio-political overtones to it. *Hunger* means economics; *sexism* means the Equal Rights Amendment; *abortion rights* means the liberals against the conservatives. Why should a church wallow into this quagmire to upset, divide, and drive away major blocks of contributing members? The return is not worth the effort.

RESPONSE: Implicit in this argument is the idea that churches should strive for uncritical harmony. Good luck. There has never been such a garden of paradise within Christendom. When two or more people are involved, conflict is natural. Ask any happily married couple. Whether or not a church decides to discuss theological ethics and possible avenues for social action, every church will experience natural, healthy conflict. *First Force* (an idea or action) always generates *Second Force* (resistance) which resolves itself in *Third Force* (synthesis).

Projects which might be considered under the category of social ethics could be as innocuous as obtaining new street lights in a high-crime area, collecting used clothing for the needy, or offering Alcoholics' Anonymous a place to meet on the church's property. However, even low-threat ideas like these will generate some Second Force. Take that as a given, and move forward lovingly. If the church begins with discussions, progressing toward easy-to-achieve projects that have a solid base of support, finally graduating to open consideration of the more controversial topics, spiritual leadership will generate a minimum of unnecessary Second Force.

We are not suggesting a church should kick off its Social Ethics program with a march on city hall. There may never again be any issues which provoke responsible Christians to take such drastic measures in our lifetimes as the Civil Rights activism did. What we are considering is the possibility of awakening the great, creative powers of Metaphysical Christian churches to the task of making this world a better place, even in some small way.

The choice should never be between spirituality and action in the real world: spirituality should help us "spring forth with a mighty faith to do the things that ought to be done."

FOUR KINDS OF ETHICS

There are many theological opinions—too many, perhaps!—but only a certain number of "schools" of thought. For example, Christian Truth churches fall generally within the broad category of Christian mysticism, whereas many mainline Protestant churches are grounded in Neo-orthodoxy and Roman Catholicism is predominantly Neo-Thomist.

Within moral philosophy/theology, there are at least four general approaches which might be called schools of ethics. Actually, they are less content and more process-oriented classifications; so we are looking at these four categories to learn how people think rather than what they think.

If we were to rank people on a scale of rigidity, for example, we might find rigid people everywhere—liberals, conservatives, or centrists. There would be rigid whites and rigid blacks, rigid women's liberation advocates and rigid traditionalists, rigid Pro-lifers and rigid Pro-choicers.

So it makes no sense to discuss the content of a "typical" rigid person's ethics because when we look at ethics from a rigidity-scale we are concerned with process. A senior longshoreman is less interested in what content his people load on outgoing ships than in how carefully they perform that loading process. For our purposes, we are going to play ethics foreman and look at four ways theologians and laypeople load their cargo of values about what is *Right, Good,* and *Proper.*

TYPE ONE: PRINCIPLED ETHICS = DO IT "BY THE BOOK."

Before beginning, we note that the word *principled* is used differently here than in the rest of this book, reflecting common ethics terminology. *Principled* here refers to functioning from a rigid set of guidelines, legalistically applying them to all cases without exceptions.

Earlier in this chapter we suggested that there were some conditions under which a normally honest person might lie or break the law. If a person functions from unbending principles, he/she might argue that violating them is never justified. Someone who proceeds from stone-carved principles has several good things going for him.

First, *eternal principles are quite reassuring in a rapidly changing world,* so the Principled Ethicist has a high degree of Certainty. He has built his house on a rock, and the winds of change will not shake its foundations.

Second, *Principled Ethicists are relieved of the burden of repeated decision-making.* Since all questions are referred to unchanging Principles which answer any circumstance, they are not creators of ethical systems but only interpreters of Divine decrees.

Third, *the viewpoints of the Principled Ethicist possess infallibility.* Because they are really not his views but God's. One of the author's seminary professors quipped that this type of person says: "You may continue to worship God in your own way; I shall continue to worship Him in His."

Finally, *he is relieved of responsibility for his actions* because the rules were made by God, and who can argue with God? I once had a disquieting discussion with an otherwise rational and likable young man whose religious group believed blacks to be spiritually inferior to whites. When I asked how he could accept such drivel, he replied, "If it were up to me, I wouldn't believe it. But it's God's law, not mine." I pursued this line of logic to its ultimate absurdity: "So, you think it's wrong," I summarized, "but you're stuck with it because God is a bigot. How can you follow a God whose ethics are inferior to your own?" He never answered satisfactorily.

We need only recall some of the terrible experiences of the human race when unbending men of "principle" came to power and sought to make the world over in their image. The Spanish Inquisition is perhaps the most infamous reign of misguided Principles our world has experienced, but burnings and beatings were not only handed down by Catholics to "heretics."

The great church reformer, John Calvin, had the Unitarian author Michael Servetus burned at the stake in Geneva. Protestant colonists killed "witches" in British America. Communist-hunting parties drove countless people from their careers during the McCarthy era. And "patriots" on both sides of the blockades in Ulster hurled firebombs and sniped at police.

These are men of unbending principle. Are terrorists who die while shooting up airports to make a religio-political statement truly evil people, or are they passionate partisans of principles which cannot be compromised or negotiated? The great danger of Principled Ethics is that it is unable to adapt itself to circumstances without forfeiting its basic principle, i.e., that rules must always be obeyed.

I knew a parent who said his daughter could not go to dances until she was in high school. He reacted predictably when she was picked to be Junior High School Homecoming Queen, and a fourteen-year-old girl sat at home crying, never to forget the disappointment of her young life. He hated himself for doing it, but he would not bend because he was a man of his word.

Certainly, there must be "tough love" that holds people accountable, but humans need better ways of solving ethical problems than a set of inflexible principles to which all the complexities of life must conform. So we find that Principled Ethics falls short because it attempts to deal in absolutes in a very relative world.

TYPE TWO: ANTINOMIAN ETHICS = DO IT IF IT FEELS RIGHT.

At the opposite end of the spectrum from Principled Ethics is a non-system of valuing called *Antinomianism*. Raised to its most respectable level, Antinomian Ethics holds that "ordinary moral laws are not applicable to Christians, whose lives, it is said, are governed solely by divine grace."[8] We find support for this position in St. Paul, but we can also see the Apostle struggling against the logical implications of Antinomianism as well.

"All things are lawful for me," but not all things are helpful. "All things are lawful for me," but I will not be enslaved by anything...Do you not know that your body is a temple of the Holy Spirit within you, which you have from God?[9]

Paul had preached that Christians were under grace and therefore not subject to the Jewish Law. Gentile Christians made the natural assumption that Christians were immune to all laws and that anything goes. When Paul heard about the wild behavior at Corinth—Las Vegas of the Roman world—he hastily dispatched a disciple with his First Letter to the Corinthians in hand. Much of the letter is devoted to settling disputes and quelling Antinomianism that was rampant in the Church at Corinth. Not only fleshly excesses, but spiritual practices had gotten out of hand. Read chapters 12-13-14 in a modern translation at one sitting and you will understand the battle Paul was fighting with the religious zealots at Corinth.

Antinominanism's great virtue is that it is flexible to circumstances. If there are no standards whatsoever, we are free to adapt our behavior to match our life experiences. So the madman with a pistol demanding to know if your friend is having tea in your house can be told a technical lie because there is no such thing as absolute truth anyway. Running red lights is acceptable behavior for Antinomian ethicists as long as no car crashes into you broadside. In fact, one often hears a kind of untutored Antinomian ethos when talking to people of the drug culture, or people who are sexually promiscuous, or people who drink too much. As long as no one gets hurt, it's okay.

But a true Antinomian Ethicist would not even concern himself with another person's pain or discomfort. If there are no standards and no responsibilities, we should just do what seems right at any given minute. Virtually any kind of behavior is ethically permitted under Antinomianism. Hitler stands beside Ghandi, Stalin walks hand in hand with Mother Theresa, because they all did what they thought was right.

Metaphysical Churches are especially susceptible to charges of Antinomianism. If God is within everyone, should not each person follow his/her own inner guide and do whatever it says, regardless of the values of society?

James Dillet Freeman answered these arguments brilliantly:

> The most important question to ask of any religion is, 'Are you a life-affirming or life-denying religion?' A religion should have beliefs that you can accept without denying your intelligence; it should motivate you to create beauty and revere joy; it should inspire you to be energetic and creative, enable you to find peace of mind and to live well; it should teach you to be kind and tolerant toward all your fellow human beings, even those who do not like you.[10]

In other words, it should call you to discipleship in the footsteps of Jesus Christ, Who is the standard by which all Christians measure the Right, the Good, and the Proper. But that is not allowable if we embrace Antinomianism, which says there are no external standards whatsoever. Christian Truth teaching, like mysticism throughout the ages, has always lived in the tension between individual freedom to follow the Christ-within and the need to follow the example of Jesus Christ. Such tension is creative, generating decision-making power while prompting us to seek out other Christians to price our ethical choices in the free market of theology.

All this presupposes some guiding principles. Even clinging to Jesus Christ requires a way of processing the raw information about Him, from Bible and tradition, into a value system which helps us make ethical choices. Again, we look to *process* instead of *content*. All Christians agree on Jesus; few agree on what it means to follow Him. Fewer still agree on how to live our lives by the light of His presence. One way to solve the problem is to boil all the verbiage down to one basic principle which serves as the staple for our whole ethical system.

TYPE THREE: SITUATION ETHICS = DO IT IF IT'S THE LOVING THING

Much maligned and misunderstood, Joseph Fletcher's book *Situation Ethics* has weathered a hurricane of anathemas from church leaders. Part of the controversy is

Fletcher's fault. He chose to include as part of his introduction to *Situation Ethics* an argument for liberalized sexual standards. Matching a new technique for doing ethics with a red-flag issue like sexuality was an unfortunate alignment, but the book attracted more publicity because of the sexual issues and probably more people became more aware of what Fletcher was trying to say through this controversy.

However, the term *Situation Ethics* has today become synonymous with libertine practice and in popular use it has become the average person's phrase for Antinomianism. Joseph Fletcher didn't say we should do whatever feels right in any given situation, as Antinomianists do. Actually, Fletcher's work sketched categories we have explored so far: Principled Ethics, which he called *Legalism*, and Antinomianism. Joseph Fletcher adds to these two polar opposites his own middle way, which he calls Situation Ethics. Let him introduce the idea himself:

> A third approach, in between legalism and Antinomian unprincipledness, is situation ethics. The situationist enters into every decision-making situation fully armed with the ethical maxims of his community and its heritage, and he treats them with respect as illuminators of his problems. Just the same he is prepared in any situation to compromise them or set them aside in the situation if love seems better served by doing so.[11]

Fletcher believes in establishing a true polar star and guiding by it in all circumstances, an all-embracing principle which calls all other values into judgment and serves as the yardstick by which we can measure ethical responses to events. For Fletcher, that standard is *Love*. He would have us ask, in every circumstance requiring a moral judgment, *What is the loving thing to do?* He calls upon an impressive array of witnesses and sources to support his ideas, including incidents from the life of Jesus, Whom Fletcher sees as the supreme example of Situation Ethics in action.

Didn't Jesus heal people on the Sabbath, eat with sinners, and converse with foreigners—all acts forbidden by the Jewish Law? And when questioned about His practices did Jesus not say that the Law was made for humanity, not humanity for the Law? What motivation other than love do we need? What better governing principle than the law of love?

Fletcher's argument is tempting, but it begs the question when assuming that everyone will agree on what is a loving act in any given situation. The anti-abortionist expresses loving concern for the unborn baby; the pro-choice counselor understands the terrible choice a mother must make and expresses loving concern for the adult female with an unwanted pregnancy that will result in an unwanted child. Which side does the Christian Ethicist endorse? Every time *Roe v. Wade* has an anniversary, devout believers hold placards on both sides of the street, a fact that each would do well to remember when demonizing their ethical-political opponents.

Fletcher offers no solution, and perhaps that is his greatest fallacy and greatest strength. No system of ethics can provide pre-fabricated answers to every life situation. We have maintained in this book that dialogue and discussion of difficult issues is the best way to arrive at answers to tough problems. Even the best answer must be held open to continual review and reconsideration because, paraphrasing Charles Fillmore, what we face today may not be the ethical dilemma of tomorrow.

We need to consider a fourth way to do ethics, a *modus operandi* which blends some of the best features of the above three. It is not a perfect system, in every circumstance, but perhaps by now you are aware that perfect systems rarely find their way into the hands of human beings.

Let's take a look at this final way of doing ethics.

TYPE FOUR: CONTEXTUAL ETHICS = DO IT IF IT APPEARS RIGHT, BASED ON A MATRIX OF VALUES AND THE MODEL OF JESUS CHRIST.

Some ethicists believe there is no single principle which can be applied in every situation, even the principle of love. To punish a criminal with lengthy imprisonment for misdeeds may result in society's protection, it may even be good for the criminal who is no longer able to harm himself spiritually by acts of violence, but we must twist the word "love" to interpret such an act of imprisonment as a "loving" deed.

Perhaps a better word is "justice" in this circumstance. Jesus showed that a *loving* person can also be a *just* person; witness His stern rebuke of the religious hierarchy and His uncompromising, drive-'em-out-with-a-whip response to the avaricious moneychangers. However, Jesus tempered justice with reasonableness, so the punishment would fit the crime: No death sentences for loitering or life imprisonment for petty theft. To be truly an act of justice, the ethical/social practice must not violate the principles of love, either.

Contextual Ethics sees a matrix of interactive values which support each other and must be understood in relationship to each other. Instead of a series of unalterable laws, Contextual Ethics speaks of "guiding principles" which support each other and give people ways to look at a problem from many vantage points. Instead of one overwhelming principle that takes precedence, Contextual Ethics offers a chorus of ideas singing in harmony and able to change pitch depending on the music that life places in our hands. A Contextual Ethicist has *principles*, but considers the real-world *situation* and lets the whole value system mull over the problem instead of doggedly trying to solve every problem by splashing love all over it.

Sometimes, love will be more important than justice, as with our mini-tragedy of the junior high homecoming queen. Other times, justice (or order) will take precedence, as with criminals facing prison for their misdeeds. The context presents the problem; the value-system lets its hierarchy of principles dialogue about possible solutions.

Of course, one of the most important questions to ask a Contextual Ethicist is what is the source of that matrix of values which will process the ethical decision?

A CONTEXTUAL THEORY OF ETHICS
FOR METAPHYSICAL CHRISTIANS

One such basis for Contextual Ethics could be Charles Fillmore's *Twelve Powers*, which we have already seen has applications beyond mere meditative introspection. Value-decisions could be considered from the vantage point of those twelve cardinal elements in the makeup of the human-divine paradox. Crowning the whole system is the Christ, the Incarnation of the *I Am* (the divinity within) which informs us of the dignity and worth of each sentient being.

Rules—such as the Ten Commandments, legal codes of the nation or community, folkways, and personal beliefs—fall under scrutiny of this value matrix and are held against the standard of the Christ-within each person. No one will ever be written off as utterly lost because the pattern of divinity dwells just below the mask of human rebellion. *Individuality*—the divine spark within each human being—will eventually triumph over *personality*, which is the summary of our current state of learning and not a statement of our eternal selfhood.[12]

Tough problems still exist. There are no clean, easy answers to ethical issues. But now we have a starting point for discussing individual and social ethics from a mystical perspective. Contextual Ethics offers Metaphysical Christians the kind of freedom we need while firmly grounding us in the Judaeo-Christian heritage.

Whether a local church launches a complete social awareness program or just a discussion group to consider world problems from the Christian perspective, the mandate for followers of Jesus to care for His sheep remains in force. How we choose to follow that command is entirely a personal matter and must be left to individual conscience.

The intent of this chapter was to spur discussion about ethical topics and suggest a basis for doing Christian theological ethics that begins and ends with the model of Jesus Christ. Whatever tools we add to our studies—Buddha's meditation on suffering or Fillmore's *Twelve Powers*—must ultimately come before the only standard of Christian faith for the final test: *What would Jesus do?* If our ethical systems can answer that question, we are well on the path to a better world.

WHERE TO GO WITH TRUTH?

Given the belief that Christianity is better than non-faith, what does that imply? Do we have a duty to teach the Christian faith to others, and if so, by what means? Our study must move beyond ethics in general and discuss one of the most controversial religious issues New Thought Churches will have to face in the twenty-first century: Shall we engage in systematic outreach to non-believers or continue to teach people sent our way by Spirit? Will our watchword change from "When the student is ready the teacher will appear," to "Go and teach all nations...?" Do Truth students have something special to say, and are they ready and willing to say it? Standby for more lovely controversy—our next topic of investigation will be *Evangelism.*

CHECK YOUR KNOWLEDGE

1. Explain/identify: *Ethics, Moral Philosophy, Christian Social Ethics, "Leaven in the Loaf" theory, First/Second/Third Force, Antinomianism, Joseph Fletcher, Matrix of Values, Legalism, Individuality, Personality.*

2. What is the philosophical definition of *ethics* given in the text?

3. Summarize the objections to discussing/doing Christian Social Ethics listed in the text.

4. What are the four kinds of ethics? Explain each.

5. Compare/contrast Joseph Fletcher's ethical system with fundamentalist Christian understandings of social principles.

6. Does the text focus on the *contents* or *process* of ethics? What's the difference?

QUESTIONS FOR DISCUSSION

1. Should local churches discuss or become involved in ethical issues? What about those areas which border on politics, e.g., Women's Rights, Racism, Pro-Life/Pro-Choice, Gay Liberation, Affirmative Action, societal violence, the environment?

2. What is the proper function of Christian Social Ethics for the Church at large? For the local church? For the individual Christian?

3. Each person list his/her ethical issues, prioritized in order of importance. Discuss the lists. Any surprises?

4. Which of the four ethical systems appeals most to you?

5. What would happen at your church if the minister announced she/he is going to take part in a demonstration about some ethical issue? What if she/he were arrested during an act of civil disobedience like the protesters were during the Vietnam War and Civil Rights era? Could your church deal with that kind of activity on the part of our clergy?

6. What low-threat social action projects could you initiate at your church? Or should the church concern itself solely with spiritual pursuits and leave social action to others?

NOTES

1. Horton & Hunt, pp. 74-75.

2. Freeman, pp. 170-171.

3. IBID., p. 169.

4. IBID., p. 170.

5. Matthew 25: 41-45 (RSV).

6. I John 4:20b (RSV).

7. Noss, *Man's Religions*, p. 121.

8. Anthony Flew, *A Dictionary of Philosophy* (NY: St. Martins's Press, 1979), p. 14.

9. I Corinthians 6:12, 19 (RSV).

10. Freeman, "Is Unity a Cult?"

11. Joseph Fletcher, *Situation Ethics* (Philadelphia: Westminster Press, 1966), p. 26.

12. Cady, pp. 72-75.

OUTREACH EVANGELISM

Chapter Sixteen

Should We Do It?

"Well, I've been coming here for over twenty years," respond-ed Jeff Reynolds, who appeared to be in his mid-forties, "but I didn't become a member until last winter when our new minister, Pastor Johnson, came and called on me and invited me to join."

"You just became a member last winter!" exclaimed a woman sitting across the table from Mr. Reynolds. "Why, Jeff, I thought you had always been a member here. I know I've been seeing you around Trinity ever since my husband and I moved here, and that's close to twenty years ago. How come you didn't actually become a member until last winter?"

"Nobody had ever asked me to join," replied Jeff Reynolds in a quiet voice...

While this may sound unbelievable to many parish leaders, some people do operate on the assumption that they are not welcome unless they have been invited.[1]

ASK AND YE SHALL RECEIVE...

Surveys show that between 70-80 percent of new members in North American Protestant churches first attended because they were invited by friends or relatives. Not only new members. A Gallup poll showed that 58 percent of all regular church members began to attend because they were invited by someone they knew. A corol-lary study done on those who do not attend church showed 63 percent of the total unchurched population have never been invited by anyone.[2]

Let's do a reality check. A show of hands, please: How many of you out there became acquainted with a Metaphysical Christian church because you were told about New Thought Christianity by a friend or relative? If you are a typical congre-gation, eight out of ten readers will raise a hand. The author's unscientific guessti-mate is that 80 percent would be a lowside number, since Metaphysical Christianity tends to be a "refugee church" comprised of a vast majority who are fleeing spiritual oppression of their childhood churches and only a few second-generation members who were born into the movement.

This suggests the most important factor in attracting new people: personal contact by someone who is excited about what is happening at his/her church. Christian Truth Churches overflow with that kind of person. Visitors report a contagious excitement, a sense of *koinonia* bubbling among members that infects even the children, who come bouncing out of Sunday school with their colored papers, announcing to pleased parents that God lives in their hearts, not in the sky.

Friendliness and positive thinking, a healthy attitude toward religion and life, practical teachings about how to overcome apparent lack or sickness or disharmony—Christian Truth churches have a lot to offer disenchanted, unchurched, alienated people. If Metaphysical Christians exude self-confidence, it is because they are convinced God is the One Presence/One Power in their lives and in the Universe and that everything is in Divine Order and will work out for the good in the end. The question we ask in this chapter is this: *Is the message which changed our lives for the better worth sharing with others?*

THE STUDENT WAS READY—THE TEACHER WENT AWOL

This very self-confidence, engendered by a strong faith in Divine Order, can sometimes mistakenly lead to complacency. If everything will work out in the end, then we can relax and let people stumble across Truth teachings by themselves. Organized effort to spread the gospel?

Ridiculous!

"When the student is ready, the teacher will appear," say the advocates of repose. *"After all, we can't really lead anyone to spiritual growth unless that person is ready and willing, and that very receptivity will attract opportunities for growth and teachers to teach the person. Any thought of intentionality about outreach is seen as a denial of the Law of Mind Action. Let people become ready in their own good time and they will find us!"*

As with other snappy clichés and folksy proverbs, ("A stitch in time saves nine...") this simplistic attitude can be countered with other truisms that lean in the opposite direction ("Haste makes waste..."). If people are ready, won't they be receptive to outreach? If not ready, they will scarcely be hurt by telling them the Good News and planting seeds in their consciousness.

How many people lived for years in towns with Metaphysical Christian churches, never hearing a word about New Thought Christianity? How many of us work, play, and live beside people who haven't the slightest idea their co-worker, friend, or neighbor ever darkens the door of a Truth churches? How many people needlessly suffer from health challenges, crushing guilt, relationship problems, lack of prosperity, un-whole-someness, or disharmony in their professional, personal, and spiritual lives? How long did you struggle upstream until someone told you how to go with the flow of God's unending torrent of blessings?

OBJECTIONS TO OUTREACH EVANGELISM

But the problem is not simply complacency or smugness on the part of Christian Truth students. There are valid theological objections to Outreach Evangelism which must be given serious consideration before launching a discussion of strategies to reach the unchurched. We must also recall the promise we made ourselves early in this study to avoid setting up straw men and women which we can easily knock down. That kind of intellectual dishonesty does little to establish the truth of one's position. We must hear and answer the strongest arguments against Outreach Evangelism before daring to propose a new way of looking at the teaching ministry in our churches, or the validity of our conclusions will be subject to justifiable criticism.

Legitimate theology asks itself the hard questions and proposes answers. Straw men and women rarely bristle with tough questions. Therefore, we shall consider eight serious objections to Outreach Evangelism which Christian theology might reasonably raise. Since we agree with Paul Tillich's dictum that good theology must be "answering" theology, each objection will be accompanied by analysis, critique, and response.

DEFINING THE TERM: "OUTREACH EVANGELISM"

To understand both sides of this controversial issue, we must first achieve a working definition of the subject we are about to discuss. We desire an exclusive rather than an inclusive definition because there are some forms of Christian evangelism which clearly fall outside the behavioral repertoire of liberal Protestantism, i.e., door-knocking, soul-winning, arm-twisting, turn-or-burn varieties of spiritual intimidation which do a disservice to the Church and Her Lord, Jesus Christ.

We also do not mean the kind of missionary activity which characterized Christian outreach during the nineteenth century, when most major North American denominations felt compelled to send spiritual imperialists to Asia in order to convert the heathen. Our definition of Outreach Evangelism must necessarily exclude those sorts of activities.

For our purposes we shall say: *Outreach Evangelism is the effort of the Christian community to share the Good News they have found in Jesus Christ with those who have no religious preference and who respond with interest to offers of information, education, and personal contact.*

There are many elements to this definition. We call the subject we are studying in this chapter *Outreach Evangelism (OE)* because of the historic connection to the latter term and the modern preference for the former among liberal churches. We say *OE* is an *effort* because it requires planning, funding, and commitment; and the effort originates within the *Christian community* as an outpicturing of their desire *to share the Good News* rather than some kind of ego-need or desire for spiritual superiority.

OE is sharing *Jesus Christ*, because Christianity is essentially a relationship between the believer and the indwelling Christ as represented by the historical/theological picture we have in Jesus of Nazareth, our Wayshower and Lord.

Outreach Evangelism directs its energies toward those who have *no religious preference* because Metaphysical Christians tend to see many paths to the same Truth. Another key ingredient is a willingness to speak to those *who respond with interest*, presumably from any sector of humanity, churched or unchurched. This disallows arm-twisting or blatant proselytizing of people who are not ready to receive what we have to teach.

Finally, *OE* represents an *offer of information, education, and personal contact*. It is an offer, not a demand. Sharing the excitement of our discovery, not slam-dunking some hapless soul into the pew.

Nonbeligerent outreach includes three distinct elements: *Information*, which relates the facts of who we are and what we believe; *Education*, which aims at improving the God-consciousness of ready souls; and *Personal Contact*, meaning we must care about people, not just peddle ideas.

This definition allows great flexibility within liberal church tradition to implement a program of Outreach Evangelism that offends none but the most flagrantly anti-activist people. It also provides opportunities for lay ministry; while spreading the Good News to others, doubtless the faith of the persons involved in *OE* will deepen as well. With this definition in mind, we shall next consider objections to any kind of outreach ministry and appropriate responses to these complaints.

FIRST OBJECTION: OUTREACH EVANGELISM IS ETHNOCENTRIC

To export one's beliefs to another group denies everything we know about the cultural bias of religious faith. Isn't it an accident of geography that makes one person a Muslim, another a Hindu? If he is born in Communist China, wouldn't't he likely be a Maoist or perhaps an old-line Confucian? How can one group try to hammer everyone else into its own image?

ANALYSIS/RESPONSE: This may be the most damaging criticism of Outreach Evangelism which can be raised. Certainly, there is an unmistakably cultural element in every religion, as this study has already indicated on numerous occasions. While we have no desire to adopt a missionary-to-the-heathen attitude toward people of other persuasions, the first line of every faith system must begin, "I believe..." We are whom we are; Truth comes to us in a way that makes us members of Western, Judaeo-Christian society.

It makes little sense for us to try to teach Hinduism, Buddhism, or Shinto if we have found the God who seeks us by faith in Jesus Christ. We can honor the teachers and prophets of other faith—learn from them, even—but all religious ideas must ultimate be brought to the yardstick of Truth which we have found works for us: Jesus of Nazareth. He is our Window to glimpse the majesty of God. However, the central thesis of this objection contains a valuable lesson for us. If other cultures find Truth through other windows, should we attempt to pry them from their perch and drag them to the Jesus-window? John Macquarrie says not so.

> I do not think that the Christian missionary should aim at convert-
> ing adherents of the so-called "higher" religions in which, as I
> believe, God's saving grace is already recognizably at work.[3]

We might even push further and insist that Christians seek only to teach the unchurched in their own backyards. But if the Truth principles are as good as we believe, then there seems to be nothing wrong with offering these ideas in a Christian missionary context among the "unchurched" or dissatisfied of the world at large. There is a difference between sheep stealing and finding strays wandering in the wastelands.

Professor Macquarrie has an even better idea:

> ...the Christian communication of Christ to the non-Christian would
> take the form of helping him recognize Christ in his own tradition
> and encouraging that tradition to grow into Christ. But clearly such
> communication would be reciprocal or dialogical. For even if Jesus
> Christ is the fullness of the divine truth, at any given time Christians
> are not fully possessed of that truth. Hence the reverence for life in
> Buddhism, the transcending of racial differences in Islam, the adher-
> ence to non-violence in Hinduism, may all be ways in which the
> pressure of non-Christian religions causes the Christian to recognize
> hitherto neglected elements in his own tradition.[4]

Earlier we said that one of the functions of theology is to *Establish Dialogue within the Theological Circle.* This dialogue can also be cross-cultural exchange, circle-to-circle. Truth is One, but there are many ways to understand the sublime Oneness. Theology should be hardy enough to withstand the trade winds blowing between the continents of the great faiths of humanity.

If we keep reminding ourselves that Outreach Evangelism is an "effort to share the Good News we have found in Jesus Christ with those who have no religious pref-erence and who respond with interest," the dangers of ethnocentrism will be substan-tially mitigated.

SECOND OBJECTION: OUTREACH EVANGELISM IS HOSTILE

Organized efforts to teach people a particular religious viewpoint creates an aggressive attitude in the teachers. Soon they stop seeing people as people and begin seeing them as big game to be bagged.

ANALYSIS/RESPONSE: Unquestionably, this is a danger. Who has not been accost-ed by a zealot peddling some religious philosophy in public? Who has not experi-enced the anxiety of strained relationships when a formerly lukewarm Christian suddenly "gets saved" and seeks to remake everyone else in her image? Zeal is praiseworthy; fanaticism is neurotic.

One evening in Colorado Springs, Colorado, the author observed a middle-aged man standing on a street corner with only a light wool jacket in a driving rainstorm. He was waving a Bible, shouting his "message" to anyone who passed by. One cannot help but wonder how many people drove by, muttering to themselves, *"If that's Christianity, they can keep it!"*

I had a flash, a wicked thought. I would go up to this howling proselytizer and say, *"I'm from the Devil—keep up the good work, you're driving dozens of people away from Christ!"*

But I don't have that kind of reckless courage. So, I approached the grinning evangelist and said, "Brother, I'm a Christian minister. You need to quit this. You're making us look like fools." He turned and demanded, "Well, preacher, what do you believe?" I just shook my head and walked away. It was a mistake, motivated by my frustrations and not out of a concern for the streetcorner crusader.

Our definition of *OE* must exclude this kind of public craziness. But a subtler form of hostility can creep into the most carefully constructed Truth-talk given to interested non-members. This kind of delicate hostility slides off the tongue in the form of put-downs directed at other churches because they are not expressly committed to Metaphysical Christianity.

Open disagreements are not necessarily dangerous, and some degree of controversy is even desirable as a corrective process to keep our theologies from straying too far from the center of the faith. However, whacking people between the eyeballs because they happen to be Presbyterians, Catholics, or Baptists is not only contrary to the spirit of Jesus but also betrays a sub rosa attitude of hostility toward people who seek Truth along a slightly different path.

Outreach Evangelism should not be attempted by people who feel hostility toward other faiths, even those faiths which teach ideas diametrically opposed to Metaphysical Christianity. One can express opposition to ideas (i.e., eternal hell) without targeting a group by name and labeling it as spiritually equal to the Neanderthal.

The author has little sympathy for fundamentalism, as anyone who has read this far already must have noticed. However, not one time did the actual name of a fundamentalist group appear in critical analysis. The issue is theological, not personal.

The only proper spirit in which to engage in teaching Truth principles is a sense of humility and gratitude. We know we have a long way to go. We are grateful that we have come this far and grateful for the teachers who pointed the way for us by their words but most of all by their lives. A popular definition of Outreach Evangelism is the image of one beggar showing another beggar where to find bread. We would like to see this scenario updated per the insights of Christian Truth studies:

Outreach Evangelism is one backyard gold miner showing her neighbor where his backyard gold mine is buried.

THIRD OBJECTION: OUTREACH EVANGELISM IS EGO-CENTRIC

There are two parts to this objection: a) I don't "save" people, God does. b) All forms of outreach are really thinly coated ego-trips where the teachers get their own sense of spiritual worth reinforced by talking down to poor, ignorant folks who don't know the Truth. There is just too much possibility for egocentric abuse in any form of *OE*.

ANALYSIS/RESPONSE: The second complaint mentioned above is not a worthy objection. *OE* can be an excuse for spiritual one-upsmanship, but people can turn almost any good into an evil by improper consciousness. Water which sustains life can drown or quench thirst depending on its use. Opportunity for abuse is no criterion for abandoning *OE*, because human beings seem to have a penchant for abusing almost everything.

The other objection (God alone saves, not me) is much more difficult to answer. If we accepted a more traditionalist definition of "evangelism" and "salvation," then we could agree that efforts to bring people safely into heaven past the fiery path to hell are fruitless unless God elects a person for salvation. But since we are talking about the path to Christ-consciousness, a freely chosen route we shall all find eventually, some kind of assistance as we stumble across the road in the darkness might be helpful.

One might argue that our own search mandates some sort of assistance to stumbling neighbors. If we have found goodness and peace, how can we justify keeping our discovery of the God who seeks us a secret? When OE begins with joyful thanksgiving, tempered by humility and willingness to allow people their right to find God along another path, the possibilities for loving service to the unchurched outweigh any dangers of ego-centrism.

FOURTH OBJECTION: OUTREACH EVANGELISM IS UNNECESSARY

All right, let's push response #3 to its natural conclusion: If Christ-consciousness is *"a freely chosen route we shall all find eventually,"* then why do *OE*? If we are truly universalists, believing in no eternal punishment, then outreach is unnecessary.

ANALYSIS/RESPONSE: This argument originates from the liberal side of the theological spectrum and at first glance it seems valid. Certainly today's religious liberals (and a lot of other Christians as well) believe that everyone will be "saved," however they define the term. Universalism is the generally held position of legitimate modern theology, despite thunderings from the theological right-wing and threats from radio and television evangelists. So, why teach the faith to the unchurched if eventually they will get it right without our help? Why not let nature take its course?

The key words in this objection are *"eventually"* and *"nature."* If we truly believe the Father will wait patiently for all prodigals to wander back home, the question shifts from if to when. As many difficulties as the author has with the pop-religious book *A Course in Miracles* (see Chapter 19), I agree with the opening lines of that work and see that the journey to Christ-consciousness is "a required course;" only the time we take to complete the program is optional.[5]

Indeed, there is nothing particularly original in this observation. The author of John's Gospel presented essentially the same idea when his Jesus said:

> "I am the way, and the truth, and the life; no one comes to the Father but by me. If you had known me, you would have known my Father also; henceforth you know him and have seen him."[6]

The constellation of verbs, pronouns, and prepositions in the Greek text suggests a variety of ways to translate/interpret this passage. In their exhaustive study of biblical language, *A Greek-English Lexicon of the New Testament*, scholars Bauer, Arndt, and Gingrich show that the words translated "except by me" could also be rendered "except represented by me." This makes greater sense considering the context. In the very next sentence Jesus claims representative status, for if they had recognized God in Jesus they would have seen what God is like.

What this means for Metaphysical Christianity is that instead of this passage working as an exclusivist proclamation whereby all people must come to the Father by Jesus, the text could just as easily mean we must come to the saving knowledge of the divinity represented by Jesus. As such, Jesus Christ becomes truly our Wayshower, the Way, Truth, and Life we must all discover before coming "to the Father."[7] However, if Jesus is the Wayshower—an example of what we all must attain—won't we find our Way without anyone telling us, like He did?

The parables of Jesus overflow with stories about lost ones finding their way back home, but not all the analogies disclose complete initiative on the part of the wanderer. True, the prodigal son did come to his senses in the pigpen of that "far country," returning to the Father on his own, but in the two parables immediately preceding, Jesus talks about seekers who look for and find lost items: shepherd and the lost sheep, woman and her lost coin (Luke 15:1-32).

Some people are further along in their spiritual development in this life, or have been given special grace to hunger and thirst after spirituality, or just seem to have been born into life circumstances which promote spiritual seeking. They are like the prodigal son: given enough time and they will come to their senses.

Others are like the lost sheep, wandering around confused, with little chance of finding their way in this lifetime. It is no act of condescension to offer help to people who can't seem to find their way. From the "show of hands" we took at the opening of this chapter, quite a few of us have fit that category at some time in our lives, the author included.

What about those sheep who are still wandering in the wilderness, seeking something, but haven't the foggiest notion of what they seek? When the shepherd (no puns, please) appears, they realize where home is and eagerly start out in that direction. You and I could be that shepherd, just as some other "shepherd" pointed the way home for most Metaphysical Christians.

Still others are like the lost coin; they are not even aware they are "lost" without God's presence in their lives. Perhaps they may lead happy, glittering lives. Perhaps they may be growing psychologically and interpersonally. But until they recognize the spiritual dimension to life, this growth is good but superficial, a staging area which can prepare someone for the journey but not the journey itself.

It is these latter two categories which *OE* aims to reach. The prodigals will be knocking on the door, and for them the old dictum about ready students and appearing teachers is highly appropriate. But the "natural" course of spiritual evolution takes some people farther afield, so far that they may need selfless shepherding from someone who has wandered into the briars and thickets.

Nothing speaks as honestly as personal experience, and this is what *OE* calls upon the individual Christian to share with her unchurched kindred. If we are willing to bless, release, and let go of those who are not ready to respond, we will be walking in the path of the Wayshower, Jesus Christ.

FIFTH OBJECTION: OUTREACH EVANGELISM IS SELF-DENYING

If the goal of life is personal salvation through Christ-consciousness, spending my time teaching others diverts important energies which could better be employed in my own search for Truth.

ANALYSIS/RESPONSE: More people feel this way than one might imagine. In fact, our emphasis on personal growth to the virtual exclusion of social action, Christian ethics, and awareness of our heritage as a pilgrim people makes this objection seem like a virtue to some Truth students. If we come to a mystical/metaphysical church seeking personal growth alone, we may find all the signposts telling us that we are right on course. Our periodicals—from *Science of Mind* and *Unity* magazines to the *Christian Science Sentinel* and the *Daily Word*—emphasize individual growth. Our books call people to private prayer, meditation, and the Silence. Worship services provide time for people to "go within" and seek God, and sermons time and again remind us that our goal is to recognize *"Christ in you, the hope of glory,"* Charles Fillmore's lifelong watchword.

To all these comments we add our wholehearted agreement. Personal spiritual growth is certainly the goal of life. Yet, just as a child cannot thrive alone but needs some kind of family arrangement, so do we grow as part of a community of faith.

You cannot be a Christian in isolation. You can certainly follow the teachings of Jesus Christ, learn great ideas and form wondrous theories about spirituality. But Christianity is no laboratory project: it is a living faith which changes, grows, and reflects the community in which it resides. All the technical manuals in the world cannot teach you how to hammer a nail. Unless you pick up a hammer, take aim at a nail, and drive the point through wood by striking with just the right amount of force, all your nailing-knowledge is just theory.

We cannot learn spirituality by reading, prayer, and even meditation alone. We must be tested in the crucible of the Christian community. For this reason, we share our faith with each other, and in sharing we learn of a surprise bonus: the joy that *koinonia* brings.

Christian growth begins with and continually must return to prayer, meditation, and worship—this is the ground of our consciousness. But we pray, meditate, and worship so that we can lead a God-conscious life, putting feet on our faith to stride through the triumphs and tragedies of human existence.

With so great a treasure as the teachings of Jesus Christ, one simply cannot rush off to a corner and hoard the faith. Part of authentic growth in Christ-consciousness is a warm, non-aggressive yearning to share the goodies with others. If we "keep the faith" to ourselves, we are truly selfish and do no justice to the model of Jesus, who taught everyone whom He found receptive.

It is significant that the following excerpt from Paul's Letter to the Colossians comes in a context of the apostle's burning desire to share the Good News with everyone:

> ...I became a minister according to the divine office which was given to me for you, to make the word of God fully known, the mystery hidden for ages and generations but now made manifest to his saints. To them God chose to make known how great among the Gentiles are the riches of the glory of this mystery, which is Christ in you, the hope of glory. Him we proclaim, warning every man and teaching every man in all wisdom, that we may present every man mature in Christ. For this I toil, striving with all the energy which he mightily inspires within me.[8]

There is an obligation implicit in receiving such a great gift. We cannot keep it to ourselves any more than we can force it upon the unprepared or the disinterested. Christianity is inherently an outreach-oriented faith.

SIXTH OBJECTION: *OE* SMACKS OF FUNDAMENTALISM

Outreach Evangelism encourages simplistic thinking and could even lead to the narrow-mindedness we left behind when we discovered Christian Truth studies. The last thing we want is an image of tent-meetings, sawdust floors, and evangelistic crusades!

ANALYSIS/RESPONSE: Amen! Couldn't agree more—but that is not what we're talking about. If *OE* means that to you, go back and re-read this chapter, because we are not communicating. We mean an organized effort to spread the Good News, undertaken consciously by a local church or a group of churches, which conforms to the definition of *OE* given on page 301, and is therefore respectful of the privacy, independence, and feelings of potential contacts. We are not out to convert the heathen; we aim to tell them they are not heathen, but children of God, princes and princesses of the Kingdom. That kind of news is a far cry from the miserable-worm/lost sinner pronouncements of fundamentalism. If any kind of outreach offends someone because some acts of blatant spiritual aggression are practiced in the name of Christ by a few of our brothers and sisters on the religious Right-wing, that is no more a logical reason to refrain from healthy outreach than it would be for us to refrain from Bible study or prayer just because others did it differently.

SEVENTH OBJECTION: OUTREACH EVANGELISM IS DIVISIVE

Rather than accepting all people as children of God, *OE* creates a dichotomy between the "saved" and the "unsaved," or, at best, between the "enlightened" and the "unenlightened." This translates into us-vs.-them thinking and divides people along religious lines.

ANALYSIS/RESPONSE: There is a certain degree of elitism in every religious group. If we believe *this* way is best, then necessarily *that* way is not so good for us. The key to controlling the tendency to us/them thinking is to recall the Divine-human paradox can be found in every sentient being. Each person is a kenotic incarnation of the Divine, as such he/she is our brother/sister.

Besides the divine identity lurking beneath the surface of every person, we have a point of departure which slants our thinking away from superiority: We have no way to know if the person is at a "higher" spiritual level than our own.

TWO LIVES CONTRASTED

Simply observing the facts of a person's life cannot give us a way to judge another's spirituality. That drunk lying in the gutter—Mr. John A. Failure—gives all the impression of spiritual bankruptcy, sin-misery-death. Ah, but what were his life-experiences? He has been struggling mightily against other problems—a battering father, a neglecting mother, a childhood spent rummaging in garbage cans for food and lonely shivering in the cold at night, homeless. Given his life-experiences, he could have become a drug pusher, murderer, or child molester—far worse than a simple drunk in the gutter. Although his life is not desirable, he is making progress.

Now let's take the case of the Reverend Doctor Aardvark O. Holiness. He graduated first in his class, went to post-grad study, and received his doctorate. He is the pillar of his community, respected, and loved by all. But Dr. Holiness's life-circumstances were so favorable—the wealthy son of a loving, spiritual family—that he has not achieved all he should have. If he applied himself, he might have become a great

Truth teacher or a bringer of peace to this troubled world, but instead he rambles on every Sunday, dishing out platitudes and currying the favor of the rich and powerful in his congregation. He never takes a risk, never does anything that might offend his wealthy contributors. He plays it safe.

Which of these two has accomplished the most, given their life-conditions? Certainly, in the eyes of the world, it is the Reverend Dr. Holiness. But we know better. Measured by the amount of growth they have achieved, John A. Failure is the real success.

No wonder Jesus insisted we should never judge anyone by appearances! God alone is the Judge, because He established the system of spiritual growth by which all sentient beings must struggle for Christ-consciousness. If we keep in mind that appearances are all relative, everyone is the image and likeness of God, and everyone will return to the Father eventually, *OE* becomes a way of sharing love rather than pitting the "saved" against the "lost."

EIGHTH OBJECTION: OUTREACH EVANGELISM IS ANTI-ECUMENICAL

It prevents cooperation between contravailing religious groups because they know each is trying to "convert" the people away from other faiths. How can we trust people who are trying to convince us their way is correct and ours wrong? At best, we can only engage in dialogue with people from religious groups which are seeking to teach their faith. There is no possibility of real unity in such circumstances.

ANALYSIS/RESPONSE: Dialogue is always healthy if it proceeds from mutual respect. There is an interesting paradox which crops up during inter-faith dialogue that might be illustrative of the real problems raise by this objection: If a person is to represent his/her faith in an inter-faith dialogue, he must believe his faith is the best. If he believes it is the best, he is less inclined toward dialogue than toward teaching the others Truth as he sees it. However, if a different representative were chosen who did not believe her faith was the best, she would not be an authentic representative of that religious community and could not participate meaningfully in dialogue.

The above scenario implies that unity among dissimilar religious groups is impossible. We are willing to concede that point, even seeing it as a strength instead of a weakness. Surely the amazing diversity of human religious institutions cannot be an accident. There are many ways to find Truth, many paths up that mountain to union with God. It is union with God we seek, not necessarily union with each other every step along the way.

In fact, if we approach the journey from different angles, unity of thought would be a disadvantage. How many people could not affirm the complicated, heavily ritualized Christianity of medieval Europe, yet had no alternative?

There certainly is a divisive element in religion, just as there is a divisive factor in every choice. When we choose one mate over the rest of the population, we have excluded all but one person from sharing the deepest intimacy of our lives.

Religion separates people into camps, and that's not necessarily bad. Only when those camps become the training ground for armies of conquest does the separation becomes pathological. Let the camps remain peaceful—church retreats instead of military garrisons—and, without fear of attack, we can invite people from other thought-compounds to visit and tell how they celebrate their spiritual lives. Of course these folks will prefer their own way to ours—we wouldn't want them to be otherwise—and the privileges we accord people from other groups we must surely allow for ourselves.

There are plenty of people wandering in the wilderness who seek, want, and need a base camp of their own. If we believe in what we are doing, we will seek to attract those wandering folks to our bivouac. We can avoid divisiveness by realizing not everyone will see reality our way and by elaborating those differences through dialogue, study, and cooperation with people of other faiths. Universalism comes to our rescue, for we can bless, release, and even learn from people who find God's brightness shining through another stained-glass window different from our own.

DISCUSSION-COMMITMENT-REVIEW-RENEWAL

These objections and their responses suffer from the obvious limitation that they originate in the mind of a person who believes in Outreach Evangelism. Hence, there may be better, stronger reasons why *OE* should not be attempted. Each group considering a program of outreach doubtless will want to hear the objections current in their circle of faith before initiating such a community project.

Indeed, the beginning stages of an effective *OE* program must include discussions among church members, the ministry team, and lay leadership about their goals in outreach. Here are some questions which must be asked:

1. Do some people have high aims to build a series of Metaphysical Christian cathedrals in the local area for reasons more personal than altruistic?

2. Are significant, powerful voices in the community of faith against any form of planned outreach?

3. Can this be a conduit for laity to express their teaching ministry, or does the church leadership plan to do it all?

4. Shall there be small-scale goals for the first few years, such as increasing the membership by five to ten percent over normal growth rates, or do the planners envision rapid, long-range expansion?

5. Do numbers count, or is the goal to plant new study groups which will grow into churches someday?

6. How far into the future does the congregation want to stretch its vision?

7. How much money are we willing to spend and how will we raise it?

8. What kind of assistance can be realistically expected, if any, from other churches or from national organizations to which this church belongs?

9. What mechanisms for feedback and course-correction are planned?

Many more questions must be answered and long hours of sometimes frustrating discussions await the church which opts for an organized program of Outreach Evangelism. But the end result will be a program in which the participants feel ownership and commitment because they have hammered it out themselves.

OUTREACH SUICIDE

The best way to kill *OE* is for the ministry team to plan in seclusion and announce the goals to the congregation at an open meeting. Even if people like the idea, they will feel little ownership in any pre-fabricated program. Without lay leadership and excitement among the people in the pews, *OE* cannot happen. A top-down program will start with a bang and end with a whisper.

Long-term planning requires Discussion, Commitment, Review, and Renewal. Attainable goals must be established and celebrations held when they are achieved. People will keep up their enthusiasm if they feel something is happening, and it's the leadership's job to remind people what the goals are and to convey a continuous sense of excited progress to the troops doing *OE*, the membership at large.

HOW TO GET STARTED: FIVE STRATEGIES

We have discussed eight tough problems which must be faced before anyone decides to embark on *OE*. Having wrestled with the angel and received his blessing, we shall now press on to consider some ways a local Christian Truth church could implement a strategy of outreach to unchurched members of the community it serves.

We shall look at five models for programs at a local church/center. The strategies below begin with the least threatening and move on to more activist programs which might be developed later if the initial phases of outreach go well.

STRATEGY #1 - POTLUCK DINNERS WITH ENTERTAINMENT

Can anything so simple be an outreach strategy? Absolutely! Lyle Schaller suggests a church could offer "Friendship Building Events" to which interested nonmembers could be invited. People would come to a potluck dinner much more readily than a worship service. Schaller writes:

> The seven common characteristics of these events are: 1) food, 2) music, 3) humor and laughter, 4) informal fellowship, 5) a structure or schedule that provides a sense of movement or progression to the event, 6) a dependable and regularly scheduled meeting date and time, and 7) perhaps most critical of all, a leader or leadership team that accepts the responsibility for planning and overseeing this type of event.[9]

When a responsive person comes to this kind of event, she meets old-timers informally, can ask questions and express her own opinions in a low-threat environment, and generally case the church to see if she wants more. Some churches are aware of this open door to new members and hold regular food-fun-fellowship events with great success.

However, a significant plurality of Metaphysical churches seem to feel that only classwork and prayer meetings qualify as legitimate extra-circular activities. We ask those persons to remember the lively, informative discussions of their recent religious past. Those who have had the privilege of study at a theological seminary or school of religion know that the mealtime is more than a place to eat. Some of the best theological discussions the author has participated in happened over vegetarian lasagna and ice tea at the crowded lunch tables of Unity Inn.

Something there is about food and drink that unites people, making conversation and therefore dialogue possible. When the author was a seminary student his class was asked to list the provisions which they considered absolutely essential to start a new church. The instructor counted the "ballots" and awarded the items listed priority based on the number of "votes" each received. First on the list—ahead of pulpit, pews, altar, songbooks or even Bibles—was a coffee pot!

Entertainment-based programming with food and informal fellowship, is the easiest way to provide an opportunity for members to invite friends, neighbors, or relatives to a gathering of the church. The next strategy builds on this simple idea.

STRATEGY #2 - FELLOWSHIP NIGHT FOR [TARGET GROUP]

Instead of a general potluck dinner/fellowship, this concept moves to a specific target group to which church wants to extend its ministry. This event does not exclude a monthly general-membership potluck/fellowship; indeed, some sort of regular gathering of diverse elements of the church in one place for food and informal chit-chat is absolutely essential if the kind of group cohesion desired for *OE* is to be maintained. A valuable supplement to the regular monthly gathering is a smaller-scale event which aims to reach specific kinds of people and bring them together with other like individuals.

Some obvious examples of groups which could be targeted are men, women, young couples, singles, widows (there tend to be more widows than widowers, but they could be grouped together), senior high students, mothers of young children (child care is a *must*), divorced persons, middle-aged couples, senior citizens, stepparents, people interested in art, music, drama, cinema, crafts, or any number of other activities. The idea is to identify a homogenous group and give them a place to gather, reflect on their common interests, have food and light programming that is related to their special needs, and invite them to come to the general potluck/fellowship later in the month.

This link is critical, because church members must have confidence enough in the value of its ministries that they will eagerly ask people to come back for a specific event at a specific time. People must be asked one-on-one, not just from the podium as part of the closing ceremonies. Pulpit announcements are reminders, not invitations. Program information is about as good as lawn fertilizer in the bag—you have to spread it by hand to get any results. Each follow-up program must be attended by committed members who understand the dual purpose of the gathering.

SECRET AGENTS?

Something must be said at this juncture about trying to be sneaky when doing *OE*. It doesn't work. People know they are attending a program at a church and that church members will want them to come back for more. If members pretend that there are no other goals than a presentation of slides or harpsichord music or a quilting demonstration, they result will probably be cagey suspicion on the part of nonmembers attending. The best tactic is to state upfront that this program is designed for such-and-such a group so they can experience the kind of people and opportunities available at First Church of Smithville.

People often report feeling welcome and wanted when members ask them to come back for other gatherings or Sunday services. However, another caution to be observed here is the polite constraint of a good host not to force the guests into religious discussions, especially if all they're interested in is needlepoint or bass fishing. If the people enjoy the program and come away with a favorable impression of your church, the goal has been achieved. Planting seeds may require patience.

So far we have considered ideas to bring people to the church building. Now we move to take the church to the people. As before, the following strategies build on programming at the local center, without which new people could not be assimilated as permanent members.

STRATEGY #3 - "FIRESIDE" PROGRAMS

This strategy creatively adapts the fellowship-gathering at the church to a home environment. It is not a new idea; several rather divergent religious groups have tried home gatherings with great success, notably the Baha'is and the Church of Jesus Christ of Latter-Day-Saints (Mormons).

Recently some Metaphysical Christian churches have adopted a similar approach and found it an exciting venture in lay ministry. Sometimes the method is called a home study group, house church, or just a "party." The following is a verbatim excerpt from an open letter to the congregation titled "Your Committee is Working!!—Unity Home Parties" in the October 1986 issue of *Unity Light Line* published by the Unity Church of Colorado Springs, Colorado:

> Do you have family members, and/or friends, and/or business associates whom you want to come to Unity Church in the Rockies, and whom you've invited, but they've never come, even though they are interested? Maybe they would come to a Home Unity Party, which can be a less "scary" intermediate step, leading to them wanting to and coming to church. Basically, the idea is you invite these people to your home to find out about our church, and a representative from the church, most usually one of the Lay

Ministers, will give a presentation and answer any questions. As you can see, the purpose of a Home Unity Party is to answer any questions that your guests have so that they can make a free and unencumbered choice about attending our church. The format would be approximately 2-3 hours long, most preferably an evening or weekend session. You as the host would probably provide some type of refreshments at the beginning of the session to allow people to get comfortable. That opening would be followed by a free-flowing interchange between the representative and the guests. Of course, you as the host would be encouraged to contribute to the presentation in whatever way you deemed appropriate. Also, if you wanted to include in the evening other church members/friends (and their guests, if applicable), that would also be fine.[10]

Details vary, but all the elements of a Fireside Program are present.

1) Private homes are used.
2) Individual members are encouraged to sponsor the event.
3) Friends, relatives, and business acquaintances are invited to an
4) Informal Presentation is given by a
5) Representative of the church.

Most importantly, the meetings will take place in a

6) Less "Scary" (Non-threatening) environment and serve as
7) an Intermediate Step to church membership.
8) Other Church Members may come if invited by the host.

The author's experience as a frequent guest speaker and host of Firesides is that an optimum ratio is about three non-members to every two members, host and speaker included. Firesides are such fun for members that they can quickly deteriorate into study groups of old-timers and lose their objective, which is to introduce Christian Truth ideas to interested seekers.

Of course, there is nothing wrong with home-based study groups, and if a Fireside metamorphizes into an ongoing program of regular spiritual deepening, then *hooray!* A different need has been discovered and met. However, our discussion centers around *OE* and ways to maintain the energy/initiative in a long-term campaign to spread the Good News to unchurched, interested persons.

Those who have tried the Fireside as an outreach tool regularly report that flooding these gatherings with eager, zealous church members only isolates the non-member and tends to shut off rather than stimulate honest questioning. If folks like Firesides so much—which they usually do—they should sponsor one in their own home or co-sponsor with another family.

Another important point, not mentioned in the excerpt, is a plan for transition from home to church. Firesides can become ends-in-themselves, which they are not meant to be. One way to control for this tendency is to limit the series of Firesides— six is a good number—then end the sessions, inviting the participants to a specific program at the local church which the leaders of the Fireside will be offering the following week.

Another possibility is to schedule the Firesides so that weeks three or four will coincide with a fellowship night or potluck program at the church, giving the participants a chance to meet informally with other church members and then return to the relative safety of the Fireside group for a week or two more. But the party must be over sooner or later if the goal is Outreach Evangelism, which brings new people into the life of the local congregation.

The next two steps move beyond Firesides into a more comprehensive program of outreach. These should not be attempted without a minimum of one year's planning, discussion, and goal-setting coupled with strong in-house education/training programs to enable the laity and religious professionals to make such large-scale projects happen. If that doesn't scare you off, read on.

STRATEGY #4 - HOUSE CHURCHES: LAUNCHING SATELLITE GROUPS

When the larger church membership accepts the concept, this project begins with the ministerial leadership and committed laypeople sitting down and looking at the map of their area to see where New Thought study groups could be started. After identifying a number of locations, people are sought who will volunteer to establish a Fireside program in those locations. Needless to say, the Fireside leaders must themselves be residents of the target area, or must have contacts who are interested enough in Metaphysical Christian studies to invite the outreach team to hold meetings in their home for an relatively extended duration, six months or more.

The goal here is to establish a house church/study group in an area where there is little or no representation in the larger congregation. New areas will provide opportunity for growth by increasing the population base. Lay leadership is important, but an energetic minister could feasibly sponsor one to three outreach groups within commuting distance of his/her primary ministry. If the ministry team is a co-pastorate, like many husband-and-wife ministry teams, or includes licensed teachers or lay ministers, the number of expansion-points can be multiplied accordingly.

Two directions can be followed after these House Churches are established. The members can continue studying/meeting during the week and attending the central church on Sundays, or they can elect to move on to the last strategy to be discussed.

This is the most comprehensive and challenging program for *OE* we shall consider. It is not for everyone and could be a true disaster if not planned carefully by all levels of church members. It could also, if properly executed, multiply the number of Metaphysical Truth churches three- or four-fold in the next decades. At least that is the idea.

STRATEGY # 5 - CHURCH PLANTING: OUTREACH EIGHT (OR SIX, ETC.)

In this approach the local church radically changes its self-image from seeking new people (an internal-growth model), to sponsoring new churches (external growth). Neighboring areas are studied by the whole congregation and an agreed number of locations tagged as places with enough people and potential to support an independent, self-subsisting New Thought Christian Church.

Look at the phone book of even a smallish town—say, 20,000 people—and see how many churches can co-exist without drying up the reservoir of unchurched people. In fact, in the United States there are 23 to 30 million adults who identify themselves as Protestants but are not members of any local church. Since liberal churches include disaffected ex-Catholics and ex-Jews as well as self-identified Protestants, the number of unchurched people who might respond to Outreach Evangelism is probably much higher.

Nor should existing church groups discourage *OE*. Studies show that churches tend to grow faster in communities with lots of churches and, surprisingly, it doesn't matter if a new church is of the same religious family as already existing, established churches in the community.[11]

Once a congregation decides to plant new churches it has changed from an inward-looking to an outward-looking community. If the people catch the vision of what a Teaching Church can accomplish and how their energies/talents can be released in service-oriented ministry, establishing six or eight fledgling churches within an hour's drive of the Teaching Church is not beyond the realm of possibility.

Such a grand dream requires comprehensive analysis, continual review and renewal, detailed planning, and a willingness to hang tough for the long run. No less than ten years will be required to complete so broad a program, and if three of eight attempts at establishing new churches is successful the project has beaten the odds. But Truth students know that One Presence/One Power stands behind everything, chuckling when disapproving nay-sayers groan about the impossibility of such projects.

No attempt will be made in this limited treatise on church growth to suggest detailed strategies to implement this kind of program. Outreach Committees bold enough to consider *OE* on such a scale do not need anyone drawing blueprints for them. The objective of this chapter was to kick *OE* into gear and hand the controls over to men and women of energy, insight, and vision who will make those dreams come true. Nothing suggested here is beyond reach for a community of faith and vision led by laity and religious professionals who let themselves aspire to great achievements in the Name of Jesus Christ.

FROM ZEAL TO STRENGTH BY PRAYER

Zeal is the Divine-human power required for *OE*, but Zeal must be tempered with compassion and patience. More than this, all our programs—teaching, healing, and otherwise ministering to a frightened and estranged world—must begin with prayer, continue in prayer, and end with prayer. Only prayer will give us the strength to make these Zeal-dreams bouncing around in our consciousness become a ministering reality.

Therefore, we shall next consider what *prayer* means from the Metaphysical Christian perspective.

CHECK YOUR KNOWLEDGE

1. What is the definition of *Outreach Evangelism* given in the text?

2. What is a *Fireside* and how does the author suggest it can be employed as a tool of Outreach Evangelism?

3. List the eight objections to *OE*. Give a brief summary response to each.

4. True or false: The author says Christianity is essentially an individualistic faith. Explain your answer.

5. How does *OE* described in this chapter differ from proselytizing done by fundamentalists in method, goals, and attitude?

6. List and describe the five strategies for *OE* in Metaphysical Christian churches beginning with the least threatening/least pro-active method and progressing to the most self-consciously "evangelistic" form of outreach.

QUESTIONS FOR DISCUSSION

1. *Outreach* Evangelism: Should we or shouldn't we? Why?

2. Which of the eight objections to *OE* makes the best case *against* a program of outreach? Which of the author's arguments makes the best case *for* it? List your own arguments pro/con.

3. How well do you think an *OE* program would be received at your church? Which level of the five strategies would represent the maximum commitment you believe your church is willing to invest? How could you nudge them to greater risk-taking in *OE*?

4. Discuss the *Fireside* as a basic technique for outreach. What are its strengths and weaknesses? Would you enjoy sponsoring this program in your home or assisting a friend to do so?

5. What kind of comprehensive church-planting program should Christian Truth churches launch in the future? Should national organizations get involved in the planning, or should it be strictly a local program?

6. Theological Reflection: From which of the Four Formative Factors (*Scripture/ Tradition/Experience/Reason*) do you find yourself responding to *OE*? What does that say about your approach to theological issues?

NOTES

1. Lyle E. Shaller, *Assimilating New Members* (Nashville, TN: Abingdon, 1985), pp. 51-52.

2. Donald McGavran & George G. Hunter III, *Church Growth: Strategies That Work* (Nashville, TN: Abingdon, 1984), p. 34.

3. Macquarrie, *Principles*, pp. 445-446.

4. IBID., pp. 443-444.

5. Foundation for Inner Peace, *A Course in Miracles Vol. I, Text* (Huntington Station, NY: Col;Coleman Graphics, 1975), Introduction. The Course comes in three volumes, the basic Text plus workbook and a teacher's guide. For further discussion, see Chapter 19, "Pop-Fad Spirituality."

6. John 14:6-7.

7. Walter Bauer, *A Greek-English Lexicon of the New Testament*, trans. and adapted by William F. Arndt and F. Wilbur Gingrich (Chicago: University of Chicago Press, 1957), p. 179a. This massive volume is still the mother book of NT Greek/English studies. It is expensive and complex, but can be mastered with a few hours of directed study. A must for all serious biblical students.

8. Colossians 1:25-29 (RSV).

9. Lyle E Schaller, *Looking in the Mirror* (Nashville, TN: Abingdon, 1985), p. 148.

10. Larry McGill, "Your Outreach Committee is Working!" in *Unity Light Line* newsletter. Unity of the Rockies, Colorado Springs, Colorado (October, 1986).

11. Lyle Schaller, *Growing Plans* (Nashville, TN: Abingdon, 1985), pp. 154-155.

CHRISTIAN PRAYER

Chapter Seventeen

A Theological Look at Centering in the Christ

Prayer is essential, not to the salvation of the soul, for the Soul is never lost; but to the conscious well-being of the soul that does not understand itself. There is a vitality in our communion with the Infinite, which is productive of the highest good. As fire warms the body, as food strengthens us, as sunshine raises our spirits, so there is a subtle transfusion of some invisible force in such communion, weaving itself into the very warp and woof of our own mentalities. This conscious commingling of our thought with Spirit is essential to the well-being of every part of us.[1]

—Ernest Holmes

There is really only one reason for Christian Prayer, and that is communion with God. Everything else said about prayer—from the educated agnostic who considers it mental house-cleaning to the frightened old woman in a nursing home who has been told God will burn her in hell for all eternity if she does not frequently remind Him how much she loves Him—is pure fancy. As James Dillet Freeman wrote in *Prayer the Master Key*:

The whole purpose of prayer—whether I pray for myself or someone else—is to unify myself with God, the Creative Spirit.[2]

Prayer is the gateway to God, nothing more. But what more do we need? If we truly glimpsed what prayer could be, we would find mountain-moving strength.

SIX MISCONCEPTIONS ABOUT PRAYER

Too many philosophers and poets place prayer somewhere between wishing and magic. It is neither. Too many modern people consider prayer a duty or a fantasy. It is not. Too many ministers believe in a God who miraculously intervenes in the world to overthrow His own rules, which makes prayer unnatural, or disbelieve in any kind of divine involvement with the real world, which makes prayer unnecessary. These misconceptions represent the attitude of the vast majority of people toward prayer.

Therefore we must discuss the six common misunderstandings before offering a new definition and model of prayer. The six are listed in couplets forming three pairs of opposites.

If sin is the willful attempt to negate divine ideas (Chapter 9), then each error-belief represents a "sinful" attitude about prayer. Instead of releasing the power of God in our lives, sin blocks the flow of divine goodness and leaves us lonely, broken, and helpless before an apparently uncaring Universe. Prayer can change all that if properly understood. But first we must examine the easy path away from effective communion with God typified by these popular but mistaken notions about prayer.

1. WISHING - MAGIC: Christian Prayer is neither *wishing* nor *magic*, and the difference between these two radically opposite error-beliefs is significant for modern religious thinking.

Wishing portrays the person as utterly powerless, a pawn of the Cosmos who can only hope that things will work out favorably. This kind of prayer is not unlike the chant of young lovers under the evening sky:

Starlight, starbright
First star I see tonight
I wish I may, I wish I might,
Have the wish I wish tonight.

To wish is to dream, and there is nothing wrong with dreaming, but dreams are not prayer. Wishing freely admits the unlikelihood of the desired outcome; no one *wishes* when he is properly prepared to deal with a situation from his own resources. Students who have studied hard for a test seldom wish for a good grade, although they might pray for clarity of thought and memory. Wishing for good grades is the desperate act of a lazy student. When we wish for ideals that seem far-fetched—world peace, happiness for all people, or the author's boyhood favorite: the Philadelphia Phillies winning the World Series—we are expressing our heartfelt desire for good to be established in our lives.

However, wishing in the place of prayer is a wasted opportunity. Wishing denies the reality of prayer, opting instead for some kind of miraculous intervention: *"If I want something strongly enough, something will happen."* Metaphysical Christians generally believe in the natural flow of good throughout the Cosmos, whenever we open ourselves to receive that good, but wishing has no real power to affect the world; "first star" hopes are understandable, but prayer to the evening star is ineffectual.

Wishing also brings false hopes. Who hasn't seen long lines at convenience stores where lottery tickets are sold? State governments which sponsor lotteries feed the wish-frenzy by slick advertisements showing average citizens with mansions, yachts, and endless tropical vacations. Yet, the odds against winning are astronomical. If the big prize is $10 million, that means the State-supported Lottery must sell $20 million in tickets to raise money, which is the whole purpose for having a lottery in the first place. Assuming one ticket wins, the odds would be one in twenty million. It's easier to attract a thunderbolt on a cloudless day.

Wishing expects to "win the lottery" instead of going back to school and getting better skills. It is innocent fantasy, wasteful of resources that could be spent in self-improvement or the betterment of others. The error-belief in wishing is that it tries to receive miraculous benefits without increasing awareness of Divine Order.

Magic, however, is not so innocuous. Those who practice magic believe there are powers in the Cosmos which can be summoned to do the bidding of the practitioner. They attempt to bend the supernatural powers of the Cosmos to their will. Looking at prayer as magic, one would believe that spoken words have inherent, value-neutral power and can be invoked for good or ill at the whim of the magician. Curses and blessings are indistinguishable in occultism, because magic is a plastic power that bends to the will of the practitioner.

This, of course, is diametrically opposed to Christian Prayer. Our task is to align ourselves with God's Will and let good things break through our walls of resistance to greater supply, vibrant health, and wholeness of life. Instead of seeking to find God's Will and grow in harmony with Him, practitioners of magic believe they can assert their will over the hidden, supernatural powers of the Cosmos.

Magic represents the ultimate ego-trip. People caught up in its web of nonsense try to make themselves greater than God by forcing Divine Power to obey them. This is a misuse of the Divine-human power of Will and represents the very definition of Sin under which we have been operating. The error-belief in the case of magic is that prayer is an attempt to manipulate God.

2. DUTY - FANTASY: These are two error-beliefs, held on the one hand by fearful people who cling to authoritarian, judgmental religion and on the other hand by cynics who consider any belief a weakness or, at best, a cheap tranquilizer for the anxieties of modern life. Young Martin Luther fits the first category, Karl Marx the second. Luther grew up in a world of dark forests populated by evil spirits. God was a terrible Judge whose holiness was so transcendent that no person dared approach Him. When his desperate search for some way to please this frowning, disapproving deity led him to embrace the monk's cowl, even the excesses of asceticism were not enough to quench Luther's thirst for God's approval. For Martin Luther prayer was an unpleasant *duty*. He almost killed himself "with vigils, prayers, reading and other works."[3]

Luther's terrible burden was lifted when he realized that God loves us whether we deserve it or not, and the sacrificial death of Jesus Christ testifies to the certainty of that ceaseless love. With this new consciousness, Luther moved from *duty* to love, and prayer became an act of joyful communion for him.

Karl Marx never overcame his hostility to religion. He observed the state-supported churches of nineteenth-century Europe as they helped keep the people under control by threatening eternal punishment and promising eternal rewards.

"Endure the inequities of this life like a good soldier, appointed by God to your lowly post, and you shall receive a kingly crown in the world to come," the religious establishment of his day told the people. Small wonder the brilliant, cynical Marx called that kind of religion the "opium of the masses." For him, prayer was *fantasy.*

Less hostile but more pervasive and more damaging to the cause of authentic Christian faith, is the patronizing attitude of modern skeptics who see prayer as a kind of *benign fantasy, daydreaming, or mental house cleaning.* This position is represented by a cliché which was floating around in religious circles a few years ago:

Q: Does prayer change anything?

A: Prayer changes people, and people change things.

At first glance this seems healthy enough. Prayer certainly *does* change people and people go forth to change the world. But implicit in this exchange is a denial that praying affects anything but the attitude of the person who prays. Psychological energies are acknowledged—spiritual energies ignored—in the interests of empiricism. One could just as easily substitute *any* kind of activity, mental or physical, in the above formula and obtain the same results:

Q: Does football change anything?

A: Football changes people, and people change things.

Q: Does eating fiber-rich foods change anything?

A: Eating fiber-rich foods changes people, and people change things.

Q: Does getting a blackbelt in Chinese karate change anything?

A: Getting a blackbelt in Chinese karate...etc.

Presumably, something more substantial happens when prayer is offered than this formula allows. To see prayer as happy fantasy substitutes psychological goals for actual power to change things in the real world because of the efficacy of prayer itself.

3. MIRACULOUS - UNNECESSARY

The final couplet originates with two schools of religious thought. Those who see prayer as invoking some kind of *miraculous* power believe God supernaturally intervenes in time and space to work spectacular deeds that are contrary to His own "laws" of science. Although the *Deus Ex Machina* is a comforting belief, Deitrich Bonhoeffer found it necessary to reject such an interventionist theology because it contradicts the New Testament image of God's power. The anthology *Letters and Papers from Prison*, printed posthumously, preserves a letter Bonhoeffer wrote to Eberhard Bethge on 16 July 1944 from Tegel Prison, containing these poignant, cryptic words:

Here is the decisive difference between Christianity and all religions. Man's religiosity makes him look in his distress to the power of God in the world: God is the Deus Ex Machina. The Bible directs man to God's powerlessness and suffering; only the suffering God can help.[4]

In Greek theater the playwrights often solved the problems of their heroes by bringing a god (*Deus*) on stage in a box (*Ex Machina*) to perform some miracle and save the day. Bonhoeffer, who has seen his country ravaged by war brought on by a madman in power, correctly observes that the New Testament knows nothing of this kind of god. The God-concept portrayed in Jesus Christ is a God so involved with His people that He experiences their suffering. Only a God so intimately involved with the world can help, because only He can speak the authentic word of Truth to us in our own language. Although Jesus Christ appears powerless in the eyes of Pontius Pilate, it is through powerlessness that His Truth is set free in the world to transform lives and move us forward toward Christ-consciousness. Miracles are not necessary if the system contains self-correcting, self-healing tendencies.

On the other extreme we have people who take Bonhoeffer literally and insist God does nothing whatsoever in the real world. God is not involved with life but stands beyond it, waiting in the wings for the final curtain. Therefore, prayer is *unnecessary*. Instead of a *Deus Ex Machina* we are left with a different heresy, Deism.

As we have already noted, because the Deists' God does not intervene in time and space, God must be beyond this realm of mechanical law. Their favorite analogy, drawn appropriately from eighteenth-century technology which was the period of Deism's heyday, was a clockwork universe which God wound up and left running. He does not return to tinker with the mechanism but trusts His creation to operate independent of Himself. Deism is out of favor in theology today, but many more people actually believe in a deistic God than theology likes to admit.

The error-belief of those who believe in a *miraculous* function of prayer stands at the stark opposite of those who hold deistic inclinations and see prayer as *unnecessary* because God leaves us entirely alone. Both, however, reject the God of the New Testament, revealed in Jesus Christ, whose power is released through living and struggling toward Oneness with the Father. It is this model to which we shall return for our definition of Christian Prayer.

WORKING DEFINITION OF PRAYER

There are so many clichés about prayer that one is tempted to rehash the best of them rather than seek a new formulation. Anthropologically, prayer is simply "addressing the supernatural."[5]

In the words of the seventeenth-century mystic, Brother Lawrence, prayer is "the practice of the presence of God."[6]

But according to the Westminster Short Catechism: "Prayer is the offering up of our desires unto God for things agreeable to His will."[7]

And John Macquarrie calls prayer "the ways in which the worshipper expresses himself verbally."[8]

All of these have value. However, Charles Fillmore gave a simple formula that encompasses all facets of prayer life: Prayer is communion between God and man.[9]

Note the two-way motion implied in the definition. This bipolarity gets lost in all the other descriptions of prayer quoted above except perhaps in the mystical insight of Brother Lawrence. Not only is prayer speaking and communicating with God, according to Mr. Fillmore it is also God's reply.

More than a reply, "communion between God and man" suggests continual exchange, first God initiating the contact, then man. Language is not required, either. Adoration of God leads beyond words to a place mystics describe as the Silence. Eventually the shadowy barriers separating God and man begin to crumble, polarities merge into unity, and we see the world with God's eyes, aware of our Oneness with Him.

WHAT CAN PRAYER ACCOMPLISH IN THE REAL WORLD?

If a man has been diagnosed with a terminal illness, could prayer heal his body? Can poverty be overcome through prayer? Marriages be healed, prison doors swing wide, childlike innocence be restored for world-weary sinful people? Can fear be conquered, jobs and housing found? Can war be avoided and world peace established through prayer?

The answer to these questions—which are really one, when distilled to their essence, namely, *Can prayer really accomplish anything in the real world?*—is *"Yes and no."*

If by "accomplish anything" we mean magically manipulating the Cosmos like a jar of modeling clay, then we must say, *"No. Prayer is not occult science, for no such power exists."*

But if we mean affecting outcomes, causing reversal of downward trends in health or prosperity, clicking coincidences into place that give us the right answer at the right time because we have opened ourselves to the power of God and let Him work in and through us, then the answer is a triumphant, *"Yes!"*

But aren't we back to miraculous intervention again? How can we say God does not operate supernaturally and yet believe He can cause connections, coincidences, healings? The answer is found in ideas advanced earlier in this work, when we considered the nature of God.

TILLICH TAKEN SERIOUSLY

In our investigation of Spirit (Chapter 6) we said that all reality has its origin in and is an outpicturing of the power of God. Only One Presence/One Power exists in the Cosmos—God's power. This means reality is an interrelated whole, not a series of separate systems operating in accidental proximity to each other but otherwise independent.

Philosophically, these ideas represent a school of thought known as *Absolute Idealism*, which was the dominant philosophy of the English-speaking world at the beginning of the twentieth century.

Theologically, we propose to take Paul Tillich seriously when he announces that God is the Ground of our being, the very Power to be. There is not a plurality of powers, God among them, but only One Presence/Power, God revealed in Jesus Christ as Goodness Omnipotent. This makes any movement of energies within the Cosmos a movement of God-power.

But power alone is useless without intelligence, and intelligence alone is helpless to prevent self-defeating actions (sin) without goodness, which is harmony with Divine Ideas. When we use God's power to attempt to negate Divine Ideas, we hurt ourselves. If we try to harm others we do more damage to our own soul-growth. Any misuse of intelligence, life, or power results in brokenness and estrangement from our true Divine-human nature. For this reason, we agree with Tillich when he declared that *sin is separation.*

The summary of all Divine Ideas about life, love, joy, faith, hope, and goodness comes to us in Jesus the Christ, our Lord, Savior, and Wayshower. Jesus reveals a God who is "powerless" and "suffering" in the eyes of the world, but the story does not end at Calvary. Jesus of Nazareth becomes Jesus the Christ, breaking the power of sin and death and showing us how it can be done. There is no powerlessness after Easter for those who believe.

Instead of a God who reaches into time and space to rescue us, Jesus shows us a God who walks the corridors of time with us and expresses the power to heal, to bring forth prosperity, to mend relationships, to overcome prejudice, to let those coincidences click into place. It is a fundamental premise of Christian theology that God acts in the world, but until we understood that God-power represents all energy, consciousness, intelligence, life, and strength, we had no tools to explain how God acted without violating the natural order.

God acts through us, because we have Divine-human powers of which most people never dream. And when we bring the Divine-within into phase with the Divine power at large in the world, seemingly miraculous things are possible. Not a movement from beyond space and time by an interventionist Supreme Being, but welling up from within every situation, circumstance, person, or event. Good planning mitigates the need for intervention by God's Hand into the Cosmos, and we must assume that God plans well. There is nothing more "natural" than God's downpour of gracious energy and creative power. When we align ourselves with this ever-flowing power, things happen which seem like miracles but which are in fact natural occurrences springing from God's Presence/Power undergirding all reality. Just as electricity seems like a miracle to primitive peoples, so these natural Divine-human powers seem miraculous to people who are unaware of their heritage as children of God.

Prayer triggers spiritual energies so vast that our limited minds cannot comprehend how pervasive and far-reaching this communion with God truly is. Mystics often say that prayer is the most powerful force in the Universe, if we only understood and used it properly. Charles Fillmore wrote:

> Prayer is the most highly accelerated mind action known. It steps up mental action until man's consciousness synchronizes with the Christ Mind. It is the language of spirituality; when developed it makes man master in the realm of creative ideas.[10]

Are we back to *magic* again, hiding our manipulative aims behind a curtain of theological gibberish about using God-power to attempt to thwart Divine Ideas? That is a real danger against which Truth students must always guard their thoughts. And in a sense, it is true that misuse of God-power can be the "sin" of attempting to manipulate some sort of plastic cosmic energy for selfish ends.

The difference is that *magic is self-conscious manipulation*, but ordinary acts of selfishness (violence, theft, deceit for personal gain) are committed by persons who are unaware that they are kenotic incarnations of God. Every atom of the Cosmos is Holy Ground; every act which seeks to destroy or negate Divine Ideas is an act of small-scale blasphemy against our true Divine nature.

THIRTY-SIX PRAYER IDEAS

Thus we have a theological rationale for prayer which reflects solid biblical principles and is philosophically sound as well. Now we turn to application, which we have continually said is the truest test of theological ideas. Prayer is such a vast subject that some kind of limitation must be placed on our investigations, so we have devised a chart (Figure 17-1) that should serve as a handy reference as we continue our study. The vertical column presents six frequent prayer goals/subjects. Horizontally across the top we have listed six methods of prayer, four well-known to Metaphysical students and two drawn from traditional prayer forms. The vertical/horizontal interfaces to form a grid, combining goals with methods in thirty-six ways.

Rather than run down the list of all thirty-six, we propose to examine briefly six goals and six methods, giving touch-and-go examples of how they can be combined to meet different prayer needs. We shall do this by taking each goal and combining it with a method, examining how they interface.

We shall be looking at *1) HEALING—IMAGERY, 2) PROSPERITY—AFFIRMATIONS/DENIALS, 3) RELATIONSHIPS—BLESSING/RELEASING, 4) WHOLENESS—CENTERING PRAYER, 5) GUIDANCE—THANKSGIVING*, and *6) ILLUMINATION—ADORATION.*

THIRTY-SIX PRAYER TYPES

	A IMAGERY	B AFFIRMATIONS/ DENIALS	C BLESSING/ RELEASING	D CENTERING PRAYER	E THANKSGIVING	F ADORATION
1. HEALING	*Healing Imagery*					
2. PROSPERITY		*Prosperity Affirmations/ Denials*				
3. RELATIONSHIPS			*Relationships Blessing/ Releasing*			
4. WHOLENESS				*Wholeness Centering Prayer*		
5. GUIDANCE					*Guidance/ Thanksgiving*	
6. ILLUMINATION						*Adoration/ Illumination*

Fig. 17-1. The column on the left represents six common themes in Metaphysical Christian prayer. Horizontally across the top are listed six types/methods of prayer. Combine the two, and the result is a grid of thirty-six prayer opportunities which represent most of the New Thought attitudes about prayer. For example, type D-5 would be "Centering Prayer for guidance." Type B-2 would be a series of Affirmations and Denials about Prosperity.

Of course, this chart is merely an artificial structure, useful only if the individual wants some ideas about deepening his/her prayer life.

We could have combined any other goal with any other method but chose to limit our discussion for the sake of brevity. Once the idea is grasped, you will be able to fill in the remaining squares. This also meets our goal of introducing new concepts which Christian Truth students can apply to concrete situations in their lives. Consider the blanks your homework for this chapter!

HEALING—IMAGERY

Significant evidence from the empirical sciences indicates that *Healing* can be powerfully affected by prayer, especially *Imagery*. Several recent scientific works have been devoted to healing through imagery, and nonscientific works about mental/spiritual healing have never been more popular. We can read about a variety of individual triumphs—from Myrtle Fillmore's victory over tuberculosis back in the late nineteenth century to the story of Noel Coward's successful assault on a fatal disease through bathing his consciousness in laughter in the mid-twentieth. We can examine the testimony of people who were healed of such dread maladies as terminal cancer like Harry DeCamp, who wrote a book about his use of imagery (*One Man's Healing from Cancer*, published by H. Fleming Revell Company).

As scientific research and popular literature begin to point to holistic healing through imagery, Christian Truth students fold their arms and say, "It's about time." These techniques have been known and practiced in one form or another for over a century.

Imagery is a powerful medical/spiritual tool which functions at the boundary between conscious control of one's thoughts and the unconscious bodily processes much the same way hypnosis does, except hypnotherapy tends to work faster and have less permanent results than imagery. Theories abound which describe why mental/spiritual healings happen, but none has captured the field. We are faced with an area where science and religion must cooperate because neither can by itself adequately explain the phenomenon, yet science and religion still consider each other skeptically.

Although we do not know why it works, we are beginning to understand what works and how to reproduce results with a fair degree of consistency. Myrtle Fillmore's testimony gives the key elements in her own words:

> I was fearfully sick; I had all the ills of mind and body that I could bear. Medicine and doctors ceased to give me relief, and I was in despair...This is how I made what I call my discovery. I was thinking about life. Life is everywhere—in the worm and in man. "Then why does not the life in the worm make a body like man's?" I asked. Then I thought, "The worm has not as much sense as man." Ah! intelligence, as well as life, is needed to make a body, Here is the key to my discovery. Life has to be guided by intelligence. How do we communicate intelligence? By thinking and talking, of course. Then it flashed upon me that I might talk to the life in every part of my body and have it do just what I wanted. I began to teach my body and got marvelous results.[11]

If this is your introduction to holistic healing, a likely response at this juncture is healthy skepticism. Talk to parts of her body? Images of a kindergarten class pop into mind: *"Good morning, Mr. Throat! Good morning, Mrs. Kneecap!"*

Of course, that ludicrous picture is not what Myrtle Fillmore meant by talking to her body. She intuitively grasped the fact that we talk to our bodies all the time— usually programming negative attitudes into them.

Doubtful? Check your memory banks and see if you've said any of the following: *I'm too fat, too skinny, too young, too old, too weak, too slow, too nearsighted, clumsy, ugly, tall, short, stupid. I catch cold easily; I have allergies; I don't sleep well; don't have any energy; I have sensitive skin, an ulcer, bursitis; I can't eat spicy food— I just can't do this!*

There is a remarkable correlation between what we think about ourselves and what we outpicture. More frightening are new studies which show that *among licensed psychotherapists*, 69 percent report feeling so personally inadequate they imagine themselves to be impostors posing as therapists! This woeful sense of inferiority which permeates our whole society has been awarded an official label by the helping professions, the *Impostor Phenomenon*. Dr. Joan C. Harvey, creator of the *Harvey IP Scale* to test for the condition, explains:

> The term "Impostor Phenomenon" was coined by two psychologists at Georgia State University, Dr. Pauline Clance and Dr. Suzanne Imes. They had been observing this phenomenon for several years, studying 150 highly successful female students and career women. Despite good grades, honors, awards, advanced degrees, or promotions, these women persisted in believing they were less qualified than their peers. They suffered from a terrible fear of being "found out" as impostors.[12]

Nor is this bad feeling endemic to females. Dr. Gail Matthews of Dominican College did a study of 41 men and women in a variety of occupations: entertainers, judges, attorneys, scientists, etc. In this mixed group 70 percent confessed to feelings of inadequacy and fears about being caught as an impostor.[13]

Coupling this disturbing data with what we know about the power of the mind to create conditions it dwells upon, one cannot help but wonder if modern society consists of a vast parade of "pretenders" hiding their terrors behind masks of gaiety and competence while inside them churn self-generated sicknesses, neuroses, emptiness. This Mardi Gras of self-doubt is marching off toward early coronaries, cancers, and broken relationships. It cannot be attacked from outside. Essentially a spiritual problem, it must be solved spiritually.

Thus the "discovery" of Myrtle Fillmore becomes one of the most important events in modern times. Listen to her gentle way of countermanding the bad programming she had fed into her bio-computer all those years:

> I told the life in my liver that it was not torpid or inert, but full of vigor and energy. I told the life in my stomach that it was not weak or inefficient, but energetic, strong, and intelligent. I told the life in my abdomen that it was no longer infested with ignorant thoughts or disease, put there by myself and by doctors, but that it was all a thrill with the sweet, pure, wholesome energy of God. I told my limbs that they were active and strong. I told my eyes that they did not see themselves but that they expressed the sight of Spirit, and that they were drawing on an unlimited source. I told them they were young eyes, clear, bright eyes, because the light of God shone right through them. I told my heart that the pure love of Jesus Christ flowed in and out through its beatings and that all the world felt its joyous pulsation.[14]

Nor did she give up easily. It took two years before Myrtle Fillmore was completely healed. But she was healed, and recovery from tuberculosis in those days was nothing short of a miracle.

Word spread. Soon others came, hungry for health and desperate to try anything which offered hope. They got better, too. In a little while the healing work expanded to general prayer, prayer meetings, Sunday afternoon services, and finally a full ministry. What began for Myrtle Fillmore in moments of quiet prayer, during her search to release Divine-human powers to quiet her fears and cure a sickly body, today has brought healing strength to millions.

And it all started as a main idea—with *Imagery*.

Imagery is a simple process which can be done by anyone, anywhere. Simply see yourself as God sees you—whole, healthy, strong, and radiant. Your true nature is spiritual, and Spirit doesn't get sick. When you realize that you are not sick—the real Divine-human spiritual being that you are—you release the image of sickness and bathe yourself in healing energy.

We know clinically this works, so if you need scientific data to back up your faith it is readily available. But the best data comes from personal experience. Work your imagery continually, seeing yourself whole and well. Read good books on holistic healing; many are available these days. But don't substitute intellectualizations for practice. Healing is no spectator sport; to get better you must work your imagery. Best of all is to let God's power work through you by nonresistance to His will for you, which is perfect health, happiness, prosperity. If everyone believed that, we would need very few hospitals indeed.

PROSPERITY - AFFIRMATIONS & DENIALS

Many people feel the finest book available on this subject is Catherine Ponder's *Open Your Mind to Prosperity*, certainly one of the most readable treatments about *Prosperity*. Written from a how-to-do-it point of view, Ms. Ponder mixes prescriptions with anecdotes to make her book lively. Before we are through the opening chapter, we've met a dozen people who grew prosperous by following the principles Ms. Ponder describes, including a pair of secretaries whom she hired to type the manuscript, but whose prosperity increased so much that they quit the typing job before the work was finished! Reading Catherine Ponder one begins to wonder if anyone need be poor. She doesn't think so. What about the idea of holy poverty, so long thought a virtue by Christian ascetics? She will hear nothing of it:

> Most people with financial problems have a psychological block about prosperity. They have been taught in the past that poverty is a Christian virtue, and that to be prosperous is somehow wicked...How in the world can poverty be a Christian virtue, when poverty causes most of the world's problems?...You can open your mind to prosperity by giving up the ridiculous idea that poverty is a Christian virtue, when it is nothing but a common vice.[15]

Surely this is an exaggeration. Or is it? Recall, our definition of sin was *any attempt to negate a Divine Idea*. If prosperity is the Divine intention for all sentient beings—if we are truly meant to be rich, healthy and happy—then poverty and the kind of conditions/consciousness which brings poverty upon humanity is, in fact, sin. This does not mean people locked into hunger, disease, and misery by conditions beyond their control are themselves sinners; it means the conditions exist which prevent the natural flow of prosperity to all God's creatures and those conditions are sin. And since poor people are caught in the poverty trap in all too many places today—from the crowded cities of the Third World to the dirt-floor cabins of Appalachia—they are made to suffer sin's burden. Lifestyles created by oppression, war, and prejudice; people held in the grip of hunger by geopolitical conflicts beyond their understanding.

Can anyone seriously doubt that poverty is ugly, maladaptive, sinful? If everyone understood the natural flow of good from God, we are prone to ponder, would there be crushing poverty at large today? Would nations which could feed the hungry dump their grain into the sea or keep their plows idle to boost prices? Can we look into the glazed eyes of a dying child and justify the sins of waste, political expediency, or regional ethnocentrisms? Catherine Ponder believes prosperity is possible for every human:

> In the beginning, God created a lavish universe, and then created spiritual man and placed him in this world of abundance, giving him dominion over it. You are only trying to open your mind to receive your heritage of abundance bequeathed you from the beginning.[16]

Prosperity contains within it much more than wealth. Peace of mind, health of the body, and wholeness in human relationships must accompany any increase in material wealth or the person is not truly free to enjoy his prosperity.

Two questions immediately step forward to bar the way to Christian prayer for prosperity and must be answered before we can proceed.

1) Can prayer actually affect our lives so practically that it puts more money in the bank?
2) Isn't it a sin to pray for riches?

1) Can prayer produce prosperity?

If we believe that God wants us to be healthy, happy, and prosperous (what kind of God would want us sick, miserable, and poor?), then if we're not prosperous we have two choices. Either *God is unable* to bring these blessings into our lives or *we are unable* to accept them. If He is unable, He is not the God of Jesus. This leaves us with the second alternative: we are somehow unable to accept the good that God is showering upon us.

Since prayer for the Metaphysical Christian means harmony with the Divine, prayer can and does bring us into alignment with what God wants for us. By prayer we unplug the channels clogged by negative thinking and let the flow of Divine blessings resume. The objective of this kind of prayer is not vast wealth (although that is certainly possible if God intends us to be super-rich); the goal is harmony with God and enjoyment of His blessings. *Quality*, not *quantity*, makes a person prosperous.

2) Isn't it sinful to pray for riches?

Certainly, if we are motivated by love of money to the exclusion of human values/virtues. That is why the rich young man in the biblical story went away sad after Jesus challenged the young tycoon to toss away wealth and follow Him. That wealthy youngster exemplified people who love things and use people instead of the healthy opposite.

However, there is no harm in praying for God's will to be done, and we have already established that God's will for all His children is health, happiness, and prosperity. Since God wants us to be prosperous, we might well be slipping into sin by accepting less!

How, then, shall we pray for prosperity? Perhaps the most effective method is a combination of *Affirmation/Denial*. It is an ancient prayer form found repeatedly in the Bible, especially the book of Psalms where prosperity prayers abound. Normally, prayer means talking to God "out there," in some spiritually distant locale. God presumably hears our prayers because, like Superman, He has long-range senses. Our prayers fall into the "up" and "down" language of the biblical cosmology with its three-story universe: earth sandwiched between heaven in the clouds above our heads and hell underground beneath our feet.

The very language we speak still reflects a prescientific worldview; why else is "highest" better than "lowest"? There is nothing particularly virtuous in greater altitude, but we talk about "lofty" purposes, "high" morals, "mountaintop" experiences, and prayer "ascending" to "heaven". We subscribed to the God-up-there thinking so completely that we translated this up-down language from physical to spiritual terms when the ancient cosmology fell apart during the Copernican revolution. Bishop John A. T. Robinson wrote in his disturbing little book *Honest To God*:

> In fact, we do not realize how crudely spatial much of the Biblical terminology is, for we have ceased to perceive it that way...For in place of a God who is literally 'up there' we have accepted, as part of our mental furniture, a God who is spiritually or metaphysically 'out there.'[17]

When we pray to the Ceiling God, do we realize the idolatry implicit in locating God in space above our heads? Metaphysical Christianity begins with God-within, which makes much of the up-down language of conventional piety meaningless. Not that God is absent from the skies or the top of the church building—the direction toward which much prayer is offered—we know God is "up there" because Omnipotent Good is everywhere, including outer space. However, God's Presence is best discovered by the individual believer at the center of our consciousness, deep within. Prayer turns a different direction, if this is our premise.

Instead of telling the Ceiling God what He presumably already knows, which in corporate prayer is really a hidden form of announcements/exhortations addressed to the congregation by the clergy *("And, Lord, Thou knowest that the offerings are down and that we needeth greater support for Thy programs...")*, this form of prayer begins by telling ourselves what God already knows. Here are some examples of conventional prayer (cp) followed by the same treatment by affirmative prayer (ap).

cp) O God, give me strength to do my best in the history test. Let my mind be clear and my memory not fail me.

ap) God's strength flows through me, clearing my mind of stray thoughts and empowering my memory. I will do well on this history test, because God never fails.

cp) Lord, if Thou wilt, let my mother be healed. She is weak, Lord, and needs Thy help. Do not turn away from her in this hour of trial!

ap) The healing presence of God's spirit surrounds my mother, bringing perfect health, wholeness, and divine strength. I see my mother as God sees her—perfect, whole, and eternally young.

Conventional prayer is a cry for help, a subject-object transaction between creature and Creator. As such, it is understandable and healthy, perhaps the most universal form of prayer; but we must move beyond these elementary notions of a Supreme Being Who can be enticed to do good deeds by petitionary prayer. Mystical Christianity has long recognized God's glorious inflexibility. He cannot do otherwise than shower His creation with good. The problem remains our inability to receive the good, and it is these blocks to Divine Grace which *Affirmation/Denial* seeks to remove.

Affirmation ("The Lord is my shepherd") tells us what is Truth; Denial ("I shall not want") points to untruth, draining these false notions of their potency. They are used in tandem in the most effective prayer sequences. Some Christian Truth teachers insist Denial must come first, cleaning house before bringing in the new thoughts, but many people find virtually any combination of Affirmation/Denial works as long as the essential elements are covered.

Those essential elements include 1) Identifying the goal, 2) Identifying and denying the power of obstacles to that goal, 3) Identifying oneself with the power of God in this situation, and 4) Remaining open and receptive to Divine surprises.

Prosperity, of course, is only one spiritual objective Affirmation/Denial can address. *Figure 17-1* shows five more, but the number of applications for this prayer form is endless, limited only by your imagination and circumstances. Nor must Prosperity work be limited to this prayer-form, as the chart shows. Imagery, for example, works quite well in bringing greater success, material wealth, and well-being.

One popular way to employ imagery for Prosperity work is the *Picture Prayer* or *Treasure Map*. A handy guide to this technique is the little book *What Treasure Mapping Can Do for You* by Mary Katherine MacDougall.

RELATIONSHIPS - BLESSING AND RELEASING

Perhaps more prayer is offered for hurting relationships than any other topic. Primary relationships of our society (parent-child, husband-wife) have never before received such wide attention and never been so deeply troubled as today. Self-help books for parents and lovers line the paperback shelves, most offering excellent advice. Countless counselors earn their daily bread working with parent-child and husband-wife problems as more and more people take responsibility for their lives and seek competent professional help.

Spiritual counselors and teachers who recognize this need can offer their special assistance. Although psychiatrists and other counseling professionals (psychologists, social workers, licensed marriage and family counselors) get most of the publicity and publish most of the best-selling books in the field, the fact is more marriage and family counseling is done by religious professionals than all the secular agencies together. A priest listens as a troubled teenager spills bitter tears while recalling the fight he just had with his alcoholic father. A Protestant minister works with a young married couple in her office at the church, gently exploring ways they can open up communication and stop yelling at each other. A rabbi talks with troubled parents whose son expresses real doubts about the Jewish faith and wants to marry a gentile girl.

In countless carpeted little rooms, clergy of every faith are doing pastoral care for their people, helping them with parent-child, husband-wife issues. We shall explore this kind of ministry more deeply in the next chapter when we look at *Pastoral Theology: God's Love with Skin on.*

Relationship problems usually arise from different ways of looking at religion, life, love, sex, money, child-raising, and role models. Conflicts are often exacerbated by differences in temperament, personalities, and backgrounds. Outside influences can be powerful levers or wedges in the relationship; peer pressure, social expectations, family, church, and school all put stress on a relationship. And whether we are talking about parent-child or husband-wife, these conditions apply.

There is not enough space in our survey to deal comprehensively with problems of this magnitude. So, we propose to offer a single prayer technique which one party can apply to most every situation, even if other participants in the problem refuse to cooperate.

Read carefully this caveat: This is not a panacea which will cure all marriage and family problems. No such elixir of Truth exists because we are all individuals with highly individual needs and complex life-circumstances. What we offer here is a simple way to start employing God-power in resolving problems through Blessing and Releasing all persons, situations, and conditions involved. At the risk of criticism for gross oversimplification, we propose an all-purpose formula which allows someone enmeshed in person-problems to avail herself of the power of this kind of prayer. The formula is not new; many Christian Truth teachers use something like this nearly every day when working with relationships.

When you have identified the person/situation/condition which is causing you grief, get quiet and center on the Christ-within. Then follow this guide:

I BLESS AND FORGIVE [NAME] FOR [SPECIFIC ACTION].

I SEE [NAME] AS GOD SEES HIM/HER, WHOLE AND PERFECT, A RADIANT CHILD OF GOD.

I RELEASE [NAME] TO GOD'S CARE, SENDING LOVING THOUGHTS TO HIM/HER AS HE/SHE GOES FORWARD TO MEET HIS/HER GOOD.

I NOW RELEASE ALL PERSONS, SITUATIONS, AND CONDITIONS INVOLVED IN THESE CIRCUMSTANCES, PLACING THE PROBLEM IN GOD'S HANDS.

(Repeat each element three times before going to the next.)

The next step is crucial. Take the above sequence and repeat the whole process, this time reversing subject/object roles.

[NAME] BLESSES AND FORGIVES ME FOR ANYTHING I MAY HAVE DONE TO OFFEND HIM/HER.

[NAME] SEES ME AS GOD SEES ME, WHOLE AND PERFECT, A RADIANT CHILD OF GOD.

[NAME] RELEASES ME TO GOD'S CARE, SENDING LOVING THOUGHTS TO ME AS I GO FORWARD TO MEET MY GOOD.

[NAME] NOW RELEASES ALL PERSONS, SITUATIONS AND CONDITIONS INVOLVED IN THESE CIRCUMSTANCES, PLACING THE PROBLEM IN GOD'S HANDS.

(Also repeats, as above.)

REVIEW: THEOLOGY OF PRAYER

Our theology of prayer began by analyzing the power of prayer to affect the world. We said prayer is effective because each and every sentient being, as a *kenotic incarnation* of the Divine-human paradox, represents a bit of condensed God-power. Prayer, then, becomes the way to unleash the flow of Divine Goodness through persons, places, and circumstances by centering on the Christ-within. This is not mere sophistry but releases real power to make connections, cause changes, and 'click' those coincidences into place. But that power does not come as intervention from the *Deus ex Machina*—we need no John Wayne God leading the U. S. Cavalry to our rescue. We need to center ourselves on the God-power already available to us and let its healing, prospering, wholeness-making energy burst forth into our lives and affairs. This is the theology behind all prayer.

Next, we shall look at the specific technique of *Centering* as it is applied to our search for *Wholeness*.

WHOLENESS - CENTERING

In a sense, all effective prayer is centering prayer if we define it as linking our consciousness with Christ-indwelling, found in every sentient being. What we are specifically looking at here is the use of Centering Prayer for the purpose of attaining Wholeness, which includes dealing with guilt, achieving forgiveness, and establishing peace with God and neighbor.

Of course, we could approach guilt-forgiveness-peace through many other avenues: *Imagery* (seeing oneself at the foot of the cross), *Affirmation/Denial*, and *Blessing/Releasing* immediately spring into mind. We are checking off techniques/goals as we travel through the chart at Figure 17-1, so our combination of *WHOLE-NESS-CENTERING* serves the dual purposes of explaining these categories and offering practical solutions to real situations.

Centering Prayer wasn't invented by modern Christian Truth students. It was practiced in the early Church and revived by medieval mystics, like Meister Eckhart. A recent Roman Catholic pamphlet discloses reasons why more people today are not aware of such mystical techniques:

> One way of entering this "secret place" is being rediscovered in our own day. It is called Centering Prayer. The name is new, but the method itself is the Church's oldest, classical form of private prayer. For at least the last four centuries this treasure of Catholic spirituality has been available only to a handful of monks and nuns in a few enclosed, contemplative communities. Numerous books on prayer (many still on our shelves) warned that this ancient prayer form was not for ordinary Christians, but only for a small number of spiritually advanced souls. The resulting spiritual loss was...great...[18]

Despite all its archaic rules, modern Catholic theology retains a never-ending ability to discover "new" ideas which in fact represent "the Church's oldest" teachings. Thankfully, the "error" was discovered and Centering Prayer is now taught widely as a private devotional technique among our Catholic brothers and sisters. However, outside the archipelago of Christian Truth churches, few Protestants ever heard of the concept.

To practice Centering Prayer requires three phases. *1) Preparation, 2) Repetition of Prayer Word, 3) Re-directing.*

1) <u>Preparation</u>. We *prepare* for Centering Prayer by getting quiet, finding a comfortable body position in a secluded location, and then saying a few simple prayers or affirmations to attune our thoughts to God's presence. Perhaps the Lord's Prayer, the

Prayer for Protection, or some other meaningful selection could be used. When we feel quiet and ready, we move to phase two.

2) Repetition of Prayer Word. Since we are praying for Wholeness, our word might be "oneness", or "joy", or just "wholeness" itself. If we are targeting guilt and desiring forgiveness, the word might be "forgiveness" or "peace". Find the word which speaks to you. The word is quietly repeated in your mind, always reaching beyond words for the Silence in which we know our Oneness with God through Christ-within. If we have difficulty maintaining concentration, move to phase three.

3) Re-directing. Whenever we become aware of outside evens, disturbances, or stray thoughts, just return gently to the prayer word. After completing our prayer time, re-direct thought to the outside world by returning through spoken or mental prayers again. Also, a period of quiet is best before leaving the prayer place.

This will not be easy at first. Stray thoughts will lead your mind far from the prayer word until you have established the mental discipline necessary. Charles Fillmore believed in regular prayer at the same time of day for a prescribed length of time, whether it went well or not. There is something to be gained from regularity, if nothing more than stretching one's ability to sit quietly for longer and longer intervals.

Other possibilities for Centering Prayer have been suggested by other teachers: Twelve Powers meditations, wordless chanting, and use of music are among these techniques. Whatever releases your mind from captivity to linear thinking and allows you to "go to headquarters" will be best for you.

Two more goals and methods remain. We'll review them together, because they're similar enough to be confusing if handled separately.

GUIDANCE - THANKSGIVING / ILLUMINATION - ADORATION

Guidance and *Illumination* are not the same. When we seek Guidance we are asking for help to decide what to do. Looking for *Illumination* means searching for ideas, insight, or understanding. Prayer for *Guidance* asks, "What can I do about this circumstance?" Prayer for *Illumination* says, "What is the Lesson in this circumstance?"

Thanksgiving means exactly that: to give thanks for some blessing, either received or on the way. *Adoration* is love expressed toward God, the Source of all good. *Adoration* differs from *Thanksgiving* in that no specific blessings need be involved; we love God because God is love-worthy. We celebrate God's goodness by *Adoration* and express appreciation through *Thanksgiving*.

If we want Guidance—i.e., help in deciding a course of action—we could use any prayer form on Figure 17-1. But, since we want to demonstrate each type of prayer through examples, let's match our desire for Guidance with prayers of Thanksgiving. We'll combine a desire for Illumination with prayer of Adoration to complete our packet of spiritual samples.

Guidance—Thanksgiving prayer might raise a few eyebrows as an unlikely match up, but if we understand Christian Truth as operating according to Principles—i.e., high-degree tendencies which function the same for everyone—then giving thanks for guidance not yet received is one of the best ways of opening ourselves to that kind of inspiration. In fact, prayers of thanks should probably accompany every other form of prayer mentioned in this chapter if we truly believe God desires all goodness, health, prosperity, and happiness for us. Jesus went as far as to assert this kind of prayer has a life of its own:

> Therefore, I tell you, whatever you ask in prayer, believe that you have received it, and it will be yours.[19]

Giving thanks for desired good is a way of greasing the chute leading from God's hands to our lives.

Illumination—Adoration prayer lets us express love to God for the insights He has provided us and will continue to provide in the future. If we are struggling with a spiritual concept, we can break the deadlock by giving praise and love to God for His blessing of understanding. Contemplate God as the Source of all knowledge, light, inspiration. Let that knowledge, light, and inspiration surround and uplift our quest for illumination, so that a dialogue begins: our praise to God and His response to our circumstances. Soon all problems fade in the love that we feel. Beyond words is the Silence, but beyond the Silence is love eternal.

NO FORMULA ALWAYS APPLIES

These prayer techniques reveal only a fraction of the possibilities for communion with God-within. Since no formula applies in every circumstance, you will need to try each for yourself, editing, and re-organizing the ideas into a network of applicable prayer principles which will put you in touch with your indwelling Christ.

LOVE IS NEXT...

Our survey of Christian Theology takes us next to love in action. We have looked at the Church and her ministries in a previous chapter (13), but now we focus upon what is perhaps the most important ministry of all: counseling people as they struggle for wholeness in their relationships. We turn now to study *Pastoral Theology*.

CHECK YOUR KNOWLEDGE

1. What is the difference between *prayer* and *wishing?* Why does the author believe *magic* is both untrue and dangerous?

2. Explain the proper use of *Affirmation/Denial* in prayer.

3. How does it help us to bless, release, and forgive someone else?

4. Describe *Centering Prayer* and tell how it can be used in daily devotions.

5. What does the author say about praying for material wealth?

6. Explain the difference between *Guidance* and *Illumination.*

QUESTIONS FOR DISCUSSION

1. Bonhoeffer said that *"only a suffering God"* can help. This is *not* a typical idea you'd find in most Metaphysical literature. What do you think it means, and do you agree?

2. How could you improve the quality of your prayer life? Does your church afford opportunities to pray outside the Sunday worship hour? What can a local ministry do to promote prayer as a way of life?

3. The author is highly skeptical of *magic* in all its forms. Do you agree? Is there some sort of power out there in the Cosmos which can be bent to do our bidding, like "the Force" from *Star Wars?*

4. Myrtle Fillmore talked to her body and was healed. Discuss this method of healing, as well as other healing techniques. What place should medicine play in healing? How is healing prayer different from a chanting witch doctor?

5. Can prayer change God's mind? If not, why bother? [Or: If God knows what your prayer will be before you say it, and knows if you'll receive your healing or prosperity demonstration or not, why go through the motions?]

6. Has anyone ever told you they were "praying for you" and you felt like someone just walked across your grave? Can prayer be a bad thing?

NOTES

1. Ernest Holmes, *The Science of Mind* (NY: Dodd, Mead and Company, 1938), p. 152.

2. James Dillet Freeman, *Prayer, the Master Key* (Unity Village: Unity Books), p. 126.

3. Martin Luther in Edith Simon, *The Great Ages of Man: The Reformation* (Alexandria, VA: 4. Time-Life Books, Inc., 1966), p. 15.

4. Bonhoeffer, *Letters & Paper*, p. 361.

5. Wallace, p. 53.

6. Brother Lawrence, *The Practice of the Presence of God*, E.M. Blaiklock, trans. (Nashville, TN: Thomas Nelson Publishers, 1982), p. 35.

7. Harkness, p. 122.

8. Macquarrie, *Principles*, p. 493.

9. Fillmore, Revealing Word, p. 152.

10. IBID.

11. Myrtle Fillmore in Freeman's *Story of Unity*, pp. 47-48.

12. Joan C. Harvey, *If I'm So Successful, Why Do I Feel Like A Fake?: The Imposter Phenomenon* (NY: St. Martin's Press, 1985), pp. 5-6.

13. IBID., pp. 6-7.

14. Myrtle Fillmore in *Story of Unity*, pp. 47-48.

15. Catherine Ponder, *Open Your Mind to Prosperity* (Unity Village: Unity Books, 1971), pp. 10-11.

16. IBID., pp. 11-12.

17. John A. T. Robinson, *Honest to God* (Philadelphia: Westminster Press, 1963), p. 13.

18. John Jay Hughes, "Centering Prayer," pamphlet (Liguori, MO: Liguori Publications, 1981), p. 7.

19. Mark 11:24 (RSV).

PASTORAL THEOLOGY

Chapter Eighteen

God's Love With Skin On

If there is any posture that disturbs a suffering man or woman, it is aloofness. The tragedy of Christian ministry is that many who are in great need, many who seek an attentive ear, a word of support, a forgiving embrace, a firm hand, a tender smile, or even a stuttering confession of inability to do more, often find their ministers distant men, who do not want to burn their fingers. They are unwilling to express their feelings of affection, anger, hostility or sympathy. The paradox indeed is that those who want to be for "everyone" find themselves often unable to be close to anyone.[1]

—Henri J. M. Nouwen

In our study of Ecclesiology (Chapter 13) we saw that ministry belongs to the whole Church, not just the professional clergy. There are some functions of ministry which can be done by either professional staff or trained laypeople, such as visiting hospitalized members; other tasks are best done by laity alone, like ushering and greeting newcomers on Sundays. But a few jobs are significantly specialized as to require the attention of clergy or lay ministers. Marriage counseling is an example of a task which needs the kind of skill a trained religious professional should bring to the job.

All these person-centered ministries of the Church can be loosely characterized as *Pastoral Care*, although it is important to reiterate that in a healthy religious community *not all the care is given by the pastor.* Indeed, we might contend that the more widely the community of faith participates in the caring ministries, the more effective a local church will be in meeting the needs of her people. If this is the case, an effective program of Pastoral Care is absolutely essential to a healthy Christian community.

The key word is *"if."*

OTHER FOLKS DISAGREE

Not everyone agrees that Pastoral Care is important. Some traditional churches see their ministry as strictly evangelical, a maximum of outreach and a minimum attention to the needs of members. Other congregations emphasize the sacraments, or intellectualized religion, or an emotional experience at worship, or lifestyle issues such as dress codes and abstinence from prohibited substances (usually alcohol, tobacco, and nonprescription drugs). These churches offer a minimum amount of Pastoral Care, so their people go elsewhere or receive none.

This lack of services is only a problem if we conclude that Pastoral Care is a vital part of the ministry to the Christian community, and we have not yet made the case for such an assumption. Indeed, some Metaphysical Christian leaders fail to see the need for an organized, ongoing program of Pastoral Care. "Our business is teaching," they complain whenever the subject arises. "We should show people Truth principles and send them forth to apply the teachings in their lives. If we hold long-term counseling with parishioners we are creating a dependency in them." These are good points which need to be addressed critically beefier we can proceed.

DEFINING TERMS - ACCEPTING THE CHALLENGE

Let's begin with a comprehensive definition: *Pastoral Care refers to those functions of ministry which seek to help people grow in their inter-personal skills, foster emotional spiritual health, and improve relationships through individual or group counseling; to support people in times of crises and difficulty such as hospitalization, health challenge, or personal loss; and to be accessible to people through the "ministry of presence" during church activities, home visitation, and regular office hours.*

This comprehensive, straight-forward definition requires little explanation. If we accept such a broad concept as our baseline for Pastoral Care, we incur an obligation to show how this much pro-active ministry is needed in a healthy program. As we go along, we will need to present honest objections to Pastoral Care as an integral function of ministry and meet these with arguments drawn from Scripture/Tradition/Experience/Reason. If we succeed in establishing the necessity for Pastoral Care, we must then propose an outline showing the essential elements of this ministry for Christian Truth churches.

We are deliberately excluding group-oriented forms of Pastoral Theology in action, such as preaching or teaching, in order to focus on person-centered ministries that generally involve some kind of one-to-one interaction, like counseling, visitation, and the "ministry of presence."

Here, then is the challenge we face in our study of Pastoral Theology. The irony of this endeavor is that Pastoral Care is so deeply entrenched in mainline Protestant churches that readers from this background will wonder what else a minister does; nevertheless, comprehensive Pastoral Care is fairly rare in Metaphysical Christian circles, so readers from those churches might wonder why a ministry should offer these services. Since the author already betrayed a bias in favor of Pastoral Care, we accept the task ahead eagerly to demonstrate his bias is well founded.

BIBLICAL BASIS FOR PASTORAL CARE

Both Old and New Testaments offer supportive images for a theology of Pastoral Care. God continually appoints leaders who help bring Israel out of one self-imposed bondage after another. Finally, Jesus appears, and His ministry is a mixture of healing, teaching, and empowering people. His charge to those who follow Him frequently involves caring/restorative functions of ministry:

> "...for I was hungry and you gave me food, I was thirsty and you gave me drink, I was a stranger and you welcomed me, I was nakedand you clothed me, I was sick and you visited me, I was in prison and you came to me...as you did it to one of the least of these my brethren, you did it to me." (Mt 25:35-36,40)

> "...but whoever would be great among you must be your servant, and whoever would be first among you must be slave of all. For the Son of man also came not to be served but to serve..." (Mk 10:43-45)

> "What man of you, having a hundred sheep, if he has lost one of them, does not leave the ninety-nine in the wilderness, and go after the one which is lost, until he finds it?" (Lk 15:4)

> "A new commandment I give to you, that you love one another; even as I have loved you..." (Jn 13:34)

Biblical motifs of servanthood, sacrifice, selfless love (*agape*), and community (*koinonia*) lend easy support to Pastoral Care. But perhaps the most powerful argument for the caring/restorative functions of ministry is the person-centeredness which Jesus demonstrated in his day-to-day activities.

Jesus of Nazareth was more than an itinerant teacher with a gift for healing; he met the needs of hurting people at the point of their suffering. Challenging those who needed to be shaken from complacency, comforting the bereaved, and liberating the self-oppressed, Jesus shows us Pastoral Care in action. He may not have had a carpeted office with soft chairs and a box of Kleenex, but Jesus Christ was a pastor.

When we move into other parts of the New Testament—some older than the gospels—Pastoral Care becomes a routine category for the authors. In fact, the non-Pauline NT letters are usually called the *Pastoral Letters*, although that is pushing the meaning a bit too far. Still, there can be no doubt that pastoral concerns motivated Paul's writing and the work of other NT authors. How can we read I Corinthians 13 and think otherwise?

TRADITION AND PASTORING

Early Church Fathers saw their roles as *defensor fidei*, Defender of the Faith. Men like Clement, Origen, and Augustine expended years of grueling labor combating "heresies" and "schismatics" on all sides, only to have their own works suspected in later ages.

What motivated their efforts, if not an earnest if misbegotten passion for the people of God? St. Augustine's *Confessions*, his thinly disguised spiritual autobiography addressed to God but aimed at the general public, carries a blatantly pastoral premise. Augustine wants everyone to learn from his mistakes and lead a whole, happy life instead of thrashing about like he did during his wild youth. Here is a sample:

> For the space of nine years (from my nineteenth year to my eight-and-twentieth) we lived seduced and seducing, deceived and deceiving, in divers lusts; openly, by sciences which they call liberal; secretly, with a false-named religion; here proud, there superstitious, every where vain. Here, hunting after the emptiness of popular praise, down even to theatrical applauses and poetic prizes, and strifes for grassy garlands, and the follies of shows, and the intemperance of desire...[2]

We might criticize both Augustine's methods and conclusions, but his longing to spare other young people the pain he suffered cannot be faulted by anyone who's raised teenagers. His failure to understand human dynamics gave him the illusory hope that exhortation might work with the young, but there is little doubt that Augustine was a practicing pastor, if not always a successful one. Caring for one another in Christ's Name became a hallmark of the Christian faith. Sometimes this meant providing food for widows and orphans; more often it meant grieving with the survivors of the Plague or nursing the bedridden back to health.

In more recent times social agencies have taken over some of the functions of the early Church, however social services workers tend to be overworked and impersonal, dealing exclusively with people from the lowest income brackets. The government may be providing care, but it is certainly not pastoral. And what agency do people call when feeling lonely and depressed, or when they need marriage counseling, or when their mother is hospitalized?

Fortunately, most modern churches understand the need for someone who can listen and offer support; counseling techniques are usually taught to young men and women entering the Christian ministry. This extension of the caring/restorative function of ministry follows naturally as more people seek opportunities for growth, wholeness, and improvement of relationships. As options increase, so does stress and the need for Pastoral Care.

For example, when divorce was uncommon, because sociopolitical factors prevented breakups, there were probably as many bad marriages as in today's easy-divorce age. When Great-great-grandmother realized she was trapped in a loveless, dead-end relationship, she had few alternatives beyond suffering in silence. If she had gone to her minister back in the nineteenth century, he probably would have told her to try harder and submit herself completely to her husband, who was thought to be biblically ordained as her lord and master.

Today, few clergy would offer similar advice. Most pastors are trained in marriage and family counseling techniques which begin with the premise of equality. That persons have alternatives to loveless, dead-end marriages is itself something of a victory for Pastoral Care. This means more people will seek healthy alternatives to suffering in silence, and the Christian clergyperson is high on the list of those sought out for guidance and comfort in times of marital strife.

The option to change has created a need for more helping persons to walk with us as we make those life-shaking decisions. This need is overloading the support-systems of society. Where can people turn, if not to the clergy?

EXPERIENCE FACTOR: THE NEED FOR PASTORAL CARE

Self-help books on pop-psychology have never been more in demand. Authors who mix pop-psychology with quasi-religion sell millions of copies to people hungry for improvement in their lives. The phenomenal success of Norman Vincent Peale and Robert Schuller indicates how deeply people hunger to feel good about themselves, to get emotionally healthy, and have long-lasting relationships. Go to a bookstore and find the nonfiction bestseller list. Odds are, a book on self-improvement, self-motivation, or self-respect is among the top ten.

Reading about personal growth, though helpful, is not enough. Real growth takes practice. Most people find that they can make greater progress if they engage in systematic in-depth counseling with a professional counselor. If the problems involve a relationship, both parties must be involved and willing to put forth the necessary effort. If the difficulties are within a system, such as a family unit, many counselors believe every member must be enlisted in the solution.

FINAL FACTOR: CONCURRENCE OF REASON

The options we have today—divorce and remarriage, abortion or carrying to term, marriage or single parenthood—create enormous difficulties for modern people. These problems are complex, fraught with emotional baggage, freighted by moral values which no longer seem to apply, compounded by society's ability to agree on what questions may be discussed, let alone which solutions are correct. When a pregnant fifteen year old comes to the door of her minister's study to talk, she is probably not interested in prosperity laws, biblical exegesis, or social ethics. She needs a pastor. Someone who'll listen rather than judge, who cares rather than cures.

OBJECTIONS STILL UNANSWERED

We have clearly established biblically, historically, and existentially the need for Pastoral Care, backing those points with reasonable arguments. Yet, the case remains open for debate on a specific type of care usually offered by today's clergy, pastoral counseling with an unlimited number of sessions. Long-term counseling causes specific problems for Christian Truth ministers, who are usually trained in short-term theory.

The trouble centers around three objections:

1) Christian Truth ministers are primarily teachers and should not pretend to be clinical psychologists.

2) Practical Christianity seeks to empower of the individual, allowing the Christ-within to emerge; all we need to do is point the person in the right direction and the Divine-human power within will take over.

3) Long-term counseling creates dependencies in counselees.

All three are worthy objections which deserve separate responses, in the course of which the goals and limitations of Pastoral Care will become apparent.

FIRST OBJECTION: TEACHER, NOT A PSYCHOLOGIST

The distinction between the role of the minister as a preacher/teacher and the counseling as a task grounded in psychology often arises among laity or incoming seminary students. Part of the misconception originates in general ignorance about what a clergyperson does during the week. Popular notions about what a profession-al minister does for a living frequently run from the fantastic to the ridiculous: Parishioners have literally expected to find their minister kneeling in ceaseless prayer, engaged in continuous Bible study or practicing sermons to an empty auditorium when they wander into the church building on Thursday afternoon. When, instead, they find her perched at the computer, cutting clip-art cartoons to paste in the Sunday bulletin or e-mailing letters to members whom she'd like to serve on the Religious Education Committee, their illusions about the holiness of professional ministry is sometimes shaken.

Even for a clergyperson who puts long, hard hours into preparation for sermons and classes, the preaching/teaching aspects of ministry take up only a small fraction of the religious professional's work week. A diligent pastor, studying the biblical backgrounds behind his text and rehearsing his sermon Saturday night, might take ten to fifteen hours preparing a well-constructed Sunday sermon. Most preachers feel like they've done their homework if they put in half that much time. If we add the usual course load of teaching carried by clergy in Metaphysical churches—one class per week—that might add another five-seven total hours of preparation/teaching. So, in the case of Superpastor who maxes out sermon and class preparation time, we could foresee over twenty hours per week alone on the preach/teach aspects of the job.

That's half-time, folks.

No minister worth a full-time salary works twenty hours a week. There are endless meetings, administrative details, notes to significant church members, hospi-tal and home visits, financial and planning sessions, composition and publication of bulletins and newsletters, supervision of church volunteers and paid staff, religious education planning and coordination, ordering supplies, recruiting workers, long-range planning, retreats, workshops, prayer meetings, clergy meetings, denominational requirements, choir/music ministries to organize and fund, offerings to supervise and bank books to balance, checks to sign, schedules to coordinate, youth activities to sponsor, telephones to answer, appointments to make... If the pastor survives this workload, he/she gets to go home and help with the kids' homework, or the laundry or wash the car, drive the family to the mall... All this is on top of sermon and class preparations. The minister is not just a preacher/teacher. These other functions must be carried out or, more appropriately, supervised by the professional clergyperson.

However, it is entirely possible that a pastor may see himself/herself primarily as a preacher, or as a teacher or administrator or any other major function of the ministry. If we're talking self-concept, there is no harm in someone leading with his strengths—as long as all the other vital functions of ministry are being accomplished under his guidance.

Setting oneself up as preacher/teacher and then ignoring church administration, finances, and people-management is a short-cut to a short pastorate. A good number of first-year ministers learn the hard way that a local church is also a business and must be run effectively or the whole organization suffers. This does not imply cutthroat business practices or laissez-faire capitalism should become our polar star; prosperity teachings have shown us a better way. It suggests that the authentic needs of the organization must be met by the pastor, so a measure of reality must seep into his/her consciousness early in the program or disaster is a distinct possibility. A fair number of fine preachers/teachers botch their first pastorates because of unwillingness or inability to grapple with the realities of managing a local church.

The other half of the objection makes a stronger case: the pastor is not a psychologist but a religious professional. Yet, if we infer from this critique that a psychologist "counsels" and a minister does not, we misunderstand the term. According to Rollo May, counseling is "any deep understanding between two persons which results in the changing of personality."[3] However, Samuel Laycock suggests that Pastoral Care involves many activities which constitute "counseling" by ministers:

> The counselor must be aware that the techniques of counseling will necessarily vary with each situation, such as, (1) a pastoral call in a home where the chief object may be to establish good human relationships with parishioners and to express the church's interest in their welfare; (2) a call on a sick parishioner where comfort and support may be the chief objectives; (3) the comforting of the bereaved; (4) the giving of information as to where a parishioner may get the help he needs; (5) referring a parishioner to other professional people—psychiatrist, doctor, lawyer, psychologist, social worker, teacher, or nurse; (6) helping people work through their problems in an interview or series of interviews.[4]

Note that "changing of personality" is not necessarily involved in each instance because there is a different emphasis here than in strictly psychological counseling. Pastoring calls for a wider, more holistic approach than clinical psychologists usually permit. It is entirely possible that "Pastoral Counseling" may consist of a chat over coffee after the Sunday sermon or a brief discussion in a supermarket parking lot with a worried father whose teenage daughter has announced she has a steady boyfriend and they want to plan marriage.

The common factor in psychological counseling is change must take place for growth; dealing with an unhealthy situation, the psychologist wants to help the counselee overcome his difficulties and make internal adjustments so he can live more effectively in the future. Psychologists try to *cure*.

However, the common factor in pastoral counseling is not the necessity for change, although change is both possible and desirable in all living, growing things. Some people need a hand to hold while they are hurting, and if the minister holds a hurting hand she is doing Pastoral Counseling without a word being exchanged. The pastor wants to walk with the counselee/parishioner as he treads the valley of the shadow or stumbles about in the darkness looking for light. Pastors try to *care*. At least one authority on pastoral counseling, Seward Hiltner, believes the role of the minister engaged in such caring/counseling can best be characterized as a kind of teaching ministry:

> The best word to characterize the attitude and approach of the pastor in counseling and precounseling pastoral work is "eductive." The pastor does not coerce, moralize, push, divert, or direct. Instead he attempts to lead out or draw out resources and strengths which can become operative only as they are helped to well up within the parishioner. The eductive approach implies an acceptance and understanding of what the parishioner is prepared to communicate, not in the sense of agreement but in receiving this as the material which must be examined if clarification is to be achieved. This approach is not passive. It does involve much mirroring of feelings expressed. But it also includes frequent definition and redefinition of the counseling situation. The counselor is a person, not a mere bit of machinery.[5]

Of course, there are similarities between psychological and pastoral counseling, especially if done in a sit-down, one-hour, appointment-at-the-office format. Although their techniques may be the same, the added dimension which religious counselors bring is the presence of the holy, representing the heritage of the Church that drifts backward through time to the primordial faith stories of our Bible. The author can testify that people seldom come to a pastor to discuss specifically religious problems. Surprisingly few walk in and say, *"I want to talk about God."* They come when they are hurting and need a friend, a shoulder to cry on, a person to help them put the pieces of their shattered lives back together.

But although religion is not the object of their quest, the pastor represents Christian faith to them, and this link is not to be dismissed lightly. People know that behind a pastor stands the unseen presence of God. Religion may not be not the topic but it is inescapably the backdrop against which pastoral counseling is done.

One further point on this first objection: Since people persist in seeking out religious professionals when they face problems, the question really isn't whether or not a minister will do pastoral counseling, it's whether he will be an effective pastoral counselor when that role falls upon him. Good pastoral counselors get training in those techniques which help them do their job. Courses in basic counseling skills are available everywhere. Although a course or two doesn't give students the right to hang up a shingle and charge $200 an hour for psycho-therapy, most mainline theological seminaries require courses in counseling of all candidates for their first professional degree.

Pastors need to know their limitations, too. One of the functions of good pastoring, listed by Laycock, is to make referrals when the presenting problem exceeds our professional abilities. The author has done this several times, and never regretted the decision to refer.

SECOND OBJECTION: GOAL IS TO LET CHRIST-WITHIN EMERGE

At first glance this appears a powerful counter-argument, especially against long-term counseling. Perhaps chatting about problems over the hood of a car in the parking lot or even sitting down for a session or two in organized counseling could be conducive to spiritual growth. But if we engage in weeks or even months of in-depth counseling aren't we losing sight of the primary goal of Christian Truth teaching, which is empowerment of the individual by helping him release his inner divinity?

To demonstrate the validity of this complaint about long-term counseling one would have to argue that *fewer* sessions are better at promoting spiritual maturity. There have been no studies which indicate that abandoning counselees after two or three sessions does anything except lighten the caseload of the counselor. Conversely, Lyle Schaller's research shows that long-term involvement tends to increase the effectiveness of the leader in reaching/teaching his people.[6]

Even if we accept the premise that a primary teaching goal of Christian Truth ministry is to educe divinity from humanity, the likelihood exists that some persons will need only brief encounters with the teacher/pastor while others may require much more one-to-one soul-coaching. Actually, the analogy of a coach working with a team is wholly appropriate when looking for models to understand pastor-parishioner relationships. The coach may not have the talent that his players display—he is hired to help others play the game, not on his ability to score touchdowns or hit home runs. Any honest pastor will admit that there are members of his "team" (congregation) who have more spiritual savvy than he does, but he is their leader because of his special skills as a leader, not because he is the most spiritually advanced member on the rolls.

The coach teaches the whole team, meets with groups of players who have special skills/needs, and offers personal guidance to athletes struggling with their performance. Sometimes a single session will improve the player's technique so radically that he needs nothing more: the coach has shown him how to release his hidden potential, and he seizes the new insight like a wide receiver racing for the end zone with the football.

Other players need more help, not because they lack talent but because their technique is flawed due to bad habits and just plain ignorance. These the coach will need to see regularly for a while, offering his expertise as they struggle to develop their potential. Of course, the athletic coach has an option which no pastor could exercise in that he can dismiss players who refuse or are unable to improve themselves. Clergy heed the rules laid down by the greatest player-coach of all, Jesus Christ, and drop no one from the squad regardless of how frustrating the task of coaching them becomes.

The key difference between counseling and coaching is that the coach is free to give advice whereas the counselor who wants to be effective strictly adheres to the eductive game plan. Counseling is not telling people what they ought to do or think. In the military, a system with which the author has some degree of   familiarity, there is an unfortunate misuse of the word "counseling" which gives it a rather abusive connotation, when a sergeant takes a soldier aside and says, "Come here, boy; I'm gone counsel you!" It also can mean the military member has been officially advised of what his proper conduct should be—"The soldier has been counseled about his duty requirements in this situation."

Modern, person-centered counseling operates from principles which oblige the counselor to function as an enabler, a person who reflects with the counselee about the matters they are discussing. Another good model for understanding non-directive techniques, especially marriage counseling, is also drawn from sports: the counselor as *referee*. In this capacity she functions as ruleskeeper of the game, ready to blow the whistle if either side refuses to play fair, either during the face-to-face sessions or outside the pastor's office. A good referee is inconspicuous, letting the team members play the game, only interceding when absolutely necessary to keep them within agreed boundaries. A good pastoral counselor provides a safe arena for people to solve their own problems, which interfaces with the clergyperson's heartfelt desire to care for all parties involved while letting the Divine-within provide each with healing energy for growth and change. Sometimes, that takes more than one or two sessions.

THIRD OBJECTION: DEPENDENCIES

But if more sessions are required, what about the last complaint, i.e., that long-term counseling creates dependencies and this flies in the face of our goals to educe divinity from humanity? The most honest response to this is, "Right."

Some people need to establish a trusting relationship so desperately that counselors do serve as a crutch for a period of time. There is nothing wrong with a crutch if a person has suffered a broken leg; there is nothing wrong with an emotional leaning-post if some part of our inner life is broken. Who has not gone to a friend in time of trouble or grief? Did we expect our friend would solve our problems? No. All we wanted was a friend to listen and to care.

Humans are incontrovertibly dependent on each other, from before we are born until we exit this mortal existence. Even Jesus Christ needed two parents to get started (or at least one, if we take biblical parthenogenesis literally). Our dependencies begin as soon as we suck in our first breath of air to cry for nourishment and do not end until a handful of friends and survivors carry our bodies to the grave. There is nothing wrong with this fact of human existence: who would want to live in a world where each person was a self-subsisting island? It may be *more* blessed to give, but it is blessed to receive, too.

What people should avoid is unhealthy dependencies, utilitarian relationships based on loveless symbiosis instead of loving cooperation and care. There is a sense in which counseling can degenerate into such an unwholesome reliance, especially if money changes hands for the counselor's efforts. This is not a plea for volunteerism in counseling ministries. Although well-trained, volunteer counselors can be a vital asset to the local church, there is no substitute for professionalism in ministries as complex as today's parish program. However, ministers who receive payment for their counseling services need to be aware of the trap of commercialization—the person feels he is buying mental/spiritual health and the only effort required is writing a check.

The opposite danger occurs when the parishioner does not pay a fee for counseling. All his life he has equated cost with quality, so when nothing is charged nothing is expected. Most churches have some kind of written policy explaining fees, love offering standards, or a statement of what is expected of the counselee in exchange for no-fee services. These stipulations may sound crudely businesslike, but the lack of clearly defined guidelines communicates disorderliness and an unprofessional attitude which does little to comfort the person seeking help. Also, many people simply do not know if they should pay the minister, give a love offering, or just plop some extra cash into the collection plate the next Sunday.

Established guidelines—even if no fee is expected—will answer those questions with a minimum of embarrassment to the parishioner. Church boards and ministers usually negotiate these matters when drawing up clergy contracts.

Short-term dependencies which occur during longer-term counseling, then, are not necessarily bad. At least one well-known psychiatrist, Dr. William Glasser, believes it is absolutely imperative that all people develop and maintain a trusting relationship with at least one significant other. In *Reality Therapy*, the name Glasser gave the school he founded, counselors encourage their counselees to form just this kind of trust-bond. Aloofness and cool detachment are not considered helpful. Warmth, understanding, and concern are the cornerstones of effective treatment.

If wholeness and mental/spiritual health are the goal, certainly long-term counseling must be considered an appropriate response to problems which are not easily dismissed. Ministers today are faced with parishioners who are more likely to seek help for deeper, more entrenched psychological/spiritual dilemmas than were brought to the attention of earlier generations of clergy.

In the first year of his/her ministry, it will not be unusual for a clergyperson to hear problems which defy the imagination of daytime television scriptwriters. During the author's first year in full-time ministry, these were some of the actual problems brought to light by walk-in counselees: Pregnant girlfriends (note the plural), abortion as a *fait accompli*, a history of shop-lifting, compulsive drinking/overeating, wife and child abuse, incest (both victim and perpetrator), adultery (caught in the act), homosexuality, compulsive bad-check writing, habitual lying, raging self-hatred, nightmares, impotence, inability to trust men/women, white hatred of blacks and other minorities, hatred of whites by blacks and other minorities, terror of going to hell, incessant fighting between married couples, divorce, premarital worries, rape, and suicidal gestures...

If a counselor tries to deal with problems like these by a three-session schedule consisting of pep-talks about the person's Divine-human qualities, he ought to turn in his ordination and open a lemonade stand at the airport, because that is the degree of involvement he is seeking. He won't be able to do his job as pastor of a congregation of struggling human beings.

Perfection is a little ways down the track for most of us, and people tend to get themselves tangled in the most incredible webs of difficulties along the way. A fundamental premise of Pastoral Care is that the pastor must *care*. This kind of caring requires involvement, and that means providing long-term pastoral counseling for those who need it.

Not every parishioner seeking long-term help will need it, but some will. Providing a multi-faceted counseling program is absolutely essential if a church wants to meet its obligation to be the body of Christ in the modern age. There is no other effective way to minister to the real needs of people today.

WHO DOES THE COUNSELING? WHAT KIND IS BEST?

Having said all that, we must now retreat somewhat from this rather Draconian pronouncement about non-counseling pastors by clarifying the role of the minister as one who *provides* these functions of ministry without necessarily doing it all himself/herself. Frankly, some pastors would be better off doing little or no counseling because they have little or no talent for it. There is nothing wrong with a person entering the pastoral ministry who has no aptitude for or interest in counseling, if he makes sure someone with the talent and energy to counsel is available to his parishioners.

The author believes we clergy should openly admit that omnipotence is later in the program for most of us. There are special skills involved in ministry, and wise pastors know they can hardly meet everyone's needs. So how can those ministers who have little talent for writing still provide a decent newsletter? By finding a frustrated journalist in the flock and turning him/her loose to create a monthly masterpiece. People will read the newsletter and say, "Isn't our minister good with words!"

How does the pastor who hates home visits get the job done? Empowering a cohort of energetic folk who love to chit-chat over coffee and will be happy to call on every member in the calendar year as the official representative of the church.

There are some jobs which the professional minister must perform, like it or not. If he leans toward *"not,"* he should locate someone to help as he works through the church financial statements, makes hospital visits, or does whatever it is he must do but doesn't enjoy doing.

Some of the more effective counseling ministries are operated by trained lay ministers or other helping professionals who work out of the local church. In this model the minister serves as senior professional advisor who coordinates a staff of counselors. Large Protestant congregations—such as Robert Schuller's Crystal Cathedral—employ a staff of full-time professional counselors who may be psychologists, pastoral counselors, or even psychiatrists.

Dr. Schuller gave up counseling years ago when his congregations grew so large that he could no longer find time to perform all the functions of ministry personally. However, he still provides pastoral care for his flock by supervising his staff of professionals.

Not every style of counseling will work in every church community, but at least two popular methods of doing Pastoral Care seem to interface nicely with the theology and worldview of Metaphysical Christianity: *Reality Therapy* and *Transactional Analysis* (called *"T. A."*). Although we do not have adequate space to provide an in-depth description of these two counseling approaches, a plethora of books is available on each.[7]

More importantly, they are simple enough to be employed by clergy or trained lay counselors without requiring that the helping person return to school for a Ph.D. and several thousand hours of supervised practice, which is the requirement for psychotherapists in most states.

SHEPHERD'S "RULE OF DUMB"

But let's get one fact very clear: *Pastoral Care is not psychotherapy.* It is care by a pastor or a representative of the Christian community. If a counselee exhibits symptoms of extreme emotional disorder, the only responsible action for the religious professional or para-professional to take is to refer that person to a qualified psychiatrist or mental health clinic, immediately! These folks are not hard to spot; your gut-instincts will tell you that the person sitting in the chair next to you is totally out of touch with reality.

For example, if a pastoral counselor has even the faintest suspicion that the counselee is suicidal, that person should be referred to a crisis intervention center or suicide hotline. If the counselee reports hearing voices, seeing visions, or any other obviously delusional tendencies, this is also a sign that the pastor is out of his league with this case.

I suggest that all pastors follow Shepherd's "Rule of Dumb." Forget your intellectual ego. Don't take chances. When in doubt, refer—refer—refer! Send anybody in whom you have the slightest hint of deep distress to competent medical facilities. When the clinic calls and says the person really didn't need hospitalization, the pastor can breathe a sigh of relief for being "dumb but safe" on this one.

ESSENTIAL INGREDIENTS FOR PASTORAL CARE

So far our discussion has concentrated on pastoral counseling. However, the comprehensive definition we gave for Pastoral Care calls for much more. Education is a major part of any program aimed at helping people "grow in their inter-personal skills" and "emotional/spiritual health." Most Truth churches do an excellent job in this, offering a bevy of classes and workshops to foster growth and a sense of community.

We must briefly mention Home Visitation, touched on above. It is probably the single biggest headache for the pastor, yet the greatest method for getting to know her congregation and enlisting their support. Here, again, the wise clergyperson knows better than to try to visit personally every member on the books during the first few months of the new pastorate. With all the energetic folks nipping at our heels, the minister has a powerful tool to multiply ourselves a dozen times and make many more home visits than we could alone.

Quite a few churches hold training sessions and then engage in a comprehensive program during which every member is regularly visited at home. Those home sessions are most effective when two-way communication happens. The pastor or church representative listens to the suggestions, complaints, and hopes of the visited member before presenting the "party line" on behalf of the congregation and pastor. Sometimes the visitor hands the member a short form to complete which asks for creative suggestions, provides space to request help for special needs (marriage counseling, etc.), and allows the parishioner to volunteer for a laundry-list of church activities and opportunities for ministry.

When the pastor and the church board sift through these records they will get a powerful indication of how they are doing and what needs are not being met. Of course, plans must include follow-up to meet those needs or the whole process will generate mistrust. ("They asked me what I wanted; I told them, but nothing happened!")

Another aspect of Pastoral Care is *"to support people in times of crisis and difficulty such as hospitalization, health challenge, or personal loss."* The author knows a military chaplain who was assigned to the 101st Division when the awful crash of that airliner at Gander, Newfoundland, took the lives of hundreds of soldiers from that famous unit. The men on that plane were a large chunk of the community of Fort Campbell, Kentucky. Not only the families of the soldiers but literally thousands of people at the fort went through the grief process. Store keepers, neighbors, teachers at the on-post dependent schools, commissary workers, postmen, military police, fire fighters, clerks at the headquarters—the loss affected them all. Even the surrounding civilian communities went through an equally tough time of trial. Just imagine what it would be like if you lived in a coal mining town and several hundred husbands and fathers died in a mining disaster. That is what happened at Fort Campbell.

The chaplains were, by all accounts, magnificent. They counseled literally thousands of people, some formally in their offices and many more informally as they moved about the stunned, grieving post. A force of less than twenty Army chaplains performed over one hundred and eighty military funerals at locations from Europe to Puerto Rico to as far away as Japan. It was a giant, complex, mind-boggling task in pastoral ministry. For weeks the ministers saw little of their own families as they went about holding hands and helping people cry through their anguish, anger, and grief.

It is our profound hope that no minister will ever have to deal with grief on that magnitude, but we can see from the aftermath of the Gander crash that pastoral ministry is not optional for the clergy in times of acute distress for his/her parishioners. It is at once an absolute necessity and a high calling, a terrible experience which no one wishes to face but which no pastor would ever shirk from meeting with faith in the God who walks with us through the valley of the shadows as well as the spring sunshine.

Tonight when you say your prayers, include a prayer of thanksgiving for men and women of the clergy who have walked such a lonesome valley with hurting souls in their charge. They are everywhere.

Equally important and sometimes overlooked are those day-by-day instances whereby the clergyperson makes herself *"accessible to people through the ministering person's presence in church activities"* as well as more conspicuous availability at the church during *"regular office hours."*

The *Ministry of Presence* ranks second only to Preaching in showing parishioners what their minister does for them. In the armed forces, chaplains leave their offices and venture into the work areas of their soldiers to greet them in the Name of the Lord. The chaplain might stroll through the motor pool during maintenance time, walking from truck to truck, chatting with soldiers about upcoming field duty, inspections, new policies, trouble spots at work and home, personal and religious problems.

Civilian clergy, who might only see their parishioners once a week, do not enjoy the daily contact which military chaplains share with their congregations. However, the pastor of a local church can maximize his visibility by a pro-active *Ministry of Presence.* Here are a few miscellaneous ideas:

1. <u>DROP IN</u>. When the ladies' group holds its Thursday morning prayer meeting, the minister drops in for prayer as a participant, not as the leader. If he does this once every other month—or more if time permits—he has established a "presence."

2. <u>OVERBOOK THE CENTER</u>. If the choir practices on a weeknight, the clever pastor schedules important, ongoing committee meetings at the same time. This will frustrate some members because they won't be able to participate in two simultaneous events, which is exactly what the pastor wants. Conflicts in the Center schedule say, *"We're busy!"* to members, establishing an activity-consciousness which translates into zeal. Those members who cannot be at both activities are invited to help find someone to fulfill the other role, multiplying involvement in the life of the church.

It also doesn't hurt church members to see the pastor at work in the evening. This kind of informal contact increases opportunities to approach the minister with personal problems without calling for an appointment. Many people just need a word or two of support and will not want to "bother" their minister with something so trivial by making a full-fledge office-hours appointment.

3. <u>THE PASTOR IS IN</u>. However, the more opportunities pastors provide for the people to speak with them, the heavier the counseling load will be. This means they must be willing to set up regular office hours and make appointments or recruit and train qualified lay counselors to handle referrals from these informal encounters. Not all the counseling has to be done by the senior minister, we have said, but the ranking religious professional must supervise the staff to insure the job gets done. That means an office schedule people can depend upon.

4. <u>GROWTH GROUPS</u> offer an exciting alternative which blend the best features of teaching and counseling. The Growth Group meets to talk about problems, challenges, and questions members might face on a common subject such as parenting, alcoholism, keeping love alive (couples), health challenges, spirituality issues, or virtually any other topics which combine a need for learning with a need for group sharing to affect growth.

If the pastor initiates a Growth Group every six months, walking with each group for about a year and then turning it over to group members to sponsor and facilitate, soon there will strong little knots of people meeting at the church and sustaining each other in Christian fellowship, the very heart of *ekklesia-koinonia*. The pastor need only drop by occasionally to renew acquaintances and see if he can meet any needs which are beyond the ken of the group. Again, many good books on this kind of ministry are available from Protestant and Catholic publishers as well as secular works on group counseling.[8]

5. <u>SOCIAL EVENTS</u> are another maximum-exposure time for the clergy. In our study of Outreach Evangelism (Chapter 16), we noted that a potluck dinner with light

programming could be the local church's most effective outreach tool. This also applies to the minister's own in-house program for outreach (in-reach?). Whether he sits down for apple pie a la mode with Mrs. Zuchovitch or a plate of chili mac with Mr. Dohner, the pastor is the pastor.

6. SHOOT THAT BULL. Newcomers to the parish ministry often complain about how their daily routine is interrupted by people who drop in unannounced at the office or who phone for no particular reason but to "shoot the bull." Veterans know that wise pastors never let a bull go unshot.

In those casual encounters the parishioner tests his minister to see if his particular bull catches the eye of the matador. Sensitive clergy know to listen carefully for off-hand remarks, jesting, and other signals that the person is in trouble. Sometimes a parishioner will laugh and say, "Yeah, Reverend, I ought to come see you myself one of these days! Maybe you could tell me how to keep my wife from complaining." Red flags ought to wave when that kind of remark is made, even light-heartedly.

Something about our society makes it difficult for some people—especially men—to ask for help, but allows them to accept unsolicited assistance. This kind of person will drop all sorts of hints, often cloaked in self-critical humor: "With my luck, I'll probably find a job but get fired for running home to nurse the baby," or "My husband is a real dream—a nightmare!" or "I don't drink any more since I bought a funnel," or "Hey, Reverend, how do you file for divorce in this state?" Gallows humor is often a tip-off that something else is likely going on.

There are jokers in every crowd, but some people use humor to surface their anxieties in a way that signals for help but gives them room to retreat if someone presses too hard. "What, divorce my wife? I was only kidding! I'd never consider divorce. Murder, perhaps." If a clergyperson cultivates a good ear and a notebook-memory, jotting down who said what at the Christmas party, she can follow up on those seemingly stray remarks later in private conversation with the persons. One minister known to the author refers to church socials as "hinting parties," an apt description.

7. CARING PERSONS REPRESENT GOD FOR OTHERS. A story was circulating when the author attended seminary which best describes Pastoral Care. A little boy was afraid of the dark, but his mother wanted to break him of the nightlight habit. After a few nights of relative success, a thunderstorm broke across the skies. Terrible flashes and crashes scared the little guy so much he ran to his parents' bedroom where he was comforted until the brief storm passed. Then Momma took him back to his dark room. When he implored her to turn on the nightlight she gently refused, saying, "Don't worry about being alone in the dark, honey. God loves you; He is here with you." The little boy replied, "I know, but I want somebody with skin on."

That is the objective of Pastoral Care: to be God's love with skin on.

LIMITED GOALS

Pastoral Care has limited goals. Although similar methods may be employed, counseling ministry is not psychotherapy. Home and hospital visitation is not deep involvement but an attempt to get to know as many parishioners as possible. Deeper commerce between ministers and individual members will happen only as these peripheral, touch-and-go encounters bring people a taste of church life and fellowship. The final choice always rests with the parishioner, but if we clergy offer a cup of cold water in Christ's Name to those who thirst we have done our part, fulfilled our calling. Just as Jesus is the Wayshower to God, the Christian clergyperson must be a Wayshower to Jesus Christ. It is a humbling, staggering, exhilarating task.

Henri Nouwen, a Catholic priest much beloved by Protestant clergy for his writing and teaching, has become the unofficial spokesperson for Pastoral Care. Father Nouwen offers our closing words on this crucial aspect of ministry:

A Chasten leader is not a leader because he announces a new idea and tries to convince others of its worth; he is a leader because he faces the world with eyes full of expectation, with the expertise to take away the veil that covers its hidden potential. Christian leadership is called ministry precisely to express that in the service of others new life can be brought about. It is this service which gives eyes to see the flower breaking through the cracks in the street, ears to hear a word of forgiveness muted by hatred and hostility, and hands to feel the new life under the cover of death and destruction.[9]

CHECK YOUR KNOWLEDGE

1. Explain/Identify: *Pastoral Care, pastoral counseling, Shepherd's "Rule of Dumb," growth groups, home visitation, office hours, ministry of presence.*

2. According to the text, what are the essential ingredients in a comprehensive program of Pastoral Care?

3. What biblical justification exists, if any, for Pastoral Care? Give several examples.

4. How does Pastoral Counseling differ from psychological counseling?

5. List the main three objections to Pastoral Care and briefly summarize the author's response to each.

6. TRUE/FALSE: The pastor must personally counsel his/her people for an effective program of Pastoral Care? Explain.

QUESTIONS FOR DISCUSSION

1. Discuss the definition of Pastoral Care given in the text. Are all the elements necessary? What other forms of Pastoral Care can you list?

2. How involved in counseling should the laity become? What can be done by trained lay volunteers?

3. Discuss three objections to Pastoral Care and the author's response. Where do you stand?

4. Is long-term counseling appropriate for Metaphysical Christians? Explain.

5. What is the difference between caring and curing? Which should be the goal of a ministering person?

6. How effective is the Pastoral Care at your church? What could be done to improve it? What can you do?

NOTES

1. Henri J. M. Nouwen, *The Wounded Healer* (Garden City, NY: Doubleday/Image Books, 1979), pp. 71-72.

2. Edward B. Pusey, trans., *The Confessions of Saint Augustine* (NY: Pocket Books, Inc., 1952), p. 45.

3. Rollo May, *The Art of Counseling* (Nashville, TN: Abingdon, 1939), p. 120.

4. Samuel R. Laycock, *Pastoral Counseling for Mental Health* (Nashville, TN: Abingdon, 1961), p. 16.

5. Seward Hiltner, *The Counselor in Counseling* (Nashville, TN: Abingdon, 1952), pp. 10-11.

6. Schaller, Mirror, p. 142.

7. Raymond J. Corsini, *Current Psychotheraphies* (Itasca, IL: F. E. Peacock Publishers, Inc., 1979), p. 316.

8. IBID.

9. Nouwen, Wounded Healer, p. 75.

MYSTICAL CHRISTIANITY AND POP-FAD SPIRITUALITY

Chapter Nineteen

Certain persons called "masters" have forged ahead of the race in their understanding and use of some of the powers of mind and have in personal egotism set up little kingdoms and put themselves on thrones. These so-called "masters" of occult brotherhoods are attracting susceptible minds away from the "straight and narrow path" and leading them to believe that there is a short cut into the kingdom. Jesus described the situation forcibly and clearly in Matthew 24:24:"For there shall arise false Christs, and false prophets, and shall show great signs and wonders; so as to lead astray, if possible, even the elect."

—Charles Fillmore, *Jesus Christ Heals,* pp. 19-20

Those familiar with the work of Charles Fillmore realize the above passage is not written in his normal tone of voice. Fillmore's admirers might even be shocked by the flagrantly combative language this kindly, broad-minded man selected when discussing teachers of the occult, especially those *"so-called 'masters'"* who by their *"personal egotism"* are trying to seduce *"susceptible minds away from the straight and narrow path"* of real spiritual growth.

As one teenager in my church said after reading the above quotes, *"Wow, Charles, chill out! Who's he mad at?"*

Mr. Fillmore, by all accounts, was a man who breathed charity for opposing viewpoints and allowed people to find their own path to Truth. He was zealous but tolerant, committed but open-minded, certain of Truth but equally certain that not everyone saw Truth's mountaintop from the same vantage point.

Here was a man of whom Emmet Fox could say:

I look upon Charles Fillmore as being among the prophets...Charles Fillmore is one of the great men of this generation...I am one of his spiritual children.[1]

Why this scathing rebuke of those who teach occult ways if "Papa Charley" was so lenient and forbearing? The only possible answer is that Charles Fillmore—religious liberal though he was—knew that every belief system must set limits. Some ideas take people from healthy pursuit of Truth into shallow, pop-fad spirituality.

These excursions to the brink of absurdity may excite the seeker temporarily, but they abandon the long path to Christ-consciousness. Some are harmless, merely diversions from the work of growth. Others are not so innocent, because they seek to negate Divine Ideas by controlling the Cosmos or by claiming to be Ultimate Authority when they are really just opinions.

That's also why Mr. Fillmore, unlike some of his teaching contemporaries, insisted that he received no special revelation from On High. Truth need not claim Divine origin to exonerate its teachings; Truth is self-validating.

FROM ELITISM TO ANTINOMINANISM: A SHORT HOP

Earlier in our study we discussed the dangers of elitism and antinomianism without showing a causal relationship between them. Looking at these two problems side-by-side it becomes obvious they are first cousins. If a religious group feels it has a unique charter from the Absolute (*elitism*) it very often begins to believe that principles which restrict behavior in "unenlightened" people do not apply to the Elect (*antinomianism*).

Israel knew this temptation intimately; time and again her special status as the Chosen people of Yahweh gave her leaders a sense of superiority and infallibility. Listen to the sheer fantasy of Psalm Two as its author imagines how highly the Lord regards the "anointed" king of Jerusalem and Mount Zion, the hill on which the Temple stands:

> Why do the nations conspire, and the peoples plot in vain? The kings of the earth set themselves, and the rulers take counsel together, against the Lord and his anointed...He who sits in the heavens laughs; the Lord has them in derision. Then he will speak to them in his fury, saying, "I have set my king on Zion, my holy hill."[2]

Time and again the prophets had to remind Israel that it was their steadfast love the Lord wanted; their special status came because He chose them to reveal His great purposes for all humanity through their history. They were not His pets who could do no wrong. Israel was chosen for a ministry, and that high calling carried with it an awful responsibility.

God has no favorites. The oral tradition recorded in Genesis recalls that as far back as the time of Abraham the Hebrews were aware their "chosen" status carried with it a missionary mandate to share the Good News with all humanity, to be the vessel from which the healing oil of God's Truth would pour out upon people of all races and religions:

> Now the Lord said to Abram, "Go from your father's house to the land that I will show you. And I will make of you a great nation, and I will bless you, and make your name great, so that you will be a blessing. I will bless those who bless you, and him who curses

you I will curse; and by you all the families of the earth shall bless themselves."[3]

No hint of Elitism can be found in this simple calling of a people to serve God, to be a prism for Divine light to flow to all humanity. The Lutheran-written Bethel Bible Series takes as its primary image from this text. On the wall over the main fireplace at Bethel's world headquarters outside Madison, Wisconsin, hangs a huge hooked-rug mural of the white light of God's Truth hitting a prism and breaking into the rainbow as it spreads out to all the nations. A Bethel Bible graduate was so impressed by the imagery of Genesis 12 that she spent countless hours creating an original rug design based on the symbol of God's light passing through the Judaeo-Christian prism.

Abraham was blessed to be a blessing, not to establish himself and his descendants as a ruling party to lord over the rest of mongrel humanity. God's kingdom has only one Ruler; all others are equal.

A more insidious form of Elitism arises when people believe they have a Special Revelation of Divine Truth. It is only a short hop from that kind of spiritual one-upsmanship to a full-blown Antinomianism.

The process works like this: *"We know our ideas are given specially to us, therefore we enjoy a special status before God. Our special status raises us head-and-shoulders above the rabble and renders ordinary moral/ethical injunctions invalid for us. What is morally wrong for 'normal' people like you doesn't apply to more 'advanced' spiritual beings like us; so we can do things which for other, less developed people would be 'sinful.' Far beyond those unsophisticated levels, we can do as we please without suffering any kind of consequences."*

That is Antinomianism, and it ran rampant in the early Church because quite a few people took Paul seriously when he told them that Christians no longer needed to follow the Law. As the news breaks of what Paul is teaching, we can almost hear them thinking: *"Oh, boy! We're not under the Law but are under grace and freedom? It's party time!"* Paul quickly fired off a flurry of letters which basically said, *"Whoa! That' ain't what I meant."* Here is a brief excerpt from his response to flagrant Antinomianism in the church at Corinth, already known as Sin City on the Aegean:

> Do you not know that the unrighteous will not inherit the kingdom of God? Do not be deceived; neither the immoral, nor idolaters, nor adulterers, nor sexual perverts, nor thieves, nor the greedy, nor drunkards, nor revilers, nor robbers will inherit the kingdom of God..."All things are lawful for me," but not all things are helpful. "All things are lawful for me," but I will not be enslaved by anything.[4]

In recent times, several quasi-religious movements have demonstrated the danger of unchecked Antinomianism. The most flagrant example came to light when the Rev. James Jones's nine hundred followers committed mass suicide in Guyana. Jones began his ministry well within the confines of orthodox Protantism but quickly factored himself out of the Christian faith by progressively more bizarre teachings and behavior. He insisted that his personal authority superseded all *Scripture, Tradition, Experience, and Reason.*

Throwing away the Bible, he preached on his own authority without regard for the larger Christian community. Harboring long-seething hostilities toward the organized Church, Jones set himself up as a false Christ and compelled stupefied followers to worship him. He allowed himself whatever sexual favors he wanted and obeyed no moral restraints other than his own whim, taking wives from members of the congregation and justifying his actions by virtue of his special status as God's Chosen. Soon, he was claiming the full rights and privileges of unique divinity, a status to which even Jesus Christ never aspired. When his flock gulped poison in an act of solidarity with this madman—mothers squirted the lethal drink into the mouths of their babies—the world rightly cringed in horror.

And would cringe again, when the fanatical David Koresh led his Branch Davidians to mass, fiery suicide at Waco, Texas. And again, when the Heaven's Gate UFO cultists committed mass suicide in California. So profound was the anti-religious backlash that several religious organizations issued disclaimers. For example, Unity School published a four-page booklet addressing the Jonestown deaths. James Dillet Freeman begins that essay: "Since the suicidal deaths in Guyana of the members of the People's Temple, Unity has received a number of letters asking, 'Is Unity a cult?' "[5]

It is a question sparked by fear of the unknown. The answer, of course, is a hearty, "No!" Like all Metaphysical Christian churches, Unity has remained firmly grounded in the Christian heritage, in particular due to the aggressiveness of co-founders Charles and Myrtle Fillmore, who maintained their ties to biblical roots and steadfastly refused to allow the lunatic fringe to capture and control the work they loved so much. Charles Fillmore even took Unity out of the International New Thought Alliance (INTA) for awhile, precisely because he felt at that time the New Thought movement was wandering too far afield from its Christian moorings. Fillmore advocated practical Christian teachings for modern men and women; he would not tolerate the movement's deterioration into a training ground for cultists. And he made certain his "followers" were not following him at all, but the teachings of Jesus Christ.

Practical Christianity today reflects long centuries of mystical Christian practices, which are only recently emerging into the light after a long hiatus of neglect. Although others may choose different paths leading to other windows to the Truth, Metaphysical Christianity stands by the light we have received through the Jesus Christ window.

ELIMINATION: A DIVINE-HUMAN POWER

Any religious system must include some kind of sorting/selecting process to weed out dangerous or unhelpful concepts. We have endeavored to establish criteria in this ongoing study which could serve such a function. If systematic theology is an attempt to make everything fit together in a coherent whole based on the guidelines one establishes for doing theology, then part of the system must include a way of identifying and eliminating unsatisfactory elements. We have done this as we go along, discussing ideas critically as we consider the various departments of Christian theology from our mystical/metaphysical perspective.

But as well as weeding the garden, a good program of religious reflection does not hesitate to fence off the area by deciding what belongs inside the faith and what falls beyond the garden wall. There is nothing wrong with fences as long as they are not arbitrary or designed to shut people off from commerce with other people. Robert Frost said, "Good fences make good neighbors," even while admitting, "Something there is that doesn't love a wall."[6]

Something there is about religious liberals, Metaphysical Christians included, that also does not love a wall. However, for the good of the garden and the mutual respect of people on both sides of an issue, some boundary lines must be drawn. Liberal-minded Charles Fillmore did not hesitate to fence out the occult fringe. Jesus Christ showed endless sympathy for the afflicted and the spiritually poor but held the religious leaders accountable for their excesses. One cannot read the New Testament without hearing the stern rebukes the Master leveled at Scribes, Pharisees, and Saducees, many of whom were lawyers and doctors of theological discourse. Jesus was gentle with the people but ferocious with those who, as Mr. Fillmore said, "in personal egotism set up little kingdoms and put themselves on thrones."

We have struggled to include as many diverse elements inside the garden of Christian faith as possible. But there stands the wall, serving its purpose. Our neighbors beyond the wall may be good neighbors, but we must tend the garden. Thus we are obligated to examine critically where we place the wall, to be sure we have not fenced out anyone who does not want to remain beyond our maximum-range definition of Christianity—and to inspect the new growth within the garden to see if flowers or weeds are sprouting. This requires the judicious application of the Divine-human power Mr. Fillmore called *Renunciation* or *Elimination*. As we approach this task, two dangers must be avoided.

ELITISM & ANTINOMIANISM REVISITED

On one extreme, stands an Elitist theology which says, *"Only those who believe exactly what I believe are saved."* So much of this One-Way thinking parades itself in public these days via the electronic media so that legitimate Christian theology is unknown to most people and the fundamentalist fringe presents itself as the only Christian Church. This kind of Christianity wants to uproot every flower in the garden which does not match its color, shape and petal arrangement. It is exactly this kind of narrow-mindedness which prompted the Apostle Paul to write chapters 12, 13, and 14 of I Corinthians. Reading these chapters in sequence is quite an eye-opener.

Elitism is legalistic, judgmental, and self-righteous. The front-page scandals about television evangelist Jim Bakker's resignation after confessing to a casual sexual encounter a few years ago demonstrates precisely the danger in Elitist theology. Well-known electronic evangelists made outrageous remarks on national TV and in newspaper accounts about how Bakker was now unfit to be in the ministry. Instead of seizing the opportunity to demonstrate God's forgiving love, they reacted predictably: ostracism, condemnation, self-righteousness. One-Way thinking produces Elitism.

But if the danger exists that we might fence the garden so snugly that only one row of monochrome flowers will bloom, a corollary danger looms in theologies which lean toward Antinomianism. We have discussed the need to stand for some religious beliefs if we are to call ourselves a community of faith. The very act of affirming a religious truth means disavowing others. If a man decides to become a Roman Catholic he has decided against Judaism, Hinduism, and Lutheranism. He need not find fault with those faiths to see they are not for him. However, if he did not see difficulties with those other faiths, by what standard could he call himself a believer?

The Japanese language has no direct way to say, *"You're wrong."* The verb they use to express the concept "to be incorrect" is *chigau,* which literally means *"to be different."* Japanese thinking recognizes differences without embarrassing people by proclaiming what's right and wrong. *"Chigaimasu!"* the instructor said when he looked at my feeble attempt to write Japanese. *"It's different!"* He was right, too. My crudely scrawled Kanji characters, convoluted grammar, and misunderstood vocabulary were all different from the Japanese language. My choices were "different." No traditional Japanese Sensei would tell me what an American instructor would have said, *"Sorry, chum. That's wrong, wrong, wrong!"*

We choose based on our different way of looking at life, and there is nothing as absolutely required by life as choosing. To live is to choose; we are inescapably bound to decide this or that, left or right, stop or go.

Freedom requires ineluctable risk. Some options will be *chigaimasu*—different from what works for us. When we encounter such ideas, we have walked to the far boundary of our religious properties, peering over the wall into a different land. Religious communities necessarily define their boundaries by the dynamics of Scripture/Tradition/Experience/Reason. Even those faiths which reject the process of faith-building must follow its basic format in order to reject that process. If we should say, in a great swoop of Antinomian generosity, *"We have no standards of belief. One may believe anything he chooses and be a Christian!",* we have just eliminated all distinctions and rendered the term *Christian* meaningless.

Inordinate openness has dissolved all identity.

Nor are we left with a big, unitive system which moves toward Oneness; without a Christ-concept there is no progress to Christ-consciousness. With a Christ-concept we must decide, evaluate, eliminate, choose. Everything outside of Metaphysical Christianity is *chigaimasu* for us.

These two extremes—Elitism and Antinomianism—must be held in tension as outer markers of our methodology. Somewhere in the middle we shall find the working principles which allow us maximum freedom to choose/eliminate while remaining as open-minded as possible. In any case, the self-righteousness of Elitism and the paralysis of Antinomianism must be avoided.

AGENDA ITEMS: THE PARANORMAL

What link is there among the various categories of Pop-Fad Spirituality which allows them to be grouped together? Almost any anthology of the paranormal will include widely divergent subjects, from Astral Projection to the Zodiac. Some central concept must unite these disparate topics. We suggest the very word *para-normal* provides a clue: the experiences generally listed under this heading describe "beyond-regular" events (Greek, *para*: "beyond;" Latin, *normalis*: "made according to the square," hence *regular*).

Flying Saucers have little in common with spirit-communications, but both qualify as categories beyond the regular flow of events for most people. Although a significant number of people indicate they have experienced something in their lives which they would classify paranormal, the fact that we recognize these happenings as extraordinary makes it possible to speak meaningfully of paranormal encounters.

In the ancient world there was no such clear line between everyday reality and the paranormal. Life did not lend itself to compartmentalization; the supernatural was seen as the motivating force behind sickness, earthquake, sunrise, and rain. We have said that after the eighteenth century Enlightenment, when rationalism and empiricism took the place of super-naturalism and religious authority, humanity began looking for natural causes to everyday events. Still, there were some things which could not be rationally explained, mysteries which even the new sciences of astronomy, physics, biology, and chemistry could not express in Newtonian mathematics. God was supposed to operate in these "gaps" in human understanding, which preserved the supernatural quality of Divine activity.

When science came to a gap in its knowledge, such as origin of human life, Christian theology stepped in to assure people that God stood in those gaps exercising His omnipotent power in direct opposition to scientific principles. Clinging tenaciously to supernaturalism, theology found itself outside of reality looking in whenever science discovered natural explanations which filled one of the gaps.

Charles Darwin's work on evolution and the subsequent, massive documentation of basic evolutionist theory put organized religion on the defensive only because religious thinkers had tried to usurp the position of research scientists in defense of supernaturalist doctrines. Darwin didn't assault nineteenth century religion; it rallied for a *Charge of the Gap Brigade* and slammed into the walls of scientific realism.

No responsible scientist denies offhandedly that unexpected events may occur, but science must function as empirical investigation and there are some categories of human experience which do not lend themselves to scientific analysis. We discussed this in detail previously (Chapters 3 and 4), but a review of the basic, necessary agnosticism of empirical research was needed before we move on to consider ways to study paranormal phenomena.

There are six categories of Pop-Fad Spirituality which have wide appeal today: 1) *Special Revelations*, 2) *ESP*, 3) *Spiritism*, 4) *"Flying Saucer" Cults*, 5) *The Pseudo-Sciences* (Astrology, Numerology, and Palmistry), 6) *Occult Studies* (Crystals, Pyramids, Witchcraft).

Each has particular dangers for Metaphysical Christians, but rather than devote ourselves to a point-by-point analysis of each we shall concentrate on category #1 because of its relevance to fringe elements operating beyond the boundary of Christian faith but nonetheless attractive to some believers.

The differences between the claims of these groups and the mystical teachings of Christianity will become apparent; as we examine Special Revelations in detail we shall see the difficulties inherent in the paranormal for Christian theology.

However, before we delve too deeply into what shall be extended critical discussion of these phenomena, the Christian Truth student is entitled to know the author's bias in such matters. Frankly, I have been fascinated by paranormal studies from my earliest childhood. There is something exciting about parapsychology, possibilities of contact with extra-terrestrial life forms and the other categories grouped under this heading. Although a firm believer in empiricism, nothing excites me more than "new" discoveries which send the scientists scrambling back to their drawing boards, scratching their heads and muttering, *"How the heck do we explain this!"*

I have never had an encounter with overtly paranormal phenomena—my wife has, twice, and she is about as level-headed and conservative as a student of Practical Christianity can be—but there is no doubt in my mind that the huge volume of reports which describe these events points to some kind of phenomenon, or more likely series of phenomena, which are not yet understood but nonetheless true.

Having said that, let me hasten to add that I believe these occurrences, though fascinating, are utterly useless and potentially dangerous for Christian theology in general and Metaphysical Christianity in particular. No responsible parent would allow a child to play with firearms or explosives, yet there are quite probably unknown energies behind some phenomena which far surpass those forbidden items in their threat to the ignorant dabbler. Although I do not believe in any sort of magical power external of God—there is only One Presence and One Power in the Cosmos, God the Good, Omnipotent—however, there are ways of releasing the unseen energies of the Divine-human paradox in a way that does harm to the individual and displays disloyalty to God's goodness. Fire can cook our foods or roast our enemies alive, depending on the consciousness by which it is employed. Could not the same be true of paranormal phenomena?

Of course, this argument could be countered, *"Yes, but we need fire. Isn't the responsible use of psychic powers and responsible pursuit of extraordinary phenomena a legitimate endeavor?"* Like many questions of theological significance, the best answer is, *"Yes and no."*

Investigation of the paranormal is certainly legitimate for those qualified individuals who take the risks seriously. However, we are a long way from understanding psychic phenomena as comprehensively as we understand fire. Listen to what Emmet Fox, who was involved in scientific research of the paranormal, said about amateur efforts in the field:

> Do not dabble in psychic things. If you wish to investigate thoroughly and scientifically, well and good, but this will be the work of years, and will call for scientific conditions. The chief objection to the running after mediums that so many people practice is that this is really a running away from the responsibilities of this life.[7]

Our purpose in discussing these beliefs/practices is to honor our commitment to pursue Truth wherever it leads us, even if that means building a wall to separate what works for us from what we regard as meaningless or dangerous. Outside that wall are other ways of looking at the Cosmos. It is not our intent to say whether those other ways are correct or incorrect. For followers of Jesus Christ they are simply *chigaimasu*, different from Truth as we know it. Charles Fillmore wrote:

> The only safety from chaos is unity with God and His Son Jesus Christ, the head of every man. If we are not anchored to this supreme and immovable reality, we shall be exposed to the storms of mortal thought and shipwrecked on the rocks of materiality.[8]

SPECIAL REVELATIONS

In our study of Sacramental Theology (Chapter 11) we discussed two views of how humanity knows about God, *Discovery* and *Revelation*. We decided that life-experiences suggest it is a combination of both; we find the God who is seeking us. We also saw that most day-to-day encounters with God (prayer, meditation, "starry night" experiences, etc.) are not normally what is meant by revelation, by which God discloses something new and about Himself to a community of faith.

Certainly, Divine Ideas are available to everyone, but those insights are personal and peculiar to our circumstances. If a person feels called by God to go to college, or visit a friend, or write an opera these worthy promptings may well be Divine in origin, but they are not the kind of burning bush event described in Exodus 3. British theologian John Macquarrie writes of this pattern in this fascinating passage from his *Systematic Theology*:

> Because of its gift-like character, revelation is a different order from our ordinary, matter-of-fact knowing of the world...in spite of

the astonishing variety of such experiences and the extravagant language in which they are sometimes described, a perfectly definite pattern runs through them all, and the basic pattern of revelation seems to be common to all the religions of the world. It can be clearly seen in such widely separated examples as the revelation granted to Moses in the desert, to the Gnostic writer who received the gospel of Poimandres, to Arjuna who receives a theophany of the god Krishna, and in numerous other cases. The basic pattern may be summarily analyzed as follows: a mood of meditation or preoccupation; the sudden in-breaking of the holy presence, often symbolized in terms of a light; a mood of self-abasement (sometimes terror, sometimes consciousness of sin, sometimes even doubt of the reality of the experience) in the face of the holy; a more definite disclosure of the holy, perhaps the disclosure of a name or of a purpose or a truth of some kind (this element may be called the "content" of the revelation); the sense of being called or commissioned by the holy to a definite task or way of life.[9]

Historic revelations are fountainheads from which flow a revitalized religious community. Native American religions allowed men to go on *vision quests* to receive personal revelations which were meant for the seeker alone. No Indian based his religion strictly on visions, viewpoints, or voices he encountered while starving himself to induce the experience. That would have violated his sense of harmony with the traditions of the grandfathers, which were the yardstick by which he measured any new insight, regardless of its source.

Time alone determines whether an allegedly Special Revelation makes such a lasting impression on human consciousness that a community of believers gathers around this new idea and it becomes the nucleus of a religious faith. Therefore, most theologians reserve the term *revelation* for the primordial communication of their religious community, God's one-on-one conversation with the founders of the faith.

Other insights may still be recognized as Divine, but these will have to submit themselves to the yardstick of that primordial revelation (often recorded in sacred *Scripture*), to the long-standing views of the wider community (*Tradition*), to the faith as it now exists as a living entity (*Experience*), and to the scrutiny of rational believers (*Reason*).

Neither visions nor voices from heaven validate a theology. These experiences have occurred throughout the history of humanity and are most certainly worthy expressions of personal faith. But they are not valid as authorities to prove doctrines which must apply to the whole community. George Fox, one of the great mystics of the Christian heritage and founder of the Society of Friends (Quakers), believed God talked to him almost continually. He chatted with God and received *"openings,"* i.e., insights on all sorts of subjects. God led him up hills, into towns, and into the company of many distinguished persons.

God also gave George Fox an endless stream of ideas which Fox took as Divine Guidance. He did not presume to take those God-to-George communications as Special Revelation. The difference is quite profound for theology. Here is an excerpt from Fox's Journal which illustrates his attitude:

> At another time it was opened in me, "that God who made the world did not dwell in temples made with hands." This at first seemed strange, because both priests and people used to call their temples or churches, dreadful places, holy ground, and the temples of God. But the Lord showed me clearly, that he did not dwell in these temples which men had commanded and set up, but in people's hearts. Both Stephan and the Apostles bore testimony, that he did not dwell in temples made with hands, not even in that which he had once commanded to be built...This opened in me, as I walked in the fields to my relation's house. When I came there, they told me Nathaniel Stevens the (Anglican) priest, had been there, and said, "he was afraid of me going after new lights." I smiled in myself, knowing what the Lord had opened in me concerning him and his brethren (the priesthood); but I told not my relations...But I showed them by the scriptures, there was anointing within man to teach him, and that the Lord would teach his people himself.[10]

Divine *Guidance* is always personal; *Revelation* carries with it a call to prophesy. Your guidance is not necessarily my guidance since that kind of insight reflects our individual learning programs. Revelation is for everyone, or at least everyone within the receiving community.

George Fox, who passionately believed in his ability to receive guidance from God, nevertheless realized his inner light was not going to convince anyone else, so he refrained from citing those personal insights as authoritative when discussing religious beliefs, even with his "relations." As the first Quaker, he set the example by arguing from *Scripture*, personal *Experience,* and *Reason.* Breaking with *Tradition*, he brought his new ideas into dialogue with those long-standing beliefs taught by the Church of England. Thus he demonstrated that responsible religious thinkers MUST engage all four formative factors in a balanced worldview, even if only to reject one of the factors as Fox rejected Tradition.

Even more remarkable is his attitude toward the "Pop-Fad Spirituality" of his day:

> Removing to another place I came among a people that relied much on dreams. I told them except they could distinguish between dream and dream they would confound all together; for there were three sorts of dreams: multitude of business sometimes caused dreams; and there were whisperings of Satan in man in the night season; and there were speakings of God to man in dreams. But these people came out of these things, and at last became Friends [Quakers].[11]

Fox rightly notes the difficulty of sifting through ideas gleaned from recollections of dreams. By what standard can they be evaluated? How does one know if the dream comes from stress, or from suppressed phobias *("whisperings of Satan"),* or from Divine guidance? Lacking a measuring stick, there is no way to tell the guidance from the garbage except by one's emotional reaction to the dream content, which is the very definition of ethical Antinomianism.

There are a number of quasi-religious phenomena which, if authentic at all, stumble along the frontier between guidance and fantasy. These include *Automatic Writing(AW)*, the use of a *Spirit Medium*, and the currently popular practice of *Channeling*. All claim to be forms of Special Revelation from the "beyond-normal." *AW* occurs when a spirit-presence allegedly writes through the hands of someone in this world. Since the medium is not involved in this writing it is said to be *"automatic."* Some theories of biblical inspiration lean toward this idea, although insisting that God does the writing and not some higher being or dead relative, which is usually the case with *AW*.

A Spirit Medium is someone through whom these spirits speak to deliver messages, often for a fee, to friends and relatives on this side of the veil. *Channeling*, which has received much attention in national news media and even served as the foil of Gary Trudeau's *Doonesbury* comic strip, takes the medium/message idea to its extreme. A *Channel* is someone who enters a trance and allows some discorporate entity to speak through him/her. Usually the channel is unaware of the message after it is delivered, sometimes for paid public audiences.

Some well known "channels" include the late Edgar Casey, known as the "sleeping prophet;" the late Reverend Arthur Ford; Jane Roberts, whose books on her spirit-guide, *Seth*, have sold millions; and Ruth Montgomery, who published her own work, then claimed to have contacted Arthur Ford after that seer died. These authors have stirred a hunger in many people for something to believe in, for hope that life does not end with death.

Channeling, though terribly trendy as this book is being written, has not yet been studied exhaustively by the empirical sciences. There are several questions which, hopefully, will be answered when such studies are undertaken. For example, one cannot help but notice the similarity between channeling and the psychological disorder known as multiple personalities. We quote from an introductory text in psychology:

> In cases of multiple or alternating personalities, the individual has more than one organization of his or her sub personalities. In one personality, the individual may be happy and carefree; in another, anxious and sullen. The personalities shift back and forth, but each retains its separate identity. Some amnesia is characteristic, so personality A is unaware of personality B, although in some instances personality B may be fully aware of personality A...In earlier centuries these changes were commonly attributed to the invasion of the body by an outside spirit, or possession. Today they

are viewed naturalistically as a split, or dissociation, within the personality.[12]

Researcher Colin Wilson describes the multiple personality syndrome in detail in his book *Mysteries* without ever making the connection between alleged spirit-guide messages through a medium or channel and this psychological disorder. Wilson's treatment of multiple personalities is comprehensive and borders on the bizarre, but every case is carefully documented. The most famous case of multiple personalities is discussed in the best-selling book *The Three Faces of Eve*, by Corbett H. Thigpen and Hervey M. Cleckley.

Let me add a personal case. The author knew a young woman who suffered from this disorder. Sharon, as we shall call her, was the wife of a sergeant at Fort Carson, Colorado, and an active member of the Little Theater group, where we became acquainted. Sharon had a history of multiple personalities—she reckoned that at one time at least twenty-two separate personalities "shared" her body. As Sharon and I became friends she related stories of the two personalities which lingered "inside" her after intense, long-term counseling. Typical of multiple personalities, both had names. One was a tough, older woman named Talula and the other a young child named Missy. Sharon told me that when she went to college she found herself unaccountably skipping class until she learned that Missy had kept her home to watch Sesame Street. She was utterly unaware what happened whenever these other personalities "took over."

One can readily see how earlier peoples identified people like Sharon as possessed of evil spirits. Is it possible that the "channels" of today—who usually go into a "trance" while the spirit-guide inhabits their bodies—are simply carriers of multiple personalities? If so, they need treatment, not a sideshow atmosphere attending their experiences. It would be interesting to see the results of psychological studies done alone these lines. Is channeling a psychic phenomenon, or a psychological disorder? Doubtless true believers will be scandalized at the suggestion.

The channeling phenomenon draws its strength from an understandable yearning. If only a source of personal inspiration, which is the essence of good religious experience, one could hardly criticize channeling. However, since this behavior has presented itself as an alternative to the Christian faith, as an authority for life after death and as a source of other religious beliefs, we are obliged to mention several serious problems with Special Revelation in any format.

First, no existential phenomenon proves a religious teaching. Every quasi-religious group in world history has pointed to "signs and wonders" as proof of its divine commission. After Adolf Hitler was not killed in the bomb-blast inside his bunker, he doubtless took it as direct evidence that God was on his side.

Just because a person can heal by touch—a fairly well-documented Paranormal experience—does not mean everything she/he says has the blessing of Divine Mind.

In fact, some of the most outrageously ethnocentric theologies of recent history were also accompanied by healings, visions, and experiences that border on the supernatural.

Power does not mean purity; neither does clairvoyance mean correctness in all categories. That is why Jesus took pains to teach His disciples principles of love, forgiveness, and justice as well as healing the sick or raising the dead. Many traveling wonder-workers walked the earth in His day. Only Jesus the Christ loved God and humanity enough to go to Calvary to prove He was right and point the way toward our own salvation through union with God.

Secondly, phenomena like these simply do not lend themselves to rational theological discourse. They belong to the realm of the parapsychologist, physicist, and behavioral scientist, not to theology. Christian thought cannot pass judgment on the validity of these experiences because they are events, not doctrines. Many events occur beyond the charter of theological investigation: astronomy, biology, physics, and human psychology are examples of legitimate ways to study the Cosmos, living organisms, matter/energy in motion, and the behavior of human beings. No theologian has any right to pass upon the validity of scientific inquiry; that got us in terrible trouble when were clinging to the "God of the Gaps."

It is their very un-theological orientation which make Special Revelations invalid as sources of religious knowledge for a community of faith. Charles Fillmore insisted that his ideas were true, not because some 10,000-year-old guru spoke through him while he was in a trance, but because he found these ideas through examination of *Scripture* and metaphysical *Traditions* of Christianity. Then he took these ideas into his own life *Experience* and proved them true, all the while using his God-given power of *Reason* to understand, both intuitively and intellectually, what worked for him. When others found similar results by applying these Jesus Christ principles to their lives, a community of faith formed which is today still struggling to understand the Gospel and apply it to everyday life.

If one of these "channels" says something of a religious nature, the Metaphysical Christian compares that bit of data to his/her criteria for determining Truth. *The question is not the validity of paranormal experiences but rather their appropriateness as sources of Truth.* Flying Saucers may very well exist, but establishing their validity falls within the realm of astrophysics and exobiology, not religious studies. ESP can be demonstrated under laboratory conditions[13], but those studies must be carried on by the empirical sciences. Furthermore, channeling, Automatic Writing and other forms of spirit-contact are the legitimate domain of psychologists and cultural anthropologists because, as phenomena, they can be studied objectively only by human and behavioral sciences at this time. Religious thinkers cannot pontificate about what is and what is not valid because *events* do not lend themselves to religious inquiry for justification.

However, if the revelatory event cannot be considered theologically, the *content* of these messages can and should be treated as appropriate data for theological investigation. If that is the case, we need only ask where the bulk of these ideas fall in relationship to the circle of Christian faith as we understand it within the mystical/metaphysical tradition. The answer is that they fall, generally, outside the circle. Few claim any connection with Jesus Christ, and those which do espouse loyalty to Him fail to validate their case because they stand beyond *Scripture/Tradition/Reason* in a bid for supremacy of *Experience* over all other sources.

Special Revelations, by their very nature, place their messages above criticism, a dangerous perch for any idea to ascend. The tools of theology are not recognized by those who avow allegiance to Special Revelations, because they recognizes no court of inquiry but their own authority. Jesus knew this was a danger, so He mixed plenty of references to *Scripture* and *Tradition* with examples drawn from everyday life (*Experience*), appealing as well to the combined power of intuitive/intellectual *Reason*.

Balanced theologies will contain all four elements in harmonious dialogue. But more importantly, as we have said previously, the Christian faith is not a series of principles to learn but a relationship to God as revealed to us in Jesus Christ. The goal of Metaphysical Christianity is union with God through faith in the Christ-within. Christians recognize an eternal relationship, not only with God through Jesus but with all sentient beings, perhaps with everything that exists. The elements of that relationship can be expressed in principles, but to say Christianity is a set of ideas is like saying Bach's *Magnificat* is a string of black marks on white paper. Divine Ideas are only so because we know about our eternal relationship with the Divine; principles of Metaphysical Christianity, Truth principles, Divine Ideas—call them what you will—simply seek to express the nature of the Christian relationship.

Pop-Fad Spirituality may churn up some dandy ideas about multi-tiered heavens or angelic beings or reincarnation on other worlds, but the hard question a Christian Truth student must ask is, *"So what? What can you tell me about my eternal, on-growing relationship to God?"*

We might add: *"Do you have anything new to say? If so, we'll listen gladly. But know that your words must meet the toughest standard of all—they must stand beside the measuring stick of Jesus Christ."*

A COURSE IN MIRACLES

One recent Special Revelation deserves special mention because of its pervasive influence within Christian Truth churches, the widely studied three-volumes known as *A Course In Miracles*[14].

Authors of the *Course* have claimed a Divine commission to prophesy unto modern humanity. More than one advocate of the *Course* has assured me that this is no mere metaphysical speculation but a new revelation from Jesus Christ. Some churches have gone as far as to include readings from the *Course* in their Sunday worship services along with the Bible, a practice which cannot help but convey unspoken messages about the authority and origin of the books to the laity.

It is not our purpose to provide a detailed critique of the content of the *Course* in this limited space; that it should be subject to critical analysis just like any other religious work, including the Judaeo-Christian scriptures, we have already established. Indeed, such an important document requires critical study if only to see if anything new is offered.

However, our concern is with the cultic aspect of the *Course* as it functions within the body of the Metaphysical Christian movement, like a kind of church-within-the-Church. Little core groups gather to study the *Course* faithfully, to practice its principles and discuss its ideas. As such there would be no harm to the Metaphysical Christian church, unless the advocates of this modernized form of Neo-platonism continue to wink and hint that their materials are a Special Revelation from Jesus Christ. These assertions are dangerous for three reasons:

1) The *Course* is both irrefutable and unprovable, thus inherently divisive. Arguments from Divine authority can neither be proved nor disproved; they must be accepted or rejected by faith. Content can be studied, and on the basis of that analysis a person could make a decision, but this decision would neither substantiate nor invalidate claims to Divine authorship. Divine Revelations are under no injunction to be rational, or Jesus Christ would not have died on the cross like a common criminal. Divine Truth need only confirm to that standard of Ultimate Goodness which is apprehended by more than rational senses. Faith is a love affair with a love-worthy Divinity, and God's love certainly owes no explanation.

Human ideas about the Divine, however, owe everyone their best explanations. That is the difference between authentic Revelation and discursive theology. When God speaks, people fall on their knees. When we theologians speak, people stand up and to cheer or to throw the hymnals at us. If Jesus Christ dictated the *Course*, we have no other appropriate response than the reply of Samuel in the Tent of the Presence, *"Speak, Lord, your servant is listening."* But since so many splinter groups claim to be receiving messages from God, the burden of proof rest on the advocates of Special Revelation. As astronomer Carl Sagan said, extraordinary claims require extraordinary proof.

This points to another reason why seeing the Course as Special Revelation is unhealthy for Christian Truth students.

2) The *Course* relies on an Argument from Authority. How strange that some people who reject biblical literalism and authority will embrace *A Course in Miracles* as a new gospel, literally true. Certainly, some people have found worthwhile ideas in the *Course* which have led them to a better understanding of their spiritual nature. The same could be said of the writing of Thomas Merton or the Alcoholics' Anonymous *Blue Book*. But *Course* loses credibility with thinking persons by proclaiming itself to be a Special Revelation, thereby claiming special Divine status. This has the effect

of undermining much of the *Course's* potential usefulness. We are done with external authorities. Let Truth stand or fall on its own merits.

3) Worst of all, advocates of the *Course* insist on seeing it as a Special Revelation and claim equality with the Bible for these lessons. The *Course* is not the Gospel. Its ideas are not truly new, and certainly not equal in importance to the Bible, as anyone but its most zealous advocates can readily see. If these books last 2,000-plus years and influence billions of lives for their collective betterment, perhaps Course-ists might have a stronger argument for its equality with the Psalms, the "Sermon on the Mount", and "Paul's Hymn to Love."

The jury of history is still out. That same jury is yet to pass judgment on the long-lasting importance of other Special Revelations—from the *Book of Mormon*, to the *Baha'i writings*, to the *Urantia Book*. And what about the endless stream of self-proclaimed perfect revelations of God's new truth for the modern age? Easternisms like the *Divine Light Mission* and Westernisms like the jungle-growth of psychics and channels are making good money marketing their prophecies and philosophies to a spiritually hungry world.

Are they equal to the Bible, too?

Since we won't know for another twenty centuries, it's a bit premature to publish a three-Testament copy of the Holy Scriptures. By the forty-first century the Bible will also be 2,000 years older and will have positively influenced billions more lives. So perhaps equality with the Judaeo-Christian scripture is not a thing to be grasped, simply because of its antiquity.

Our Bible—for better or worse—represents the "recorded memories of our ancestors in the faith," the events and conceptual framework of the primordial Revelation which created our Western religious heritage. By virtue of its posture as one of the four tent posts holding up the Christian faith, the biblical library is *nonpareil*, truly without peer or equal. It alone must remain the basic textbook for all expressions of Christian faith including Metaphysical Christianity. Any work which claims equality with the Bible faces a long struggle to authenticity.

AUTHENTIC OR FLAKY?

Which raises another question about the whole business of the paranormal that must be considered before we move on: What makes a spiritual practice "authentic" and another one, to use a common colloquialism, "flaky"?

Metaphysical Christianity has fought long and bravely for recognition of its status as a legitimate expression of Christian faith. Charles Fillmore realized that a movement so open-minded was bound to attract the lunatic fringe, so he repeatedly called for his branch of the Christian Truth movement to remember its roots deep within the Judaeo-Christian heritage. He would brook no compromise with those who wanted to move "beyond" Christianity into either the normlessness of syncretism or the netherworld of dependency to psychic phenomena.

In 1906 the Fillmores went to Chicago to attend the convention of the International New Thought Federation, which is today called the International New Thought Alliance (INTA). At that time, Mr. Fillmore was dismayed by what he perceived as a drift away from the teachings of Jesus Christ toward the establishment of a hybrid, non-Christian religion:

> It dawned on me that the name "New Thought" had been appropriated by so many cults that had new theories to promulgate that it had ceased to express what I conceived to be absolute Truth. The New Thought Federation is attempting to carry this load of thought diversity, and I can see no success in it... [15]

Today, *New Thought* is an umbrella term describing a diversity of organizations. Some are avowedly Christian; others seek a synthetic Western equivalent to Eastern spirituality. When we use the term "New Thought" in this work, we refer to the Christian elements in the movement as a whole.

Setting aside the theological arguments against reliance on the paranormal for religious information or becoming tied too closely with those practices because of their threat to personal growth, the plain fact still remains that to the vast majority of people Flying Saucers, Astrology, and channeling are not religious experiences at all but represent, at best, the "Far Side" of life. At worst, these are things we are accustomed to read about in those goofy newspapers sold at supermarket checkout stands rather than in Sunday school lessons.

While there is certainly cause for expanding our consciousness and getting religion involved with all aspects of life, we risk becoming a comical caricature of religion by harboring cultic practices that the general population believes are one squirrel short of nutty. When TV evangelist Oral Roberts announced that he needed to raise $8 million or God would take his life, religious liberals laughed derisively and conservatives called him all manner of unChristian monikers. Yet, Roberts simply claimed to be the bearer of a Special Revelation, no more.

What is the difference between Oral Roberts proclaiming that God will kill him if people didn't contribute money and some trance-state "channel" babbling about cosmic consciousness in front of a paid audience? If Rev. Roberts was guilty of anything it was outrageous honesty. Obviously, he passionately believed that he has received a Special Revelation and passed the message on to the world bluntly, blatantly. There's the rub: No theological tool exists to evaluate the *authenticity* of Special Revelations: which makes them utterly meaningless for anyone but the receiver.

The dangers explicit in paranormal experience were often mentioned by Fillmore in his writings. In *Atom-Smashing Power of Mind* he calls as his witness the Bard of Avon:

> Shakespeare was familiar with all the superstitions of his age. His characters are witches, seers, soothsayers, astrologers; he shows familiarity with forces that in our day are considered occult and spooky. They believed in signs and omens, the control of men by

the sun, moon, and stars—astrology. Yet the fallacy of such concepts of mortality was usually pointed out.[16]

Mr. Fillmore's position on these "superstitions" did not waver, as his compendium *The Revealing Word* shows:

ASTROLOGY—"The pseudo science which treats of the influence of stars upon human affairs..." Astrology represents the belief in man that his good depends wholly on something outside himself—his ruling star, fate, providence—instead of depending on the power of his own thoughts...[17]

OCCULTISM—The belief that secret and mysterious powers can control the visible world. This procedure is not the way of the Christ Mind.[18]

PSYCHIC—Pertaining to mental powers not common to ordinary man; mental powers outreaching the scope of the physical man, but not yet quickened to the standard of Spirit...[19]

BREAKING THE "OCCULT CONNECTION"

The very word "mystical" in our self-designation as the "mystical" branch of the Church causes the Christian Truth student to be suspect because, unfortunately, alternate meanings of the word equate mystics with occult practitioners. Here is the complete definition from the 1980 *Random House College Dictionary*:

MYSTIC—adj. 1) spiritually significant or symbolic. 2) of occult or mysterious character, power, or significance: a mystic formula. 3) of or pertaining to mystics or mysticism.—n. 4) a person initiated into mysteries. 5) a person who attains, or believes in the possibility of attaining insight into mysteries transcending ordinary human knowledge, as by immediate intuition in a state of spiritual ecstasy.[20]

Mystical Christianity has always smacked of occultism, ergo heresy, in the eyes of hyper-orthodoxy, perhaps because some "secular" mystics did dabble in occult studies. But Christian mysticism eschews the occult, which is an attempt to manipulate psychic/magical "forces" to do the will of the individual. The goal of Christian mysticism absolutely contradicts all occult questing, because the Christ-centered mystic wants to let God's power—the One and only Power—flow through and transform the individual.

We are conformed to Christ; Christ is not conformed to us.

For this reason Charles Fillmore and other early modern Christian Truth teachers rejected the word occult and disavowed concepts which grow from an avowed intention to practice arcane lore. In this they brought their brand of mysticism into line with this definition found in the same source as cited above:

MYSTICISM—n. 1) the beliefs, ideas, or mode of thought of mystics. 2) the doctrine of an immediate spiritual intuition of truths believed to transcend ordinary understanding, or a direct, intimate union of the soul with God through contemplation and love.[21]

KEEPING AN OPEN DOOR TO INNOVATIVE IDEAS

It is easy to see how genuine mysticism presents us with similar problems as Special Revelation. If a person receives *"immediate spiritual understanding of truths believed to transcend ordinary understanding,"* how do we evaluate the validity of those truths for our belief system? History tells of a long struggle between the mystic and the Church precisely because mystical awareness is individualized instruction and Church teaching must teach/reach the masses.

When trying to represent Divine Truth to a large membership, some degree of systematization is required. However, we have repeatedly asserted that any system will offer, at best, a symbolic representation of reality, not to be confused with the Reality which the system seeks to symbolize. The city model is not the metropolis; the map is not the countryside.

When the Church confronts the mystic with charges that he/she is violating the model by which its community of faith presently defines itself, the mystic replies that he/she is in contact with the Reality the model represents and therefore stands above criticism. The Church often responds by blacklisting or excommunicating the mystic. Friction between Church and mystic cannot be avoided, but it can become the source of growth for both if the institution and the individual mystic engage in dialogue based on commonly held criteria.

We have attempted to establish the criteria for such ongoing discussions between experimental Christianity and the greater community of faith to which Christian Truth churches belong. This allows exciting possibilities without abdicating our responsibility to follow the path of Jesus Christ. Let all "Special Revelations," new beliefs and mystical insights stand before the bar of *Scripture/Tradition/ Experience/Reason* and meet the strict requirements of fidelity to the Truth revealed/discovered in Jesus of Nazareth, the Christ. But let Metaphysical Christianity remember that it is not and never shall be an "occult science." Our task is to help all sentient beings grow to awareness of their oneness with God, not to remake the Cosmos in our own image or fly after every Pop-Fad fantasy which hits the newsstand. That kind of behavior is the very model of idolatry found in the Bible.

If we follow a vigorous program of theological examination based on dialogue and critical analysis, Metaphysical Christianity shall be able to keep its distinct identity as a wholly Christ-centered movement which keeps the door open to innovative ideas about Christian spirituality. These magnificent words of the prophet Jeremiah provide closure to our discussion of Pop-Fad Spirituality:

> Thus says the Lord: "Let not the wise man glory in his wisdom, let not the mighty man glory in his might, let not the rich man glory in his riches; but let him who glories glory in this, that he understands and knows me, that I am the Lord who practices steadfast love, justice, and righteousness in the earth; for in these things I delight, says the Lord."[22]

CHECK YOUR KNOWLEDGE

1. Explain/Identify: *elitism, antinomianism, Elimination/ Renunciation, "chigaima-su," occult, paranormal, nonpareil, Special Revelation, Emmet Fox, George Fox, openings, automatic writing, channeling, INTA, mystic, spirit medium, "God of the Gaps," idolatry.*

2. Why does Special Revelation pose a danger to authentic theology? List and explain the problems mentioned in the text.

3. Why did Charles Fillmore withdraw Unity from INTA and cease calling himself a "New Thoughter"? What was his position on occult studies in general? Did Emmet Fox agree?

4. What psychological disorder closely parallels "channeling"?

5. Explain this quotation from the text: "Not the validity of these particular experiences but rather their appropriateness as sources of Truth and subjects of metaphysical inquiry is what we challenge here."

6. Why does the author believe the assertions of the Course in Miracles as a Special Revelation from Jesus Christ are dangerous to the credibility of Metaphysical Christian Churches?

QUESTIONS FOR DISCUSSION

1. What is the difference between legitimate theology and paranormal studies?

2. Should Christian Truth churches teach paranormal phenomena as part of their religious education program? What is the proper forum for interested persons to investigate these subjects?

3. Do you agree with the author that Special Revelations are not valid sources for religious knowledge except as individual insights?

4. Have you had an experience of the paranormal? What kind?

5. Should Metaphysical Christian churches use readings from *A Course in Miracles* as part of their worship or prayer services? Do you believe the *Course* is a special revelation from Jesus Christ?

6. What do you believe about the "Channeling" phenomenon? Is it authentic spirit-guide communication or something else?

NOTES

1. Emmet Fox in Wolhorn, p. 165.

2. Psalm 2:1-2, 4-6 (RSV).

3. Genesis 12:1-3 (RSV).

4. Romans 6:9-10, 12 (RSV).

5. Freeman, "Is Unity a Cult?", p. 1.

6. Frost, "The Mending Wall," p. 94.

7. Fox, p. 211.

8. Charles Fillmore, *Jesus Christ Heals* (Unity Village: Unity Books, 1939), p. 21.

9. Macquarrie, *Principles*, pp. 7-8.

10. George Fox in Capps & Wright, *Silent Fire*, p. 167.

11. IBID.

12. Ernest R. Hilgard and Others, *Introduction to Psychology* (NY: Harcourt, Brace & Jovanovich, 1979), p. 163.

13. IBID., pp. 151-153.

14. See Note 4, Chapter 16.

15. Charles Fillmore in Freeman, *Story of Unity*, pp. 103-104.

16. Charles Fillmore, *Atom-Smashing Power of Mind* (Unity Village: Unity Books, 1949), p. 113.

17. Fillmore, *Revealing Word*, p. 17.

18. IBID., p. 141.

19. IBID., p. 159.

20. Stein, *Random House College Dictionary*, p. 882.

21. IBID.

22. Jeremiah 9:23-24 (RSV).

THEOLOGY FROM A GALACTIC PERSPECTIVE

Chapter Twenty

With a third or a half a trillion stars in our Milky Way Galaxy alone, could ours be the only one accompanied by an inhabited planet? How much more likely it is that technical civilizations are a cosmic commonplace, that the Galaxy is pulsing and humming with advanced societies, and, therefore, that the nearest culture is not so very far away...Perhaps when we look up at the sky at night, near one of those faint pin-points of light is a world on which someone quite different from us is then glancing idly at a star we call the Sun and entertaining, for just a moment, an outrageous speculation.[1]

Astronomer Carl Sagan, quoted above, said that even a conservative estimate of the number of advanced civilizations in *our Milky Way Galaxy alone* runs into the millions. And our half-trillion (500 billion) stars represent one of billions of galaxies in the Cosmos, each with hundreds of billions of stars. Even given conservative estimates, the likelihood that earth is the only inhabited world in that vast ocean of galaxies appears to be incomprehensibly slight.

In our last chapter we looked at Pop-Fad Spirituality, one phase of which is the "Flying Saucer cult" phenomenon. We deliberately avoided extensive comment on this topic because we wanted to discuss the implications of extra-terrestrial life at length. Cultic aspects of UFO sightings continue to find an almost inexhaustible market; books and other publications fan the flames of imagination and hope. The Internet buzzes with extraterrestrial lore. At this writing there are 130 "UFO Clubs" on *YAHOO.com* alone. One well-visited website declares:

"We are interested in discussing the topics of mystical events such as ghosts/spirits and UFO sightings. Sharing of personal experiences and discussing all opinions on the subject with others."

(http://clubs.yahoo.com/clubs/ufoandmysticalevents)

Popular UFO authority Paris Flammonde says in his book *UFO Exist!* that the craze has spawned over a hundred organizations since World War II. Centers devoted to research and study of UFOs have multiplied around the globe. Flammonde lists names and address of five in the USA and thirty-one in other countries, including nine in Australia alone.[2]

Passionate, true believers all around the world meet regularly to discuss details of extra-terrestrial cultures, non-human races, and alien philosophies. Books and articles have been written by people who claim to have taken rides on alien starships—some with astonishing details. Virtually every issue of those supermarket scandal sheets—the kind we've become accustomed to glancing at while waiting in the checkout line—offers more insider knowledge about extra-terrestrials.

Published reports have claimed that the U. S. Government is suppressing information about hard, physical evidence which it allegedly has that confirms UFOs are real. One book claims that comedian Jackie Gleason was shown the bodies of aliens who died when their spacecraft crashed.

> It may be hard to swallow, but according to Beverly Gleason, wife of TV star Jackie Gleason, it is all true, because she recalls a night in 1973 when her husband arrived home late and slumped into a chair, ashen-faced. "I've seen the bodies of some aliens from outer space," he claimed. Gleason was a good friend of then President Richard Nixon and is known to have had a deep interest in UFOs. Nixon is supposed to have set up the visit to the air force base where the four beings were...Jackie Gleason himself has refused to confirm or deny the story.[3]

Past and present advocates of a conspiracy theory of history are legion, from Karl Marx on the ultra-left to Adolf Hitler on the ultra-right. However, one overwhelming factor in American political life mitigates against the arguments of a government conspiracy to suppress UFO evidence: the slip-shod track record our government has at keeping anything secret very long. Investigative reporters would kill for a story like this. The man or woman who broke the news of a government plot to cover up evidence that UFOs exist would be an instant superstar among journalists, candidate for a Pulitzer Prize, able to negotiate for book and screen rights to the story, offered lucrative TV appearances, and be in a position to demand a top-dollar salary for the rest of his/her life. Anybody who thinks the Nixon White House could have kept the wreckage of a UFO and the bodies of aliens a secret from the electronic news media probably spent the 1970s in a monastery in Outer Mongolia.

Carl Sagan maintains that there "is no credible evidence for the Earth being visited, now or ever."[4] He suggests that there are many reasons why we have not been visited, or if visited not officially contacted, the most intriguing of which is an idea popularized by science fiction. Perhaps there exists a "Lex Galactica, some ethic of noninterference with emerging civilizations" which keeps alien starcraft from touching down on the White House lawn.[5]

While we agree extra-terrestrial contacts are possible, Sagan's conjecture that we probably haven't been visited seems valid for two further reasons.

LET'S GET SERIOUS...

First, the density of stars in our galaxy alone is so great that few science fiction authors have ever accurately represented its enormity. Sagan mentions that a civilization only two hundred light-years away could find itself sorting through two hundred thousand star systems in the neighborhood which extends from them to us. Even allowing them the luxury of Faster-than-Light travel—which is by no means an assured technology of the future—such a "local" civilization would require hundreds of centuries to weed through the closest stars.

Our Galaxy is so vast that it is entirely possible a world with star flight capability could exist for tens of thousands of years and *never* encounter another technologically advanced culture, even given the probability that millions exist in the Milky Way alone. Finding our world in its spiral arm of the Galaxy would be like finding a needle in a haystack somewhere on the earth's surface from a vantage point beyond our solar system.

Another reason we likely have not been visited by UFOs is known as the "Postage Stamp Theory." There are billions of star systems in the Galaxy far older than our own. Perhaps intelligent life has existed with starflight capability somewhere in the Cosmos for as long as our earth has orbited the sun. If we were visited at all, it might have been millions or perhaps even billions of years ago.

To illustrate the problem in relation to extra-terrestrial visitors, let the Empire State Building represent the geological history of the earth. On top of the radio tower poking above the great building let's place a one-foot ruler to represent the million-odd years of human life on this world. Next, put dime flat on the top edge of the ruler; this stands for recorded history, approximately the last seven thousand years. Finally, lick a postage stamp and stick it atop the dime; it will represent modern times, Renaissance to the present.

That thin slice of paper compared to the great Empire State Building must be our period of visitation by alien cultures. In fact, we are really only talking seriously about visits after the dawn of the twentieth century. If earth were visited sometime in its geological history by more advanced races the great likelihood is that the fly-by occurred on the fifty-eighth floor, or some other point in the dim, unrecorded past. Perhaps the vessel took pictures of our dinosaur-ruled surface and decided this was a nice place to visit but they wouldn't want to live here. Perhaps they never came back.

If the incredible volume of UFO sightings contain even a grain of truth, this planet must straddle the trade routes and be considered quality entertainment for the amusement of star flight civilizations. Two visits every hundred years would make this corner of space as busy as Chicago's O'Hare International Airport at Christmas.

THEOLOGY AND EXOBIOLOGY

Interesting as it may be to speculate about UFOs and alien intelligences, we are engaged in a study of Christian theology, therefore you may have rightly suspected some ulterior motive for trotting out all this data on the possibility of extra-terrestrial life. Alien life forms are the province of the infant science known as Exobiology, and if we are to take seriously what the exobiologists and speculative astronomers like Sagan have said, we are not alone in the Cosmos. So far, few Christian thinkers have lifted up their eyes to the heavens and taken a look at how Christian theology must be affected when viewed from this new, Galactic Perspective.

We propose to discuss the rough outlines of how Christian theology must change as we look to the stars, predicated by the firm belief that Divine Mind is active wherever there is life, energy, and love. We propose to view theology from that Galactic Perspective. Rather than try to establish the existence of alien life forms through further argument, we shall taken their existence as a given. We shall also assume that definitive contact between humanity and other sentient beings remains for the future, despite all the sightings of UFOs and the hosts of cultists who believe contact has been made. Perhaps it has; there is no way to refute or substantiate the claims of true believers.

However, we shall proceed on the assumption that Definitive Contact, open discourse between our species and races from other worlds, will occur sometime in the future but shall not speculate on the journalistic questions—*who, what, when, where, and why*. Let science fiction play with timetables and scenarios. Our task will be to ask Christian theology to reevaluate itself in the light of humanity's quite probable loss of status as an only child.

IS THIS APPROACH VALID?

One might justifiably ask if a program to shift from an anthropocentric theology to a multi-species, Galactic Perspective is intellectually tenable. We know nothing of civilizations among the stars; why not concentrate on the known and deal with the human condition as it is today?

The answer to this objection is that one often gains a better view of subjects by bringing them up against a higher perspective. Life becomes more precious when taken to its limit by considering finitude and death. Our inter-faith dialogues disclose hidden ethnocentrisms which become apparent only when we meet others who think differently, benefiting both parties. The same could be said of any effective cross-cultural interaction, like the Christian-Jewish dialogue underway today in Europe after the historic declarations of Pope John Paul II about the Church's sin and culpability in the persecution of European Jewry throughout the centuries.

Perhaps the best example is the language we speak.

Ordinarily, we become aware of our native language only when we find ourselves adrift in a sea of non-English speaking people. When the author found himself downtown in Seoul, Korea, and unable to communicate or even read the signs in Korean script, my unconsciousness dependency upon language became self-conscious helplessness.

When preparing remarks to make to a New Thought Christian group in London, England, I began to wonder how many "Americanisms" I took for granted. (Example:

Is *"take for granted"* a British expression, too?) Somewhat apologetically, I began the talk, *"You'll have to excuse me. I don't speak English; I'm an American."*

It was an interesting exercise in linguistic introspection but one that never would have occurred to me if my Colonial English had not been brought before its Mother Tongue. (If you promise not to laugh, I'll confess that only then did I realize why they call that great set of reference books the *Encyclopedia Britannica*.) Comparison deepens understanding.

REVOLTING DEVELOPMENT

Christian theology has undergone frequent revolutions in its long history, although most are now taken for granted. We mentioned previously that the up/down language of the ancient world—which the biblical authors took as actual spatial references, since God lived "up there" in the clouds and the land of the dead was "down there" below the flat earth—has been spiritualized by most Christians ever since the earth lost its place as the center of the universe after Copernicus. God is no longer *physically* "up there" but has moved to another dimension, *spiritually* "up there." Beyond the shrinking fundamentalist fringe, no reputable theologian takes Genesis literally. It, too, has been spiritualized to mean "God created everything" without the crude mechanics of mud-scooping and rib-snatching to bring about man and woman.

Revolutions in Christian thought are barely beginning to seep down from the walls of the ivory towers to the people in the pew. Reading twentieth century theology, we discover people like Rudolf Bultmann, who insisted we must "demythologize" the biblical message of its pre-scientific worldview; Paul Tillich, who said God does not "exist" but is the very Power of existence itself; and Pierre Teilhard de Chardin, who held that sentient life evolves because God has programmed the very atoms of the Universe to yearn for union with Him.

With "revolting developments" like these just beginning to draw the attention of the laity, perhaps there is hope for Christian theology after all. Provided, of course, that all the folks turned off by fundamentalism and literalism have not already abandoned Christianity for secular philosophies or Pop-Fad Spirituality by the time these "new" ideas reach the people at First Downtown Church.

Fortunately for Metaphysical Christianity, new ideas are not generally a threat to the kind of seeking person who wanders into a Christian Truth church. However, before we descend into elitism, we hasten to add that there are vast numbers of people in Protestant, Roman Catholic, and Orthodox churches who are equally eager to hear the old, old story told in the language of today. Courageous clergy of every denomination are doing just that, even though they expose themselves to criticism and risk their job security by chipping away some of the comfortable crust of centuries. With pro-active pastoral care and a well-balanced theology, priests and ministers are struggling to bring the Truth of Jesus Christ to people who live in a space age world.

If we take the modern world seriously, we must ask our religious insights to operate in the light of a radically different Cosmos than faced our ancestors a few generations ago. Is it not, therefore, an acceptable risk to look forward and outward to find still another method of comparison which might give us pause to reconsider our deepest beliefs?

If we take the modern world seriously, that means accepting the strong likelihood that humanity is not the only intelligent species in the Cosmos. Serious speculation from this vantage point will call for some profound changes in Christian thought.

We quoted Professor John Macquarrie on this subject in another context, but his point is worth repeating because it tolls like a bell at midnight:

> The overwhelming probability is that countless billions of "histories" have been enacted in the cosmos, and a space-age cosmology calls for a vastly enlarged understanding of divine grace and revelation.[6]

We shall look boldly forward and outward, accepting John Macquarrie's challenge to enlarge "our understanding of divine grace and revelation." Although one could re-write an entire systematic theology from the Galactic Perspective, we shall limit our discussion to three areas: *Christology, Soteriology*, and *Social Ethics*.

FIRST PROBLEM: CHRISTOLOGY

The assumption that the Cosmos is teeming with sentient life calls for a radical reorientation in the orthodox position on the nature and person of Jesus Christ. Given the probability of intelligent life on other worlds, the claim that the Jesus-event represents God's definitive self-disclosure for all time and space makes little sense. Without raising the issue of non-human intelligences, theologians today are already asking hard questions about His uniqueness. John Macquarrie believes God works through other faiths to bring the same kind of Good News that Jesus Christ represents to us. It is only a slight extrapolation to conclude God is also at work in all locations where sentient beings yearn for Truth.

Classical Trinitarian Christology will not bend this far. A uniquely divine, pre-existent Son of God does not translate easily into a reproducible paradigm for alien worlds. If the man of Nazareth was the Second Person in the Trinity, He and He alone partaking of full divinity with the Father and the Holy Spirit, then extra-terrestrial religions could be nothing but philosophical constructs offering neither grace nor revelation. "Discovery," at best, could be found in their religious views, provided they stumbled on some of the principles revealed by Jesus in His onetime appearance on earth. Authentic commerce with God would be ruled out because non-terrestrials have no access to the sole point of contact between sentient beings and Omniscient, Triune Divinity.

With Classical Christology, we are locked into an elitist view which says, in effect: *The only Son of God was born in a small town on the eastern shore of a small sea of a small planet lost somewhere in a spiral arm of an average-sized galaxy.* One incarnation of God for millions of potentially inhabited worlds in our galaxy alone, in a Cosmos of perhaps 100 billion galaxies? When we raise Christology to a Galactic

Perspective, the unique divinity of Jesus becomes not just impossible to defend rationally. It becomes ridiculous.

However, if the divinity of Jesus were taken *as typical* rather than *unique*, which is the position virtually all Metaphysical Christian teachers have advocated, then it does not matter whether the person is a human being or an alien lifeform, he/she/it will possess the Christ-within. If the true nature of all sentient life is spirit, the outer form is almost irrelevant, an outpicturing of organic evolution tempered by climate, chance, and chemistry.

Would the music of Handel, Brahms, and Beethoven be less breathtaking if created by gifted marsupials on a ringed world with ten moons? Would the sublime concepts of mathematics or the majesty of the Psalms diminish if non-human hands scratched the ideas in an unknown script under a double-sun? Certainly, some types of knowledge would be powerfully affected, notably social sciences like sociology and anthropology, but intelligent beings of any form would need psychologists and counselors to help them with their problems, philosophers and theologians to wrestle with the hard questions of life, artists and musicians to bring beauty to their world.

Where there is life, love, and intelligence, there is God. Charles Fillmore wrote in *Keep a True Lent:*

> God-mind is located and appears wherever it is recognized by the mind of man. It thus follows that whoever gives his attention to Spirit and seals his identification with it by his word (the Son) starts a flow of Spirit life and all the attributes of Spirit in and through his consciousness. To the extent that he practices identifying himself with the one and only source of existence, he becomes Spirit in expression, until finally the union attains a perfection in which he can say with Jesus, "I and the Father are one." [7]

Rather than creating a problem, raising Christology to a Galactic Perspective validates the deepest theological insights of Metaphysical Christianity into the nature of the Divine-human paradox. We would need only to modify our terms and begin speaking of the "Divine-sentient being paradox." We would then be ready, with Alice Meynell, to listen eagerly to "a million alien gospels" tell "in what guise He trod" the face of other worlds.[8]

SECOND PROBLEM: SOTERIOLOGY

Once again, classical theology crash-lands in difficulties when its ethnocentrisms are raised to the Galactic Perspective. Let us state the problem fairly without puffing up straw men: *Universalism* (the belief in salvation for everyone) contradicts the necessity for Christian commitment, yet both are necessary for Christianity in the modern age. The problem breaks down into two sub-points.

1) Modern theology does not believe in hell. It is somewhat frustrating that we must reiterate this point continually to groups of Metaphysical Christians and other religious liberals who, armed with their own frustrations at the vociferous presence of

TV evangelists proclaiming archaic "turn or burn" doctrines, simply refuse to believe heaven-or-hellfire is not the viewpoint of most mainline Christian thinkers. In pervious chapters we have repeatedly said that universalism is the dominant theological position of mainline Protestant and liberal Catholic thinking today. As we make this point one more time, we are certain that someone holding this book is shaking his head in disbelief.

2) <u>One-Way or No Way</u>? Even with theology's almost unanimous universalism there remains a hidden problem implicit in any Christocentric system: If Jesus Christ is the way to knowledge of God, how can a person find God without Jesus Christ? And if He is not the only way to God, why *this* way instead of some other? We have discussed this problem earlier, but the complaint becomes quite critical when raised to the Galactic Perspective. How can an alien come to a "saving knowledge" of God without Jesus Christ? Raising the old spectre of gnosticism (i.e., *knowledge* is not required, *faith* is) merely substitutes terms without changing the equation. Instead of this formula:

SALVATION = KNOWLEDGE x JESUS CHRIST

Gnostophobics among us insist on this sequence:

SALVATION = FAITH x JESUS CHRIST

Neither removes the difficulty for the liberal Christian confronted by a non-Christian culture, terrestrial, or ET. Nor does softening the consequences of non-belief get us out of trouble. If we say there is no hell, we must at least allow that belief in Jesus Christ provides *some kind of benefit*, or what right do we have to call it "saving" anything? Perhaps the benefits are a better life, warmer relationships, peace of mind, or some sort of empowerment. The goal is almost irrelevant. The question is whether salvation, however defined, comes exclusively through the agency of Jesus, which is essentially the same question as asked about the well-read Hindu who rejects Christian faith because it won't work for him in his milieu.

Classical theology would have snorted at him, *"I hope you like warm climates!"* But today's liberal Christians are caught in a bind; they know there is no hell, but they feel that faith in Jesus is nevertheless the best way for everyone.

If saving knowledge/faith comes only through God's self-disclosure in Jesus Christ, as Karl Barth and others insisted, there is no possible way an alien being could be held accountable for lack of faith. Yet, what alternatives are left? Can we say faith in Jesus a) is not required for salvation of any kind (which invalidates the need to follow Jesus), or faith in Jesus b) is required for salvation (which binds God's Truth to geography and accident of birth)?

Even a benign One-Way theology based on universalism is still a One-Way theology; but a limp heterodoxy which calls for commitment to Jesus makes no sense. This is a profoundly difficult question and the ambivalence of mainline liberal clergy on this issue can be felt in their sermons, prayers, and programs. Is there any way out of this predicament? Once again, we return to theology's favorite battle cry when riding the horns of a dilemma: *Yes and No.*

If we maintain the *unique divinity* of Jesus Christ as the gateway to salvation (enlightenment, better life, whatever), the answer is *no*, for all the reasons discussed above. If Jesus is the one Key which unlocks the door to eternal life, love, and happiness, we are forever trapped in the logical inconsistency of Christian universalism as an avenue to spiritual benefits not obtainable elsewhere. With neither penalties nor rewards for ejecting/embracing Christianity, doesn't the faith become a moot point?

Is there any value in embracing a religion which fails to distinguish itself from other worldviews by its mindless open-mindedness? However, if we distinguish between faith in Jesus and faith in the Christ, we hear theology's *"Yes!"* to the question, "Is there any way out of this predicament?" The solution lies not in the search for answers but in the problem itself. If we accept the equation:

SALVATION = FAITH/KNOWLEDGE x JESUS

there is no resolution for Christian universalism. However, if we reprogram our theology with a different equation, the difficulties dissolve:

SALVATION = FAITH/KNOWLEDGE x THE CHRIST-WITHIN

Christian Truth students will immediately grasp the difference. This new equation allows us to see the Christ in every sentient being. The classical viewpoint requires every sentient being to see the Christ in Jesus *exclusively*. If Jesus represents unique divinity, all intelligent life forms must come to Him—the historical Jesus, revealed through the New Testament—or suffer some sort of spiritual shortfall. Dowsing hellfire does not solve the problem, because the elements of exclusivism remain intact. Only when we eliminate the *exclusive* divinity of Jesus of Nazareth does Christian universalism make sense.

The other extreme to avoid is deleting all divinity from Jesus by insisting he was exclusively human. We noted before that, although radical unitarianism *(Jesus possesses no divinity whatsoever)* and docetism *(Jesus possesses no humanity)* are easier to defend philosophically, Christian theology has rightly insisted that Jesus represents a *hypostasis*, a union in which His divine and human natures are fully integrated to form one unitive being. We would call that union *Christ-consciousness* and see it as ultimately normative for all thinking/feeling entities, human or extra-terrestrial. Christ-consciousness, as the basic goal of all sentient lifeforms, validates both historic Christianity, in its grasp of the Divine-human paradox represented by Jesus of Nazareth, and modern Christian theology with its profound insights about the universality of God's love.

Only Christian universalism grounded in Christ-consciousness allows us to look upward and outward to unknown races without the smug superiority of bygone eras when rival factions within the Christian camp pronounced anathemas upon each other with self-righteous confidence that their piece of the Cosmic puzzle constituted the whole.

Metaphysical Christianity welcomes the chance to discover Truth which the Christ-within has spoken to nonhuman religions, even while fully committed to our Wayshower of Christ-consciousness, Jesus of Nazareth. This leaves us with only one more point in our mini-survey of theology from a Galactic Perspective.

THIRD PROBLEM: SOCIAL ETHICS

War and peace issues dominated social ethics during the twentieth century, which indicated theology was attempting to grapple with the real problems of life. On May 3, 1983, the National Conference of Roman Catholic Bishops of the United States approved their now-famous pastoral letter on war/peace issues entitled *The Challenge of Peace: God's Promise and our Response*. This letter is built on the 1963 encyclical of Pope John XXIII known as *"Pacem in Terris" (Peace on Earth)*. Both called upon Christians and non-Christians alike to make all reasonable efforts to reduce the risk of nuclear war by multilateral disarmament.

John XXIII wrote:

> Justice, right reason and harmony...urgently demand that the arms race should cease; that the stockpiles which exist in various countries should be reduced equally and simultaneously by the parties concerned; that nuclear weapons should be banned; and that a general agreement should eventually be reached about progressive disarmament and an effective method of control.[9]

The bishops went beyond this to recognize no peace is possible unless the *"effective method of control"* included more than promises of on-site inspections. Their letter hints that peace must be accompanied by some sort of political union:

> We support, in an increasingly interdependent world, political and economic policies designed to promote the human rights of every person, especially the least among us. In this regard, we call for the establishment of some form of global authority adequate to the needs of the international common good.[10]

Social ethics includes all areas of human interaction where moral values come into play. Certainly, the greatest issue humanity faces today is the threat of regional conflicts in a world where too many nations have nuclear weaponry. That it is a moral issue cannot be denied. Ethical choices made by world political leaders can create a climate of stability where peace flourishes or mistrust and instability leading potentially to the end of the human species. All other ethical concerns, important as they are, pale in comparison to the vision of nuclear Armageddon.

Classical theology places barriers between peoples: *If our religion is faithful adherence to God's unique revelation in Jesus Christ and all other forms merely towers of Babel, no meaningful dialogue can transpire between Christians and non-*

Christians. Social ethics becomes social evangelism. Efforts for World Peace become dreams of a Christendom coextensive with human civilization or, at best, peaceful coexistence with those unenlightened souls who have it all wrong. If the Christian faith represents God's exclusive revelation to this Universe, then the Crusaders were more logically consistent than the Peace Corps, and we should not rest until every- one embraces our form of religiosity. Then, after we have a Christian world, we could eliminate all the heretics within the Church and bring about a Christian Utopia. The nasty images creeping into your mind right now should indicate how awful this argu- ment is. But, based on the exclusivist premise, it is perfectly logical.

Christian Social Ethics raised to the Galactic Perspective must reflect the kind of tolerant confidence which characterized our discussion of Christology. If the spirit of God resides in every sentient being, there is no need of unanimity. Rather, we can see in the clash of ideas a healthy contrast, an opportunity for creative insights. If I find God-within through Jesus of Nazareth and someone else discovers his/her divine nature through other prophets, teachers, or messiahs—human or not—why should my piece of the puzzle invalidate the other pieces? Granting that we might not see how two dissimilar ideas about Reality could be reconciled, could we not learn from the contrast and agree to disagree without destroying the other? Would not both be stronger, wiser for the exposure to alien doctrine?

And how shall we present ourselves to other races in the Cosmos? As Americans? Russians? Japanese? Arabs? Shall we not begin to see ourselves as one species, inhabiting one world?

The only possible long-term preventative for national conflicts is, in the words of the American Bishops' letter, "...the establishment of some form of global author- ity adequate to the needs of the international common good." That means one human government, world unity. It is an idea fraught with peril. It is an idea whose time has not yet arrived. It will be the most important sociopolitical issue facing humanity for the next few centuries.

The dangers implicit in world unity are second only to the dangers of continued national anarchy in a world with nuclear technology. Because humans hate each other so viciously, many years will pass before the urge toward pan-humanism becomes the driving force of world political opinion. Our squabbling—Arab against Jew, Irish Catholic against Irish Protestant, tribe against tribe, West against East—will likely continue to dominate the politics of this world for generations.

To put this fratricide in proper perspective, let's allow ourselves a flight of science fiction/fantasy and ask, *"How would an intelligent alien look upon a car bomb exploding in the Middle East, killing women and children in the name of God?"* Perhaps the theory of a Lex Galactica placing this world off limits is less for our protection against contamination of new technologies before we are ready and more for the protection of Galactic civilization against Homo sapiens violence.

ONE WORLD

If we step away from earth and look back at our home planet from the Galactic Perspective, the pettiness of these conflicts snaps into focus. There are no lines drawn on the face of this world to separate one segment of humanity from another. The spectrum of human races moves gracefully from the darkest Australian Bushman to the palest Swedish blonde, so that no one can say where one race ends and another begins. We are one species, one race, one family. But we are a family embroiled in seemingly endless feuds, brother against brother, cousin against cousin, ideologue against ideologue, true believer against true believer. Humans are the only form of life on earth that kills for "love." Could any attempt to negate Divine Ideas—which is our definition of sin—be more perverse?

No sober person believes heaven on earth will be achieved through sociopolitical union, but at least the hellfire of nuclear holocaust will be forever avoided. Yet, as we have noted, there are great dangers to face along the road to world unity. There is the danger that human consciousness will not grow rapidly enough, that we shall destroy ourselves before a vision of the Oneness of humanity captures the imagination of the peoples of the world. There is also danger that force might be used to compel some nations to join the world federation, defeating the very goal of union, which is to preserve the peace.

The greatest danger of all, the one to hold constantly before our eyes, is the potential tyranny of world-wide dictatorship, an Orwellian nightmare in which some power-hungry demagogue seizes power and rules by force rather than through international law. For this reason there must be no compromise on the basic principles of representative democracy. Fundamental rights to freedom of religion, speech, the press, and other individual liberties of all the peoples of the world must be protected by a full charter of political freedom, like the Bill of Rights to the U. S. Constitution. Economic rights, too, must be addressed, but from a framework which encourages individuals to profit from their own inventiveness and fosters free trade for personal prosperity. This will require a delicate balance between the needs of centralization for stability and order vis-à-vis the rights of the individual world citizen to private enterprise and civil liberties.

"THE EARTH IS ONE COUNTRY..."

We repeat: establishing a world federal government based on representative democracy will take centuries. It is the unique opportunity of Metaphysical Christian churches to stand in the forefront of this long-term struggle for lasting peace and prosperity through world unity, but we do not stand alone. Men and women of good will in all the cultures of earth have seen the vision of One World. Over 150 years ago the Persian mystic/prophet Baha'u'llah, founder of the modern Baha'I Faith, sounded the call for world democratic union when he proclaimed:

It is not for him to pride himself who loveth his own country, but rather for him who loveth the whole world. The earth is but one country, and mankind its citizens.[11]

Metaphysical Christianity, which emphasizes the dignity of the individual while stressing our right to prosperity, freedom, and corporate oneness in God-consciousness, is uniquely suited to play a leading role in the movement for world unity. Looking down the ages, we see not only socio-political union but eventual spiritual union with all sentient beings as we grow back to full awareness of our in-dwelling Divine spirit. I hold that no other movement within the body of Christ can better respond to this long-term call to lead the Christian faith, as it challenges humanity to move toward unity, than the Truth Churches. Our work lies ahead of us; the finest hours of Metaphysical Christianity are yet to come.

True Christianity looks backward and forward: backward to the primordial revelation of God in the history of Israel and in the person of Jesus Christ, forward to the establishment of the Kingdom of God. We know our images of both are tainted by cultural and historical biases, but there is an integrated whole obtainable when we bring our ideas into dialogue with both Christian and non-Christian thinkers who are grappling with morality, survival, and quality of life issues facing humanity.

Not a perfect set of doctrines distilled into a creed but an ongoing dialogue, a continuous review and re-working of our religious ideas in the light of new knowledge from the social and physical sciences and new insights from *Scripture, Tradition, Experience,* and *Reason*, all mediated through the model of God-consciousness given to us in Jesus of Nazareth.

Problems facing humanity are great, but not insurmountable. We began this study by quoting a hymn of faith. It is entirely proper that we end our discussions with these words from another great old hymn which, if you grew up a Protestant, you will doubtless recognize:

O Jesus, you have promised
To all who follow you
That where you are in glory
Your servant shall be too;
And, Jesus, I have promised
To serve you to the end;
O give me grace to follow,
My master and my friend![12]

CHECK YOUR KNOWLEDGE

1. According to astronomer Carl Sagan, how does the size of the Cosmos affect the likelihood that intelligent life exists on other worlds? How does it affect whether we have been visited by UFOs?

2. Describe the "Postage Stamp Theory" of UFO visits to this world.

3. What is "exobiology"?

4. What new Copernican Revolution does the text envision?

5. If astronomer Carl Sagan is right, name the three areas of theology which this chapter says will come under attack.

6. Explain what theologian John Macquarrie means when he says: "The overwhelming probability is that countless billions of 'histories' have been enacted in the Cosmos, and a space-age cosmology calls for a vastly enlarged understanding of divine grace and revelation."

QUESTIONS FOR DISCUSSION

1. The author says: "If we take the modern world seriously, that means accepting the strong likelihood that humanity is not the only intelligent species in the Cosmos." Do you agree?

2. Read and discuss the poem by Alice Maynell:
   > Doubtless we shall compare together, hear
   > A million alien gospels, in what guise
   > He trod the Pleiades, the Lyre, the Bear.

3. What will happen to Christianity if "definitive contact" is made with intelligent, non-human species from other worlds?

4. How do you believe the Christian Faith will change in the future?

5. What areas of progress might be a threat to some people's religious faith?

6. Do you share the author's enthusiasm for "a world federal government based on representative democracy"?

NOTES

1. Carl Sagan, *Cosmos* (NY: Random House, 1980), p. 298.

2. Paris Flammonde, *UFO Exist!* (NY: Ballantine, 1987), pp. 448-454.

3. Jenny Randles, *Beyond Explanation* (NY: Bantam, 1987), pp. 78-79.

4. Sagan, pp. 307-308.

5. IBID.

6. Macquarrie, *Principles*, p. 172.

7. Charles Fillmore, *Keep A True Lent* (Unity Village, MO: Unity Books, 1953), pp. 17-18.

8. Alice Meynell quoted by Macquarrie, *Principles*, p. 172.

9. Dean C. Curry, *Evangelicals and the Bishop's Pastoral Letter* (Grand Rapids, MI: Eerdmans, 1984), p. 3.

10. IBID.

11. Baha'u'llah, *Summons to the World's Religious Leaders*, available online at http://metalab.unc.edu/Bahai/Texts/EN/PB/PB-60.html#Page%20116

12. "O Jesus. I have Promised,": words by John E. Bode, *Book of Worship for U. S. Forces*, p. 410.

AFTERTHOUGHTS

The tasks of theology never end. Every generation must re-interpret the Ancient Faith for its children, who will of course reject their parents' conclusions and struggle to come up with a cleaner shadow of the Divine, only to be rejected as hopelessly out-of-date by the next generation. This work has attempted to lay down a baseline for future thinkers, not in any false hope that this represents the final word, a Summa for Metaphysical Christian thought, but that it will provide ample opportunities for future theologians to spend long summer evenings wrestling with the Divine in the playing fields staked out in this first systematic theology of our Metaphysical Christian tradition.

The author is convinced that God loves us, even those of us who are cursed with the interminable need to do theology, the passion to grapple with and come to some kind of understanding about the interplay of life, death, humanity, morality, and the Cosmos with the One Presence/One Power undergirding and causing all existence. The lighthouse belief of this effort has always been that God would not have given us an intellect if we were not supposed to use it, which Jesus Christ emphatically declared as a worthy pursuit when He told His disciples to "love the Lord your God with all your heart, and with all your soul, and with all your mind..." (Mark 12:30)

This book aims at franchising the struggle to know God with our minds, not to the exclusion of intuitive-meditative searching, but as a supplemental and balancing process. Mind and heart, thinking and feeling--these are the two wings by which the human soul can learn to fly.

When I presented some of these ideas at a small church in the Florida Keys, a young woman came up to me with tears in her eyes. She took my hand and said, "I have always felt guilty because I've wanted to understand more." She thanked me for saying aloud from the pulpit that it was okay to use the head as well as the heart in our spiritual quest.

It is an endless task, because it is utterly impossible. We simply cannot understand God with our minds; the Divine is too vast, too immeasurably wondrous for mortal consciousness to comprehend. However much we learn, more will be unknown. In this respect, the vastness of the Universe itself is an allegory for the knowledge of God. The process of stretching toward the Unreachable must in some way provoke and promote growth.

Certainly, we can never love God enough, yet we leap forward in spiritual growth as we attempt the impossible. In ages to come, as humans sail into the Cosmic ocean, our descendants will learn more and more about God's handiwork without exhausting its delights and diversity. Doubtless, their starships will have computer libraries, and in those memory banks humans will transport the collected wisdom of earth, to include the words of the Son of Man, Who said as He looked into the skies on the last day of His mortal existence, "Father, into your hands I commit my spirit." (Luke 23:46)

Into those same Divine Hands do we prayerfully commit this first effort at Systematic Theology from a Metaphysical Christian point of view. We trust Divine Mercy and the good will of generations yet unborne for the outcome of these rudimentary efforts.